LANDLORD AND TENANT IN
URBAN BRITAIN
1838–1918

Landlord and Tenant in Urban Britain 1838–1918

DAVID ENGLANDER

CLARENDON PRESS · OXFORD

1983

Oxford University Press, Walton Street, Oxford OX2 6DP

London Glasgow New York Toronto
Delhi Bombay Calcutta Madras Karachi
Kuala Lumpur Singapore Hong Kong Tokyo
Nairobi Dar es Salaam Cape Town
Melbourne Auckland
and associates in
Beirut Berlin Ibadan Mexico City Nicosia

Oxford is a trademark
of Oxford University Press

Published in the United States
by Oxford University Press, New York

British Library Cataloguing in Publication Data

Englander, David
Landlord and tenant in urban Britain, 1838–1918.
1. Ladlord and tenant—Great Britain—Social
aspects—History   2. Landlord and tenant—
Great Britain—Economic aspects—History
3. Great Britain—History—19th century
4. Great Britain—History—20th century
I. Title
333.33'8'0941   HD7288.72.G7
ISBN   0–19–822680–2

Printed in Great Britain by
Hazell Watson & Viney Ltd,
Aylesbury, Bucks.

Preface

Along with unemployment, housing was the most intractable of problems with which the labour movement had to deal. The former has attracted a good deal of scholarly attention; the latter remains virtually *terra incognita*. Studies of housing policy frequently note the working-class presence without pausing to explain the attitudes or activities of working people. In short, the assumption is that these are of no account. The focus of social history upon the worker as producer rather than consumer has allowed this erroneous impression to pass without challenge. The fundamental antagonism of propertied and non-propertied does, however, represent an important aspect of the experience of the urban working-class. The 'cash-nexus', if it defines the character of master and servant, employer and employee, capitalist and proletarian, is no less central to the relation of landlord and tenant. This book is concerned to examine that relation, to explore the tensions and conflicts generated by the operation of a free market in the provision, ownership, and control of working-class housing, and to show how the politics of tenancy transformed the politics of housing. From this perspective the activities of working-class tenants were of rather more importance in the formation of policy than is usually allowed.

This book is a revised version of a doctoral thesis prepared in the Centre for the Study of Social History and submitted to the University of Warwick. Staff and students at the Centre were from first to last an unfailing source of support: generous, patient, enthusiastic, critical, and scholarly. I am grateful to them all. A special debt is owed to Tony Mason, an affable and extraordinarily good-humoured supervisor, who saved me from numerous errors and might have saved me from more had I been more attentive. Professor Royden Harrison, Director of the Centre, provided advice, encouragement, and invaluable assistance at all stages. Professor J. F. C. Harrison, an examiner of the thesis, suggested many useful improvements. I am also grateful to the President and Fellows of Corpus Christi College, Oxford, for a congenial climate in which to research and write during my tenure as P. S. Allen Junior Research Fellow.

Various scholars, wittingly and unwittingly, have contributed to this volume: some passed on references, some scrutinized sections in draft, and some cheerfully allowed me to bend their ears. My good friends Laurence and Jo Marlow have done all three without complaint. In this connection too I must thank Chris Fisher, W. J. Fishman, Brian Harrison, Christopher Harvie, Joseph Melling, Avner Offer, James Osborne, Fred Reid, Michael Shepherd, Stan Shipley, Charles Webster, and David Wilson. Ian Donnachie made research in Scotland both pleasant and instructive. The Arts Faculty Research Committee of the Open University provided financial assistance at the right time and in the right amounts.

I am grateful to the editors for permission to reproduce, in altered form, material which first appeared in the *Bulletin of the Society for the Study of Labour History*, the *Journal of the Scottish Labour History Society*, and *Midland History*. I should also like to acknowledge the courteous and efficient service provided by the staffs of the following institutions: Bodleian Library, Oxford; British Library (Colindale); Public Record Office; Scottish Record Office; University of Birmingham Library; Strathclyde Regional Archives; Mitchell Library, Glasgow; Leeds City Archives; Birmingham Central Reference Library, and Tower Hamlets Central Library. Beverley Brittain and Angela Raspin of the British Library of Political and Economic Science were exceptionally helpful. I am also grateful to the Librarian of the Labour Party, to the directors of the Peabody Trust and to the officers of the British Property Federation (formerly National Association of Property Owners) and the National Housing and Town Planning Council for ready access to material in their possession. I am grateful to the University of Birmingham Library for permission to use the Neville Chamberlain Papers. The two drafts of the manuscript were typed with exceptional celerity and admirable accuracy by Mrs Brenda Vaughan and Mrs Peggy Mackay; Rosemary O'Day read the proofs. My thanks to them all. This book, though, is dedicated to my parents for whom no thanks can ever be sufficient.

The Open University   David Englander
September 1981

Contents

List of Tables

Introduction

Victorian London, a city proud but cursed, its imperial glories blighted by the material and spiritual poverty of its working-class citizens: millions of people sentenced at birth to a life of hard and unremitting toil, to dreadful deprivation, infinite squalor, and death in the workhouse. Few tried to escape and even fewer succeeded: the slum-dwellers' 'machine-like perseverance' was considered astonishing.[1] 'Why did people stand it?' Wells, writing at the turn of the century, thought he had posed the key question with which future historians would be preoccupied.[2] He was wrong. Until quite recently, historians have shown little interest in the housing of the working classes and, with few exceptions, have concluded that the people did 'stand it', that their views were largely irrelevant or incapable of retrieval.[3]

Those whose aspirations were commensurate with the length of their purse, for whom unrestricted market forces made more or less satisfactory provision, and whose condition did not pose a menace to society, have also been neglected by historians. The housing of the middle classes has been consigned to an oblivion from which it is at present being rescued.[4] This is all to the good; but it is not the

[1] Thomas Holmes, *Known to the Police* (1908), pp. 154-6.
[2] H. G. Wells, *Anticipations* (1902), p. 24.
[3] See, for example, W. Ashworth, *The Genesis of Modern British Town Planning* (1954); W. Vere Hole, 'The Housing of the Working Classes in Britain 1850-1914' (University of London Unpublished Ph.D. thesis, 1965); S. D. Chapman, ed., *The History of Working Class Housing* (Newton Abbot, 1971); G. E. Cherry, *Urban Change and Planning, A History of Urban Planning in Britain* (Henley-on-Thames, 1972) J. N. Tarn, *Five Per Cent Philanthropy* (Cambridge, 1973); Enid Gauldie, *Cruel Habitations, A History of Working Class Housing 1780-1918* (1974); D. J. Olsen, *The Growth of Victorian London* (1976); and J. Burnett, *A Social History of Housing 1815-1970* (Newton Abbot, 1978).
[4] On this, see V. S. Doe, 'Some Developments in Middle Class Housing in Sheffield, 1830-1875', in S. Pollard and C. Holmes, eds., *Essays in the Economic and Social History of South Yorkshire* (Barnsley, 1976); S. M. Gaskell, 'Housing and the Lower Middle Class 1870-1914' in G. Crossick, ed., *The Lower Middle Class in Britian 1870-1914* (1977); J. N. Tarn, 'French Flats for the English in Nineteenth Century London', in A. Sutcliffe, ed., *Multi-Storey Living: The British Working Class Experience* (1974); M. A. Simpson and T. H. Lloyd, eds., *Middle Class Housing in Britain* (Newton Abbot, 1977); John Burnett, *A Social History of Housing*, Chs. iv and vii.

stuff of politics. The Housing Question does not, after all, reflect the success of the free market.

The extent of that success has rightly been the focus of much of recent scholarship. Space permits no more than a bald summary.[5] Until the third decade of the nineteenth century house-building had kept pace with the expansion of population.[6] Thereafter, the countryside began to disappear at an alarming pace. The decennial rate of population growth during the 1820s in Liverpool, Manchester, Birmingham, Leeds, Sheffield, and Bradford never fell below 40 and generally exceeded 45 per cent.[7] The labouring classes, overwhelmed by the viciously accelerating growth of industrial capitalism, huddled in dark, filthy, fetid centres of industry and commerce: the 'age of great cities' had arrived.

The townscape reflected the play of unbridled market forces, nowhere more so than in the maldistribution of such benefits as could be obtained from grossly inadequate investment in social expenditure.[8] The needs of the commonalty were sacrificed to the formation of new capital: pressure on working-class consumption was ruthless, intense, and unrelenting. The resultant absence of effective demand hastened the deterioration of the environment as workers and their families were packed, layered, and compressed like sardines into the made-down houses of the wealthy, forsaken by their original inhabitants for the safety of the suburbs, or crowded into such accommodation as the speculative builders were willing to provide. The trend towards higher densities, already evident in the last decades of the eighteenth century, now became more strongly pronounced: infilling took place on a colossal scale. Herein lay the origins of the ubiquitous back-to-back, of the perilous backlands of urban Scotland, of the claustrophobic courts and alleys of Birmingham and Liverpool, and of the dank, unwholesome cellars of Manchester, so numerous that 'it might well be considered a city of

[5] A valuable survey of the field is presented by Anthony Sutcliffe, 'Working Class Housing in Nineteenth Century Britain: a review of recent research', *Bulletin of the Society for the Study of Labour History*, No. 24 (1972), pp. 40-51.

[6] C. W. Chalklin, *The Provincial Towns of Georgian Britain: A Study of the Building Process 1740-1820* (1974), pp. 304-8.

[7] R. Price Williams, 'On the increase of Population in England and Wales', *Journal of Statistical Society*, III (1880), p. 468.

[8] See *Fifth Annual Report of Poor Law Commissioners* (PP 1839, XX), app. C, p. 106; and S. & B. Webb, *English Local Government, Statutory Authorities for Special Purposes* (1922), pp. 274, 314-15.

cave dwellers'.[9] In London the subsequent stagnation of these impoverished districts owed something to that complex procedure, brilliantly and dramatically anatomized by Shaw, concerning the extraction and transfer of the rents of the poor to help finance the housing of the suburban bourgeois. The slums of Victorian London were the consequence of this exploitative process.[10]

The slums of urban Britain constitute a massive indictment of unregulated capitalism, one which has undoubtedly obscured the real progress registered during the nineteenth century, a period which experienced an over-all improvement in standards of accommodation together with a marked reduction in overcrowding towards the end of Victoria's reign. The slums and their inhabitants represented a minority, but a minority composed of millions.

A function of a low-wage economy, the worst slums were concentrated in the major centres of casual employment, in Liverpool, Glasgow, and London.[11] Life in such quarters, often nasty and brutish, was generally short. Although no formal definition exists, abnormally high death rates can be regarded as axiomatic in the definition of the slum.[12] Not surprisingly these non-remunerative areas were frequently proscribed by the life insurance companies.[13] However, they possessed a coherence more palpable than that confirmed by the mournful sight of the seemingly ever present

---

[9] M. W. Beresford, 'The Back-to-back in Leeds, 1787-1937', in Chapman, *History of Working Class Housing*, Ch. iv; I. C. Taylor, 'The Court and Cellar Dwelling: the eighteenth century origin of the Liverpool Slum', *Transactions of the Historic Society, of Lancashire and Cheshire*, CXII (1970). On formation of Scottish backlands, see *Eighth Report of the Medical Officer of the Privy Council* (1865) (PP 1866, XXXIII), p. 212. Quotation from E. D. Simon, *How to Abolish the Slums* (1929), p. 22.

[10] This theme is explored more fully by H. J. Dyos and D. A. Reeder, 'Slums and Suburbs', in H. J. Dyos and M. Wolff, eds., *The Victorian City*, 2 vols., (1973), I, Ch. xv.

[11] On this, see I. C. Taylor, 'The Insanitary Housing Question and Tenement Dwellings in Nineteenth Century Liverpool', in Sutcliffe, ed., *Multi-Storey Living*, Ch. iii; James H. Treble, 'Liverpool Working Class Housing 1801-1851', in Chapman, *History of Working Class Housing*, Ch. v; John Butt, 'Working Class Housing in Glasgow 1851-1914' in Chapman, *History of Working Class Housing*, Ch. ii; G. S. Jones, *Outcast London* (Oxford, 1971); A. S. Wohl, *The Eternal Slum: Housing and Social Policy in Victorian London* (1977).

[12] An important discussion of this peculiarly indeterminate concept coupled with a valuable bibliographical review is presented by H. J. Dyos, 'The Slums of Victorian London', *Victorian Studies*, IX (1967).

[13] Fabian Tract No. 5, *Facts for Socialists* (1899), p. 15; Dundee Social Union, *Report on Housing and Industrial Conditions and Medical Inspection of Schoolchildren* (Dundee, 1905), p. 5.

hearse. Inside frontiers etched by commercial developers, street improvers, and railway promoters, there existed an insular world composed of poverty and destitution, an environment starved of capital, condemned to a living death, lingering thus and rotting until such time as the next round of improvements began.[14] Anchored by the nature of their calling, casual labourers and low-paid outworkers were forced into a hopeless competition with commerce and industry for the use of scarce building land. Improved transport offered them no relief. Even for the more prosperous artisan, inadequate suburban rail services prevented any significant outward migration from central London until the last decade of nineteenth century. Herein lies the crisis of the 1880s.

The 1880s, it is now clear, mark a turning-point that failed to turn. There was no assumption of national responsibility, no unilinear progression towards the welfare state. The assimilation of housing reform to 'politics' did not take place.[15] The voluntarist ethos underpinned the tacit agreement of both political parties to do nothing of significance. This consensus, though dented in places, remained substantially unbroken down to the eve of the Great War.

The teleological bias which informs much of the historiography of housing reform fosters other kinds of distortion. The apparent indifference of the labour movement has at times aroused reproachful exasperation in certain scholarly breasts.[16] The absence of popular demand for municipal housing has been conflated erroneously with the absence of interest *tout court*. The Chartists, it is true, were often dismissive of sanitary measures and public health reforms.[17] But, as one of them once remarked, if it were not to obtain regular employment, decent housing, good food—and plenty of it—what was the point of the Charter? The attainment of citizenship was the means not the end of endeavour.[18]

In the years which followed the demise of Chartism, working men were encouraged to turn to the building society rather than

[14] J. R. Kellett, *The Impact of Railways on Victorian Cities* (1969), pp. 16-17, 292-3, 337-46.

[15] For an alternative view, see A. S. Wohl, *Eternal Slum*.

[16] Cf. David Eversley, *The Planner in Society: The Changing Role of a Profession* (1973), pp. 77-8; also see B. S. Townroe, *The Slum Problem* (1928), p. 31.

[17] V. Zoond, 'Housing Legislation 1851-1867' (University of London Unpublished MA thesis, 1931), p. 48; F. B. Smith, *Radical Artisan William James Linton 1812-1897* (Manchester, 1973), pp. 40-1.

[18] Donald Read, 'Chartism in Manchester', in Asa Briggs ed., *Chartist Studies* (1967), p. 34.

the state.[19] Home ownership represented the realization of that independent status prized by all working people, but vital to the position of the would-be labour aristocrat. Amongst artisans it long remained a dominant aspiration.[20]

It is a curious fact that, notwithstanding the voluminous literature on the housing question, it was not until shortly before the Second World War that any systematic survey was made of working-class opinion.[21] It is also unfortunate that historians have often been too ready to step into the breach to pronounce upon 'working-class apathy and helplessness' or, having stumbled across evidence to the contrary, to respond in tones of barely concealed amazement.[22] These unhelpful reactions do, however, underscore the formidable problems involved in the re-creation of popular opinion. Some of the difficulties are obvious. A non-literary culture bequeaths few records, and angry sentiments, when voiced, were often unprintable. Popular suspicion of official inquiries deprives the historian of an otherwise rich and informative source.[23] Again, priorities were not

[19] *Royal Commission on Friendly and Benefit Building Societies* (PP 1871, XXV), qq. 3652-3, 3892-900, 3974, 5125; *Second Report of Commissioners of Friendly and Benefit Building Societies*, Part I (PP 1872, XXVI), p. 17. W. L. Arnstein, *The Bradlaugh Case, A Study in Late Victorian Opinion and Politics* (Oxford, 1965), p. 27; *Select Committee on the Present Scarcity and Dearness of Coal* (PP 1873, X), qq. 7411-12, 7382-4, 5878-81; A. S. and E. M. Sidgwick, *Henry Sidgwick, A Memoir* (1906), p. 495; *House and Home*, 12 Feb. 1881; S. J. Price, *Building Societies, Their Origin and History* (2nd edn. 1959), p. 140; V. S. Berridge, 'Popular Journalism and Working Class Attitudes, 1854-1886, a Study of *Reynolds's Newspaper, Lloyd's Weekly Newspaper* and the *Weekly Times*' (University of London Unpublished Ph.D. thesis, 1976), pp. 364-5.

[20] *Select Committee on the Savings of the Middle and Working Classes* (PP 1850, XIX), q. 413; Report of a Committee of Working Men, *Improved Homes for Working Men in London* (1866); *Select Committee on Town Holdings* (PP 1887, XIII), qq. 9475-6; Stedman Jones, *Outcast London*, pp. 226-7; R. Q. Gray, *The Labour Aristocracy in Victorian Edinburgh* (Oxford, 1976), p. 96; G. Crossick, *An Artisan Élite in Victorian Society: Kentish London 1840-1880* (1978), pp. 146-50; W. Glennie, 'Become Your Own Landlord', *A. S. E. Monthly Journal*, October 1898; *Property Owners' Journal*, July 1906; W. Newton to Commodore, Superintendant, Rosyth, 17 Jan. 1917 (PRO Adm. 116/2170).

[21] Mass Observation, *An Enquiry into People's Homes* (1943).

[22] Quotation from Enid Gauldie, 'The Middle Class and Working Class Housing in the Nineteenth Century', in A. Allen Maclaren, ed., *Social Class in Scotland Past and Present* (Edinburgh, 1976), p. 13; and for a more cautious though equally negative, appraisal, see John Smith, 'Public Health on Tyneside 1850-80', in Norman McCord ed., *Essays in Tyneside Labour History* (Newcastle, 1977), pp. 39-40; and for a somewhat startled response, compare R. Lambert, *Sir John Simon and English Social Administration*, (1963), p. 399.

[23] On the 'blue' language occasioned by urban redevelopment, see William Kiddier, *The Old Trade Unions* (1931), pp. 186-7; on popular suspicion, compare *Report of*

constant. The superficial observer might unwittingly come away with a misleading impression of working-class inertia. The National Housing Reform Council, which received generous financial assistance from the organized labour movement, especially the North Eastern miners' unions, understood this well enough. 'The present time', its fund-raising secretary told his executive in the autumn of 1908, 'is by no means the best as many societies are finding a drain on their funds from dispute and out-of-work pay so heavy as to encroach on their reserve funds.'[24] Timing, then, was crucial. 'The passing of the Miner's Eight Hours Bill', he later remarked, 'will set a good deal of reforming energy free amongst miners and it should be possible for us to arrange a special campaign against bad housing in colliery villages.'[25] These important qualifications (and others can be made) indicate that the undoubted advance in the demand for improved housing was neither uniform nor continuous. The artisans who formed the backbone of the labour movement were often vexed by the absence of a spontaneous desire for improvement.[26] Scottish trade unionists regarded themselves as missionaries and tutors to the more backward elements within the working class. Although deprecating the use of corporal punishment on schoolchildren, they were not slow to reach for the tawse when it came to the sanitary education of their parents.[27] If the expectations of the activists were wildly unrealistic, it does not alter the fact that, as Edward Thompson has remarked, Christ's poor were not always pretty.[28] The brutality and degradation of slum life is not a figment of overwrought imagination. It was real. It still awaits the gifted historian to penetrate its meaning.

The silence of the poor is deceptive. The non-realization of ambition is not in itself evidence that none is possessed. Even the denizens of the vilest slums were not insensible of their environment, although to most contemporary observers the fact was not always

---

the General Board of Health on the Administration of the Public Health Acts (PP 1854, XXXV), p. 36; *Fifth Report of the Select Committee of the House of Lords on the Sweating System* (PP 1890, XVII), p. xxi; *Royal Commission on the Aged Poor* (PP 1895, XV), qq. 10193, 10198-200.

[24] Minutes of National Housing Reform Council, 23 Oct. 1908.

[25] Minutes of Quarterly Meeting of National Housing Reform Council, 7 Jan. 1909.

[26] *Royal Commission on the Housing of the Industrial Population of Scotland: Minutes of Evidence*, 4 vols. HMSO (Edinburgh, 1921), qq. 354149, 35493-4.

[27] *R. C. Housing in Scotland*, qq. 26651, 26872, 33047, 33108-26, 33186.

[28] E. P. Thompson, *The Making of the English Working Class* (1963), p. 59.

immediately apparent. The bulk of the literary evidence is, in consequence, often little more than a register of revulsion suffused with a Hogarthian grotesqueness and characterized by a fixation upon the pathological, a fascination for the curious. The men of letters or even the more hard-nosed quantifiers, compilers of blue books and the like—moral statisticians, as they liked to regard themselves—were in this respect barely distinguishable. The working man, it was generally agreed, was a rather brutish creature, insensitive and without culture, a fugitive from an Arnoldian nightmare, who had to be moralized lest civilization be trampled beneath the weight of his barbarous boot. When purged of such prejudice, however, this literature reveals something of the critical attitudes which animated the poor.

The want of basic amenities—adequate drainage, proper sewerage and paving, lavatories, a constant, or indeed any, supply of running water—provoked a good deal of resentment. 'The complaints of labouring men and of their families on these heads are very common and distressing,' observed Dr G. T. Robinson of Newcastle. 'It is impossible to converse with them on the subject without hearing accounts of hardships and privations, the infliction of which no plea of economy can justify.'[29] These and similar observations, on the extraordinary pains taken by working people to 'keep up appearances' in the most frightful conditions, are far too frequent to be dismissed as exceptional.[30]

The non-participation of working people in the sanitary reform movement is not evidence of a want of interest in such questions. The sociologically ill-informed programme which characterized that movement was itself a sufficient inhibition. Popular intransigence—the seemingly perverse hugging of the city centre, opposition to ticketing and similar attempts at sanitary regulation—must be read in this light. The extreme voluntarism of Victorian social science

[29] *Report of Commissioners enquiring into the outbreak of Cholera in Newcastle, Gateshead and Tynemouth* (PP 1854, XXV), q. 4058.

[30] See, for example, *Fourth Annual Report of Poor Law Commissioners* (PP 1837-8, XXVIII), app. A, pp. 85-6, 91, 95-6; Hector Gavin, *Sanitary Ramblings* (1848), p. 78; *Morning Chronicle*, 24 Sept. 1849; *Report to Board of Health in reference to the Sanitary Condition of Agar Town, St Pancras and other parts of the Metropolis* (PP 1851, XXIII), p. 33; *Second Report on Operation of Common Lodging Houses Act* (PP 1854, XXXV), pp. 5, 7; *Report of Commissioners on Cholera in Newcastle etc*, qq. 5026, 5031, 7169, 7213, 7234-337; R. A. Lewis, *Edwin Chadwick and the Public Health Movement* (1952), pp. 221, 285; *First Annual Report of Medical Officer of Health, St Pancras* (1856), p. 13; *Royal Commission on Physical Training (Scotland)* (PP 1903, XXX), q. 13777.

meant that 'improvement' invariably rebounded upon the heads of the poor. Its benefits were always problematical. Opposition of a discrete and non-programmatic kind should not, therefore, be projected as a universal hostility to some abstract beneficent entity, 'the sanitary idea'. By so doing we perpetuate error and prejudice.

The poverty of British architecture is nowhere better evidenced than in the design of the model dwellings. The shapes and structures of philanthropic capitalism, however, were more than a reflection of economic stringencies or architectural ignorance. These buildings, wrote Henry Roberts, architect to the Society for Improving the Condition of the Labouring Classes, 'appear to act as silent monitors, reproving disorder and encouraging cleanliness and propriety'. The severe lines, the grim, flat, almost punitively monotonous exterior, redolent of prison, barrack, hospital—anything but home—did not accord with the popular taste. The rejection was so complete that it later required the elaboration of a new ideology to rid flatted accommodation of 'its unsavoury nineteenth century image' in order to commend multi-storey living to working people.[31]

But criticism extended beyond the appearance of the buildings, much of it directed at their decidedly cramped interiors, the glacial, spartan finish and primitive sanitation.[32] These unsatisfactory features were the source of 'considerable indignation' amongst tenants of Katherine's Buildings, Stepney, 'the aborigines of the East End', who deeply resented the insufferable arrogance of the youthful Miss Potter, their less than competent landlord.[33] The historian of working-class housing is not, then, confronted by an absence of popular interest. The evidence, though scattered and

[31] Quotation from Henry Roberts, *The Physical Condition of the Labouring Classes Resulting from the State of their Dwellings* (1866), p. 9. Cf. W. G. Blaikie, *Heads and Hands in the World of Labour* (1865), p. 102; also see *Select Committee on Artisans' and Labourers' Dwellings Improvement* (PP 1882, VII), qq. 2050-3. On subsequent ideology, see Alison Ravitz, 'From Working Class Tenement to Modern Flat: local authorities and multi-storey housing between the wars', in Sutcliffe, ed., *Multi-Storey Living*, Ch. v.

[32] J. N. Tarn, 'The Peabody Donation Fund: the role of a Housing Society in the Nineteenth Century', *Victorian Studies*, X (1966-7), p. 14; *S. C. Artisans' and Labourers' Dwellings Improvement* (PP 1881, VII), q. 3971; *The Correspondent*, 3 May 1865; J. Symington, 'The Working Man's Home', in James Begg, *Happy Homes for Working Men and How to Get Them* (1866), pp. 169, 179-80; *S. C. Artisans' and Labourers' Dwellings Improvement* (1882), q. 2941.

[33] Joseph Aarons to Beatrice Potter, 3 Mar. 1886 (Passfield Papers, British Library and Political and Economic Science). Quotations from Beatrice Webb's Unpublished Diaries, 22 Feb. 1886 (Passfield Papers) and *My Apprenticeship* (Penguin books edn. 1971), p. 272.

difficult, is not unyielding. It is sufficient to indicate the existence of a broad spectrum of critical opinion on which the impoverished labourer and more prosperous artisan both have a place. The principal difficulty was to translate aspiration into effective political action. It is this aspect of the Housing Question with which this book is concerned.

The history of housing reform, in so far as it takes cognizance of the working class, has been written in terms of the SDF, the Fabians, the Workmen's National Housing Council, land reformers, and the Labour Party.[34] The tendency to assign significance only to those attitudes and activities which had a positive effect on legislation excludes much that is of importance. The Small Tenements Recovery Act, 1838, one of the most Draconian measures ever enacted, which until recently formed the basis of the law of summary ejectment in England and Wales, was, for example, passed in response to the frequent communal rent riots of the early nineteenth century. The relation of landlord and tenant, however, has been ignored by most scholars. The first part of this study is concerned to repair the omission, to provide some account of the ordinary relations of tenants and landlords.

In addition to the better control of contumacious tenants, the desire to protect house property—the coping stone of local authority finance—against ever rising assessments, provided a continuous impulse towards organization on the part of property-owners. The relation between rates and rents, which is explored below, constitutes a unifying framework essential to an understanding of the conflict between landlord and tenant. House property, under almost continuous pressure throughout the nineteenth century, entered a crisis in its closing stages. Rates soared alarmingly from the 1890s onwards. Landlords, faced with diminishing returns, sought without success to reduce local expenditure and redistribute some of the rate burden away from house property. The attempt to raise rents at a time of declining real wages proved equally futile. Property owners were, in fact, the victims of an inequitable system of local taxation that was

[34] See, for example, A. T. Mallier, 'Housing in Coventry The Development of Municipal Action, 1890-1908' (University of Birmingham Unpublished M. Soc. Sc. thesis, 1969); David Englander, 'The Workmen's National Housing Council, 1898-1914', (University of Warwick Unpublished MA thesis, 1973); A. S. Wohl, *Eternal Slum* Ch. xii; P. R. Wilding, 'Government and Housing: a study in the development of social policy 1906-1939' (University of Manchester Unpublished Ph.D. thesis, 1970).

increasingly unable to shoulder the burden of social and civic reform heaped upon it by central and local government.[35] Much of the conflict examined below arose from this predicament.

The focus of this study is upon the activities of working-class tenants in relation to the development of state-subsidized housing policies. Tenants' agitations deserve attention, not only because they illuminate an otherwise largely inaccessible reality of social and property relations, but also because of their retrospective importance as harbingers of wartime and inter-war reforms. This study will show that, before the Great War, attempts at formal organization amongst such tenants were more widespread than has been suspected. The intervention of the state in 1915 marks an abrupt shift in focus. Private conflicts henceforth became matters of public policy. The dramatic nature of the transformation obscures certain underlying continuities. The introduction of rent control, following the wave of rent strikes which reached a crescendo in the autumn of 1915, represents in some degree the conjunction and culmination of several pre-war rent struggles. Indeed, the growth of tenant militancy presents an added dimension to the 'labour unrest' that began before the war and finally ran its course in the early twenties. The parallel movement of the rents agitation, with which this study concludes, proved sufficiently powerful to prevent the raising of controls at the end of the war and thereby frustrated the re-establishment of housing upon an economic footing. The assumption of state responsibility for the provision of housing was neither planned nor desired. The ubiquitous council house was one price of post-war stability in Britain.

[35] For a first-class analysis of this and cognate matters, see Avner Offer, *Property and Politics 1870-1914* (Cambridge, 1981).

PART 1

Landlord and Tenant in the Late Victorian City

Houses, lines of houses, streets, miles of pavements, piled up bricks, stones. This owner, that. Landlord never dies they say. Other steps into his shoes when he gets his notice to quit. They buy the place up with gold and still they have the gold. Swindle in it somewhere.

James Joyce, *Ulysses*

1

Possession

Entering London from the West, footsore and weary, the traveller halted and stood awhile in the twilight. Then, gently easing the straps of his tool-bag over a still-aching shoulder, he turned off the Edgware Road into Sovereign Street and pushed open a door: inside there was warmth, refreshment, news of the trade and a bed; for this was a house of call: its name, the *Sign of the Rent Day*.[1]

On arrival in the central area early next morning our tramping artisan might have chanced upon a number of suspicious looking carters, glancing furtively as they scurried along, their careworn and anxious features betraying the all-too obvious fact that theirs was no legitimate furniture removal business.

A man of culture and refinement, our obscure Jude, now in lodgings and regular employ, devotes his leisure to self-improvement. He visits a picture gallery. 'Distraining for Rent', if he saw it, leaves little impression. Perhaps it was the painter, possibly the prosaic subject-matter. Whatever the reason, the artist is no longer acclaimed. Who now remembers David Wilkie?[2] Douglas Jerrold, prolific author and bohemian, somehow found the scene moving. His play, *The Rent Day*, first produced at Drury Lane in 1832, was one of the earliest of a genre the subject-matter of which later became a staple of popular melodrama. But by then our weary traveller was no more. Master and Servant had meanwhile all but disappeared, but Landlord and Tenant, like pain and fear, seemed eternal. With Marie Lloyd his children and grandchildren gaily sang *My Ol' Man Said Follow the Van* and laughed nervously. Monday, rent day, was always just round the corner, and who knew what untoward event might occur in the interval? Outside the music-hall the distance between lyric and reality narrowed appreciably.

Until quite recently home ownership was unattainable by all but a privileged or incredibly abstemious minority. Perceptions of

---

[1] *Trades Newspaper & Mechanics' Weekly Journal*, 2 Apr. 1826.
[2] Cf. T. S. R. Boase, *English Art 1800-1870* (Oxford, 1954), p. 154.

working-class home ownership in Victorian and Edwardian Britain bear little relation to reality. The temptation to conflate labour aristocratic aspirations with fact must be resisted. George Shipton of the London Trades Council, for example, waxed lyrical upon the virtues of home ownership before the Royal Commission on the Housing of the Working Classes, but confessed that he actually knew few owner-occupiers. The admission is hardly surprising. Almost twenty years later, the Chairman of the London County Council's Local Government Committee, a gentleman whose knowledge ought to be reliable, claimed that in the whole of the Metropolis there were a mere 14,000 owner-occupiers, a derisory figure.[3] There is a good deal of scattered evidence which indicates that, elsewhere too, working-class home ownership was negligible.[4] On the eve of the Great War owner-occupation accounted for approximately 10 per cent of *all* dwellings.[5] The Chamberlainite conception of a property-owning democracy was premature. The search for the 'urban cow' proved as elusive as the crew of the *Marie Celeste*. The British working-class experience was pre-eminently one of rented accommodation.

Surprising therefore that, outside of legal textbooks, virtually nothing is known of this, the oldest, most common and, perhaps because of it, the most neglected of contractual relations. The absence of organized protest is deceptive. The object of the agitation mounted by the Soho O'Brienites in the early 1880s was, in the words of one luminary, 'that all over the Metropolis there might be circulated that outward expression of that discontent which the working classes inwardly felt with respect to rents and

[3] *Royal Commission on the Housing of the Working Classes* (PP 1884-5, XXX), qq. 12, 886; *Estates Gazette* (10 July 1913), p. 123.

[4] See, for example, 'Report on the Condition of the Working Classes of Bristol', *Journal of Statistical Society of London* II (1839), p. 372; 'Report upon the Condition of the Town of Leeds and its Inhabitants', *Journal of Statistical Society of London*, II (1840), p. 410; F. J. Kaijage, 'Labouring Barnsley 1816-1856: A Social and Economic History' (University of Warwick Unpublished Ph.D. thesis, 1976), pp. 48-51; Patrick Joyce, *Work, Society and Politics: The culture of the factory in later Victorian England* (1980), p. 122; R. M. Pritchard, *Housing and the Spatial Structure of the City* (Cambridge, 1976), pp. 70-1; B. S. Rowntree, *Poverty, A Study of Town Life* (1901), p. 201; R. Furbey, 'National and Local in Social Class Relations—Some Evidence from Three Scottish Cities', *Social & Economic Administration*, VIII (1974), p. 217.

[5] See E. J. Cleary, *The Building Society Movement* (1965), p. 185; *Economist* (26 Aug. 1939), p. 394; Building Societies' Association, *Facts & Figures* (Jan. 1975); Sean Glynn and John Oxenborrow, *Interwar Britain: A Social and Economic History* (1976), p. 221.

apartments'.[6] The failure of that campaign underlined the virtue of a prudential silence. The insistent tenant was easily disposed of.[7] Nevertheless, rent strikes, though rare, were not unknown in nineteenth-century Britain. One of the earliest occurred in Bolton in 1826, impoverished hand-loom weavers there having 'got a notion that they were to pay no more rents'. This extraordinary action, it appears, arose not out of any dissatisfaction with the available accommodation, but rather from 'a diffusion of discontent and political agitation accompanied by the very worst features of infidelity'.[8] No doubt research will reveal further examples, but in the main the struggle against urban landlordism was conducted on a more personalized basis. An examination of the forms, meanings, and consequences of such conduct will help to establish the legal framework and is a necessary prelude to a study of the rent strike proper.

I

In perceptual terms the landlord was an ogre, the hardest of hard-faced men, one who preyed upon and tormented the lives of millions. Damocles might take comfort from the knowledge that only one sword was suspended overhead: death at least is the end of experience. For the working-class tenant there was no such finality. The threat of eviction did not recede by virtue of its having once occurred. The weekly exaction of Danegeld kept the brokers at bay. And yet, invasion did not automatically proceed upon the failure to receive tribute. A cursory glance at national income statistics immediately compels qualification.

House rents rose continuously down to 1914. Rent, however, absorbed an ever increasing share of earnings. At the beginning of the nineteenth century, house rent probably accounted for 5 per cent of GNP: in 1851 it contributed 8 per cent, and fifty years later 9 per cent. In the period 1880-1900 rents rose anything between 13 and 17 per cent, depending on the preferred method of calculation.[9]

---

[6] *Daily Chronicle*, 2 Aug. 1880.

[7] R. C. *Housing of Working Classes*, qq. 1919-20. 3360, 5536, 5626-7, 9524, 10686; *West Central News*, 21 Aug. 1880; *Clarion*, 7 Jan. 1899. Cf. *Report of the Committee on Housing in Greater London* (PP 1964-5, XVII), pp. 166-7.

[8] Quotation from *Select Committee on Handloom Weavers*, (PP 1834, X), qq. 4984-90; also see E. P. Thompson, *The Making of the English Working Class* (1963), p. 320.

[9] John Burnett, *A History of the Cost of Living* (1969), p. 219; Arthur Shadwell, *Industrial Efficiency*, 2 vols. (1906), II, p. 190; *Memoranda, Statistical Tables and Charts Prepared by the Board of Trade etc, Changes in the Cost of Living of the Working Classes in Large Towns* (PP 1905, LXXXIV), p. 98.

The smaller the income the higher the proportion devoted to rent. The working class formed the higher-rented section of the community, and the poorest the highest. In Edwardian Britain rent swallowed up a third of the income of the very poor.[10] The social consequences were sickening. Of the homes of such persons, one investigator wrote: 'The bareness of the room and the thin famished faces of the people, coupled with their scanty clothing, are evidence that though their clothes are at the pawnshop, and they have had no regular food for days, they have never escaped from the phantom of the rent collector.'[11] In an age of unfettered capitalism, of violent and frequent trade fluctuations, of obscene poverty, it is scarcely credible that rent could be paid regularly. How then did the working man keep a roof over his head?

There were landlords who were quite prepared to evict or distrain upon a defaulter at the drop of a hat. In the slums of Victorian Edinburgh, for example, there stood clusters of ancient tenements, some of them 400 years old, owned by jobbing capitalists, known locally as 'ruin lords', and let to 'the most debased classes'. The substantial rents of these single-apartments were, however, 'exacted with merciless rigour every Monday morning, on pain of being turned out instantly to the street'. From metropolitan dockland came a similar tale. As one casual worker put it: 'There is a remedy in the East End if you do not pay: they know how to get their money very quick ... with the working man in London, if a man cannot pay the second week, the broker is in safe enough. That is a matter of course.'[12]

Landlords were not sentimentalists; they pressed hard for their money. It is by no means axiomatic that eviction was the best means of securing it. Here we enter unknown territory, a land of which there are few maps, an undulating terrain in the declivities of which much lies concealed. Statistical guides are rare. When management is vested in solicitors, estate agents, auctioneers, and others, the pattern of property-ownership makes but a poor compass. How

[10] On rent as a percentage of income, see *Report of Royal Commission on Housing of Working Classes*, pp. 16-17; *Statement of Men Living in Certain Districts of London* (PP 1887, LXXI), pp. xiv-xv; B. S. Rowntree, *Poverty*, p. 201; *Report of Urban Land Enquiry* (1914), pp. 42-4; A. L. Bowley and A. R. Burnett-Hurst, *Livelihood and Poverty* (1915), pp. 23-4.

[11] Mary Jeune, 'The Homes of the Poor', *Fortnightly Review*, XLVII (1890), p. 67.

[12] *Report on the Condition of the Poorer Classes of Edinburgh* (Edinburgh, 1868), pp. 53-4; *Royal Commission on Labour*, Group B (PP 1892, XXV), qq. 225, 227.

many owners continued to supervise personally the management of their holdings? What degree of latitude were agents allowed? Even if we possessed the answer to these kinds of questions we should still remain ignorant of the experience of that vast army of sub tenants who shared multi-occupied dwellings. Still, something can be learned, however incomplete the evidence at present available.

Landlords were not without compassion. In the absence of adequate data as to the number of evictions and distraints levied, it ought not to be assumed that individual acts of kindness were unknown or gratitude rather than hostility displayed. Shortly after the passage of the Reform Act of 1867, a mass meeting convened by tenants of Columbia Square buildings, adopted the following resolution: 'That it is the opinion of this meeting that Miss Burdett Coutts is deserving the grateful thanks of us, her tenants, in having aided us obtaining the benefit of citizenship, and having defrayed all pecuniary expenses attached to our being put upon the electoral roll, and entitling us to a vote ...' It was also agreed that the buildings be illuminated 'in honour of her generosity, being the first to defend her tenants' rights, and to show the world that working men can appreciate such a boon as has been conferred upon them'.[13] It was from such obsequious behaviour that philanthropic housing managers derived satisfaction and confirmation that the personal touch provided the best medium for the recreation of desirable class relations. In an earlier age gratitude went farther, too far. Roxana's landlord, 'a Man that had but a little while ago been my Terror, and had torn the goods out of my House like a Fury', was unusual in making complete restitution in addition to a years' free tenancy, on learning of her circumstances.[14] Sympathy was not, of course, without a price, and no doubt the pleasures of the flesh continued to be taken in lieu of rent.

'Rarely in the poor quarters is a house empty at all', wrote George Haw. 'People get to know when the out-going tenants are timed to leave; so you have the two vans at the door at the same time: the one unloading the furniture coming out; the other unloading the furniture going in. Should it rarely happen that a house is left empty then you get as many as twenty to thirty applications a day.'[15] In the worst slums people came and went with telegraphic

[13] *East London Observer*, 21 Dec. 1867; also see 'A Generous Landlord', *Eastern Post*, 11 Aug. 1881.

[14] Daniel Defoe, *Roxana*, ed. Jane Jack (Oxford, 1964), p. 26.

[15] George Haw, *No Room to Live* (1899), p. 4.

rapidity: the landlords were hardly ever apprehensive about empties.[16] In the lowest class of accommodation turnover rates were astounding. Marx wrote of lodging houses 'whose personnel changes as quickly as the billets in the Thirty Years War'. Occupancy of Glasgow's farmed-out houses averaged 5¾ months.[17] Amongst the nomadic poor, however, removals fluctuated sharply with the seasonality of production, and these natural rhythms were well understood by the keepers of low lodging-houses and the like.[18] But, in the main, the migrations of the casual poor were circular and confined to a narrow radius.

Frequent removal was not restricted to the lowest stratum. A high rate of residential mobility appears to have been prevalent before the advent of rent control. In London more than one in five of all council tenants removed annually. In Liverpool 26 per cent of all Corporation tenants on average left each year. Turnover rates of this order were an electoral agents' nightmare: something between 30 and 40 per cent of the urban electorate in Edwardian Britain had removed by the time registration was complete.[19]

The haunting vision of wandering bands of footloose vagrants and semi-criminal mendicants who were reputed to comprise the 'dangerous classes' of urban Britain led to a confusion of mobility with instability. Among those peripatetic masses, however, was to be discovered not only the tramping artisan, but the artisan in search of a better home. The high rate of residential mobility in part represented the respectable working man trying to remain respect-

[16] On residential mobility in Victorian London, see studies of St. Margaret and St. John, Westminster, St. George's, Hanover Square and St. George's-in-the-East in *Journal of Statistical Society of London*, III (1840), p. 24; VI (1843), p. 22, and XI (1848), p. 219; also see Howard Martin, 'On the Recent Proposals to Enable Working Men to Purchase their Dwellings etc.', *Surveyors' Institution, Transactions*, XXXI (1898-9), pp. 385-6.

[17] *Glasgow Municipal Commission on the Housing of the Poor* (Glasgow, 1904), q. 798. Quotation from Karl Marx, *Capital* 3 vols. (Moscow, 1965), I, p. 662.

[18] Raphael Samuel, 'Comers and Goers', in Michael Wolff and H. J. Dyos, ed., *The Victorian City*, 2 vols. (1973), I, pp. 123-53.

[19] London County Council, *London Statistics* (1914-15), p. 158; *Annual Report of Medical Officer of Health, Liverpool* (1915), p. 117; Neal Blewett, *The Peers, The Parties and the People: The General Election of 1910* (1972), p. 361; P. F. Clarke, *Lancashire and the New Liberalism* (Cambridge, 1971) p. 430; Paul Thompson, *Socialists, Liberals and Labour* (1967), p. 72; see too *Unemployed Workmen Act 1905: Distress Committee of the City of Glasgow, Report for 1908*, p. 16 (Webb Local Government Collection, Vol. 347, British Library of Political and Economic Science; also the excellent discussion of mobility in Martin Daunton, *Coal Metropolis: Cardiff, 1870-1914* (Leicester, 1977), Ch. viii.

able. Unlike the casual poor whose purse was not commensurate
with their aspirations, better-off workers could, and did, exercise
the sanctions of a free market–at least until overcrowding in London
reached saturation point. A Poor Law Board official who studied
the problem for purposes of electoral reform was firmly convinced
that frequency of removal was a hallmark of respectability. 'The
respectable class', he insisted,

are the persons who remove because they like a clean house: ... I found that
the ordinary rule amongst the better class of artisans who occupied houses
was to change their residence once every six months, and the reason for
doing it was, that it was the only chance of getting any repairs done. When a
house becomes vacant the landlord cannot let the house until it has been put
in proper order, and immediately a man whose house has become shabby
sees a house across the street which has just been put in repair, he goes and
takes it.[20]

   This restless search for improvement was continuous in aim only:
unemployment, a lengthy industrial dispute, the death of the bread-
winner—all or any might suddenly deprive the working-class family
of the ability to maintain its momentum. Unemployment initially
resulted in a lowering of housing standards. The substantial workers
who comprised the South Wales Tin Plate Workers' Union were,
according to its secretary, forced to sell or heavily mortgage their
own homes to tide them over the slump of 1894/5. In the contraction
of the armaments industry following the Boer War, Woolwich
artisans, unable to meet their mortgage repayments, were likewise
compelled to economize either by becoming or taking in lodgers.
Overcrowding increased in industrial Lancashire during the Cotton
Famine for much the same reasons.[21] In areas already densely
over-populated, the scope for this form of economy was more
limited. Here the desperate struggle for survival intensified as rent
collectors became ever more insistent. In these circumstances, the
temptation to abscond might become irresistible.[22]
   Flitting, the most common form of rent evasion, was a necessarily

[20] *Select Committee on Registration of Voters* (PP 1868-9, VII), qq. 2970, 2973;
also see *Forty First Annual Report of Medical Officer of Health, St. Pancras* (1896),
p. 52.
   [21] *Select Committee on Distress from Want of Employment* (PP 1895, IX), qq.
9450-60; *Woolwich Pioneer*, 7, 14, and 21 Apr. 1905; J. Parry Lewis, *Building Cycles
and Britain's Growth* (1965), p. 94.
   [22] Cf. *Distress Committee for Burgh of Glasgow: Report for 1906-7*, p. 5 (Webb
Local Government Collection, Vol. 347).

permanent feature of the economy of the poor. A good deal of the coming and going in poorer quarters can be explained by reference to this economic imperative. 'The difficulty of tracing these removals', an electoral agent told the *Manchester Courier* in 1910, 'is enhanced by the disinclination of neighbours to assist in giving information—from reasons of delicacy maybe'. In order to overcome the problem, he continued, 'a strong hand of ladies had been formed, the reason being that the wives of working men are more open in dealing with their own sex among whom there are, as yet, no bailiffs'. The fact of his speaking thus is a reminder that 'shooting the moon' was not a peculiarity of the poor. Faced with destitution following a prolonged period of unemployment, the respectable artisan too was inclined to adopt a similar course.[23]

At all times he would do so with extreme reluctance. The restraints were considerable. First, the underhanded character of the operation was an affront to his sense of independence. Second, it invariably entailed a descent into inferior accommodation from which escape could be difficult; the taint of slumdom frequently proved indelible. Of 944 occupants of farmed-out housing in Glasgow, nearly one-fifth, when questioned assigned the want of a factor's line (i.e. reference) as the principal cause of their present whereabouts.[24] In this respect, the obstacles confronting the would-be defaulter had greatly increased. The growth of property owners' associations, locally up to the 1880s and nationally thereafter, represented an organized attempt to reduce these kinds of losses, principally through the insistence upon a character reference or clear rent book signed by the former landlord and the creation of a register of 'bad tenants'. Landlords of superior working-class dwellings looked askance at applicants from poorer quarters and all took a jaundiced view of their offspring whom they considered the very worst despoilers of property. This 'Malthusian horror of children' was itself a sufficient disqualification. Even with a character reference suitable accommodation could be difficult to secure, but without such testimonial it was simply not worth entering an appearance at the agent's office. Obtaining a decent home thereafter became an exercise in subterfuge and deceit repugnant to the tenant's

---

[23] B. S. Rowntree and Bruno Lasker, *Unemployment, A Social Study* (1911), p. 231. Quotation from Clark, *Lancashire and the New Liberalism*, p. 122.

[24] John Butt, 'Working Class Housing in Glasgow, 1851-1914', in S. D. Chapman, ed., *The History of Working Class Housing* (Newton Abbot, 1971), p. 77.

self-respect.[25] Finally, and most important of all, the temporary escape from indebtedness gained by flitting had to be weighed against the loss of a credit connection and the dismal prospects that awaited the inevitable recurrence of those circumstances that had brought the tenant to his current predicament. In the main, those who had either lost or failed to establish such connection were compelled to abscond with arrears outstanding.

Credit was vital to the working class: without it the casual labourer could not survive the winter; without it the artisan would be swept perilously close to the workhouse in the wake of periodic trade depression. A bond of debt united landlord and tenant. Arrears accumulated during the winter for repayment by instalments the following summer were, for the casual labourer, one of the few regularities in an otherwise unpredictable existence. If he had less frequent recourse to this syncopated pattern of expenditure, the artisan was nonetheless familiar with its workings. When to permit arrears was a major decision that was determined by circumstances and the degree of rational economic calculation amongst property-owners.[26] Competent management could do something to arrest the often rapid depreciation of working-class property (due in large part to the fragmentation of ownership and the inadequate resources of the proprietors) and reduce loss of income during periods of acute depression. A discreet lowering of rentals during a crisis often paid in the long run. But such interventions required skill and judgement: errors were costly and not easily rectified.[27] When demand was high landlords might please themselves. Such times were propitious for the 'weeding out of undesirables'.[28]

For the astute observer of human nature, indebtedness need not

[25] On this, see Percy, Greg, 'Homes of the London Workmen', *Macmillans' Magazine*, VI (1862), p. 66; *Select Committee on Artisans' and Labourers' Dwellings Improvement* (PP 1882, VII), qq. 2055-60, 2285; *R. C. Housing of Working Classes*, qq. 63-6; *Fourth Annual Report of Medical Officer of Health, St. Pancras* (1859), p. 4; George Haw, *Britain's Homes* (1902), pp. 157-9; Thomas Holmes, *Known to the Police* (1908), pp. 149-50; Corporation of Birmingham, *Report of Special Housing Enquiry* (1914), Schedule A, Evidence of Birmingham Socialist Centre. Quotation from Thomas Beames, *The Rookeries of London*, 2nd edn. (1852), p. 182.

[26] The movement of working-class rents and arrears over an eighteen year period forms the subject of a remarkable study by E. C. Howarth and Mona Wilson, *West Ham, A Study in Social and Industrial Problems* (1907), Chs. iv-v.

[27] Cf. statement of H. E. Williams, *Commission of Enquiry into Unemployment in the City of Liverpool* (Liverpool, 1894), esp. p. 102.

[28] Montague Price Williams, 'Some Urban Housing Problems', *Surveyors' Institution, Transactions* XLV (1912-13), p. 286. Quotation from *Tottenham & Edmonton Weekly Herald*, 31 Dec. 1913.

necessarily be disadvantageous: city financiers and bankers thus grow fat. The impecunious tenant, if blessed with sufficient insight, and possessed of the gambler's temperament, might also manipulate his debt to advantage. A tenant or lodger of proven record possessed a certain market value. Arrears not only mirrored the vicissitudes of trade and industry; they were the landlord's protection against total loss of income, against the vicious destructive elements who might otherwise obtain a tenancy, and against vexatious fluctuations in rentals. Those tenants who were not only conscious of, but chose to exploit the reciprocity of indebtedness cannot be measured. But some were. 'A landlady who has allowed herself to get into the position of being owed nine weeks rent feels more pleased when she unexpectedly receives rent for one week than she does when the rent is paid soberly and regularly', remarked one lodger who, during the depression of the inter-war years, had mastered the art.[29] Similar forms of manipulation may have been practised widely before 1914. If so, tenants had the wisdom to remain silent. Nevertheless, it was a particularly hazardous form of brinksmanship. To less adventurous sorts arrears imposed a crushing burden on body and soul. Besides going without adequate diet, there was always the dreadful uncertainty as they tried not to contemplate the future. 'I'm expecting notice to quit every Monday; and when the collector comes I feel I could sink through the floor', said one wife desperately trying to pay off £2 arrears. Her husband might find work before the worst happened. Rafferty's situation was hopeless. A respectable labourer, he had always managed to repay the back rent in the summer until incapacitated by consumption. Although his landlady had been extraordinarily lenient the family was £3 behind, and as he himself said: 'it ain't in reason that she should let it go forever'.[30]

II

What eviction meant is difficult to convey: words can but inadequately express the feelings experienced as homes, however humble, were tossed into the street to rot, police and vestry refusing to accept responsibility for storage or removal. The homeless themselves appear to have been nonplussed, seated amongst the ruins of their homes, a vacuous expression betraying the futility of

[29] Max Cohen, *I Was One of the Unemployed* (1945), p. 231.
[30] Rowntree and Lasker, *Unemployment*, pp. 246, 256.

vigilance.[31] A disconcerting scene was this, an alfresco existence constituting a massive indictment of a society devoted to the sanctity of private property. The accusing presence of the homeless produced an unsettling effect in the neighbourhood. Local residents, half-sensing it, complained of obstruction to the public highway and the police were apprehensive lest a disorderly crowd assemble.[32]

In an earlier period the collective sanctions of a sympathetic crowd might have quickly mobilized against injustice of this sort as, for example, occurred in eighteenth-century Edinburgh when, following distress and eviction, the unfortunate tenant committed suicide: 'The common people, being informed of this act of oppression, assembled about the landlord's house, broke open the door, brought everything movable into the street, set fire to the pile, and burnt the whole to ashes, not sparing money, notes, nor even the poor bird that hung in the cage, having execrated all the cursed things belonging to so merciless a wretch.' The landlord was reported to have made a timely escape 'otherwise it is probable that he would have shared the same fate with his effects'.[33] An isolated incident perhaps; although more than two generations later Celtic landlords were still to be found at the receiving end of a hostile crowd.[34] Moreover, Dr Jones assures us that, outside industrial conflicts, landlords and bailiffs were 'the most obvious targets' for scotching.[35]

The battle against political economy was lost in the early nineteenth century. But its triumph was never total—not, at any rate, amongst the labouring poor. Time did not dim popular notions of morality: the whole debate on rent control would otherwise be incomprehensible. The outraged sentiments provoked by the unjust and extortionate claims of the slum landlord, once voiced in the street ballads of the 1840s and 1850s, were echoed faithfully during the long campaign in defence of the Rent Acts.[36] And while spontaneous forms of collective protest did not entirely die out, particularly among the very poor, they become socially less visible as the

[31] See photograph, G. R. Sims, *Living London*, 4 vols. (1901), I, p. 208.

[32] PRO Mepol. 2/257.

[33] *Annual Register* (1767), pp. 92-3; *Scots Magazine* (1767), p. 325; also see Robert Chambers, *Traditions of Edinburgh* 2 vols. (Edinburgh, 1825), II, p. 146.

[34] *Monmouthshire Merlin*, 7 Aug. 1841.

[35] D. J. V. Jones, *Before Rebecca, Popular Protest in Wales 1793-1835* (1973), p. 104.

[36] On street literature, see Martha Vicinus, *The Industrial Muse* (1974), pp. 30-2; also *Quarter Day: Being a Curious and Laughable Dialogue which Occurred between the Landlord and his Tenants* (British Library Pressmark 1162 i.k. 51-435).

century wore on, although the sight of injustice in late-Victorian London could still incite demonstrative crowds, as many a bruised bailiff was ready to testify.[37] Retribution, of course, brought no respite to those evicted or sold up. Sojourn on the pavement was, however, short-lived. More often than not, the unfortunates were taken in by friends and neighbours and given shelter in their already cramped homes; if not, the workhouse beckoned.

Eviction rarely excited interest outside of the locality and in the main, the evicted went quietly. But there was a stubborn, and perhaps sizeable, minority who refused to yield without a struggle. 'In some of the worst neighbourhoods of Manchester', wrote Edwin Chadwick,

'the whole population of a street have risen to resist the service of legal process by the civil officers: I was informed by the superintendent of police of that town, that one of the most dangerous services for a small force was attending to enforce ejectments. This they had often to do, cutlass in hand, and were frequently driven off by showers of bricks from the mobs. The collection of rents weekly in such neighbourhoods is always a disagreeable service, requiring high payment.[38]

Debt collectors entered the Irish quarter with trepidation. 'In Angel Meadow or Little Ireland, if a legal execution of any kind is to be made, either for rent, for debt, or for taxes, the officer who serves the process almost always applied to me for assistance to protect him', the deputy constable of Manchester told the Poor Law Commissioners, and, he added, 'in affording that protection my officers are often maltreated by brickbats and other missiles'.[39] In poor districts defensible space was of more than academic interest. The popularity of the cellar dwelling, which in early Victorian Liverpool housed something like 20 per cent of the working population—some 39,310 people—can be partially explained in these terms. The Head Constable noted the strategic advantage obtained by the occupants: 'It renders them independent of their landlords. It is a complete dwelling in itself; the inhabitants enter and leave by their own door, and not by the landlord's door, and

[37] See, for example, *Estates Gazette* (8 Sept. 1894), p. 275 and for an earlier instance, *Shoreditch Advertiser*, 8 Aug. 1868.

[38] *Report on the Sanitary Condition of the Labouring Population of Great Britain, 1842*, ed. M. W. Flinn (Edinburgh, 1965), p. 300.

[39] *Poor Enquiry—(Ireland) Appendix G, Report on the State of the Irish Poor in Great Britain* (PP 1836, XXXIV), pp. 73-5.

consequently ejectment is not only a difficulty, but in many cases an impossibility without pecuniary compromise.'[40] To describe the relation between landlord and tenant as strained at the time of Victoria's accession would be a gross understatement. At this juncture when, in the absence of a summary mode of proceeding, to raise an action for ejectment cost a small fortune and took the best part of a year before execution, it was more like a medieval seige. Complaints by property owners were legion, and from them can be glimpsed something of the tumultuous nature of the tenants' tactics.

Cumbrous procedures for the recovery of possession, Manchester property owners claimed, 'do not afford to the landlords of small tenements that security which is requisite for the full enjoyment of their property', a defect which, so they said, was 'often taken advantage of by refractory tenants, who are thereby induced to commit acts of the most aggravated fraud towards their landlords, whom they often, with impunity, set completely at defiance'. It was alleged that 'numerous instances occur where tenants not only refuse to pay their rent, but withhold from their landlords possession of the premises after the expiration of legal notice to quit, conscious that the expense of any remedy would in many instances, exceed the value of the property sought to be recovered'. Meanwhile, the tenant was at liberty to commit 'all kinds of waste and depredation'. These 'instances of hardship have been so frequent', Mancunian proprietors informed Parliament in 1836, that they were 'long ago feelingly convinced that the laws, as they now stand, leave them entirely at the mercy of the tenant'. Similar sentiments were voiced in nearby St. Helens. In Ashton, the protracted ejectment procedure was held to afford 'a means of successful, audacious and impunitive defiance by unprincipled tenants' to beleaguered owners seeking the exercise of their legitimate rights.[41]

Turbulent tenants were not peculiar to industrial Lancashire. In 1835 the Scottish Law Commission recommended the introduction of 'a cheap mode of proceeding for the recovery of small tenements, in order to avoid the oppression and ruin which frequently attends the process now in use ... in rendering this class of debts effectual to landlords'.[42] In London, where it was agreed that disputes between

[40] *Report of a Committee of the Manchester Statistical Society on the Condition of the Working Classes in 1834, 1835 and 1836* (1838), p. 10. Cf. *Moral Reformer* (1831), p. 116.

[41] *Reports of Select Committee of the House of Commons on Public Petitions* (1836), app. 1887, No. 5429; app. 679, No. 1853; (1837), app. 567, No. 6137.

[42] *Second Report from Law Commissioners, Scotland* (PP 1835, XXXV), p. 26.

landlord and tenant led to 'constant riots and disturbances and assaults', landlords claimed to 'sustain most grievous loss and injury from unprincipled, worthless and litigious persons, retaining unjust and adverse possession'; that 'in many instances they have had to submit not only to a ruinous diminution of their limited incomes by the protracted and expensive recovery of possession by action of ejectment, but that they receive much more serious and aggravating mischief during the occupancy by the perpetration of most wilful and deliberate damage, without any adequate law to prevent it, to award compensation after its committal, or to punish the offender'. They urged the House of Commons to 'enact some wholesome measure whereby these frequent causes of grievance, oppression, broil and disturbance between owners and occupiers ... may be considerably lessened, if not wholly averted'.[43]

The tumult and disorder occasioned by the want of a summary mode of redress in small disputes between persons in humble life had long been a cause of concern amongst metropolitan magistrates and none more so than disputes relating to landlord and tenant. 'We very frequently witness the departure of applicants from the office under a burning sense of injustice on learning that there is no redress accessible to them,' Henry Wedgwood informed the Select Committee which examined the problem in 1838. 'Nothing in my opinion would tend more than such a jurisdiction to encourage in the common people a habit of looking to the law for protection, a consideration which, I think, can hardly be over valued.'[44] That Committee, like its several predecessors, accepted the case for extension of civil jurisdiction to the inferior courts: 'Though the subject matter of dispute may often in these cases be very trifling, yet the hardship and mischievous consequences arising from the want of a prompt and suitable redress are subjects of grave importance. Even their multitude, be they ever so insignificant, makes them worthy of attention'.[45]

London justices, however, balanced their call for summary eject-ment and a tightening of the law against wilful damage with a proposal for a prompt and more effective redress against landlords

[43] *Select Committee on Metropolitan Police Offices* (PP 1837, XII), q. 693; *Report of Select Committee on Public Petitions* (1837-8), app. 76, No. 237.

[44] *Select Committee on Metropolitan Police Offices* (PP 1837-8, XV), app. No. 2, p. 198.

[45] *Report of Select Committee on Metropolitan Police Offices* (PP 1837-8 XV), p. 27.

and brokers in cases of unlawful, excessive, or irregular proceedings when levying distress, so that 'at least the harshness of the law shall not be aggravated by injustice'.[46] In this they enjoyed the support of the Home Office.[47] But in its final shape the measure which emerged reflected the wishes of proprietors rather than any concern for equity and justice.

Hitherto the Law Officers of the Crown had frowned upon attempts at emendation promoted by the parliamentary representatives of the small house owners.[48] In the absence of a general enactment summary eviction clauses were often included in the numerous local bills for the establishment of small debts courts which regularly came before Parliament. In 1833, however, the Law Commission lent its authority to the emergent reform movement. Henry Aglionby, MP for Cockermouth, prepared a bill accordingly which, despite vicissitudes, became the Small Tenements Recovery Act five years later.

Opposition was limited to a handful of dissidents. Thomas Wakley, Radical MP for Finsbury, considered it 'a most arbitrary measure', one that would prove 'most disastrous'. 'He was convinced the Bill must be a bad one, as it was so very palatable to a large majority of that House.'[49] The Member for Chester agreed: 'He was satisfied that this was a landlords' Bill, that it was an oppressive measure which established invidious distinctions between the rich and the poor.' Surely, he added, 'was not a measure oppressive which provided that as regarded the poor, a magistrate was a sufficient tribunal, whereas as regarded the rich the sanction of the law was necessary?' If it became law, he concluded, 'it would subvert the whole rule of ejectment and the common law of the land'. This precisely was the intention.

Hitherto the law on ejectment recognized no distinctions as between different kinds of tenancies. The rich man in his castle and the poor man at his gate were both subject to trial by jury in which the plaintiff was required to prove his title to possession of the property in dispute. The Small Tenements Recovery Bill promised to revolutionize this procedure. Upon expiration of due notice to quit, landlords of small tenements (defined as premises rented at

[46] *S.C. Metropolitan Police Offices* (1837), app. No. 1, p. 186.
[47] *S.C. Metropolitan Police Offices* (1837), qq. 142-8.
[48] Correspondence of Lord Sandon MP and William Ewart MP, *Liverpool Mercury*, 10 Apr. and 24 May 1833.
[49] *HC Deb.* 3s xxxviii (1837), 1460.

less than £20 per annum) henceforth need only apply to the nearest magistrate to obtain an order for possession. All that was required was that the applicant prove termination of tenancy. The grounds for such termination were deemed irrelevant: the magistrate became a mere cipher.

Not surprisingly some were profoundly disturbed by so sweeping a transformation. William Theobold, a barrister of the Inner Temple, and the only person to petition against the bill, predicted that it would 'operate with peculiar harshness on the poor, and will make the magistracy and police odious as the instruments of powers which cannot fail to be regarded by their objects as a reckless and unmerciful tyranny'. It was, he considered, a measure 'more harsh than the law of imprisonment for debt, to which it bears a strong analogy; for it entitles the landlord, upon his own affidavit, to turn out of doors not only the tenant, but his lodger and family'. The right of action reserved in cases of unjust ejectment was 'a mere mockery'. Finally, he warned that 'the class of landlords most eager in demanding are most likely to abuse, and least fit to be trusted with such harsh and extraordinary powers'.[50] Sir Edward Sugden MP, himself a substantial land owner, felt much the same way. Speaking on the Second Reading, Sir Edward expressed 'great alarm, lest a feeling of suspicion should be engendered in the minds of the people of England that, in sanctioning such a measure, they were thinking more of their interests than of the justice of the case'.[51] But of the honourable Members who heard him, there was scarcely one who shared this viewpoint. Shortly afterwards the bill received the Royal Assent.

The mischievous consequences of the Small Tenements Recovery Act, although self-evident, can hardly be overemphasized. Yet, it is curious that those who were most affected, appear to have been quite ignorant of its implications. Some, indeed, may have welcomed the new measure. The member for Cockermouth claimed to have taken 'the opportunity of sending the Bill to every place throughout the country—not to landlords alone but every mechanic's news-room of which he had the slightest knowledge, and the only complaint he had heard against the Bill was, that it did not go far enough for the protection of small landlords'.[52] Of course, we do not know

[50] *Reports of Select Committee of the House of Commons on Public Petitions* (1837), app. 734, No. 7538.
[51] *HC Deb.* 3s xxxix (1837), 1050, 1054.
[52] *HC Deb.* 3s xliv (1838), 297.

just how slight Mr Aglionby's knowledge really was; but it is clear that working-class response, if that not be an over-generous description, was such as not to deter others from commending it to the sons of toil. In one of its many publications 'containing information especially calculated to advance the intelligence and better the condition of the working classes', the Society for the Diffusion of Useful Knowledge said:

It is of great importance that the provisions of the above Act should be widely known. The change in the law is certainly favourable to the honest tenant, and also it may be said to those who are otherwise disposed, as it will compel them, if they mean to keep a house over their heads, to be very careful how they dissipate the means of paying their rent. Formerly with tenants of this description it was of little use issuing a distress ... and the expensive process of ejectment generally fell upon the landlord, while the dishonest tenant laughed at the matter in which the law supported him in his contest with the owner of the premises. The plan of doubling the rent, unroofing the tenement and other oblique courses will no longer be necessary ...[53]

Octavia Hill was just a little girl, but the notion that summary eviction and rational behaviour went hand-in-hand was already well established.

An act which confined the magistrate to a ministerial rather than a judicial function was not the kind of measure originally contemplated by metropolitan magistrates. Elsewhere too the bench was less than enthusiastic. Mr Maude, a Manchester justice, thought it 'a very arbitrary act of Parliament and ... it was necessary that magistrates should put the most liberal construction on the powers invested in them by it'.[54] In Liverpool, a senior police magistrate, fearful lest it encourage great false swearing, decided that before granting an order for possession, he would require the 'strictest proof' of tenancy, and deemed the evidence of the landlord insufficient and inadmissible for this purpose. In the opinion of this sagacious gentleman: 'It was as foolish an Act of Parliament as ever was passed.'[55] He was right too. A most serious defect resided in its ambiguity as to whether its provisions extended to lodgers occupying

---

[53] *The Working Man's Companion or Year-Book* (1839), p. 138. Cf. *Birmingham Housing Enquiry*, q. 1059; Paul Thompson, 'Voices from Within', in Wolff and Dyos, eds. *The Victorian City*, I, p. 78; and R. White to J. S. Middleton, 4 Oct. 1917 (War Emergency Workers' National Committee Papers, Labour Party Archives).

[54] *Manchester Times*, 22 Sept. 1838.

[55] *Liverpool Mercury*, 21 Sept. and 5 Oct. 1838.

rooms or part of a house from a tenant holding from a superior landlord. In consequence some magistrates had refused to grant possession while others had freely done so. The opinion of Sir John Campbell, the Attorney-General, was taken. Notwithstanding Sir John's declared view to the contrary, a number of magistrates persisted in refusing to grant possession orders in such cases until an authoritative ruling from the Court of Queen's Bench was obtained.[56] This, in due course, was forthcoming. But in general, whatever their feelings, there was little the bench could do for the tenant. At best a magistrate might delay execution of an ejectment for a fortnight; to go further was to exceed his authority.

The Act of 1838 was frankly a disappointment to most landlords. True, it conferred immense power but it offered him no express protection against the unruly tenant. Wilful and malicious damage may even have increased. So long as their poverty compelled tenants to consider the non-payment of rent as a necessary form of income redistribution, resistance was inevitable. If it limited the scope for certain kinds of defiance, the Small Tenements Recovery Act was powerless to prevent, and may well have encouraged, more frequent recourse to flitting. In London moreover, where furnished accommodaton was fairly common among the poorer classes, absconding tenants were prone to pawn the furniture in the process.[57] The year following the passage of the Small Tenements Recovery Act brought fresh legislation designed to curb such practices. Section 67 of the Metropolitan Police Act, 1839 decreed that 'it shall be lawful to any constable to stop and detain, until due enquiry can be made, all carts and carriage which he shall find employed in removing the furniture of any house or lodging: between the hours of eight in the evening and six the following morning, or whenever the constable shall have good grounds for believing that such removal is made for the purpose of evading the payment of rent'.[58] The London 'bobby' was not, perhaps, at his best during those particular hours: 'shooting the moon' remained a standard form of evasion.

The Small Tenements Act, 1838 was perhaps more sucessful in helping to curb the open warfare between owner and occupier which had necessitated its introduction. Of the 9311 warrants for

[56] *The Times*, 10 Nov. 1838.

[57] M. D. George, *London Life in the Eighteenth Century* (1966 edn.), p. 100.

[58] The registration of furniture removals was no less pressing outside the Metropolis: see *Fourth Annual Report of the Birmingham Landlords' Association* (Birmingham, 1859), pp. 6-7.

possession issued by magistrates in the Metropolitan Police District between 1886 and 1890, nearly 10 per cent required the use of force to give the warrant effect but in only nine cases was that force resisted.[59] Nevertheless, rent-collecting in working-class quarters remained an unenviable task.

A month before the Armistice, the *Glasgow Property Circular* announced: 'The end of the European War marks the beginning of the Rent War'.[60] The commencement of hostilities, however, long antedated the landlords' formal declaration of war; antedated the Great War, the Crimean War, even the Revolutionary and Napoleonic Wars. Ever since the needs of the many became profits of the few, landlord and tenant had been locked in a ferocious, if silent, struggle. There were on average 5,594 evictions each year in Edwardian Scotland.[61] This figure excludes Glasgow. There the struggle was fought with a peculiar savagery. In 1902 all but three of the 17,000 applications for ejectment, lodged in the Burgh Court, were granted; in 1906 all but nine of the 20,887 applications were similarly approved. In the two years preceding the outbreak of the Great War, 52,290 petitions for ejectment were taken in the courts of the city and 10,000 evictions were sanctioned.[62] More remarkable still, these figures understate the full extent of the problem: on average, an additional 2,107 evictions were sanctioned annually in the Sheriff's Small Debt Court.[63] We may be sure therefore that a contemporary estimate of 20,000 petitions for ejectment per year in Edwardian Glasgow is not far off the mark.[64]

[59] *Returns on Evictions, London and Suburbs* (PP 1888, LXXXII) and (PP 1890-1, LXIV).

[60] *Glasgow Advertiser & Property Circular*, 8 Oct. 1918.

[61] Calculated from *Civil Judicial Statistics for Scotland* (1899-1914), table xxxiii, cols. 25 and 26.

[62] *GMC*, qq, 2071, 2080; *Minutes of Evidence of Departmental Committee on House-Letting in Scotland* (PP 1908, XLVII), q. 5502, *HC Deb*. 5s clxxii (1924), 1449.

[63] Calculated from *Civil Judicial Statistics for Scotland* (1899-1914), table xxxiii.

[64] Robert Renwick, *Glasgow Memorials* (Glasgow, 1908), p. 181.

2

Distress for Rent

In Victorian England the action of distraining or distraint described the common law right of a landlord to seize, without legal process, the personal chattels of his tenant for non-payment of rent.[1] All things were distrainable with the following exceptions: perishable articles, fixtures, wearing apparel and the instruments of a man's trade or profession in actual use at the time the distress was made. Goods belonging to subtenants and other occupants were, until the passing of the Lodgers Goods Protection Act, 1871, also liable to seizure.

The procedure regulating the distress was not without complications. A distress could not—and indeed still cannot—be made after sunset and before sunrise, i.e. in the night, nor on the day on which the rent became due. Although the outer door of the house could in no circumstances be broken open, the person distraining might, if the outer door be open, justify breaking open an inner door or lock to find any goods distrainable.

The distress might be made either by the landlord himself, or by an authorized agent, the bailiff, under a warrant of distress. An inventory of as many goods as were judged sufficient to cover the rent distrained for, and also the charges of the distress had then to be made, and served personally on the tenant, together with a notice of the fact of the distress having been made, and the time when the rent and charges must be paid, or the goods replevied.[2] It was customary precaution, following the distress to impound the goods immediately, and in the notice to acquaint the tenant whither they had been removed. In the event of clandestine or fraudulent removal in order to avoid distress, landlords were empowered to

---

[1] In presenting the following outline I have been guided by the various editions of two standard authorities: *Woodfall's Law of Landlord and Tenant* and *Redman's Law of Landlord and Tenant*

[2] *Replevin* describes the restoration or recovery of goods taken in distraint upon the tenant affected giving security to have the matter tried in a court of justice and to return the goods if the case were decided against him.

follow the goods within thirty days of their removal from the premises. Goods taken in distraint could not be sold before the expiration of five days. Prior to sale an appraisement had to be made by two appraisers. Any surplus accruing from the sale had to be handed over to the tenant. The foregoing thumb-nail sketch, though it might not satisfy a lawyer, is sufficient description for the purpose of this study. It is with the practical operation of the law of distress that this chapter is concerned.

I

Contempt for the landlord was exceeded only by that of his *alter ego*, the broker or bailiff. An essayist, writing in 1638, numbered him among 'the very offscum of the rascal multitude', one of 'a rabble of such stinkardly companions'.[3] In succeeding centuries his standing does not appear to have risen. His particular services were not, of course, confined to matters arising from the non-payment of rates and rents. In addition, distress warrants might be issued for a multiplicity of purposes relative to the recovery of small debts and enforcement of appearance. There were all sorts of abuses. The Law Commission of 1833, reporting upon the extortionate activities of the bailiffs employed by the inferior courts, described 'a vicious system of practise ... in consequence of the duty being usually executed, not by regular bailiffs, but by casual agents of the lowest description, it is in fact frequently exercised in a violent and oppressive manner'.[4]

Tenants too had to contend with similar predacious behaviour, rent bailiffs misconducting themselves in much the same manner as court officials.[5] The tenant's unfortunate predicament arose, in part, out of the legal reforms undertaken in the course of the previous century. The cumbersome and archaic procedure under the old law offered the tenant some guarantee against hasty and unlawful action in that any one irregularity nullified the whole. But from 1689 onwards a series of amendments swept away such protection as hitherto existed, however limited it may in practice have been. Procedure for the levying of distress was simplified, and

---

[3] Quotation from *OED*.

[4] *Fifth Report of the Commissioners appointed to enquire into the Practice and Proceedings of the Superior Courts of Common Laws relative to Provincial Courts in England for the Recovery of Small Debts* (PP 1833, XXII), p. 8.

[5] Correspondence of 'A House Agent', *Estates Gazette* (25 Feb. 1888), p. 91.

restriction on the things liable to seizure greatly relaxed. Summary powers of sale were introduced.[6] The consequences can be quickly summarized. Goods were seized to a value far greater than the arrears outstanding and fictitious appraisements issued. Auctions were rigged and extortion prevalent. Tenants might be ruined at a whim.

Parliament was not unaware of the humble householder's precarious situation. An act of 1817 (57 Geo. III c. 95), designed to regulate distress proceedings, bore the following preamble: 'Where as diverse Persons acting as Brokers, and distraining upon the Goods and Chattels of others, or employed in the course of such Distress, have of late years made excessive Charges, to the Oppression of Poor Tenants and others; and it is expedient to check such Practises ...' The measure prescribed a fixed scale of charges and fees (payable by the tenant) for the execution of a warrant, as well as penalties, including imprisonment, for contravention of the scheduled costs.

The enactment was scarcely worth the paper on which it was printed. In the words of R. E. Broughton, a London magistrate, it was 'so trifling, so insignificant in itself that it really leaves us nearly powerless'. Nearly everything relative to the legality of the distress, the regularity of the proceedings with regard to the impounding and disposal of the goods, and the accounting for the proceeds, remained matters subject to costly forms of redress; and as Mr Broughton put it: 'a weaver, toiling hard fourteen or fifteen hours a day, for 14s or 15s a week, cannot even talk with an attorney; it would take half his week's earnings to do so'. In any case, the nub of the matter was not the broker's extortionate charges, but the turning of a man and his family into the street, and the sale of his bed and tools into the bargain:

... as the law stands, it tends to impoverish tenants; I have seen many cases of the destruction of a family, by carrying away the beds, tables and chairs, and everything that they had; one broker calls in another, and they what they call condemn the articles; they fix their own price, often not one tenth of the value of the goods, and hardly ever send them to auction; and when stripped of all their property by the conduct of the landlord or brokers, they come to us, and we have to remedy.[7]

[6] Frederick Pollock, *The Land Laws* (1883), p. 141.

[7] Quotation from *Select Committee on Metropolitan Police Offices* (PP 1837-8, XX), qq. 239-40; also see *Select Committee on Metropolitan Police Offices* (PP 1837, XII), qq. 690, 889.

In the face of such glaring inadequacies, not all magistrates found it possible to maintain that sense of detachment and composure expected of those charged with the administration of justice. Mr C. K. Murray, for example, was troubled by his own difficulties in this respect.

I wish to state [he told an official enquiry in 1834] that much oppression takes place at present on the part of brokers, in cases in which we have no power to interfere; the only jurisdiction that we possess over them is in the case of their exceeding the amount of costs allowed by statute; but our jurisdiction is so imperfect, that although the Act enables us to impose a fine upon the broker who makes an overcharge in his account, it gives us no power to compel delivery of that account. There is a low class of brokers who occasionally seize and sell all the goods, perhaps worth three times the rent, and put the whole balance in their pocket; for this there is no remedy but by action; and the result of the broker's conduct being the entire ruin of the poor tenant, of course no action can be brought. In one instance of this kind, which was attended by gross oppression, I could not refrain from putting a strained construction on the law; and having assessed the costs allowed by the Act, I treated the surplus as an overcharge retained by the broker out of the proceeds of the sale, and fined him accordingly three times that amount. It would be useful if we were relieved from the temptation of resorting to these doubtful constructions of the law, by definite remedies for these and other acts of oppression.[8]

Although the Metropolitan Police Courts Act, 1839 provided a summary form of redress against unlawful distress,[9] the 'definite remedies' for which Mr Murray called were a long time coming. Attempts to introduce a more equitable arrangement called forth opposition from the most influential quarters. A proposal to exempt lodgers from the seizure of their property in case of default by the tenant, a common occurrence, which came before Parliament in 1869, was rejected out of hand. The Lord Chancellor sympathized with 'the great inconvenience' which lodgers suffered, but felt that the bill would encourage tenant and lodger to enter into collusive arrangements and thus permit 'the grossest frauds being practised on the landlord'. But there were more substantial reasons: 'A right, however, which had been vested in the landlord from the remotest time as a security for his rent', his lordship concluded, 'ought not to be lightly interfered with.'[10] The Lord Chief Justice thought other-

[8] *Select Committee on Metropolitan Police* (PP 1834, XVI), q. 2475.
[9] 2 and 3 Vict. c. 71, s. 39.
[10] *HL Deb.* 3s cxvi (1869), 563.

wise. The law, he maintained, was 'harsh and cruel'. Mr Justice Hannen concurred. In the light of these opinions, the Liverpool *Porcupine* ventured to suggest that the days of the 'exclusive and tyrannical privileges' of the landlord class were at hand.[11] But the fruits of the reformers' efforts, the Lodgers' Goods Protection Act of 1871, looked more impressive on paper than in its practical application.

The depredations to which brokers had become habituated continued unabated for many years. In 1881 Stuart Rendel, Radical MP for Montgomeryshire, introduced a bill designed to curb some of the worst excesses. Rendel's initiative foreshadowed the subsequent campaign organized by Edmund Robertson, a distinguished lawyer who sat for Dundee and twice held office as a junior naval minister in various Liberal administrations. Robertson had been a good deal in the United States on legal business and formed a favourable opinion of the homestead and exemption laws of that country. Shortly after entering parliament in 1886, he had been instrumental in the formation of the Homestead Law Association, a non-party pressure group which conducted the agitation for the extension of the American principle to British legislation.[12] A bill to exempt personal goods to the value of £20 from seizure or sale had been canvassed in the working men's clubs and was supported by the popular Radical press.[13] It was introduced into Parliament in 1887; property owners were horrified.[14] The following year the government acted.

The Law of Distress Amendment Act, 1888, marks the first serious step towards the elimination of the worst kind of abuse. Following the precedent established under the Agricultural Holdings Act five years earlier, landlords were henceforth restricted to the employment of bailiffs whose appointment had been approved by a county court judge. Where not satisfied as to the character of the applicant, the judge was empowered to withhold the now mandatory certificate for the execution of a distress. Unlicensed persons distraining for rent were guilty of trespass. The act also provided

[11]   *Porcupine* (20 Apr. 1871), p. 57.

[12]   On the operation of the American law, see *Further Reports from Her Majesty's Minister at Washington on the Homestead and Exemption Laws in the United States* (PP 1887, LXXXI).

[13]   On the Homestead Law Association, see leaflets (1887-8) in the British Library of Political and Economic Science; see also *Club and Institute Journal* (1887).

[14]   *Estates Gazette* (5 Nov. 1887), p. 599.

that tools and implements of trade, wearing apparel, and bedding to the value of £5 was absolutely exempted from distress.

It is difficult to assess the degree to which the new law was successful. Unfortunately, the Crown Office of the Treasury considered unimportant the collection of statistical data relative to the number of certificates granted or refused. However, the student of the period cannot but fail to be impressed by the frequency with which cases of illegal distress appear in the 'Police Intelligence' columns of the local press. The recourse to further amending legislation in 1895 and 1908 suggests that this impression is not without foundation. The Homestead Law Association continued to advocate the exemption of personal property from distress and execution, a policy subsequently adopted by the SDF.[15] Meanwhile, tenants persisted in their traditional means of resistance. 'Breaches of the peace often arise from the oppressive and improper acts of brokers', Mr Murray told the Select Committee on the Metropolitan Police in 1834; it was an observation which, in 1914, still retained its validity.[16]

II

It had been thought that, through the effective regulation of their proceedings, brokers might become 'a more respectable class'.[17] It seems unlikely that this hope was ever realized. Nothing appears to have raised the tone of brokerage which remained the most despicable of callings. 'The general public', an informed solicitor observed, 'always had a bad word for the bailiff who was generally looked upon as a vulgar man possessing brute strength, no heart and no brains ... Many men, even magistrates who had to deal with the subject ... often unjustly supported the popular prejudice.'[18] Henry James MP, a barrister with considerable experience in these matters, considered 'that the class of persons executing such a process, it not being a very agreeable occupation, is formed generally of persons who are for the most part insolvent, and who are not certainly sufficiently careful with respect to the due performance of

---

[15] Robertson's Homestead Bill is reprinted in *Estates Gazette* (6 June 1896), p. 824; and for the outraged proprietorial opinion it evoked, see issues of (13 June 1896), p. 876. On socialist response, see *Report of 26th Annual Conference of the SDF* (1906), pp. 19-20.

[16] *S.C. Metropolitan Police*, q. 2480.

[17] *S.C. Metropolitan Police*, q. 2477.

[18] *Estates Gazette* (17 Dec. 1898), p. 1058.

their duties'.[19] Auctioneers and estate agents usually combined rent-collecting with broking duties; the broker's man, however, tended to be recruited from the lumpenproletariat, or the stratum closest to it. According to the first historian of the North Eastern miners, the 'ruffian auxilliaries' who assisted the police in the work of eviction during the Great Strike of 1844 were 'low, mean, ragged fellows'. Thomas Burt remembered them, the candy men, as 'a dirty blackguardly lot' collected from the slums of Newcastle and other Tyneside towns: 'a regiment of ragged, ugly-looking, ill-bred, ill-mannered fellows'. Almost twenty years later, the same 'wretched ragged lot', who were 'offensively rough and insolent in the discharge of their functions', were again employed during the Cramlington Strike of 1863.[20] Such persons were beyond redemption and they knew it. As Mr Bung, the broker's man, put it: 'a broker's man is not a life to be envied ... people hate them and scout 'em because they're the ministers of wretchedness like, to poor people'.[21]

Sometimes they were employed to recover possession without the delay and expense of litigation. Lady rent-collectors, such as the youthful but less than charitable Miss Potter, were, for example, not averse to the use of intimidation. In Katherine's Buildings, where she served her apprenticeship, Miss Potter records being approached by a broker—'typical Jew'—to whose services she had recourse. 'Was I done?', she wondered. 'Paid 5s for three warning visits. If he gets two disreputable women out without further charge, I have made a good bargain.'[22]

Brokers themselves took the view that their material rewards were not commensurate with the risks they ran and that the statutory costs, in theory chargeable to the tenant,[23] were insufficient recompense for their labour. One London landlord who regretted having 'frequently to requisition the services of a local bailiff', considered them 'a rapacious class' of persons: 'I have not come across one who will work for the scale provided by law', he complained.[24] The brokers' reluctance to

[19] *Select Committee of the House of Lords on the Operation of the Law of Hypothec in Scotland* (PP 1868-9, IX), q. 55.

[20] Richard Fynes, *The Miners of Northumberland and Durham* (Blyth, 1873), pp. 72-3; Thomas Burt, *Autobiography* (1924), pp. 34, 178.

[21] Charles Dickens, *Sketches by Boz* (1890, edn.), p. 19.

[22] Beatrice Webb, *My Apprenticeship* (1971), p. 274.

[23] The statutory limitation on costs chargeable to the tenant did not preclude a private arrangement between bailiff and landlord for higher remuneration: see *Redman's Law of Landlord and Tenant* (sixth edn., 1912), pp. 480-1, and Appendix C.

[24] *Property Owners' Journal*, Aug. 1903.

distrain upon working people owed nothing to an atavistic human-itarianism. It was rather a matter of fine calculation. Where poor people were involved there were bound to be difficulties in recover-ing costs, the sale of their homes frequently proving insufficient to cover the expense of distraint (a reputable South London bailiff claimed, in 1898, to have received payment for only 112 of the 652 distraints levied in the previous year),[25] besides which, the fact that intimidation and harassment had evidently failed, that the tenant was an uncommonly obstreperous type, had also to be considered. Indeed, respectable auctioneers were extremely reluctant to under-take such work. As one of them explained: 'The levy fee of 3s. for distresses under £20 is quite inadequate to the risk run, but good firms have to do this work to keep in touch with their clients and solicitors.' 'It is not a matter of choice that auctioneers take up a bailiff's certificate', a colleague added, 'but rather for the con-venience and necessity by those having rent collections and the management of estates.'[26] The fear of losing ground to more obliging rivals had also to be considered. The head of a brokerage firm, stung by the critical correspondent to whom reference has been made above, put the case for his colleagues candidly:

In the first place bailiffs have to be certificated by the County Court Judge once a year and their conduct is always liable to review, and consequently their living is a precarious one, seeing the possibility of the suspension or cancellation of their certificate is always before them. Secondly, they, in a sense, differ from every other class of men, and as possession men are not noted for their probity (or they would not have descended the social scale to hold such a position), the bailiff is continually in fear and trembling as to what enormity they may commit or what duty omit, resulting in damages at the suit of an angry tenant.

Thirdly, the services of the bailiff are seldom requisitioned till after all kinds of entreaty, coaxing and threats have been exhausted, so that he enters upon his admittedly unpleasant duties with a bias against him, resulting in many cases in the expenditure of much brain exercise in how to obtain a legal entry for which, according to your correspondent, no payment should be made. It frequently happens that a bailiff has to leave his bed two or three hours before he usually rises, to circumvent some tricky defaulter, and as no costs are payable before the levy is made, can it seriously be supposed that 3s for levying the distraint pays a man who has to qualify to hold a certificate and keeps an office and staff for the convenience of those individuals who

[25] *Estates Gazette* (8 Jan. 1898), p. 52.
[26] *Estates Gazette* (12 Oct. 1895), p. 498.

like your correspondent, would ... fail to remunerate him for his work? No Mr Editor let us be fair between man and man and let the socially ostracised bailiff have reasonable reward for his onerous work.[27]

Truly, a bailiff's lot was not a happy one.

III

Before the First World War landlords in England and Wales were at liberty to distrain for rent in arrears without the intervention of the courts. In consequence it is impossible to measure the extent of the practice. Although the practical operation of the law was (from the tenant's point of view) immaterial, Scots law differed both juridically and with respect to procedure. The common law right of hypothec in urban Scotland, unlike the English law of distress, arose out of a tacit contract and was therefore an implied condition of tenure. It meant that the tenant's furniture, furnishings, and tools were liable to sequestration even though no arrears were outstanding. It was a form of privileged coercion guarded jealously by the proprietors.[28] Enforcement, however, required the prior approval of the sheriff courts. Thus, Scottish tenants were still sold up except that, in consequence of this formality, there was a capable official to record the transaction.

'The enforcement of hypothec in a small house', a philanthropic landlord once observed, 'is the enactment of a tragedy.'[29] How many such tragedies were enacted each year? We cannot be certain. Civil Judicial Statistics record the aggregate annual value of the sums sequestered but do not enumerate the number of petitions for sequestration nor identify the class of tenant most deeply affected. However, the limited evidence available is consistent with the commonsense view that this was an overwhelmingly working-class problem. Of the 21,402 petitions for sequestration in the period 1867-74, one-fifth were for the security of rent to become due; of the remainder ninety-five per cent involved amounts for less than £25 rent; while eighty-three per cent were for rents below £10 per annum.[30]

[27] *Property Owners' Journal*, Sept. 1903.
[28] See evidence of John Whitton, Secretary to the Glasgow Landlords' Association, *Select Committee on the Law of Hypothec in Scotland* (PP 1868-9, IX), qq. 1576-94.
[29] *Minutes of Departmental Committee on House-Letting in Scotland* (PP 1908, XLVII), qq. 5083-4.
[30] *Hypothec Scotland: Return of Sequestrations for Urban Subjects* (PP 1874, LIV), pp. 4-5.

On average sequestration for rent accounted for one-sixth of the annual value of all small debt business in Scotland. Sequestration for rent in Glasgow, however, comprised on average 42 per cent of the annual value of all such sequestrations. Table 1 suggests that, in spite of the many thousands of vacant dwellings in the city, landlords were reluctant to permit arrears during the severe unemployment of 1904/5 and 1908/9. The persistence of an extravagantly high level of empties in conjunction with an improvement in trade thereafter

Table 1: Sequestration for Rent, 1900–14

Year	Sequestration for rent in Scotland	Sequestration for rent in Glasgow	Percentage increase or decrease	Unoccupied houses in Galsgow
	£*	£*		%
1899	23,159	9,479	—	—
1900	25,411	10,818	+ 14.1	2.97
1901	27,012	10,878	+ 0.5	2.66
1902	28,136	11,409	+ 4.8	2.97
1903	30,362	13,092	+ 14.7	3.82
1904	34,496	14,517	+ 10.8	5.88
1905	36,435	15,020	+ 3.4	7.51
1906	33,583	14,528	− 3.3	7.77
1907	35,393	15,602	+ 7.3	8.28
1908	45,807	20,858	+ 33.6	9.34
1909	47,182	21,517	+ 3.1	9.48
1910	43,147	19,556	− 9.2	10.71
1911	36,706	16,450	− 15.9	10.72
1912	28,599	11,239	− 31.7	10.35
1913	11,230	4,522	− 59.8	9.25
1914	9,430	3,660	− 19.1	6.94

* figures rounded to nearest £

Sources: *Civil Judicial Statistics for Scotland*, Table XXXIII, cols. 4 and 7, (PP 1900, CIII); (PP 1902, CXVII); (PP 1904 CVII); (PP 1905, XCIX); (PP 1906, CXXXV); (PP 1908, CXXIII); (PP 1909, CIV); (PP 1910, CXI); (PP 1911, CII); (PP 1912–13, CX); (PP 1914, C); (PP 1914–16, LXXXII); figures on empties from A. K. Cairncross, *Home and Foreign Investment 1870–1913* (Cambridge, 1953), p. 16.

brought about a moderating reaction. In view of the fact that the sale value of the furniture and tools of the more prosperous English working man was—on the most generous estimate—no more than £32,[31] it is certain that the number of working-class tenants in Edwardian Scotland who were sold up each year must have run into the thousands. It was not for nothing that the programme of the Scottish Labour Party (1888) included a Homestead Law to protect furniture and tools to the value of £20 from seizure for debt.[32] It was to be a recurrent motif in the politics of labour thereafter.[33]

[31]   H. Clay, *The Problem of Industrial Relations* (1929), p. 287.

[32]   Programme of Scottish Labour Party reprinted in R. H. Campbell and J. B. A. Dow, ed., *Source Book of Scottish Economic and Social History* (Oxford, 1968), pp. 209-10.

[33]   See, for example, *Report of Departmental Committee on House-Letting in Scotland* (PP 1907, XXXVII), pp. 15-16; also, see *Forward*, 13 Mar. 1909.

3

Landlords, Tenants, and the Law

Before the Great War the legal relation of landlord and tenant in Britain, as in Europe, was non-problematical. The operation of the laws of supply and demand bolstered by extraordinary legal privileges for securing the rent defined a juridical framework that was largely unchalleneged by most housing reformers, and indeed, by most respectable tenants.[1] The non-respectable elements—excluding Socialists—were, however, too poor to offer assent to this system, and too weak to challenge it. Their aim was to survive. This chapter will explain how they fared.

I

Until the last decade of the nineteenth century the slums of urban Britain were perceived as an amorphous mass predisposed towards mischief: a seething bubbling cauldron, brutal, ugly; a volatile mixture which, should ever it explode, would leave the corpse of civilization rotting beneath the blood-stained trail of its vile effluence. After 1890 the tocsin ceased to sound. Social imperialists continued to toll the alarm, but the slums and their inhabitants were no longer viewed as a violent threat to the state—just centres of vice, degeneracy, and, criminality: still an evil, but one amenable to reform. The age of social administration had dawned.

Every city had its Jago—congeries of dark courts and labyrinthine alleys, forbidding closes and fearful backlands; areas whose topography not merely encouraged loitering with intent but seemingly made it irresistible, almost mandatory—areas in which violence was endemic. These were districts to be avoided by all but professional reformers. From the haven of villadom the aspiring bourgeois faintly applauded the efforts of the Hills, the Booths, and the Barnetts, but no one, except the Oxbridge narodniks—frightened, guilty and, of

[1] International Labour Office, *European Housing Problems Since the War* (Geneva, 1924), pp. 6-7.

course, green—seriously sought to emulate them. 'Who would be even conscious of change, if, say, Wandsworth or Hoxton vanished with tomorrow's sunrise?' Charles Masterman wondered.[2] Even those charged with their administration tried to give the 'rough' quarters as wide a berth as possible. Indeed, one senior official spoke of them in terms of 'no-go' areas.[3]

The constabulary's reluctance to enforce the law left the upright citizen of these districts at the mercy of all sorts of importunate vagabonds. 'I have complaints over and over again about respectable householders not being able to get rid of these men and women in back courts', said the Chief Inspector of the Poor for the parish of Glasgow. 'I have known a man expose his chest—I know the man—and call down all the purgatories upon the people because they did not throw coppers at him.'[4] Landlords too had to shift for themselves. A casual labourer who rose to become a man of property, on being asked the secret of his success, replied:

There wasn't much secret about it; I know most of the tenants and their ways and means. Where it was a case of pay but wouldn't, I brought their nose to the grindstone with a firm hand; in most cases it was only a matter of doing with less drink, and I used to think, 'The less drink you have my beauties, the better for you; so here goes for a good tight turn of the screw on you' ... Knowing my customers well, I could generally tell when there would be an attempt to shoot the moon as they say; and I used to be on the look-out for it, and in most cases managed to stop it. If they did succeed in running the blockade with me, I could generally find them out and make it warm for them; in short, one way or another, I made not paying so unpleasant to such gentry that they used to pay as being the less of the two evils. Other landlords hearing of my success, gave me their collecting to do, and the more I had the easier it was to do in proportion, for then the cut-and-run sort often found it a case of out of the frying pan into the fire, giving me the slip in one place only to find themselves under me in another, for you see, people of this class must move in a very limited circle. This street that I live in was the worst paying one in all the neighbourhood. The fact was the roughs had stormed the garrison, and not only wouldn't pay rent, but were given to knocking about those who went to ask for it, and to pretty well tearing the house to pieces. So bad was the property that some of the owners actually kept out of the way altogether, to avoid having to pay rates on it. I knew that most of them would be only too glad to get rid of it at

[2] C. F. G. Masterman, *In Peril of Change* (1905), p. 163.
[3] *Glasgow Municipal Commission on the Housing of the Poor* (Glasgow, 1904), qq. 5208, 5210.
[4] *GMC*, q. 4859.

any price, and as it struck me I could manage it, I went in for buying it up by degrees after my collecting business had grown to be large enough to enable me to save money out of it. When I did get hold of the property, my first step towards reclaiming it was to come and live in it—sort of carrying the war into the enemies' country you know.[5]

The military leitmotiv underlines the existent state of belligerency that was a necessarily permanent feature of the slums. 'It is an art and a boast with a considerable number of tenants as to how long they can live rent free', one landlord told his assembled colleagues.[6] And so no doubt it was. In the Southwark Police Court, Mr Taylor, the presiding magistrate, was heard to have remarked 'that it seemed to be a custom of a good many people never to pay rent after the first two or three weeks of their tenancy', an opinion with which the prosecuting agent fully concurred: 'we lose hundreds of pounds every year through that class of people'.[7]

Such persons were frequently violent. More often than not tenants came off the worse from such encounters, but not always. One landlord, a widow with a few properties, claimed to have received only two weeks' rent in two years because of bad tenants.[8] Others bore the scars of battle. Octavia Hill was told of an alley 'where the people had lived for many years without paying rent, for the landlord had deserted them through fear ... Such was the danger and difficulty that his wife was then suffering from an Irish attack of poker and broomstick'.[9] However, to be successful threatening behaviour had to be employed with care. Some tenants were clearly negligent in this respect. In Dod Street, Blackfriars, for example, the occupants, having received notice to quit, went too far. In court the landlady explained:

Well, they have pretty well torn the place to pieces. They have burnt and destroyed the woodwork and sold anything that would fetch some money. They locked me up in a room and threatened to murder me; and it was only through someone going for the police that I was released. I am in fear of my

[5] The Riverside Visitor [Thomas Wright], *The Great Army: Sketches of Life and Character in a Thames-Side District* 2 vols. (1875), II, pp. 136-7.
[6] *Report of 16th Conference of United Property Owners' Association of Great Britain* (Bradford, 1903), p. 41.
[7] *Southwark Recorder*, 3 June 1899.
[8] Corporation of Birmingham, *Report of Special Housing Enquiry* (Birmingham, 1914), q. 472.
[9] H. O. Barnett, *Canon Barnett: His Life, Work and Friends* (1921), p. 74; see too Thomas Wright, *The Great Unwashed* (1868) p. 147.

life as I get into the streets; in fact, they are a regular pack of Hooligans, about as bad as any I ever knew.[10]

In these districts landlords generally showed scant regard for the law. Nobody really cared: landlord and tenant set their own standards of misconduct. Perhaps the most common form of intimidation was the issue of 'blue frighteners'—notice to quit similar in appearance to court summonses.[11] Harassment and intimidation were not only widespread but even considered commendable. Mr Baron Robin of the North East London Property Owners' Association, for example, was rather proud of his particular technique:

Now we don't go to court with all these small tenants. A practice I carry out very frequently is to 'bounce' them (Laughter). I take a van up to the house and threaten to take the goods away under a legal distress. I then let them offer to have the use of the van to take goods away, and thus get rid of them (Laughter). I have no doubt my experience will be borne out by every agent or auctioneer in London who has to deal with this class of property.[12]

Others made no pretence at legality. In East London where there was nothing worth distraining upon, 'landlords or their collectors summarily "bundled out" old non-paying tenants'. 'These ejectments', said Revd. Thomas Wright, 'were often very painful affairs.'[13] 'Man after man reveals the lawless conduct of landlords', Canon Barnett wrote his brother in 1899, shortly after the formation of the Toynbee Hall Tenants' Defence Committee, 'and our lawyer tells them how to resist and force them to use legal methods of eviction.'[14] But the 'Poor Man's Lawyer' spread slowly, too slowly.[15] In 1913 a Birmingham estate agent, 'handling one of the largest collection of weekly and monthly houses in the city', told a local inquiry: 'I have many times taken the law into my own hands, but the tenants know the law too well now.'[16]

[10] *Southwark Recorder*, 29, Sept. 1900.
[11] London Reform Union, *Annual Report* (1892), p. 12.
[12] *Report of Special Conference of United Property Owners' Association of Great Britain at Westminster Palace Hotel* (Bradford, 1902), pp. 6-7.
[13] Riverside Visitor, *Great Army*, I, p. 133.
[14] Barnett, *Canon Barnett*, p. 519.
[15] In any case the identity of its beneficiaries often remains problematical. Cf. *5th Annual Report of Mansfield House University Settlement in East London* (1896), p. 39.
[16] *Birmingham Housing Enquiry*, qq. 3001, 3038.

II

Until quite recently, the alienation of the wage-earner from the law was almost total. The law was a rich man's conspiracy, its victims were the poor; the courts a source of oppression, the cost of justice prohibitive. 'What do magistrates know about the law?', exclaimed one angry worker:

> They know what sentences they can give, an' how much they can fine 'ee an' that's about all. An' what do 'em know about life—how us be situated— 'cepting what they picks up in police courts, which is pretty place for to learn it in? ... I don't say the magistrates can help o' it altogether. Some o' em's nice nuff gen'lemen, an' tries to listen an' weigh it all up, an' do their best; only naturally they leans towards their own sort o' people, an' looks down on the likes o' us ... No doubt they do know about the likes o' theirselves, but they don't know our ways an' our feelings. How can 'em? So they listens to lawyers an' clerks, an' bobbies. It saves 'em trouble ...[17]

Moreover, the courts dealt with criminals, drunks, peevish spouses, and general ne'er-do-wells, not the sorts of people wth whom the respectable working class cared to be identified.[18] Such people shrank from the ordeal of a court appearance, often to the detriment of their own interests. 'They are as much afraid of being in the court as plaintiff as they are of being there as defendant', said Revd Henry Williamson. Amongst the Dundee jute workers this reluctance to prosecute claims for industrial injury came as a welcome boon to negligent employers. Time and again Williamson found that a woman worker would refuse to press her suit when urged to do so. ' "Oh", she says, "dinna gang there. I would rather let them keep the money." '[19]

If only suspicion, timidity and disenchantment with the law equalled ignorance of its provisions landlords might have been better pleased. Although the law offered the tenant no express or positive protection, the complex procedure governing eviction and distraint constituted a legal minefield. Its tortuous and ill-defined paths threaded faintly through a treacherous landscape pitted by the craters of those who had stumbled carelessly in the dark. The

---

[17] Stephen Reynolds, R. & T. Woolley, *Seems So! A Working Class View of Politics* (1911), pp. 93, 103; and for a discussion of these attitudes, see Henry Pelling, *Popular Politics and Society in Late Victorian Britain* (1968), Ch. iv.

[18] Cf. Central Billeting Board, Report on Workington, 14 Mar. 1918 (PRO Mun. 5/97).

[19] *Royal Commission on Labour*, Group C (PP 1892, XXV), qq. 11055, 11148.

stream of handbooks published for their guidance invariably warned landlords of judicial fastidiousness in this respect, and of the penalties to which they were exposed should they succumb to temptation and ignore due process. Tenants were by no means unmindful of the obstacles confronting their landlords. Indeed, it was less the existence of a popular reform movement which property owners found disquieting but rather that individual tenants too frequently displayed a knowledgeable determination to ensure that eviction proceedings complied with the strict letter of the law. 'The poorer classes of tenant are now so well versed in the law as between landlord and tenant, and often defy the owner to serve an ejectment order, well knowing that they then have immunity for paying rent for some weeks', said one landlord.[20] Another characterized the relation with his tenants as analogous to that of teacher and pupil with himself cast as the latter.[21] Thomas Binnie, a much respected Glasgow landlord and valuer, found the audacity of his tenants startling: 'At present they know their position so well that, after sitting for a long time without paying any rent, I have had a tenant come to ask me how much I would pay him to leave the house, in order that I might be saved the expense of getting an ejectment.'[22] Binnie's assessment was not wildly inaccurate. Indeed, the scale of sequestrations and evictions in that city was such that a nodding acquaintance with the law on landlord and tenant was well nigh unavoidable.

Tenants in Glasgow were impossible. 'They won't pay the landlord, the temptation to cheat the landlord, and their knowledge of being able to do so, are so strong.'[23] In this they were exceptional. In the opinion of experienced proprietors, weekly tenants in Liverpool were nowhere near as well informed of their position as their Glasgow counterparts.[24] Landlords responded with exceptional severity. Table 2 indicates that, in Victorian Glasgow, iron discipline was habitually enforced to secure the rent, and that such discipline was applied without regard to the state of the housing maket. This is unique.

[20]   *Birmingham Housing Enquiry*, q. 2694.
[21]   *Royal Commission on Housing in Scotland: Minutes of Evidence*, 4 vols., HMSO, (Edingburgh, 1921), q. 21838.
[22]   Presbytery of Glasgow, *Report of Commission on the Housing of the Poor in Relation to their Social Condition* (Glasgow, 1891), pp. 154-5.
[23]   *Glasgow Presbytery Commission*, p. 120.
[24]   *Glasgow Presbytery Commission*, p. 139.

Table 2: Summary Ejectment Proceedings, Glasgow

| Number of warrants granted in | | | |
Year	Sheriff Courts	Burgh Court	Total
1875	1,481	2,780	4,261
1880	1,316	6,376	7,692
1885	1,647	8,760	10,407
1889	1,900	10,350	12,250

Source: James Nicol, *Vital Social and Economic Statistics of Glasgow* (Glasgow, 1885), 138; idem, *Vital Social and Economic Statistics of Glasgow* (Glasgow, 1891) 232; Presbytery of Glasgow, *Report of Commission on the Housing of the Poor in Relation to their Social Condition* (Glasgow, 1891), 96.

Whatever its cause, the endemic strife between landlord and tenant in Glasgow was not a simple function of the size or growth of the population. In London, for example, the average number of summary ejectments granted by magistrates in the period 1886-90 amounted to a relatively modest 2,327 per year.[25] In 1913, that most prosperous of pre-war years, police courts in England and Wales heard 18,996 applications and granted 18,197 orders for possession.[26]

An adequate explanation of the peculiar conflict between landlord and tenant in Glasgow would require a comparative analysis of patterns of investment, ownership, and management of property. It would also have to take account of that dispossessed peasantry who came from the Highlands and Ireland to swell the casual labour force. The presence of these impoverished tenants evidently highlighted the authoritarian aspect of Scottish culture.[27] Landlords everywhere in the United Kingdom pressed for more summary powers of ejectment; but only in Scotland did they enjoy the support of 'respectable' opinion, and only in Scotland were their claims conceded.[28] To enumerate such factors, however, is relatively

[25] *Returns on Evictions, London and Suburbs* (PP 1888, LXXXII) and (PP 1890-1, LXIV).

[26] Departmental Committee on the Operation of the Rent Acts: MS Minutes of Evidence, 8 Mar. 1920, p. 42 (PRO HLG. 41/5).

[27] G. F. A. Best, 'Another Part of the Island', in Michael Wolff and H. J. Dyos, ed., *The Victorian City*, 2 vols. (1973), I, pp. 398-400.

[28] In Scotland the right to evict a weekly tenant in arrears on 48 hours' notice that was to be embodied in the House Letting & Rating Act of 1911, had previously been supported by the Glasgow Presbytery Commission on the Housing of the Poor (1890), the Glasgow Municipal Commission on Housing (1904) and the Departmental Committee on House-Letting in Scotland (1907). In England and Wales, by contrast, the 'indiscriminating attacks which have been made against the owners of working class property as a class', it was claimed, had undermined investment in such property.

simple; to explain them is a more daunting task. The following paragraphs provide some information from which a more adequate account might eventually be constructed.

Under the Sheriff Court Act, 1838, the function of the presiding judge, in cases of summary ejectment, was administrative rather than judicial unless the tenant could show title to possession, or, alternatively, on payment of a sixpenny fee, lodge written 'answers' contesting the landlord's claim for warrant of ejectment.[29] In Glasgow, a long-standing grievance arose from what was considered the unauthorized assumption of discretionary powers on the part of successive sheriffs in the conduct of these proceedings. In combination with the Association of House Factors and Property Agents, the Glasgow Landlords' Association protested against these persistent irregularities:

Your Memorialists have been informed that the tenant frequently states such defences as that the premises are in disrepair or insanitary, or asks that an arrangement to accept arrears of rent be made, and the petition dismissed. The Memorialists respectfully submit that such statements by the tenants are irrelevant.

The petition for warrant to eject is not one for payment of rent, but for possession ... The practice which has been followed in some cases of adjourning the hearing of the petition till the Sanitary Inspector has reported as to the condition of the premises, that the Court may judge whether the tenant ought to have withheld his rent, is, in your Memorialist's opinion, irregular; and if the tenant has a claim against the landlord he must bring it in a competent form. He is not entitled without a title to possession, to retain possession against the landlord ...

The landlord may be considerate or inconsiderate, in making his demand, but he is, in either case, entitled to his legal rights.[30]

It was alleged that, in consequence of this want of uniformity, bad tenants 'systematically take advantage of the various views taken by the individual judges, and thereby not only does serious loss fall

---

'These attacks have not been confined to newspapers, and the tendency has been to induce the better class of landlords, who are most sensitive to public opinion, to withdraw from a business in which they are liable to receive more than their share of opprobrious epithets to another class of investment where the return is at least equally good and safe, and where their operations are not the subject of public condemnation.' Reconstruction Committee [Printed] Correspondence on the Question of Housing After the War, ii, p. 7 (Christopher Addison Papers, Bodleian Library, Oxford, Box 72).

[29]   1 & 2 Vict. c. 119, ss. 12-13.
[30]   'Memorial of Glasgow Landlords' Association and the Association of House Factors and Property Agents', 15 Jan. 1900, *GMC*, pp. 348-50.

upon the landlords and factors, but the tenants are demoralized. These tenants, mostly uneducated and of the poorest class, find that the terms of their contracts of lease can be disregarded with impunity'. As a result, landlords often lost from one to three months' rent.

More serious still was the conduct of affairs in the Burgh Court where business was confined exclusively to summary ejectment proceedings. Even more than the Sheriff, magistrates were held to show partiality towards tenants in the performance of their duties. Not only where they inclined to give credence to the most outrageously contrived defences, but were held to encourage tenants in such preposterous extravagance through the ease with which the lodging of answers was permitted, reducing what ought to have been a careful process of inquiry into the merest formality.

Amongst the poor, the compassionate character of the local bench was thought to be a subject of mirth and cynical exploitation. Inevitably the tenant's wife appeared suitably dressed for the occasion: a shabby, lugubrious woman, clasping an emaciated infant (borrowed from an obliging neighbour, of course!), while another disappeared into the folds of her skirts, who proceeded to deliver a few well-rehearsed lines, a faltering lachrymose performance which rarely failed to excite the tender-hearted (feeble-minded, some would have said), gentlemen peering down on them. The class theatre of the criminal law found its counterpart in the inferior civil courts, albeit in an attenuated melodramatic form, except that here the roles were more ambiguous. The plebs are still part of the cast, to be sure, but many landlords felt that they were also the directors!

Table 3 shows at a glance that the landlords' complaints were not without foundation. The spectacular increase in warrants for ejectment and the growing tendency to challenge such applications was in large part a function of changes in the administration of justice. The take-off into quindigital evictions coincides with the renaissance of the Burgh Court. Ever since the late 1880s when, at the request of the factors, that ailing institution had been revived and regularized in twice-weekly sittings, the number of defendants lodging answers had grown at an alarming rate.[31]

This lodging of answers, landlords protested, tended to diminish the value of the Burgh Court which otherwise was faster and cheaper

---

[31] *Minutes of Departmental Committee on House-Letting in Scotland* (PP 1908, XLVII), qq. 5505-6.

Table 3: Burgh Court Glasgow: Warrants for Ejectment and Answers

Year	Number of Warrants for Ejectment	Number of Answers	Percentage of Answers to Ejectments
1870	3,624	17	0.46
1875	2,780	6	0.21
1880	6,376	52	0.81
1885	8,760	226	2.57
1889	10,350	—	—
1892	12,181	981	8.05
1902	17,000	6,916	40.68
1906	20,887	7,736	37.03

Source: Strathclyde Regional Archives, Memorial of Glasgow Landlords' Association to the Lord Provost and Magistrates, 22 Dec. 1893, MP26.52; Presbytery of Galsgow, *Report of Commission on the Housing of the Poor in Relation to their Social Condition* (Glasgow 1891), p. 96; *Glasgow Municipal Commission on the Housing of the Poor* (Glasgow, 1904) QQ.2071, 2076; *Departmental Committee on House Letting in Scotland* (PP 1908, XLVII), Q.5502.

than proceeding in the sheriff courts. Many ascribed this irksome development to the emergence of a disreputable class of lawyers 'who made a point of going to people and advising them that by lodging answers they were certain to get delay'.[32] The bush telegraph had certainly been crackling. In Edwardian Glasgow more than one-third of the warrants for ejectment were challenged. In consequence, monthly tenants gained an additional eleven days in which to remove; weekly tenants generally received from three to five days grace. This irregular procedure, for that is what it was, represented a practical solution to the complete breakdown which would otherwise have occurred had the magistrates attempted the minute inquiry into each of the 300 cases which on average came before the Burgh Court every week.[33]

Glasgow landlords were incensed by such conduct. As early as 1893 they drew attention to 'the startling increase' in the numbers lodging answers. 'On finding that additional days of grace are given to those who lodge answers', they protested, 'unscrupulous defaulters readily enter objections, simply as a move to gain time.' Moreover, although invariably awarded against the tenant, the costs of ejectment in practice fell upon the landlord as tenants generally possessed neither funds nor furniture worth sequestra-

[32] *House-Letting in Scotland* (1908), q. 5509.
[33] 'Report by the Town Clerk as to Procedure in Cases of Ejectment brought before the Burgh Court', 21 Dec. 1904 (Strathclyde Regional Archives, MP34.59).

tion.[34] It was calculated that in 1904 the delay in getting ejectments carried out involved an aggregate loss to the owners of 'more than 570 years' rent', besides the large arrears which had accumulated before proceedings were instituted. The legal costs in that year alone exceeded £8,000.[35] But what, from the landlord's point of view, was all the more alarming was that it prolonged the dangerous interlude between the service of notice to quit and execution of warrant for ejectment in which vengeful tenants were prone to vandalize the property.[36] The significance attached to the matter was such that Glaswegian landlords were not only willing to countenance more exacting standards in public health administration but even prepared to acquiesce in the dreaded Sassenach practice of compounding the rates (i.e. the rating of owners in lieu of occupiers) if, in return, they obtained an unfettered summary power of ejectment.[37] The House Letting and Rating Act of 1911 represented just such a trade-off.

It might have been thought that the stratospheric level of evictions disclosed in the preceding analysis was such as to propel the legal relation of landlord and tenant to the forefront of working-class politics. Apart from the Scottish colliers who, like colliers elsewhere, had long campaigned against eviction in trade disputes, there is little evidence to suggest that eviction was in fact perceived as an urgent problem. The evicted were socially visible, to be sure. 'Those of us', wrote John Maclean, 'who have crossed St. George's Square on a keen biting winter night, and have seen the mass of misery huddling together on the seats and plinths of monuments, can comprehend the full significance of ejection to many of those hundreds remorselessly driven from shelter by the hell-hounds of capitalism.'[38] The evicted, however, were drawn from the poorest sectors of the working class.[39] Respectable tradesmen, the foundation of the labour movement, were worried by high rents rather than eviction. Those with homes to lose were more concerned with hypothec and sequestration rather than eviction and with the peculiarities of the onerous house letting system. It was the 'Massive Question', a question whose resolution affected the more substantial

[34] 'Memorial of Glasgow Landlords' Association to the Lord Provost and Magistrates', 22 Dec. 1893 (Strathclyde Regional Archives, MP26.52).
[35] Memorandum of Thomas Binnie, *Report of Departmental Committee on House-Letting in Scotland* (PP 1907, XXXVI), p. 25.
[36] *Glasgow Presbytery Commission*, pp. 115, 117; *GMC*, q. 10419.
[37] *Glasgow Presbytery Commission*, pp. 113, 117-18.   [38] *Forward*, 10 Mar. 1910.
[39] For analysis of eviction statistics, see my article, 'Landlord and Tenant in Urban Scotland: the background to the Clyde Rent Strikes, 1915', *Journal of Scottish Labour History Society*, No. 15 (1981), pp. 10-12.

elements among working people, that was to prove a principal source of radicalism amongst tenants in Edwardian Glasgow.

III

If the lodging of answers represented a means by which unprincipled defaulters sought to thwart their landlords, proprietors could draw comfort from its limited application. A universal source of resistance, and one far more galling, was the intimidation to which they were subjected by officious bureaucrats egged on by vindictive tenants. 'I know perfectly well that if you get an undesirable tenant, the moment the landlord or the agent threatens to distrain ... they go to the Council House and complain that the house is unfit for habitation and in the case of hundreds of houses', one agent complained, 'that has resulted in the Housing Committee visiting the property in question. If it had not been for the tenants these houses would never have been brought to your notice at all.'[40] Owen Williams, Chairman of the Liverpool Land and House Owners' Association, stated that 'the owners are now powerless to compel their tenants to keep the houses clean, and even in some cases to pay their rent. If they attempt to do so the tenants go to the Health Officer and in a few days the owner receives notice to clean the houses.' Members of the Liverpool association complained that they 'are thus put to such an expense that they no longer care to interfere with the tenants'.[41] The contempt for cleanliness and subordination coupled with the general antipathy towards the rights of property could, however, assume more serious forms.

Octavia Hill argued that the crux of the housing problem was the need to reform the depraved character of the slum-dweller. It was a view which received widespread assent. 'Weekly tenants', said Mr Justice Eve, 'are the people who take the bannisters for firewood', a legal definition with which, the *Birmingham Daily Mail* remarked, 'owners of small house property, in slum districts at least, will be disposed wholeheartedly to agree ... The class of tenant referred to is the bane of many a landlord'.[42] Although the word had not yet entered common usage, vandalism was already considered a major

[40] *Birmingham Housing Enquiry*, q. 2966.
[41] Borough of Liverpool, *Reports of Dr Parkes and Dr Sanderson on the Sanitary Condition of Liverpool* (Liverpool, 1871), p. 64.
[42] *Birmingham Daily Mail*, 18 Mar. 1914.

social problem. In some properties, for example, it was alleged that wilful damage consumed 30 per cent of the rental. 'The vast amount of wanton destruction of property ... well nigh amounts to a national loss', one authority declared.[43]

Children, in particular, were amongst the very worst offenders. Notorious for their destructive propensities, landlords despised and feared them. Still more troublesome were those who dwelt on the fringes of the urban economy, peripheral characters for whom the unoccupied house provided a shelter, and its components an income of sorts. Such persons cared little for statutory provisions against forcible entry and detainer; neither were they impeded by the penalties against malicious damage to property. Uninhabited houses were thus entered and stripped of all valuables: piping, lead, copper, zinc, sash-weights—anything in fact for which a few coppers might be obtained.[44] The scrap-metal market of late Victorian and Edwardian Britain has yet to find its historian, but no doubt he or she will find house-breaking or 'junking' an important source of supply.

Property-owners were constantly on guard against these proletarian asset-strippers. But there were others, squatters, who were equally as bad, if not worse, on whom fortune smiled now and then. The occupants of Three Tuns Court, Whitechapel were so blessed. In its fifteen houses were crammed some 150 persons, with one privy and no water, except what could be begged from neighbours. And yet these fifteen houses were considered desirable residences by the occupants because the owner was in prison for debt and the local authority careless. In St. Margaret's, Westminster, too, some seventy families squatted peacefully while the courts slowly—ever so slowly—set about establishing rightful ownership amongst rival claimants.[45] Others, however, did not restrict themselves to the slums.

In February 1914 Mr James Cheverton Brown, President of the United Property Owners Association of Great Britain, told the Royal Commission on Housing in Scotland a tale of destruction which Grahame Greene would be hard put to it to equal:

[43] *Glasgow Presbytery Commission*, p. 101; *R.C. Housing in Scotland*, qq. 14884-9. Quotation from Pascoe Fenwick, *Better Dwellings for the Workmen of London* (1884), p. 12.

[44] Examples are numerous, but see 'Housebreaking', *Porcupine* (22 May 1869), p. 66.

[45] *First Report of the Metropolitan Sanitary Commission* (HMSO, 1848), p. 109; 'Report of an Investigation into the State of the Working Classes in the Parishes of St. Margaret's and St. John's, Westminster', *Journal of Statistical Society of London* III (1840), p. 21.

About seven or eight years ago [he said], I was interested in a block of property in the city of Hull, consisting of about 200 houses. It was new property; each house had four rooms. They were fitted with gasfittings, they had back-yards, each house had a separate privy, and each house had a back-way and a back-door. They were well fitted with drawers and cupboards, and every convenience and accommodation that a workman's family could require. They cost an average of £200 each, and they were all let to working men at rentals of from 3s. 6d to 5s a week. They were new, and in every sense in excellent condition. About that time the Corporation of Hull were clearing away certain areas ... and breaking up slums, with a view to city improvements. Our slums up till then in Hull had been fairly well centralized and segregated; everyone knew where they were, and every one avoided them so far as possible. Now, when these slums were broken up, and the slummers who had occupied them, and who were of the shiftless, thriftless character that I am referring to, split up into many different districts throughout the town; and one notorious family from among them succeeded, with a forged rent book, in getting possession of one of the houses in the neighbourhood which I have just described. From that day the decent tenants began steadily to leave. Within a few weeks thirty or forty of them had gone; and as fast as they went, more and more slummers kept arriving, mostly surreptitiously and by night-time, taking possession of these houses without anyone's official knowledge—generally by breaking in from the back yard.[46]

The Commissioners were flabbergasted. Surely there were policemen? 'Oh yes; there were policemen who went up and down the streets.' And no caretakers? 'No, not in that class of property. We employ collectors who simply go round once a week to collect the rents; and it took us a few weeks to fully realise what was going on. The decent tenants, as I say, left; and the houses became, apparently shut up; ... and these people break in—usually on a Saturday night, or some other evening after it is dark—at the back. Generally it is done by breaking a window in the scullery and undoing the catch of the window.' But has not the landlord powers to protect himself? 'He does not know that they are there for a time; perhaps for several weeks. They live at the back; and they have no furniture, except a dirty mattress or two, and perhap an orange box.' Could they not have been turned out? 'Not without great difficulty once they get in. When you find that there is an individual of that class, he usually has a plausible story that the house was sublet to him by the tenant that left.'

[46] This quotation and the following account are from *R.C. Housing in Scotland*, qq. 25768-80.

David Gilmour, an official of the Scottish Miners' Union, and a member of the Commission, was stunned. 'You are putting a state of affairs before us', he told Mr Cheverton Brown, 'that we have never had given us before.' It reflected the feelings of his colleagues. Landlord and tenant relations in Scotland were not what you might call good, but lawlessness as practised in England seemed unheard of. The witness continued:

As regards this property, when it was brought to our knowledge, and when we realised that this had happened, I went down myself, and I saw this property, and I was amazed at the alteration in it; there was hardly a window that was not broken and stuffed with rags; the grates had been removed; the drains were stopped, and the woodwork damaged ... It was all over this district and the property. We had to get the assistance and goodwill of the police, and in the end we did go down, and by the cooperation of all the landlords in the neighbourhood we ejected every one of these objectionable persons; but it costs us hundreds of pounds to restore the property to anything like its original condition, we had to change the name of the street, and it took us four years to get the neighbourhood back to anything like the respectable reputation that it had enjoyed before this occurred.

Landlords had every reason to magnify their difficulties. The widow Codlyn, it will be recalled, considered her seventy cottages 'an affliction, a bugbear, an affront, and a positive source of loss', although the rent provided a comfortable income. 'Invariably she talked as though she would willingly present them to anybody who cared to accept–"and glad to be rid of 'em!" ' To which Bennett, who knew a thing or two about the business, adds: 'Most owners of property talk thus'.[47] Nevertheless, even if its incidence cannot be measured with any precision, violent acts against house property were committed with sufficient frequency as to be socially visible. The meaning of these acts, however, remains far from clear. Playful, though destructive, children and acquisitive house-breakers present few problems; while some kinds of destruction appear to represent a grotesque parody of socially approved behaviour.[48] Moreover, a good deal of what was defined as problematic was not so much the physical destruction of property as its misuse. The absence of necessary amenities in most working-class houses, particularly in the poorest quarters, easily presented a menacingly chaotic appearance to the casual visitor of middle-class origin to whom dirt, disease, and

[47] Arnold Bennett, *The Card* (Penguin books edn. 1975), p. 24.
[48] Cf. Riverside Visitor, *Great Army*, I, p. 134.

destruction were a single continuum. Landlords were more precise. From their own accounts, it is clear that house-wrecking was anything but the random expression of depraved minds and warped intellects.

In his evidence before the Presbytery Commission on the Housing of the Poor, William M'Bain of the Glasgow Landlords Association, explained: 'It costs a month's rent and much delay to eject bad tenants, and whoever requires to be ejected must get notice to quit, and as soon as he gets notice to quit he retaliates, so to speak, by doing as much damage as he possibly can to the property.' It is the timing of such incidents which affords some clue as to their meaning. The Commission itself was much interested in this problem of motivation. 'It is the drink tendency that causes them to destroy houses after receiving notice to quit, and not because of any feeling of revenge or want of moral tone?' enquired Mr Mather, pursuing the subject. M'Bain replied somewhat sweepingly: 'My answer is that the two go hand-in-hand; you find in the drink all the cause of the trouble'.[49] Mr George Donald, caretaker to the Glasgow Workman's Dwellings Company, was more circumspect:

Some of the tenants may be fair to your face when asking for a house or trying to get leave to remain after being warned away, but when they know they are to go, knowing the course of ejection, they are openly defiant. They turn round and distinctly say to your face that you cannot put them out and they wait until the last moment. They know all about 'answers' and that they can get another week sitting in the house for 6d and they make up excuses about illness to get further time. That is the time when the damage is done to the property as a rule—to the dresser, gas bracket, automatic gas meters, and also money extracted from them.[50]

Tenants did not take lightly to eviction even if, and perhaps because, there was little they could do to prevent it. To many it must have seemed that through no fault of their own, they were unable to pay the rent and likely to be deprived of a roof over their head. The landlord seemed harsh, society unfeeling. But self-respect demanded something, some protestion, however muted, some satisfying act of retribution, and one moreover in which the chance of detection and punishment was slight.[51] This desire to square accounts for wrongs committed, real or imagined, had parallels in intriguing phenomena

[49]   *Glasgow Presbytery Commission*, pp. 115, 117.
[50]   *GMC*, q. 10419.
[51]   Cf. *Glasgow Presbytery Commission*, p. 96.

such as industrial sabotage. A missile hurled at the malefactor's window was probably more usual. The resounding crash of broken glass followed by the dull thud of a brick at the end of its trajectory; the receding clatter of hobnails moving rapidly over cobbled streets—this may well have been the most common form of property destruction. And should it exist, a colloquialism encompassing such action would surely be on the most thumbed page of the dictionary of the inarticulate. But there need not be violence. Old Jo Philpot, sneaking time off the job for an illicit smoke and drink, and remarking to himself: 'This is where we get some of our own back', is not all that far removed from the poor tenants with whom we are concerned.[52]

Many proprietors were convinced that tenants behaved thus merely to spite them, that they retained possession after expiration of notice to quit largely to indulge a malicious satisfaction in compelling the landlord to commence legal proceedings before their surreptitious disappearance. There is no doubt something in this line of reasoning. At the same time, it must be noted that, though powerless to prevent eviction, pernicious procrastination might none the less assist materially in finding a new home. In order to avoid the expense and the attendant risks consequent upon the delay in summary ejectment procedure, many gave way to untoward pressures. As one reformer noted with disapprobation: 'the "making-up" of rent books is a common practice of certain landlords who, wishing to get rid of tenants from whom they have failed to extract any rent, and with a view to persuading them to go without giving trouble, offer to enter up in their rent books all the rent as having been regularly paid when due'.[53] Although repeatedly condemned, this tendency to off-load unsatisfactory tenants on to the nearest competitor frequently proved irresistible, even for the most enthusiastic advocates of combination. Addressing his comrades in conference assembled, a spokesman for the Barrow Property Owners' Association strongly urged the need for effective organization proudly pointing to the 'good work' thus far achieved: 'Tenants who have for many years evaded the landlord have found their wings clipped by the united actions of Property Owners, and in Barrow we have been successful in driving our worst tenants into

---

[52] Quotation from Robert Tressell, *The Ragged Trousered Philanthropists* (Panther books edn. 1965), p. 38.

[53] *Charity Organization Review* (July 1885), p. 297.

the country where houses are more plentiful and owners innocent!.[54]
Some local associations of proprietors were, however, more positive
in their thinking.

[54] *Report of 19th Conference of United Property Owners' Association of Great
Britain* (Liverpool, 1906), p. 50.

4

Property-Owners' Associations

Nothing like enough is known of the structure of property-owership in Victorian Britain but such information as is readily available seems consistent with the familiar image of the small houseowner as a person drawn from the 'trading classes': builders, publicans, shopkeepers, etc. Although concentration of ownership was, one suspects, more pronounced in the early stages of industrialization and perhaps remained so in those industries where custom, geography and the needs of a stable labour force compelled industrial magnates to enter the housing market on their own account, a more diffuse pattern of ownership appears to have prevailed.[1] In mid-Victorian Liverpool, for example, landlords of working-class property held on average between six and eight dwellings each, a pattern not at all dissimilar to that which has been found in some of the adjacent cotton towns, or indeed, in places as different as Cardiff, Ramsgate, Bilston, or Newcastle-under-Lyme.[2] These properties were purchased primarily as an investment. In mid-century Leicester, only 4 per cent of all houses were owner-occupied while in Ramsgate 80 per cent of dwellings were for renting.[3] The contemporary adage 'as safe as houses' was an evocation of the security of the investment, not a reference to the quality of construction.[4]   That security was undermined by the growth of local

[1] See John Bateman, *The Great Landowners of Great Britain and Ireland* (4th edn. 1883), p. 315; *Report of Urban Land Enquiry* (1914), p. 81.

[2] John H. Treble,'Liverpool Working Class Housing 1805-1851' in S. D. Chapman, ed., *The History of Working Class Housing* (Newton Abbot, 1971), p. 213; J. D. Marshall, 'Colonisation as a factor in the planting of towns in North West England', in H. J. Dyos, ed., *The Study of Urban History* (1968), p. 228; M. J. Daunton, *Coal Metropolis: Cardiff 1870-1914* (Leicester, 1977), pp. 118-20; R. S. Holmes, 'Ownership and Migration from a Study of Rate Books', *Area*, V (1973), pp. 242-51; G. J. Barnsby, *A History of Housing in Wolverhampton 1750-1875* (Wolverhampton, n.d.), p. 24; F. Bealey, J. Blondel, and P. McCann, *Constituency Politics, A Study of Newcastle-under-Lyme* (1965), p. 41; also see *Select Committee on Local Taxation* (PP 1870, VIII), q. 4792; P. Joyce, *Work, Society and Politics* (1980), pp. 121-2.

[3] R. M. Pritchard, *Housing and the Spatial Structure of the City* (Cambridge, 1976), p. 40; Holmes, 'Ownership and Migration', p. 246.

[4] *Report of Committee on Housing in Greater London* (PP 1964-5, XVII), p. 23.

taxation. Rates levied upon real property, the foundation of local authority finance, grew by leaps and bounds. During the course of the nineteenth century an extraordinary transformation had occurred in the relative positions of land and other classes of property, a revolution from which urban housing emerged as the principal prop to local taxation.[5] Property-owners, in the main small men of slender resources, were loath to play Atlas. They formed the vanguard of an emergent petty bourgeois radicalism which found episodic expression in those ubiquitous ratepayers' associations of whom Professor Hennock has written.[6]

Combination for political purposes, a theme explored below, was not the sole means employed by proprietors to relieve this crushing financial burden. Property-owners were no more, and no less, honest than any other section of the community. But they were not noted for their probity. Where the opportunity was present many were prepared to take improper advantage. Thus, owing to fraudulent claims for fictitious improvements, tax relief on real estate was discontinued in 1806 and not restored until 1894.[7] In the municipal vineyard, however, the grapes were always full and ripe to the touch; pickings were easy, fruit abundant. 'The owners of rateable property might, at least, be expected to be favourable to any change which should avert their impending ruin', wrote the Poor Law Commissioners of 1834. 'But we have seen that of the property liable to poor-rates, there is a portion ... of considerable importance ... which not only is in practice exempted from contributing to the parochial fund, but derives its value from the maladministration of that fund. This property consists of cottages or apartments inhabited by the poor.'[8] Rate evasion was, in fact, rampant.[9] Not only was a vast amount of property grossly undervalued but, consequent upon the negligence of indolent and corrupt overseers, frequently working in collusion with local landlords, much was simply not rated at all.

[5] See Edgar J. Harper, 'The Bases of Local Taxation in England', *Journal of Royal Statistical Society*, LXXXI (1918), pp. 428-32.

[6] E. P. Hennock, 'Finance and Politics in Urban Local Government in England, 1835-1900', *Historical Journal* VI (1963), pp. 212-35.

[7] Josiah Stamp, *British Incomes and Property* (1934), pp. 60-1; and for examples of rate evasion before the Great War, see PRO HO. 45/10511/1130281.

[8] *Report of Royal Commission on the Poor Laws* (PP 1834, XXVII), p. 178.

[9] See, for example, *Report of Select Committee on the Poor Laws* (PP 1817, VI), pp. 94, 139; *Report of the House of Lords Committee on the Poor Laws* (PP 1818, V), p. 160; *R.C. Poor Laws, Reports from Assistant Commissioners* (PP 1834, XXVIII), app. A part ii, pp. 128, 917; also *Select Committee on the Rating of Tenements* (PP 1837-8, XXI i), qq. 112, 127-30.

The problem was aggravated by the inexorable growth of a mobile urban population. Rating authorities were prone to waive all claims upon an impoverished class of occupants from whom recovery was often difficult. The tenant derived little or no benefit. The relief thus obtained was immediately converted by the landlord into an equivalent increase of rent and the deficit recouped from the remainder of the community in the form of higher rates.[10]

In order to minimize these growing losses rating authorities, by way of local enactments, had increasing recourse to some system of compounding, i.e. the rating of owners in lieu of occupiers. Under this arrangement, systematized by the Poor Rate Assessment and Collection Act, 1869, owners were paid substantial allowances for the collection of rates on behalf of the local authority.[11] Working people found the conjoint weekly payment of rates and rents convenient. And so long as they believed that, on balance they had the best of the bargain, landlords too were satisfied.

The compounding system nevertheless became a source of contention. True, the position of the weekly tenant was marginal to the issues which dominated the mid-Victorian debate on the incidence of rates. But in the hope of arresting the continued upward spiral in municipal expenditure, contemporaries began to reconsider his situation.[12] The working-class ratepayer, if properly instructed, might yet be mobilized on the side of 'economy'. This was not a vain expectation. Working-class enthusiasm for municipal housing and other desirable social reforms was certainly constrained by the implications of the increased local indebtedness which such projects invariably entailed. It was not for nothing that the Workmen's National Housing Council concentrated its energies upon the financial basis of housing reform.[13] Rates absorbed a not inconsiderable proportion of working-class rents and about 5 per cent of income. The regressive nature of this form of taxation, moreover, meant that the contribution of the working-class family to local taxation

[10] *Report of Poor Law Commissioners on Local Taxation* (PP 1843, XX), p. 36.

[11] On this, see B. Keith-Lucas, *The English Local Government Franchise* (Oxford, 1952), pp. 64-74.

[12] On the marginal position of the working class occupier in the mid-Victorian debate on rates, see G. J. Goschen, *Reports and Speeches on Local Taxation* (1872), pp. 168-9.

[13] See Norman McCord, 'Ratepayers and Social Policy' in Pat Thane ed., *The Origins of British Social Policy* (1978), Ch. i; David Englander, 'The Workmen's National Housing Council, 1898-1914' (University of Warwick Unpublished MA thesis, 1973), pp. 222-6.

was no less than that of the middle-class family, and a good deal in excess of the contribution of the families of the wealthier classes.[14] The perception of the burden, it was felt, was obscured by the compounding system. The assimilation of rates and rents disguised the more frequent fluctuations in rates and so did nothing to stimulate an enlightened self-interest which might act as a check to the rise in local expenditure. It was a plausible but flawed argument.

The reversion to direct rating was, for working people, a far from attractive prospect. Experience showed that landlords were inclined to use such occasions to adjust rents upwards. Local authorities, though keen to secure economies, were, on administrative grounds, also reluctant to dispense with compounding. Instead they sought to scale down the exceedingly generous permissible allowances, a policy to which property-owners often took exception. Although card-carrying members of those innumerable middle-class 'economist' parties which made such an impact on local politics, property owners were more concerned with the incidence rather than the volume of local taxation. The short-term gains often prevailed over the long-term benefits in their calculations. Those who cavilled at municipal extravagance were at the same time steadfast opponents of reform and retrenchment where communal advantage outweighed the immediate gratification of self-interest. Working-class occupiers were willy nilly embroiled in the ensuing struggle between landlord and local authority. Indeed, much of the tenant radicalism examined below was an echo effect of this conflict over the administration and division of rates.[15] Opposition to the reduction of compounding allowances also indicates the relative isolation of the proprietors. The advocates of personal payment of rates spoke on behalf of middle-class rate-paying occupiers rather than the owners of small house property. This isolation, as the present chapter will show, proved fatal to the defence of proprietorial interests.

I

The growth of combinations amongst property owners is difficult to chart with any accuracy. Many were ephemeral bodies while documentation, even for their more robust number, is either insufficient

---

[14] *Report of Urban Land Enquiry* (1914), pp. 522-3; F. W. Kolthammer, *Some Notes on the Incidence of Taxation on the Working Class Family* (1913), p. 16.
[15] See chapters 5, 6, and 7.

or not readily accessible. The United Property Owners' Association, the first national combination, founded in 1888, was based on a handful of local groups drawn mainly from the North East which, by the turn of the century, had managed to secure the allegiance of some fifty affiliates.[16] But whether this represents a significant secular trend is, for all practical purposes, impossible to determine. Although the eighties witnessed an increasing awareness of their exposed position, reflected in the frequency of attempts at organization, the fact remains that active local associations flourished long before that troubled decade. In 1907, for example, the 129 gentlemen who comprised the Darlington Association for the Protection of Property, assembled in conference to reflect upon the previous years' progress, as indeed they had done annually since its formation forty years before.[17] The sixties in fact saw the emergence of some of the most stable and influential property-owners' associations. The fusion of the hitherto separate land and cottage-owners' associations in 1859 was consummated in the birth of the Liverpool Land and House Owners' Association.[18] Three years later, a new and vigorous body was formed to replace the crumbling alliance of creditors heretofore institutionalized in the Glasgow Merchants' and Landlords' Association. In December 1865 the directors of the new body, the Eastern District Landlords' and House Factors' Association, resolved to extend the sphere of action across the whole city: a new constitution was drawn up, president and executive elected, and vigilant committees established in each municipal ward. The Glasgow Landlords' and House Factors' Association was thus born. It proved a most formidable combination.[19] And, as already suggested, associations such as these played no small part in the genesis of the Small Tenements Recovery Act, 1838. The preservation of property, like the liberty with which it was equated, required constant vigilance.

The Small Tenements Recovery Act, however, had not given complete satisfaction. Its restrictions notwithstanding, contumacious tenants, it was felt, were still permitted far too much scope. The desire to curtail their malicious activities provided a continuing

[16] *Gazette of the National Federation of Property Owners and Ratepayers*, Jan. 1931.

[17] *Estates Gazette* (21 Dec. 1907), p. 1093.

[18] On formation, see 'The Liverpool Association', *Gazette of the National Federation of Property Owners and Ratepayers*, Nov. 1931.

[19] *Glasgow Herald*, 19 Oct. 1907.

stimulus towards organization. The 'chief objects' of the Nottingham and Nottinghamshire Owners' and Agents' Society for the Protection of House Property, formed in the summer of 1850, were, for example, described as:

> ... the preventing, if not the cure of the system of *moonshining*, which has become so prevalent by a confederate system already matured, which will, if carried out, prevent dishonest persons from getting a domicile, either in the town or neighbourhood. The arrangement made will also be calculated to check if not effectually put a stop to the serious depredations so frequently practised upon the owners of household property of low rentals ... The owners and agents of house property ... have the power to prevent their houses, as is frequently the case, being turned respectively into dovecots, dog-kennels, and rabbit-warrens; the cellars of their houses from being converted into pig-styes and manure-vaults, and the pantries from being made the receptacles for the ashes and filth of the family, which every owner knows to be too frequently common.[20]

The general plan adopted in fulfilment of these objects was to compile a register of 'bad tenants' and to insist upon the production of a character reference from the previous landlord prior to granting a new tenancy. In addition, a small fund was to be established through the members' subscriptions to furnish rewards to informants, and to cover the costs of exemplary prosecutions against despoilers of property brought before the magistrates courts each year. By these means a good deal of the expense and vexation was to be removed from the business of house management. In its first year, the Newcastle Property Owners' Association recovered £228 in rent arrears and in nearby South Shields, the secretary of the local association was reported as having collected £250 by distress and other means.[21] However, these modest provincial efforts were completely dwarfed by the energetic North East London Property Owners' Association which over the years claimed to have saved its members from £10,000-£12,000.[22]

The success of such bodies depended, to a very considerable degree, upon the enterprise of the principal officer. In this respect, affiliates could do no better than to recruit someone of the calibre of their own Mr Rotherford, secretary of the national property owners' association, whose commitment was by any standards extraordinary. When did he find time to sleep, his colleagues wondered? 'Some

   [20] *Freeholder*, 1 July 1850.
   [21] *Report of 2nd Conference of United Property Owners' Association of Great Britain* (Sunderland, 1889), p. 7; *Estates Gazette* (30 May 1898), p. 782.
   [22] *Estates Gazette* (26 July 1902), p. 155.

said he put his clothes to bed instead of going to bed himself.'[23] In addition, the ideal secretary ought to have been possessed of an extensive knowledge of legal and taxation matters connected with the ownership and control of residential property. As a consequence, these posts tended to be filled by solicitors, estate agents, and auctioneers. Moreover, such persons frequently comprised the rank and file of the association. The 300 or 400 members of the Liverpool Land and House Owners' Association, half of whom represented small property in the city, also included 'a very large number' of agents who were not proprietors.[24] In Nottingham and Glasgow, to which reference has already been made, the local associations represented an amalgamation of proprietors and agents or factors. Although not usually formalized in such manner, these are indicative of the close relations and shared community of interest amongst such groups.

How effective were such associations? On the face of it the rather low membership figures—123 in South Shields in 1898, 149 in 1899; 60 in Darlington in 1863, 129 in 1907; 72 in Birmingham after six years of continuous recruitment; 100 in Stoke-on-Trent; 82 in Ashton-in-Mackenfield; and a couple of hundred in Liverpool and Glasgow—do not appear to reflect the broad diffusion of property characteristic of the period.[25] The specialist press is in fact studded with references to the apathy and inertia of the possessing classes from which it is tempting to conclude that the 1,000-strong Hull Property Owners' Association, or the equally impressive Workington Association, supported by owners of not fewer than 1,000 houses in a town of fewer than 14,000 people, were exceptional, as indeed were the two associations which together represented 'fully three fourths' of all compounded properties in Manchester, Hulme, and Salford.[26] The Birmingham Property Owners' Association, which in its early years could not afford the rent of permanent offices or the services of a full-time secretary, is more typical in this respect.[27] The frustrated outpourings of the secretary of the Edinburgh

[23] *Report of 3rd Conference of United Property Owners' Association of Great Britain* (Sunderland, 1890), p. 11.

[24] *Royal Commission on Local Taxation* (PP 1898, XLV), qq. 6425, 6510, 6513-15.

[25] Membership of South Shields Property Owners' Association, *Estates Gazette* (2 July 1900), p. 126; of Darlington, *Estates Gazette* (21 Dec. 1907), p. 1093; of Birmingham, *Gazette of National Federation of Property Owners and Ratepayers*, Oct. 1931; of Stoke-on-Trent, issue of same for Jan. 1932; and of Ashton-in-Mackenfield, issue of Jan. 1933.

[26] *Report of 27th Conference of the United Property Owners' Association of Great Britain* (Liverpool, 1912), p. 7; *Estates Gazette* (4 Dec. 1886), p. 673; *Select Committe on Poor Rates Assessment* (PP 1868-9, XI), q. 2765.

[27] 'The Birmingham Association', *Gazette of the National Federation of Property Owners and Ratepayers*, Oct. 1931.

and Leith Property Owners Association is no less instructive. 'I have found it to be uphill work to persuade property-owners, in large numbers, that it is in their interest to become members', he explained. 'The main difficulty in getting property owners to unite is, however much they may feel their burdens, yet they have a sort of fatalistic feeling that there is no remedy.' In consequence, membership was 'not numerous' representing something less than one-fifth of the annual value of the city's total rental.[28]

This kind of quantitative expression might, at first glance, be considered deceptive. In terms of ability to dominate the local housing market control rather than possession of working-class housing might be considered of greater importance. The agent, who often controlled or managed hundreds and sometimes thousands of tenancies, was a more significant figure in such associations than, say, the proprietor of a half-dozen tenements. On reflection, however, it appears that the agent's expertise in reducing the depreciation of working-class property was consistently diminished by the frequent buying and selling of such property. In West Ham, for example, 'an agent might be managing a hundred houses one month, and perhaps only a dozen the next, and vice versa'.[29]

The repression of malicious misconduct on the part of the tenants was recognized as being beyond the unaided capacities of even the most enterprising local association. Official support was necessary to secure an expeditious reform of the law of ejectment, universally acclaimed as *the* solution to such difficulties. Much as they might have wished, such associations could not exist as private conspiracies. They had to enter the political arena. This alone might serve to explain the rather prickly self-consciousness which increasingly appeared to characterize their proceedings. Obstruction of all social expenditure, as a matter of course, was no longer sufficient, although it remained their stock-in-trade, albeit conducted with greater subtlety than heretofore. Landlords were compelled to clothe naked self-interest in appropriate moral fig-leaves.

A favourite ploy was to identify summary eviction as a progressive instalment of sanitary reform and thus to pander to the prejudices of the age. In a submission to the Lord Chancellor representing 'the urgent necessity' of amending the law, Manchester Property Owners'

[28] *Report of 3rd Conference of the United Property Owners' Association of Great Britain* (Sunderland, 1890), pp. 38-40.
[29] E. G. Howarth and Mona Wilson, *West Ham, A Study in Social and Industrial Problems* (1907), pp. 61-2.

Association singled out 'destructive, dirty or disorderly tenants' as those for whom nothing short of summary eviction would suffice.[30] Had not Octavia Hill and umpteen medical officers of health said as much? Fortunately, it was understood that these vague discriminatory categories would, in practice, have a universal application. The occupant of the Woolsack remained unmoved.

Virtually all local associations persisted in seeking to identify their cause with one version of municipal progress. If nothing else, it was a useful complement to the campaign directed at parliament by the national body. Moreover, it was not without some success. The reader will not readily have forgotten the staggering number of evictions sanctioned by Glasgow magistrates in 1912/13. This in part reflects the persistence of the Glasgow Landlords' Association in opposing the adoption of some form of compounding unless accompanied by a summary power of eviction after 48 hours' notice, an extraordinary concession that was to be embodied in the House Letting and Rating Act, 1911.[31] In the following year Birmingham Watch Committee proposed the insertion of clauses designed to expedite the ejection of unruly tenants in the Corporation's forthcoming General Powers Bill.[32]

Influential persons holding positions on sensitive bodies such as the watch committee were always worth cultivating.[33] The police had to be kept up to the mark however distasteful they may have found the work of eviction.[34] When, however, the protection of property combined with a proper respect for the observance of the Lord's Day, action became imperative. Thus, the secretary of the Workington Property Owners' Association was 'instructed to write to the Superintendent of Police asking him to take action in regard to card playing in empty houses on Sundays'.[35] A similar concern to uphold correct spiritual values was even more marked amongst the members of the Glasgow Landlords' and House Factors' Association who, on being approached by the Sabbath Protection Association,

[30] *Estates Gazette* (27 Aug. 1898), p. 378.

[31] Presbytery of Glasgow, *Report of Commission on the Housing of the Poor in Relation to their Social Condition* (Glasgow, 1891), p. 113; 1 & 2 Geo. 5 c. 53. ss. 5-6. See above p. 176.

[32] *Birmingham Gazette*, 14 Nov. 1912.

[33] See *Fourth Annual Report of Birmingham Landlords' Association* (Birmingham, 1859), p. 6.

[34] Cf. correspondence of James Timewell, *Justice*, 28 Oct. 1899.

[35] *Estates Gazette* (8 Oct. 1910), p. 607.

agreed to co-operate in suppressing Sunday trading amongst the 2,000 shops over which they held some dominion.[36]

II

The resort to political action was no new departure. Property-owners had always been closely involved with the management of local affairs. Indeed, a good deal of the odium from which they suffered derived from the unsavoury character of that connection. Local administration not only provided opportunities for the manipulation of assessments, but also the chance to exert a moderating influence upon the activities of over-zealous public health officials. So long as they remained local appointments, denied security of tenure, medical officers of health were acutely conscious of the untoward pressures emanating from their municipal masters in vestry assembled. Legislation was wanted, said one of them, 'which will enable you to work without getting into constant hot water with the owners'.[37] Sometimes the temperature reached boiling point: 'In Bermondsey a newly appointed sanitary inspector was refused a house by dozens of landlords. They would not have anything to do with sanitary inspectors, so they said. Things got to such a pass that the Vestry was urged by one of its members to build the inspector a house itself'.[38] As guardians too, the owners of small tenements were notorious for making the security of their rent the first call upon the parish chest. It was not for nothing that Lord Derby, when mounting relief operations during the Cotton Famine, considered the involvement of such persons highly prejudicial to the cause. 'A knowledge, moreover a suspicion, that any portion of the funds was devoted to the payment of rent, would at once check the flow of public charity', his lordship declared.[39] Not that members of his own class were untainted, as many a small owner was ever ready to testify.

Although apocryphal stories abounded, proprietors bent on winning a parliamentary contest were known not only to resort to intimidation but, where necessary, to avenge themselves and evict recalcitrant tenants. These, however, were generally persons of

[36] *Glasgow Herald*, 30 Jan. 1875.
[37] *Select Committee on Artisans' and Labourers' Dwellings Improvement* (PP 1881, VII), q. 2817.
[38] George Haw, *No Room to Live* (1899), pp. 89-9.
[39] John Watts, *The Facts of the Cotton Famine* (1866), p. 86.

rank and substance, Lancashire mill masters, gentlemen, and the like.[40] The expansion of the municipal electorate under the Small Tenements Act, 1850, was thought to have encouraged small owners too to engage in this kind of activity. In consequence of the lax procedure under this act, registration of electors became almost exclusively dependent upon the whim of the landlord. In this way thousands were thought to have been disenfranchised. Proprietors were quick to deny the charge: the pattern of ownership, they declared, was such as to vitiate all deliberate attempts to exert undue influence by such means. But the drift of opinion was against them.[41] That it was not without some justification is evident from certain events in East London.

In the dying years of the nineteenth century, Labour came to power in West Ham pledged to an extensive programme of municipal housing. Local property owners, terrified by the energetic administration of the public health acts, and alarmed by the speed and vigour with which the new authority proceeded to embark upon costly building schemes, began to mobilize a determined resistance to these dangerous innovations. Although rates actually fell during the period of Labour supremacy while rents rose spectacularly, property owners were quick to raise the usual hue and cry, snapping at municipal extravagance and mounting indebtedness. Shopkeepers, manufacturers, brewers, and temperance reformers combined in an unholy Municipal Alliance for electoral purposes. The proprietors chipped in with a concerted attempt to intimidate voters. Socialists retaliated by threatening to raise assessments on landlords who increased their rents. In the Channelsea district, a notorious slum area and the prime target of the socialist housing reformers, the threat of increased rents was sufficient to constrain the impoverished inhabitants. In other parts of the borough belligerent landlords delivered stern warnings to their tenants. The following letter, one of several issued by small owners, requires no comment:

Sir—we regret very much that on and after Monday next, the 30th day of October, 1899, the rent of the house you now hold of us, will be raised by 6d per week.
This course is rendered necessary by the increased and ever increasing rates

[40] H. J. Hanham, *Elections and Party Management: Politics in the Time of Disraeli and Gladstone* (1959), pp. 43, 67, 79, 85.
[41] See *Report and Minutes of Evidence of the Select Committee of the House of Lords on the Rates and Municipal Franchise Acts* (PP 1859, VII), qq. 301, 306, 309-10, 326, 480-2, 586-91, 594, 726-7, 794-800, 1294-5, 1680.

coupled with higher assessments of property and demands made upon the owners of Small House Property by the Sanitary Authority.

If you wish, as you surely must, to stop this constant raising of your rents, your remedy is by removing from office those who, by their extravagance in dealing with *your* money compel *you* as the very natural result to 'pay the piper'.

Support men on the Council of standing and intelligence and by so doing decrease your burdens instead of adding to them, as your present Labour members are doing.

Yours &c...

Simpson & Co.,

House Property Owners.

This kind of pressure ultimately told against the reformers. Labour's brief reign came to an end after twelve months.[42]

West Ham was not an isolated example. But, in the main, organized landlordism was compelled to rely upon the exercise of more legitimate forms of pressure. The very dynamism of the infrastructure of advanced capitalism, provided ample scope for these associations of apprehensive proprietors. For the municipality not only gave promise of becoming a significant financial institution, an attractive haven for the modest savings of the small investor looking for a safe if unspectacular return on his capital, but an institution which, moreover, was administered by a burgeoning bureaucracy, increasingly professional in outlook, champions of the public interest, innovators, able and willing to countenance forms of labour reproduction in which the role of private enterprise housing might be considerably diminished. 'No one seems to have noticed that side by side with the labour movement has grown up what might be called the professional movement', wrote George Haw. 'With the advent of the artisan into public life has been the advent of the professional man. It is singular too, that these two classes, both benefiting from each other, work well together, but that neither get on very well with the old order.'[43] Such persons, members of the *nouvelle couche sociale*, were by their class situation a menace and landlords were quick to understand the threat which they posed.

[42] On Labour in West Ham, see Paul Thompson, *Socialists, Liberals and Labour: The Struggle for London, 1885-1914* (1967) pp. 130-5; on landlord-tenant conflict, Howarth and Wilson, *West Ham*, pp. 315-16; *Justice*, 2 Dec. 1899. Quotation from *West Ham Citizen*, 20 Oct. 1899.

[43] On comparative returns on municipal stocks, see A. W. Flux, 'The Yield of High Class Investments', *Transactions of Manchester Statistical Society* (1910-11), pp. 103-38. Quotation from Haw, *No Room to Live*, pp. 136-7.

Meanwhile, the daily struggle against 'municipal socialism', a convenient shorthand which could, and did, encompass all measures calculated to increase local taxation or otherwise reduce income from property, continued unabated. There was much to do. The enemy attacked on many fronts, and always seemed to have fresh reserves. The permissive character of so much important legislation, as anticipated by its framers, formed a political terrain that was destined to be churned up time and again by contending forces in each of the local theatres of war. These 'side-shows' still have not received the attention which is their due but they affected the lives of many. In West Ham, local property-owners, ever alert in defence of self-interest, discovered that under the Borough Funds Act 1872, a poll based on an anachronistic property qualification could be invoked to legitimate municipal expenditure Bills. By such means they defeated a plan for the acquisition of 100 acres for house building. The property qualification gave some owners as many as twelve votes apiece. Analysis of the result disclosed a majority of 2,409 voters in favour of the scheme but a majority of 529 votes cast against it.[44] In Manchester too the Corporation had been similarly thwarted, the property-owners' association again insisting upon a plebiscite for which careful preparation had been made.[45] The rewards which accrued from the tenacious defence of self-interest were not insubstantial. Nearly every property-owners' association could point to some Corporation Bill or proposed regulation which had been suitably amended or even withdrawn in consequence of its intervention. The negligible amount of municipal housing built before 1914 is not a testimony to the unaided efforts of such bodies but it bespeaks something.

Victory rarely came cheaply or easily. Organized landlords in Glasgow, for example, managed at one point to raise a special fund of £339 to oppose legislation promoted by the local authority. Birmingham proprietors spent 'over £400' for the same purpose. The Burnley Property Owners' Association, having spent £500 fighting the Corporation, was reduced to such straightened circumstances that it was compelled to introduce stringent economies to stave off bankruptcy including resignation from the national association.[46] Success, moreover, was purchased at a cost not to be

---

[44] *Labour Leader*, 19 May 1900.

[45] *Estates Gazette* (29 Dec. 1906), p. 1190.

[46] *Glasgow Herald*, 21 Jan. 1892; Birmingham and District Property Owners' Association, *Twentieth Annual Report* (Birmingham, 1921), p. 111; *Report of 23rd Conference of United Property Owners' Association of Great Britain* (Liverpool, 1910), p. 17.

computed in mere monetary terms alone. In moving the adoption of the annual report for 1898, the chairman of the Glasgow Landlords' Association expressed relief that members 'were saved the expense and worry of a parliamentary fight such as they had the previous year'. The effort expended in opposing the Corporation's City Improvement Bill during that time had stretched its resources to the utmost.[47]

These, the most important kinds of conflict, were invariably resolved in London, and not entered into in any light-hearted spirit: in fact they were dreaded. A compromise solution was always sought for at first. It was only after 'the Police Commissioners were found difficult to manage' that, for example, the Glasgow association decided to oppose the Corporation's Police Bill, 1895.[48] Such a course involved raising extraordinary funds in order to brief counsel and prepare witnesses to testify before the appropriate select committee at Westiminster. The lawyers fees were considerable. In defence of its Improvement Bill, Glasgow Corporation retained 'no fewer than four of the leading members of the parliamentary bar' and fought all opposition 'with a total disregard of expense that only access to the ratepayers' pockets could explain'.[49] Against such a lengthy purse how could opponents compete? These limitations, it was agreed, had 'seriously interfered with the efficiency of the opposition' offered by Glasgow landlords to the Police Bill, 1890. The want of a senior counsel, the result of its financial embarrassment, prejudiced the Association's cause. The Law Agent explained:

Mr Fitzgerald was all that could be desired as a counsel, but men such as Mr Littler and Mr Pember have immense weight with the Committees, and are not afraid to put things strongly when necessary, or to keep counsel on the other side in order. It was always quite apparent, both in the Commons and the Lords, that Mr Pope was a man of immense influence with them, and whenever our counsel came into conflict with him the Committee backed up Mr Pope invariably. With a senior I am quite confident that we would have secured a good deal more than we did.[50]

The mounting expense of these increasingly frequent and protracted legal encounters influenced the structure of Glasgow's property owners' associations. In 1895 the Association of House Factors and Property Agents decided to seek incorporation under the Companies Act, a course duly followed by the Landlords' Association two years

---

[47] *Glasgow Herald*, 19 Jan. 1899.   [48] *Glasgow Herald*, 23 Jan. 1896.
[49] *Glasgow Herald*, 20 Jan. 1898.   [50] *Glasgow Herald*, 1 Aug. 1890.

later in order 'to give members greater facilities for defensive work and more definite legal status in opposing parliamentary bills and Provisional Orders'.[51] Finances were also reorganized and placed on a sounder footing. A special reserve fund was established to defray the cost of extraordinary expenditure instead of relying as hitherto on desperate fund-raising drives to meet each individual emergency as it arose.

Before the formation of the United Property Owners' Association, the struggles in which house owners engaged were characterized by *ad hoc* alliances and a limited degree of co-ordination with similar groups outside their own locality. Imperial issues—compounding, the reform of taxation, leasehold enfranchisement, the repeal of obnoxious stamp duties and other imposts—usually drew forth a spate of petitions or an occasional deputation to lobby ignorant or indolent MPs, including those of Ministerial rank, who sometimes condescended to grant their humble constituents an audience. In the main, these formalities served to advertise the weakness rather than the strength of the yeomen of urban Britain.

The formation of the United Property Owners' Association indicated a heightened awareness of the exposed position of property and a new determination to obtain something like adequate protection. In addition to the difficulties arising from soaring local taxation and increasingly effective sanitary administration, property-owners felt even more threatened by the growth of democracy. These factors were not, of course, unconnected. A spokesman for the Glasgow Landlords' Association stated their predicament with brutal clarity: analysis of the municipal register disclosed one owner to every thirty-five occupiers. Ever since the Reform Act of 1867, it was clear that the balance of power had been tipped decisively against the owners of real property. To be sure, working people would not enter into their inheritance for many a year, but the writing was on the wall and whatever their defects, property-owners were not illiterate. The meaning of the independent labour movement that gradually emerged in the last quarter of the nineteenth century was crystal clear. As R. L. Foster, secretary of the Sunderland Property Owners' Association, put it: 'there exists between Socialism and our Association an open warfare which it would be sheer insanity on our part to pretend does not exist'.[52] As early as

[51] *Glasgow Herald*, 19 Oct. 1907.
[52] On proportion of owners to occupiers in Glasgow, see *Surveyors' Institution,*

1876 Lord Wemyss, founder of the Liberty and Property Defence League, broached the idea of a national combination of landed properties in a correspondence with the chairman of the Liverpool Land and House Owners' Association.[53] It was the beginning of what proved to be a contentious connection from which the United Property Owners' Association later sought to extricate itself; a desirable but impractical move, as it transpired.

The United Property Owners' Association never acquired great wealth. Although in due course it came to represent £200 millions'-worth of small property, or so it was claimed, the new organization could never rival the fabulous riches of pressure groups such as the United Kingdom Alliance. Indeed, it could not afford to maintain a London office with a salaried staff. It was not until the sixth annual conference that such a course was discussed and agreed to, but the association was in existence for forty years before the move to the capital was finally accomplished. Until 1928 the General Secretary remained a part-time post. Criticisms directed at the inadequate measures for monitoring parliamentary proceedings were often voiced in conference. In fact, so long as affiliates refused to dig deeply into their pockets, the association was compelled to rely upon the parliamentary services provided by the Liberty and Property Defence League. This attachment not only reinforced the United Property Owners' Association's marked provincialism, but also perhaps tended to accentuate its faintly comic profile.[54]

From the outset the two bodies had sensed a mutual attraction. In 1896 Frederick Millar, the League's secretary, was reported to have 'practically acted as our Parliamentary agent'. The position was subsequently regularized though not to the satisfaction of all, or many, affiliates. One advantage of establishing its own journal, a much discussed proposal, was that, in addition to fostering a sense of mutuality and purpose amongst members, it might go some way towards freeing them from exclusive dependence, at least during

Scottish Supplement to Professional Notes, XII (1903-4), p. 68, and *Glasgow Presbytery Commission*, p. 94. Quotation from *Report of 9th Conference of United Property Owners' Association of Great Britain* (Liverpool, 1896), p. 11.

[53] Edward Bristow, 'The Liberty and Property Defence League and Individualism', *Historical Journal*, XVIII (1975), p. 764.

[54] *Report of 25th Conference of United Property Owners' Association of Great Britain* (Liverpool, 1910), p. 10; *Report of 6th Conference* etc. (Sunderland, 1893), p. 9; *Report of 16th Conference* etc. (Bradford, 1903), p. 20; 'Our Federation, 1888-1938', *Property Owners' Gazette*, Feb. 1938.

the parliamentary session, upon information furnished by the League. But unless the projected publication could achieve a circulation of some several thousands, such a rash venture, Millar hastened to predict, must turn out 'a bad speculation'. He was right. Until removal to London the United Property Owners' Association was not in a position to publish a regular journal.

Increasingly, however, the public identification with so doctrinaire a body was considered an obstacle to the pragmatic defence of the proprietor's more limited interests. The Liberty and Property Defence League, it was felt, was not sufficiently concerned with the particular problems of cottage property. The course of a long debate reviewing the advantages of retaining their unsatisfactory political agent disclosed the existence of an underlying antipathy towards the Property Defence League. The merest hint that the two bodies might amalgamate brought forth the unequivocal opposition of the delegate from the influential Liverpool association. 'I cannot go as far ... in advocating that we should become fully identified with the Liberty and Property Defence League. Some of us are property owners, and some of us are moral reformers, and we do not care for indiscriminate blocking of bills'. Another, deprecating the League's extremism, suggested that Millar's services be henceforth confined to non-controversial chores, such as the arrangement of parliamentary deputations etc. But on reflection, he added: 'We cannot touch the Liberty and Property Defence League without our name being involved. The fact that we use them would mean a certain amount of obloquy.' Alderman Hindmarsh, founder and president of the property-owners' association, was even more emphatic. 'My only fear is that if we did identify ourselves ... with the Liberty and Property Defence League many members would withdraw altogether.'[55]

Although they might champ at the bit, these diffident gentlemen, uneasily aware of their indeterminate position within the class structure, envied the legitimacy enjoyed by the Liberty and Property Defence League and similar bodies graced by aristocratic patrons which helped to displace the scorn and derision which might otherwise have attached to those seeking to unite theory and practice on the fringe of politics. The League could arouse strong feelings, but

[55] *Report of 9th Conference of United Property Owners' Association of Great Britain* (Liverpool, 1896), pp. 4, 14-15; *Report of 15th Conference* etc. (Bradford, 1902), pp. 30, 32. *Report of 16th Conference* etc. (Bradford, 1903), p. 59.

never that peculiar contempt which Englishmen of all classes reserve for the *petite bourgeoisie* which brusquely dispenses with the cultivation of silent ambition, and thereby makes public that which taste and convention renders private. The members of the United Property Owners' Association were acutely conscious of the idiocy of *petit bourgeois* life: its deprecation of collective self-reliance, the exclusion of forms of political action incompatible with the upkeep of a genteel mien, the envy and loathing of the aristocracy and its plutocratic retainers, and worst of all the recognition and coming to terms with the vile proletariat and its despicable agitators, organizers of those malevolent and seemingly omnipotent trades unions and political parties. Gissing and Masterman knew these people well and understood their apprehensions. So too did Wells, and the interested reader must consult their eloquent accounts.[56]

It required unusual courage to persist in the face of the taunts and sneers invariably heaped upon a newly-formed association. 'At the beginning', one landlord recalled, 'they had felt that the Association was rather ridiculed and attempted to be laughed down'. 'When the Sunderland Association was formed', said another, 'it was sneered at but gradually came to be more and more respected until its communications instead of finding their way to the waste paper basket, were carefully considered.' Although presenting themselves as associations, it was the labour movement rather than the professions to whom they turned for inspiration. If only property owners would organize, what power they would wield, what respect they would command:

Not to say a single word about what a combination of the Irish tenants had realised, there is almost daily evidence of what labour combinations had been able to accomplish in a question with capital. Not a great many years ago who would have dreamt that a poor labourer would have been in a position of dictating terms to his master, and handicapped as he is, we find that carried into effect every day.

If this was a little too abstract, another speaker conjured a vision in which the down-trodden bourgeoisie would inherit the earth, or at least that portion over which the municipality chose to exert dominion:

[56] He (or she) should also consult Geoffrey Crossick, ed., *The Lower Middle Class in Britain* (1977).

... if we will increase and unite, there is no union in England that would have so much power as the Property Owners' Association. They would be able to say to the Corporation 'If you don't prevent your nuisance inspectors from coming to us and compelling us to do things which put us to unnecessary expense, we shall have to call a meeting of our members, and we shall have to advance the rents.'[57]

Notwithstanding its more fantastic features, this discordant trade union mimetic served in some respects to increase that sense of isolation which no doubt afflicts all prophets, but especially those trying to surmount the inhibitions of an ingrained individualistic culture. The activists were certainly conscious of the distance separating themselves from their natural constituents and while the break was not as sharp as the reformed drunkard trying to transcend his proletarian background, it was still felt keenly. The secretary of the Edinburgh and Leith Association had few illusions on this score:

Another difficulty in getting property owners to unite is the feeling that what is everybody's business is nobody's business. We have in our midst a large class who may be regarded as silent men, taking an active interest in no public affairs, ... and I am sorry to think that that represents the largest class of property owners, men well contented to leave things as they are, and holding a sort of fatalistic view that they cannot be made better.[58]

This isolation had a broader aspect. It was a reflection of material realities. Property-owners were patently *of* but not *for* the middle class. At the end of the Great War it was middle-class as much as working-class pressure which was decisive in preventing the raising of rent controls.[59] Organized landlords were not moved by the same passions or fears as their *petit bourgeois* tenants. Although 'the Trade' might have been elevated as an appropriate precedent for continuous collective action, the property-owners' moth-like fixation upon the trade union movement is indicative not of a politically maladroit posture, but of a basic contempt for the ideological sensibilities of the heterogeneous elements that composed the middle classes. These were not namby-pamby white-collar workers assured of a place in the sun of an advanced capitalism, and struggling

[57] *Report of 3rd Conference of United Property Owners' Association of Great Britain* (Sunderland, 1890), pp. 41, 43; *Report of 2nd Conference* etc (Sunderland, 1889), p. 42; *Report of 14th Conference* etc. (Liverpool, 1901), p. 38.
[58] *Report of 3rd Conference of United Property Owners' Association of Great Britain* (Sunderland, 1890), p. 40.
[59] See below, pp. 292-4.

meanwhile to reconcile their individualism with their unions. On the contrary: the survival of pre-industrial forms of capitalist enterprise in an increasingly complex society was highly problematical. Residential property considered purely as a speculation was vulnerable to the economic and political pressures which that formation generated. From the eighties onwards small property-owners felt themselves to be on trial and there is no place more lonesome than the dock.

IV

In nineteenth-century Britain, land conferred status. Parvenus bourgeois were drawn to it like mice to cheese. Towards the trappings of gentility, displayed in possession of a country estate, the *arriviste* aspired.[60] The social character of the urban landlord forms a curious contrast. Where the pastoral tradition evoked power, influence, opulence, and comfort, the residential property-owner inspired loathing, opprobrium, and scorn, condemned alike by crusty Tory and progressive Liberal, indignant cleric, and Radical free thinker, philanthropic busybody and the casual reader of the *Daily Telegraph*. This strange disdainful consensus rested upon a contrived squeamishness larded with a good deal of hypocrisy. 'Members must beware of the great clan "Sartorius" ', a Fabian socialist warned. 'Owners of property may call themselves "Progressive" and may be active Gladstonian Radicals; but when additional Sanitary Inspectors are required to look after their property, they will desert their Party and vote for dirt and disease as the most "moderate" of Tories'.[61] It was the unsavoury business of housing management rather than any meaningful criticism of proprietorial right which was considered offensive to the good taste and quiet dignity of the drawing room. As Shaw's Cokane put it: 'There is something peculiary repugnant to my feelings in the calling of a rent collector.' And Dickens venomous description of the slum landlord at work captures that degree of repugnance like no other.[62]

Property owners were themselves acutely conscious of their isolation. A striking feature of the 'trade papers' is an imminent

[60] Cf. Cobden to Bright, 1 Oct. 1851, John Morley, *Life of Richard Cobden* (1910), p. 561.

[61] *Fabian News*, May 1893.

[62] G. B. Shaw, *Widowers' Houses* (Bodley Head, 1970), p. 81; 'Up a Court', *Household Words*, V (1852), p. 510.

sense of foreboding, an incipient paranoia, like a quivering fox balanced on the brink of perennial fear. Everyone was against the landlord. 'By some he is regarded as a social outcast and his regeneration prayed for, by others he is looked upon as fair spoil for the unscrupulous and by a third set as a butt for all the Parliamentary satire and Municipal sarcasm that fevered rhetoric can produce.'[63] East End Jewish landlords quicky discovered that, against such prejudice, ethnic solidarity was no protection. As one of them observed: 'When I go to the synagogue I am a Jew; when I come for my rent I am a *goy*.'[64] Landlords fancied themselves beset by wicked tenants determined to evade their legitimate obligations, mindlessly destructive and ungrateful for all that was done for their comfort and well-being. But tenants were only part of the tribulations that had to be endured. Local government officialdom was even worse, something akin to a municipal Gestapo:

The abject serfdom of property owners is proverbial. They are the vassals arbitrarily ruled by diploma holders of self constituted sanitary institutes: few hold, in addition, medical qualifications, but mostly the awe inspiring word on coat, collar or cap 'Sanitary Inspector' discloses authority sufficient to command compliance to unreasonable and unjust demands. The Inspector's power is severely felt, as trifles are relentlessly magnified, and their abatement or removal ordered.[65]

It was the need 'to mitigate the evils of super inspection and resist the tyrannical oppression of Borough Council officials' that prompted the formation of the Incorporated Association for the Protection of Property Owners.

An even greater threat was posed by the growing power of organized labour to which the so called natural defenders of private property seemed increasingly unresponsive. 'Today', said one landlord, 'the *Working Man*, I mean the *Manual Labourer*, is the *Politicians Pet* and if you want to get a hearing on any platform today you must be careful not to say anything against the interests of the so called *Working Man*.'[66] 'This prejudice against house-owners is growing at an alarming rate', said another. Speaking to the annual

[63] *Property Owners' Journal*, Nov. 1904.
[64] C. Russell and H. S. Lewis, *The Jew in London* (1900), p. 174. Similar tensions evidently existed in the smaller provincial communities: see Corporation of Birmingham, *Special Housing Enquiry* (Birmingham, 1914), qq. 1113-15.
[65] *Property Owners' Journal*, Feb. 1903.
[66] *Report of 19th Conference of United Property Owners' Association of Great Britain* (Liverpool, 1906), p. 48.

conference of the United Property Owners' Association, he continued: 'It is a remarkable fact and much to be regretted that not
only adventurers, but responsible political leaders, and even ministers of religion, vie with each other in the wholesale condemnation
of landlordism.' Local councillors were the worst offenders in this
respect: 'These men ... are now endeavouring to sow the seeds of
discord between landlord and tenant, teaching the latter to look
upon the former as his greatest social enemy. It is considered a
crime to own a house, and however well-earned have been his
savings, when he invests them in brick and mortar, a man loses all
credit of economy, and almost his character for humanity'.[67] And
when a British Chancellor of the Exchequer, and a former solicitor
to boot, could declare: 'The claws of landlordism rend the flesh, and
the sores fester even more in our town system than they do in our
country system'—the end of the world may well have seemed
nigh.[68]

These feelings of inferiority, never fully conquered before 1914,
were aggravated by the difficulties repeatedly encountered in the
search for support among the two national political parties. The
middle classes, it has been suggested, turned increasingly to the
Conservatives during the late nineteenth century.[69] Property-
owners, as a fraction of a fraction, took care, however, to adopt a
bipartisan stance in the day-to-day conduct of their affairs. It is true
that Lord Salisbury's speeches, particularly those reproving the
contemners of private property, foul-mouthed Proudhonist critics,
who numbered house-owners amongst the semi-criminal elements,
were frequently cited with approbation. But property-owners
understood well enough that, for all his disdainful aristocratic
hauteur, his lordship, was in the vote-getting business and that it
was the Disraelian image which the Party had to keep to the fore if it
was to continue in governance of the democratic masses. At the end of
the day, the Tories would never sacrifice the substance for the
shadow: if need be, the small house owner would be forced to the
wall.

[67] *Report of 14th Conference of United Property Owners' Association of Great
Britain* (Liverpool, 1901), p. 13.
[68] *The Urban Land Problem—Housing—Wages, Speeches of David Lloyd George
at Middlesborough, 5 November 1913* (Liberal Publications Department, 1913), p. 3.
[69] See James Cornford, 'The Transformation of Conservatism in the late Nineteenth Century', *Victorian Studies*, VII (1963-4), pp. 35-6; Henry Pelling, *Social
Geography of British Elections 1885-1910* (1967), p. 41.

In this respect, a cursory glance at the activities of Sir Arthur Forward, leader of the Liverpool Tories, might have given pause for reflection; and, should that prove an insufficiently convincing exercise, the sceptic might be referred to the career of Colonel Kyffin Taylor, MP a gentleman to whom the most rabid of Fabians (and according to the property-owners, most Fabians were afflicted with hydrophobia), would have extended the warmest of welcomes. Kyffin Taylor, chairman of the Liverpool Corporation Housing Committee, was in no sense a solitary eccentric, but the representative of a still vibrant tradition of pragmatic *étatisme* which, if it was not the dominant strain in Edwardian Conservatism, was a growing force that could not be ignored.

In Queen Victoria's last Cabinet this tradition, adorned with suitable imperial embellishment, was represented by Radical Joe Chamberlain, then at the peak of his career, less of a Radical than heretofore, perhaps, but still champion of a programme well in advance of anything that property-owners or their parliamentary spokesmen could possibly stomach. Even so innocuous a measure as the Small Dwellings Acquisitions Act, 1899, which Chamberlain piloted through the House of Commons, provoked the most unreasoning opposition.

In its practical application, the Act was a complete failure. The amount of money sanctioned by the local authorities for the expansion of home-ownership among the working class, the object of the measure, proved negligible. A faint echo of his pre-Tory past, the Small Dwellings Bill had hung fire since the middle of the decade, thwarted repeatedly by unthinking and inflexible opponents. Those possessed of a more panoramic view, regarded such intransigence with disdain. The authoritative *Estates Gazette*, had, for example, warmly approved of the measure when introduced in 1896. To the objection that it was a form of State Socialism, this much-respected journal answered:

So it is; but what does that matter? ... let us remember that there is Socialism and Socialism ...

It is an honest and well conceived endeavour to bring about an eminently desirable state of things. In a country where a large proportion of the working classes own their own dwellings, the subversive nonsense of agitators has very little chance of a hearing. No doubt large numbers of working men already do possess their own houses, but their number is insignificant when compared with those who have not been subjected to the steadying influence which come from having something to lose.[70]

[70] *Estates Gazette* (29 Feb. 1896), p. 291.

It returned to the subject eighteen months later to condemn Wemyss for his 'being so impractical and irreconcilable' towards a measure calculated to be productive of good.

If unreliable, the Conservatives were at least acknowledged to be committed to the defence of private property. From the Liberal Party and its increasingly vociferous left wing, property-owners expected little and feared much. Organized property-owners frequently shared Radical enthusiasms. They were not averse to the enfranchisement of urban leaseholds and pricked an ear at proposals for the taxation of ground rents which promised to affect a diminution in rates at the expense of the superior landlord. At the same time such sympathies were checked by the anxieties, assiduously cultivated by the Conservative press since the early eighties, that income accruing from Radical proposals for the taxation of site values and the levying of a betterment tax would be reserved to finance extensive municipal housing programmes.[71] Although at first it declined to join the Land Union, the United Property Owners' Association eventually affiliated in 1911. The Land Union, formed to fight Lloyd George's confiscatory budgets, possessed a Council graced by thirty-four MPs and this, property-owners hoped, might give them a more effective voice on the floor of the House.[72]

Neither political party, then, appeared likely to provide that security requisite to the full enjoyment of property. The dependence of the United Property Owners' Association upon the Liberty and Property Defence League was symptomatic of this predicament. But, if alienated from both Liberal and Tory, there are few indications that organized proprietors were estranged from democratic politics. On the contrary: it was often suggested that local associations ought to engage as candidate-running bodies, a sure means of enhancing their social and political status. In an opening address to the annual conference of 1899, the Lord Mayor of Liverpool observed that the delegates assembled were not a numerous body but, he added, 'if you represent the ratepayers, even to a very moderate extent, you have a constituency numbered by scores of thousands'.[73] His Worship's valuable suggestion had, in fact, been

[71] Cf. Birmingham and District Traders' and Property Owners' Association, *Eleventh Annual Report* (Birmingham, 1912), pp. 9-10.

[72] *Report of 26th Conference of United Property Owners' Association of Great Britain* (Liverpool, 1911), p. 20.

[73] *Report of 12th Conference of United Property Owners' Association of Great Britain* (Liverpool, 1899), p. 4.

anticipated. The desire to broaden the base of their support was reflected in the adoption of a new title. Henceforth the national body was to be known as the United Property Owners' and Rate-payers' Association of Great Britain. It was a strategy that was later pioneered by the London Municipal Society with some success. The property-owners, however, never got beyond the change in nomen-clature. The ratepayers' associations whom they were supposed to represent remained fictitious bodies, a useful letter heading at best.[74]

The United Property Owners' Association was born in the North of Britain. Its centre of gravity remained firmly fixed in the provinces. London proved stubbornly resistant to all efforts to arouse property owners to a just appreciation of the dangers with which they were confronted. The failure to penetrate the capital constituted a source of weakness, psychological and material. Unlike some earlier pressure groups, the United Property Owners' Association was not a crusade righteously hurling its thunderbolts at the centre of sin and power. It possessed neither the means nor the morality, nor indeed the inclination, to conduct the kind of histrionic campaigns that characterized the Anti-Corn-Law League and the numerous nonconformist bodies that patented themselves upon it. It did, however, share the same self-conscious provincialism of its illustrious predecessor. But whereas the Anti-Corn-Law League embodied a new confident middle class progressivism, property-owners were on the whole a more timorous breed, fearful of the future, and conscious that the form of property they sought to defend was vulnerable because it was no longer seen as vital to the continued health of British capitalism. The significance of Cham-berlain's Small Dwellings Acquisitions Act lay in the recognition that it was possible to draw a distinction between the virtues of owner-occupation and acquisition for speculative purposes and that the state was not necessarily best served by the latter.

London was certainly not without an organized landlords presence. But until the turn of the century coverage remained patchy and action uncoordinated. There were some minor successes. The London Freeholders' and Leaseholders' Defence Association, which was formed following the passage of the Customs and Inland Revenue Act, 1890, to urge uniformity amongst medical officers of health in the granting or withholding of house duty exemption

[74] Cf. 'Our Federation, 1885-1938', *Property Owners' Gazette*, Feb. 1938.

certificates, lent its weight, however light, to the campaign already begun for the repeal of that contentious measure.[75] It appears to have made a favourable impression upon the Chancellor of the Exchequer.[76] Others, however, were whistling in the dark. In 1894 the secretary of the newly-formed Middlesex Property Owners' Association claimed that, within twelve months of its foundation, his 150-strong association was operating throughout the metropolis.[77] His was one of several attempts to organize upon a regional basis. Frederick Millar's announcement that he too was in process of forming just such an association gave rise to an interesting correspondence which unearthed numerous bodies, not all of which could be formally described as property-owners' associations, but which nevertheless fulfilled some of their most important functions.

The London Association for the Protection of Trade was one of them. The Association, Mr George Maddox, its president, explained:

... has from time to time rendered good service to property owners in obtaining reliable information as to the character of persons proposing to rent property. Owners of property can, for the trifling subscription of one guinea per annum, obtain complete protection from the schemes of any gang of rent robbers.

The Association's register contains the names of thousands of such swindlers, while its connections are so extensive and its correspondence so numerous that the most exhaustive enquiries can be made into every case.

This kind of work, he added, had been 'carried on quietly and unobtrusively since 1842'. Similar work, it also transpired, was undertaken by the North London General Landlords' Protection Association, a limited company formed in 1890 which, according to its managing director, possessed a register of defaulting tenants that 'already contains over 3,000 names, and is being increased daily'.[78] Although the casual labour problem militated against effective combination in the worst slum districts, elsewhere metropolitan landlords might not have been quite as helpless as they liked to suggest in the struggle against difficult tenants.

The decentralized structure of metropolitan government, and the consequent absence of a focal-point on which to concentrate resources, was often considerd a more important retardative factor. At the annual conference of the United Property Owners' Asso-

[75] *Estates Gazette* (18 July 1891), p. 59.
[76] *Estates Gazette* (1 Aug. 1891), p. 109.
[77] *Estates Gazette* (27 Oct. 1894), p. 462.   [78] *Estates Gazette* (20 Oct. 1894), p. 434.

ciation, held deliberately in the heart of Empire, in order 'to stir up the London property owners to action', Councillor J. B. Kyffin of the North East London Association compared the situation with other centres thus: 'In a moderately sized provincial town you are in touch with your Corporation but it is very different in the case of London, and the consequence is that the Authorities deal with us single-handed, one by one, and up to the present they have always got their own way.'[79] No one appeared to notice the irony in the fact that it was a Tory Cabinet which carried the London Government Act, 1899, a measure designed to balkanize the metropolis in the belief that by such fragmentation property would be preserved from the hands of extremists.[80] This less than satisfactory enactment did little to convince small house-owners that their interests could be entrusted to the Conservative Party without further ado. The Party's languid response to the relative radicalization of metropolitan politics, which marked the advent of the London County Council, scarcely inspired confidence. It was not until 1895, following two successive Progressive victories, that the London Municipal Society was formed to organize the Conservative vote.[81] In the interval an obstructive strategy was pursued by the Property Protection League, an organization liberally funded by London's great landowners, working in alliance with the Liberty and Property Defence League and miscellaneous ratepayers' societies. In the short run these were not without effect, but by the turn of the century the Progressives were back in office and under pressure from their radical constituents. The resurgence of the housing agitation spearheaded by the Workmen's National Housing Council and the National Housing Reform Council were events which could not be ignored. There seemed no substitute for self-reliance.

The formation of the Incorporated Association for the Protection of Property Owners, in 1901, was the result of the last of several initiatives previously undertaken by the North East London Property Owners' Association. The latter, flushed by a recent victory over the late and unlamented Hackney Vestry, a body 'ruled by a bitter and avowed hatred towards landlords', had not only prevented an arbitrary reduction in the compounding allowance, but hoped that

[79] *Report of 14th Conference of United Property Owners' Association of Great Britain* (Liverpool, 1901), p. 22.

[80] W. A. Robson, *The Government and Misgovernment of London* (2nd edn., 1948), Ch. x.

[81] On this, see K. Young, *Local Politics and the Rise of Party* (Leicester, 1977).

it had helped to establish a new association that would constitute 'a strong Central Organisation with influential local Committees, that shall be a great and serious power in this wealthy metropolis, a power which shall make itself known, felt and even feared by those agitators...'[82] Not all of these hopes were to be fulfilled. But much progress was made. The new organization, which came to represent millions of pounds' worth of property, grew steadily and managed to maintain a regular publication of its own, the *Property Owners' Journal*. Although relations appear free of friction, it did not amalgamate with the United Property Owners' Association until shortly after the outbreak of the Great War.

The numerous local victories obtained by such bodies, however, were not matched by a comparable success in the key battles waged in parliament. The property-owners somewhat negative stance helped to obstruct several measures, some of them quite important, but failed to convince vote-hungry politicians that they possessed policies with attraction sufficient to still an ever clamorous electorate. Moreover, such concessions as were gained, were always granted in such a mean grudging spirit as to inhibit the growth of a relaxed and generous self-confidence within their ranks. The repeal of the Inhabited House Duty, a tax assessed upon tenements let at an annual rental of £20 and above, had, for example, been repeatedly urged upon the Treasury both by the United Property Owners' Association and a society specially devoted to that purpose. The Chancellor of the Exchequer, though not unmoved, was cautious in appraising the claims submitted. The tax, he was willing to concede, was neither desirable nor just. Henceforth, exemption was to be made dependent upon the issue of a certificate by the medical office of health if satisfied that the property in question was in proper sanitary condition. This shrewd proviso prevented the owners of multi-occupied slum properties from reaping the advantage of a rent increase additional to the proposed tax reduction. It was much resented.[83] The campaign continued.

Paradoxically, however, success too tended to accentuate the sense of isolation from the centre of power. Year after year property-

[82] *Report of 14th Conference of United Property Owners' Association of Great Britain* (Liverpool, 1901), pp. 15, 18; also see *Gazette of National Federation of Property Owners and Ratepayers*, Dec. 1931.

[83] *Report of 2nd Conference of United Property Owners' Association of Great Britain* (Sunderland, 1889), pp. 4-5, 7, 13; *Report of 5th Conference* etc (Sunderland, 1893), p. 5; *Report of 6th Conference* (Liverpool, 1895), pp. 5, 11-12.

owners managed to obstruct the ambiguously titled Rating of Machinery Bill.[84] It was feared that the measure, promoted by manufacturers and designed to relieve certain classes of machinery from the burden of local taxes, would be accompanied by a corresponding increase in the rating of house property. Other interests were no less disturbed. The bill, when first introduced, had been vigorously opposed by a combination of North Eastern Poor Law authorities. But the United Property Owners' Association remained the most implacable foe. Not only did it resist any move towards the de-rating of machinery, but pressed for a thorough review of the whole tax structure.

The appointment of the Royal Commission on Local Taxation was considered a major breakthrough, a reward for its unremitting pressure. But there the advance halted. The Commissioners listened patiently, and not without sympathy, to its spokesmen and their demands for the transference of the poor and education rates to the imperial exchequer, and for a more equitable system that would extend the bases of local taxation to embrace hitherto exempted sources of personal and industrial wealth. These claims were not unjustified; house property was unfairly penalized, and rates were crippling. But the persistent effort to transfer the burden on to capital's unwilling shoulders did little to command the expositors to the captains of industry or to their parliamentary subalterns. It is not without significance that it was one of the largest of Clydeside shipbuilders who, when confronted by militant tenants in 1915, first suggested that they press for controlled rents.

This sense of isolation was further heightened by the chilly atmosphere which seemed to settle over St. Stephens whenever the occasion arose for a just consideration of the proprietors most important claims.[85] The Lord Chancellor, for instance, when receiving a deputation from the United Property Owners' Association

[84] The following two paragraphs are based upon *Report of 2nd Conference of United Property Owners' Association of Great Britain* (Sunderland, 1889), p. 7; *Estates Gazette* (13 Feb. 1897), pp. 249-50; Liverpool Land and House Owners' Association, *Memorial to the Right Hon. W. E. Gladstone M. P. on Local Taxation* (Liverpool, 1882); *Minutes of Evidence, Royal Commission on Local Taxation* (PP 1898, XLV), pp. 233-5, 239-42; *Minutes of Evidence, Royal Commission on Local Taxation, Scotland* (PP 1899, XXXVI), pp. 64-9.

[85] The following three paragraphs are based on *Report of 17th Conference of United Property Owners' Association of Great Britain* (Bradford, 1904), pp. 5-6; *Report of 19th Conference* etc (Liverpool, 1906), pp. 17-18; *Report of 21st Conference* etc (Liverpool, 1908), p. 6.

in 1899, was certainly genial, indeed most affable, but apart from mouthing sweet nothings, refused to contemplate seriously their proposals for the reform of distress proceedings. In vain did they try to appeal beyond him. But of the county court judges who were circularized only five vouchsafed an opinion.

In political terms landlords were a liability. Members of Parliament hastened to flee from before them as if from a plague. It was found impossible to obtain their support for amending legislation. A year after it had first been mooted, the executive of the United Property Owners' Association had to admit that the proposed deputation to the Commons had not been assembled 'on account of the unwilling- ness already shown by Members of Parliament who had been asked to take this matter in hand to lead the way'. Notwithstanding its recondite matter, a bill to register compulsorily all furniture removals as a precaution against flitting was also dropped on the realistic grounds that this was unlikely to receive a sympathetic hearing. Although not insensible of the advantages which greater respectability would bring to the defence of their interests, landlords seemed incapable of repairing their tarnished image. So long as the Government refused to sanction a power of summary eviction, they continued to oppose every attempt towards the liberalization of distress proceedings, all to no avail. Legislation reached the statute book in 1888 and again in 1895. The United Property Owners' Association delayed the passage of the Distress Amendment Act, 1908 by one year.

Even greater exertion, however, was necessary to master the fierce rolling tide of legislation issuing from the last Liberal Govern- ment, especially with Mr Lloyd George in the ascendant. Clause 51 of his National Insurance Bill was considered particularly vicious.[86] This clause, which prevented the levying of distress or eviction during the occupant's illness, was 'worse than Socialism', for, it was claimed, 'if Socialists promoted the Bill they would have provided for the Government paying the rent during the sickness of the tenant'. If passed, he added, it would create 'a new race of "Weary Willies" and "Tired Tims" and "Artful Dodgers" who would prac- tically live rent free'. Another considered it a gratuitous insult. Landlords he protested, 'are most human and considerate and sympathetic to their tenants whenever they meet with adversity':

---

[86] 'Clause 51 of the National Insurance Bill, Memorandum by the Council of the Surveyors' Institution, July 1911', *Professional Notes*, XVII (1911), pp. 253-4.

invalids were invariably allowed to run up arrears, the landlord 'in many cases ... cannot find it in his heart to distrain ... and he forgoes his claim and looks upon the transaction with a cheerful countenance'. The United Property Owners' Association joined with the Building Societies' Association and the Liberty and Property Defence League in seeking its deletion. The Welshman agreed to re-draft but not expunge the offending clause.[87] On reflection, however, the provision was not to be without merit. Landlords would suffer no hardship. Those fortunate enough to let exclusively to better-off workers would gain inasmuch as insured tenants would be better able to meet their obligations during illness. It made no difference for the unskilled majority.

This was not the sole manner in which Mr Lloyd George had come to the aid of the small owner. Until the introduction of the 'People's Budget', the United Property Owners' Association seemed to have lost its way. At the turn of the century it was on the verge of collapse. Of its fifty-five members 80 per cent had disaffiliated between 1900 and 1902. At the same time there were said to be sixty local associations of proprietors who had never bothered to affiliate in the first place. Before the First World War its single success, according to an early historian, was a small depreciation allowance granted in the form of a tax relief on income.[88] The Budget of 1909 brought about a miraculous revival. Organized property owners were infused with a new sense of direction and purpose, and thereafter membership began to pick up. At the end of the Great War the National Federation of Property Owners and Ratepayers, as it had then become, was a substantial body of some importance. But by then the proverbial horse had long since bolted.

[87] *Report of 25th Conference of United Property Owners' Association of Great Britain* (Liverpool, 1911), pp. 7-8, 14-21; *Report of 26th Confernce* etc. (Liverpool, 1911), p. 7.

[88] 'Our Federation: Its Origins and Growth', *Gazette of the National Federation of Property Owners and Ratepayers*, Jan. 1931.

PART 2

Tenants' Defence Associations

England was governed by landlords and the voice of
the tenants was never heard unless combinations
were effected to remove particular injustice and
oppression.

F. W. Soutter, Secretary, Bermondsey Tenants'
Protection League, *Southwark Recorder*, 31 Aug.
1901.

5

Rents, Rates, and Reform

In a previous chapter it was suggested that widespread rent evasion represented a necessary form of income redistribution practised informally and sometimes collectively amongst the poor. It was commonly thought to have had an inflationary effect upon house rents. It also underscored the importance of combinations amongst property owners. Tenants, however, found it even more difficult than their landlords to engage in continuous organization. Nevertheless, the *ad hoc* movements that emerged, however fragmentary and ephemeral, are not without significance. A synoptic view of their character and activities forms the essential prelude to the more dramatic struggles of 1915.

I

The poor Rate Assessment & Collection Act of 1869 restored the peace. It marked the end of the crisis precipitated four years earlier by the resurgent campaign for universal manhood suffrage. The history of that campaign, its disputed relation to the genesis of the second Reform Bill, is relatively familiar.[1] Inept ministerial improvisation needlessly prolonged the turmoil. The famous amendment proposed by Grosvenor Hodgkinson, MP for Newark, and accepted rather unexpectedly by Disraeli in May 1867, swept away compounding and made the occupier alone responsible for local rates. It virtually established complete household suffrage as the basis of the borough franchise in England and Wales. It also caused havoc between landlord and tenant. No arrangements were made for the estimated half-million compounders, who previously had paid rates to the landlord in instalments with the weekly rent.[2] In

---

[1] The most comprehensive analysis is provided by F. B. Smith, *The Making of the Second Reform Bill* (Melbourne, 1966). Rival interpretations of the place of the popular agitation are advanced by Royden Harrison, *Before the Socialists* (1965) and Maurice Cowling, *1867: Disraeli, Gladstone and Revolution* (Cambridge, 1967).

[2] Asa Briggs, *Victorian People* (Pelican Books, 1965), p. 291.

fact Disraeli's acceptance of Hodgkinson's amendment initiated an extension of the extra-parliamentary agitation that was finally arrested by the aforementioned Assessment Act and the resultant restoration of the compound householder. Recent research has in general focused upon the events preceding the passage of the Reform Act. The subsequent transformation in the character of the agitation has been noted but not explored in depth.[3] The volte-face represented by the Act of 1869, however, was the direct result of unprecedented tenant militancy, a mass campaign, albeit one that was neither as definite nor as orderly as that directed by the Reform League, but of real significance none the less. It was the first major victory for collective tenant action.

Disraeli's rash commitment to Hodgkinson's amendment, subsequently incorporated as section 7 of the Reform Act, was greeted with dismay by local government officials.[4] The leader of the Conservative Party, however, who knew little and apparently cared even less for the minutiae of local taxation, remained unmoved by their remonstrations. Gladstone, irked at the prospect of being dished by a more unscrupulous rival but unwilling to prolong the crisis, could offer them no encouragement. 'There has been a great deal of idle talk and jeering about the compound householder, as if he were a chimpanzee or ourangoutang' [*sic*] he told a deputation of anxious local officials.[5] It formed part of a fine display of oratory, characteristically verbose and Radical in tone, but poor consolation to apprehensive occupiers faced with a bleak winter. In addition to the local administrators were others who hoped it might not represent Mr Gladstone's final word. In October 1867 the *Bee-Hive* urged him to reconsider. 'We have no doubt the intense feeling now growing up on the subject will culminate in a giant agitation, exceeding any that took place prior to the passing of the Reform Bill', ran one editorial. It was confident that nothing could withstand the mounting pressure, and that 'even before the Reform Bill is brought into operation, the total repeal of the ratepaying clauses will take place, and the pernicious system of personal payment of rates be abrogated'. It was also confident that Mr Gladstone, like all 'true Liberals', would wish to place himself at the head of the popular

---

[3] The best brief account remains Charles Seymour's *Electoral Reform in England and Wales* (New Haven & London, 1915), pp. 354-7.

[4] Smith, *Making of the Second Reform Bill*, p. 201.

[5] *Tower Hamlets Independent*, 15 June 1867.

movement, and therefore called for 'the unmistakeable support of the people out of doors' in order to help him fulfil his task.[6]

The 'intense feeling', to which the leader referred, was no exaggeration. Section 7 of the Reform Act which abolished compounding, was based on the expectation of a rent reduction proportionate to the sum previously absorbed by the rates. Should landlords be tempted to act otherwise, it was confidently assumed that market forces would come to the tenant's rescue. Temporary difficulties might be experienced during the period of readjustment, but these were of no concern and would subside rapidly. The free market could not be burked. Angels and political economists might fear to transgress these self-evident truths but not landlords. R. D. Baxter, the statistician, was perplexed by their irrational conduct. In spite of the prevalent distress, landlords in East London were actually raising and not reducing rents. Goschen, chairman of the Select Committee on Local Taxation, was equally baffled. Baxter thought hard. In the absence of a deficiency of accommodation in the district, there could but be one explanation. 'I suspect', he concluded, 'that it was rather a little bit of trade unionism on the part of the landlords.'[7] Attempts to thwart the play of the market were not confined to the East End. Throughout the autumn and early winter of 1867 meetings of property-owners were held up and down the country to consider the position. It was generally agreed that no reduction was to be permitted. Notices to quit were issued by the thousand in order to create a fresh tenancy, thereby depriving tenants of their statutory right to deduct the old rate from the new rent.

Three weeks before the *Bee-Hive* had first invited Mr Gladstone to take up the cudgels on the tenants' behalf, the newly-formed Tower Hamlets Liberal Registration Committee announced its intention of holding a series of public meetings in order to encourage tenants to resist the new rents. In adjacent Bethnal Green plans for what, it was hoped, would prove 'an obstinate resistance' were already in preparation. A Tenants' Mutual Protection Association had been formed on the initiative of a group of politically advanced working men operating from taverns in the proximity of Victoria Park where they were accustomed to assemble. The resolution, carried by universal acclamation by the 2,000 persons who attended

[6] *Bee-Hive*, 23 Oct. 1867.
[7] *S.C. Local Taxation* (PP, 1870, VIII,) qq. 5795-8.

the inaugural meeting, left no doubt as to the strength of local feeling: 'That this meeting view with great regret the unscrupulous, selfish, and impolitic attitude assumed by the landlords, and parochial authorities ... and is prepared to firmly resist any unjust impost that the tyranny or avarice of the landlords may feel disposed to put upon their already high rented tenants.' Its proposer then proceeded to support the resolution with arguments condemned by the otherwise sympathetic *Bethnal Green Times* as 'the most atrocious folly and stump oratory gone mad'. In short, he advocated rent-free accommodation. This extravagant language sufficed to alienate Revd. Septimus Hansard, an influential Guardian, who contemptuously spurned their advances. Mr John Holmes, Radical candidate for Hackney, of whom much had been expected, also declined to appear on their platform, a refusal which was reported as having excited 'turbulent displeasure'. But the struggle continued. In Blackburn 'a strong feeling' against the landlords was said to exist. In Birmingham tenants began to organize for mutual protection. At one meeting it was agreed that those landlords who were also shopkeepers would henceforth be the object of a boycott. It was also unanimously resolved: 'That a committee be formed in this ward to co-operate with the committee formed in St. Georges ward to carry on the defensive scheme against the aggression of the landlords.' In London Fields, Hackney, a torchlight demonstration drew 1,000 people. Proceedings were of an 'orderly character' and resolutions protesting against the offending clause were forwarded to the Home Secretary.[8]

The leaders of the Reform League realized that the obstructive rating qualification threatened more than an intensification of landlord tenant conflict. If not expunged, it would vitiate much for which they had fought. The General Council, confronted by unmistakable signs of burgeoning and possibly uncontrollable grassroots fury, decided to defer the banquet that had been planned to celebrate the passing of the Reform Bill. The agitation would be renewed. Its spokesmen—'dealers in stale sedition, wandering minstrels who sing the glories of the mob, ... petty thunderers, ... and strike-jobbers'—returned to the stump. Radical suspicions were fully aroused. James Acland, the ex-Chartist Vice-President of the

[8] *Tower Hamlets Independent*, 21 Sept. 1867; *Bethnal Green Times*, 5 Oct. and 7 Dec. 1867; *The Times*, 1 Oct. 1867; *Birmingham Daily Gazette* 23 Oct. 1867; *Bee-Hive*, 5 Oct. 1867.

Reform League, subjected Disraeli to 'the gravest censure' for his having placed the people 'in the power of the lowest class of landlords—the scum of the middle class—to deprive the working classes of their rights'. Beales told an East London audience 'that it seemed as if this was intended as a punishment on the poor man for having taken part in the proceedings of, or sympathised with the objects of the Reform League; or else its aim was to disgust them with the vote altogether'. In Hackney a petition drawn up by unhappy tenants and frustrated citizens spoke of the hardships and injustice inflicted upon the people as a result of the facilities for extortion which had been granted by the Conservative Government in consequence of which 'a spirit of antagonism between landlord and tenant has been engendered'.[9]

The Reform League represented the best of the artisanal element, organized in trade unions and familiar with politics. The bulk of the working classes were beyond their ken.[10] These harassed and impoverished occupiers, downtrodden and ignored, impatient and fearful, determined to seize the initiative. The claims of citizenship were of secondary importance: the struggle to keep a roof over their heads remained the higher priority. The reception of notice to quit held sufficient terror. The coincidence of a severe trade depression, however, turned worry into fear, fear into anger, and anger into violence. And as had been foreseen, it was the parochial official who bore its brunt. In October 1867 the first rate under the new regulations fell due.

The overseer, like the policeman, the school board, and the sanitary inspector was never a welcome presence in the poorest districts: '... a collector of rates or taxes is not exactly the sort of person who is received with open arms. He has a hard-looking face and carries his octavo-size book in his hand as if it were an insignia of power and position, or an instrument of torture, that has only to be seen to be dreaded.'[11] In these quarters all authority was suspect. The jobbery and corruption attendant upon local administration for so much of the nineteenth century left a sour taste, an uncertain feeling that moneys paid over went straight into the rate-collector's pocket.[12]

[9] Minutes of the General Council of the Reform League, 19 Oct. 1867; *Tower Hamlets Independent* 26 Oct. 1867; *Bethnal Green Times* 4 Apr. 1868; *Bee-Hive*, 28 Mar. 1868.

[10] Harrison, *Before the Socialists*, p. 118.

[11] *Radical*, 12 Feb. 1881.

[12] Cf. R. Thompson, *The Laws Respecting Landlords, Tenants and Lodgers* (1841), p. v.

There seemed to be incontrovertible evidence that, whatever the ultimate destination, such funds as were remitted to the parish chest were not disbursed for the improvement of the masses. Paving, adequate sanitation, and refuse collection always seemed to cease at, and thus to define, the districts inhabited by the poor. Not surprisingly many wage-earners simply turned their backs on their accursed municipal masters.[13] The neglect of the early nineteenth century was in due course succeeded by ill-informed official intrusions into these quarters all of which in the short-term, the only term which mattered, were detrimental to their inhabitants. The agreeable Queen Anne style introduced by the London School Board and much lauded since by architectural historians,[14] was a symbol of oppression to those who, in consequence of its operations, were rendered homeless. The civil style of these public buildings may have accorded with the notorious infidelism of the population, but there is little evidence to suggest that its secular character evoked any commitment to the new civic consciousness embodied therein. 'So lawless were some of the inhabitants' of Eagle Court, Clerkenwell, wrote E. R. Robson, architect to the Board, 'that on the first commencement of the new schoolhouse, which now occupies its northern side, ... it became necessary to protect the workmen from violence by a guard of police'.[15] These operations, like the cutting of Corporation Street, Oxford Street, and other impressive thoroughfares, were, in Henry Pelling's felicitous phrase, nothing more than a form of 'municipal Stalinism'.[16] Behind the violence directed at the overseer lay the pent-up frustrations of a generation at which it is only possible to hint but not to pass over in silence.

Resistance was widespread. Ratepayers simply ignored the demand note. In one street, the town clerk of Wolverhampton explained, the overseers were 'surrounded by a lot of noisy lads hooting and shouting at them, and on the opposite side of the street would stand the women and men making foolish remarks, inciting the boys to make a noise, and when the overseers went into a house they held the doors, put to the shutters, and annoyed them very

---

[13] Cf. S. & B. Webb, *English Local Government: Statutory Authorities for Special Purposes* (1922), p. 436.

[14] See, for example, M. Seaborne, *The English School* 2 vols. (1971-7), and Mark Girouard, *Sweetness and Light, The 'Queen Anne' Movement 1860-1900* (Oxford 1977).

[15] E. R. Robson, *School Architecture* (1874) pp. 315-16.

[16] Henry Pelling, *Popular Politics and Society in Late Victorian Britain* (1968) p. 3.

much indeed, and if the overseers had not acted with great forebearance I believe they would have met with personal violence!' The womenfolk, he added, 'were more noisy and have been more demonstrative against the rate than even the men, as a rule'. In Norwich, where before the Reform Act there had been 13,500 tenements the occupiers of which were subject to composition, the same difficulty was experienced. A memorial representing the considered views of the overseers of 42 parishes, declared: 'In many instances the greatest opprobrium has been freely heaped upon us, and even threats of personal violence used towards us, and we find an almost universal refusal by such occupiers to pay the rate or any part of it.'[17]

In East London the harsh winter plus the severe industrial depression following the collapse of Thames-side shipbuilding combined to give the popular resistance its peculiar intensity. Landlords and overseers appeared to compete for possession of the poor man's home. 'Rent is a sore subject', a commentator observed, 'Nothing can exceed the iron harshness of some of the landlords: the people grimly say of them that they collect their money weekly in coppers, going from house to house with a barrow.' The landlord probably fared better than the parish official. A journalist who visited the area left a hair-raising account of the difficulties which the overseers encountered. 'The collection of rates in Bethnal Green has never been an easy matter', he wrote, 'but the present distress combined with the abolition of compounding has made it a frightful affair.' The enforcement of the law had, he claimed, become 'a perilous matter':

In the ward where most of the defaulters are found the collector is now thoroughly well known and cordially detested. One part of this district, Hope Town, is in 'open rebellion against the rates'. The moment he shows himself the boys gather at his heels and shout along the streets, 'Shut your doors'. Unfortunately many of the streets are closed at one end, so that the collector is at the mercy of the foe, and has little chance of catching his people unawares. He is hissed, hooted, and groaned at in the most vehement style. We should add that there are very few Irish in the parish, so that the explanation of such a scene is not to be found in the superior excitability of the Celtic race. Threats are not wanting and there is too much reason to fear that personal violence is really intended.

This report was confirmed by the Vestry Clerk in evidence before

[17] *S.C. Poor Rates Assessment* (PP 1868-9, XI), qq. 1128-30, 4844.

the select committee appointed to investigate the problem. 'There has been an organised opposition', he told his interrogators:

The moment a collector is seen approaching, every door is shut; two or three times we have had recourse to the expedient of getting six policemen to accompany the collector because it is actually dangerous to his life to attempt to distrain; and unless the landlord is in some way coaxed into it, there are certain parts in which we shall never get the rate ... The difficulty seems to be growing, for this reason; a man who has paid finds that his neighbour has not paid, and he meets the collector with the imprecation that he will see him damned before he pays again.

The police were, however, reluctant to become involved and who could blame them? 'The collector is face to face with a class whom he had never met before—some of them rough and rude enough to be exceedingly formidable'. Our intrepid reporter contemplated the future with apprehension. 'We should not be surprised if this rate-enforcing business were to end in some rather serious disturbances'. In the event local officials were compelled to bribe landlords willing to pay the occupiers rates with the offer of reduced assessments.[18]

At first, however, the threat of insolvency and contempt of the law posed by this popular intransigence was countered by the wholesale prosecution of the offenders. The harrowing and at times riotous scenes at the court-house left a deep impression on those who witnessed them:

Ten o'clock was the time fixed for holding the sessions, but long before that hour an immense crowd had assembled ... A large number of females were among the crowd, and suffered severely from the pressure, several being removed in a fainting condition, and more than one in a fit of hysteria, the screams of the latter being distinctly audible in the court, and producing a painful impression in the minds of the Bench and the parochial officers present.

The Hackney magistrates dealt with these cases with 'marvellous rapidity'. The total number of summonses issued exceeded 5,000, and by the end of the first sitting at 2 p.m., 1,000 cases had been disposed of. In Birmingham 'the number of summonses issued for the recovery of the poor rates was so great as to be almost incredible'.

[18] Anon, 'Anecdotes about the London Poor', *Macmillan's Magazine*, XX (1869), p. 400; *Standard*, 6 Jan. 1868; *S.C. Poor Rates Assessment*, qq. 2641, 2645; *HC. Deb.* 35, cxiv (1868-9), 318; and for the industrial crisis, see G. Stedman Jones, *Outcast London* (Oxford 1971), pp. 100-6.

It was reckoned that two thirds of the small householders were summoned, 'as many as six or eight hundred summonses being issued in a day'. 'The warrants of distraint', the same course added, 'were proportionately numerous, two or more officers being constantly out with a van effecting seizures'. Similar proceedings took place up and down the country. Some authorities, overwhelmed by the fast rising tide of destitution, agreed to grant wholesale exemptions while others defiantly reintroduced compounding. But many pressed for their pound of flesh. By the end of 1867 137,000 summonses had been taken out and 29,000 distress warrants issued.[19]

The efforts of the nascent tenants' associations and those of the National Reform Union and the Reform League were to some extent eclipsed by these dramatic events. East London, scene of bread riots at the beginning of 1867, continued to dominate the headlines. During the summer tension mounted as misplaced fears of a revolutionary alliance between its turbulent population and the respectable forces marshalled behind the Reform League gained currency. The passage of the Reform Act momentarily defused the crisis. The volatility of its wretched inhabitants, however, gave cause for continuing alarm. The menacing scenes outside the magistrates courts tortured the middle-class imagination. 'The excited demeanour of the vast crowds which assembled about the town halls of these places, the signs which onlookers noted of sullen and deep-seated resentment and of a disposition to tumult, the curses, groans, and threats to destroy buildings, which were muttered are symptoms which a wise statesman would not disregard. The sense of injustice acting upon the sense of hunger, and embittering the despair of poverty, is a state of mind of bad augury for the public peace.'[20] In this poverty-stricken environment, the attempted politicization of the question foundered, overtaken by the tumultuous spontaneity of its desperate inhabitants.

It all stood in sharp relief to the situation in the once fearsome manufacturing districts, a contrast which to some extent had been concealed by the nervous fixation upon the particular problems of East London. In Wigan, for example, the formative meeting of the tenants defence association attracted 'a large attendance of the

---

[19] *Bethnal Green Times*, 7 Mar. 1868; *Manchester Examiner & Times*, 4 Feb. 1868; J. T. Bunce, *History of the Corporation of Birmingham* (Birmingham 1885), II pp. 41-2; Seymour, *Electoral Reform*, pp. 354-5; Smith, *Making of the Second Reform Bill*, p. 201.

[20] *Daily News*, 2 Mar. 1868.

more respectable class of working men'. Even in Salford where the rate-collectors were relentless in their exactions, even to the point of refusing exemption to cellar-dwellers already in receipt of outdoor relief, and where the Mayor expressed the hope that the overseers would have regard to the capacities of the New Bailey, no fears of tumult or disorder were aroused. The 'crowd of defaulters' at the Salford Borough Court, a batch of 250 drawn from 'the poorest class', presented 'a spectacle such as one would never willingly witness a second time'. But they inspired pity rather than terror. 'The order-loving disposition of this population', it was observed, 'has come too victoriously out of previous trials for any combined outbreak of violence to be apprehended in this emergency'.[21] Indeed, in the Manchester area tenants displayed hitherto unsuspected capacities for the prosecution of a protracted and ultimately successful campaign.

The Manchester and Salford Land and House-Owners' Association was a long established federation with several suburban affiliates. It claimed to represent 75 per cent of all properties in the area that were subject to composition.[22] In September 1867 meetings of proprietors were held in anticipation of the re-introduction of direct rating that was due to take effect at the end of the month. These deliberations were 'very numerously attended'. No tears were shed for the abolition of compounding which was condemned as a 'pernicious practice'. It was agreed that members should seek indemnity against litigious tenants through the creation of fresh tenancies; and in Hulme alone the secretary personally issued 1,000 notices for this purpose. It was also resolved that a 'just and equitable' rent reduction should be made, the conditions and amount of which were to be determined as the landlord thought fit.[23]

In his testimony before the Select Committee on Poor Rates Assessment, seven months later, William Griffiths, an overseer who also happened to be secretary of the Hulme Property Owners' Association and a prominent figure in the central Land and House-owners' Association, tried to minimize the popular unrest which had, in consequence, been engendered. It was all a storm in a teacup, over within 'a month or two' once the tenants had mastered

[21] *Manchester Examiner & Times*, 20 Jan. 1868; *S.C. Poor Rates Assessment*, q. 2822; *Salford Weekly News*, 7 Mar. 1868.
[22] *S.C. Poor Rates Assessment*, q. 2765.
[23] Cf. *Manchester Examiner & Times*, 27 Sept. 1867; and *S.C. Poor Rates Assessment*, qq. 2766-8.

the new system under which the rates were to be paid in regular instalments. The ill-informed and prejudiced tenants were, he explained, 'more frightened than they were hurt, in reality'. Personal payment would, moreover, encourage provident habits and a much-needed civic spirit among the lower orders. Indeed, it had already begun to do so. The whole inquiry appeared superfluous, although he had the good sense not to say so. At this point Mr Shaw Lefevre became suspicious. The unprecedented increased participation in vestry affairs to which the witness averred, in truth had little to do with the growth of a new civic awareness. Griffith was forced to confess that the new interest related solely to the election of those who would support the repeal of the rate-paying clauses. But such piffling qualifications were of no account. The honourable Members did not appear to appreciate the role of outside 'agitators' in leading the tenants astray. Griffith sought to enlighten them: 'It rests with a few; there are a few men belonging to the National Reform Union, headed by a man who has got some working men together for the purpose of agitation in the town; ... it is not really the feeling of the township.' None the less he was confident that, before its expiry, the current rate would be paid in full, an optimism for which, as Mr Shaw Lefevre again demonstrated, there was not the slightest foundation.[24] There was in fact very considerable tension among the occupiers.

In his attempt to place the best construction on events, Griffiths was prepared to concede that some landlords had at first intended to 'deal harshly' with their tenants, but this minority was quickly brought to heel. 'I do not believe that there are half-a-dozen now who have dealt fairly with their tenants; and I may say that now almost universal satisfaction prevails where nothing but turmoil was the rule.'[25] This generous and somewhat roseate view of recent local history will not bear close scrutiny. In Salford, to which he referred specifically, fair-dealing was conspicuous by its absence.

In the second week of October 1867, the Salford Property Owners' Association met to consider their attitude towards the rate-paying clauses of the Reform Act. It was coolly resolved to pocket the rates. No reduction in rent would be allowed. Mr Abraham Helm thought the conduct unbecoming. Mr Helm, a gentleman, was understood to say that he would be 'acting as a rogue' if he behaved

[24] *S.C. Poor Rates Assessment*, qq. 2769-71, 2774-83, 2808-13, 2849-70.
[25] *S.C. Poor Rates Assessment*, qq. 2826-7.

accordingly. Mr Wild too opposed the motion. He had good tenants and was reluctant to lose them by the adoption of so unnatural a course. 'The resolution', he declared, 'would bind all the property-owners in a kind of trade union' and that would never do. But it was to no avail and the motion was carried.[26]

By this stunningly maladroit display, the property-owners con-trived 'to attract to themselves as much odium as the occasion would admit of'. In the outcry which followed landlord and tenant appealed to public opinion for support. *The Salford Weekly News*, having weighed the merits of each case, was ready to pronounce judgement. Whether or not rising costs had outstripped the, in some instances, 20 per cent increase in rents obtained in recent years—factors emphasized by landlord and tenant respectively—could not, it felt, be resolved by abstract computation alone. The owners, it was observed:

... hint that the doctrine of Free Trade applies even to the question of house rents. Those who do not feel willing to pay the increased rent, it is stated, have the 'privilege' of leaving the houses. Now we cannot say that this is not, in a sense, true, and if the owners had not engaged in controversy at all, and had not mixed up the rise of the rent with the alteration of the rating system it would not have been easy to prolong the debate. As a matter of abstract political economy it is necessarily as open to the owners of houses to plead the law of supply and demand in face of criticism of their rate of profits as it is for the merchant and trader. But then this is not a mere matter of pure theoretical speculation; the rate of rent, while men are men, will never be calmly regarded as a mere natural phenomenon, rising and falling like the tides. A little feeling would be excited even in case of tides, if associations were formed for the purpose of regulating their ebb and flow.

Here, we apprehend, is the grievance of the occupiers. They consider that the owners and agents have banded themselves together for the purpose of enforcing higher rents. Well, we know what there is to be said on the question of the rights of association ... Still, we fancy that we should have to expend a good deal of time in illustrating the principles of economical science before we convinced people that corn factors and millers were warranted in holding back food for the purpose of benefiting by starvation prices. That gives us the clue to the final consideration of this matter. It is quite true that these abstract rights exist, but it is also true that they do not override our moral duties ... The question of acting with fair moderation—of not taking the full limit of an advantage—has not been wholly precluded by the organisation of political economy ...[27]

[26]   *Salford Weekly News*, 19 Oct. 1867
[27]   *Salford Weekly News*, 26 Oct. 1867

In the weeks that followed the local press published a spate of letters from irate tenants, all expressing support for some kind of collective counter-response.[28] One of them included an intervention from a Mr Malcolm Macleod, Secretary of the Salford Tenants' Association. Meetings, he explained, had been arranged 'to organize against the injustices and tyranny' of the property-owners. The Tenants' Association, he added, 'would be most happy to form an alliance with friends in Manchester and elsewhere'. 'The property owners have already formed such an alliance and we must fight them with their own weapons.'[29] A similar body had in fact already been formed in nearby Pendleton. Shortly afterwards occupiers in a neighbouring suburb united to found the Hulme Weekly Tenants' Defence Association, and early in the new year Hulme Town Hall, a popular meeting-place, was the venue for the founding of yet another association, the Hulme Registration and House Occupiers' Protection Association.[30] In the main these combinations eschewed the proto-socialism of the Bethnal Green Mutual Protection Association. The Salford Tenants' Association, for example, adopted a far more restricted view of its responsibilities. Its objects were clearly stated in a widely publicized circular. The Association, it declared, aimed:

To use all legal and lawful means to prevent property owners or agents taking any advantage of their tenants, such as causing tenants to pay rates both to them and the tax collector—to watch over the interests of the ratepayers and prevent any encroachment by the landlords' combination—to aid by all possible means the erection of improved working men's dwellings, with a view to such dwellings becoming the property of the tenants, by monthly repayments in the shape of rent—by keeping a 'house-register', and by other means to aid in tenanting the cottages owned by honest landlords, and to encourage tenants to quit the houses of landlords who under the pretence of carrying out the spirit and intentions of the Representation of the People Act, have caused their tenants to pay an increased rental or double poor rates. By monthly contributions of two pence and upwards to defray the working expenses of the association.[31]

The emphasis upon home ownership requires comment. Owner-

[28] See, for example, correspondence of 'A Working Man', 'A Porter', 'A Weekly Tenant', 'One who Can't Afford to Pay', and 'A Working Man', *Manchester Examiner & Times*, 19, 22, 29 Oct. 1867 and 21, 26 Dec. 1867.

[29] *Manchester Examiner & Times*, 30 Oct. 1867.

[30] *Salford Weekly News*, 2 Nov. 1867 and 11 Jan. 1868; *Manchester Examiner & Times*, 7 Jan. 1868.

[31] *Salford Weekly News*, 7 Dec. 1867.

occupation in Hulme, for example, was not widespread. In that township, with some 11,500 houses let at an annual rental below £10, there were not more than 1379 owners.[32] In Salford, generally considered a residentially inferior area, there is no reason to believe that a similar pattern did not obtain. At one level this faith in home-ownership represented a kind of emancipation, one that embodied those virtues of thrift, discipline, and self-restraint for which the Lancashire working man was much praised; at another it probably represented professional self-interest. Macleod, an active Liberal and member of the National Reform Union, was also the district manager of the Manchester branch of the Artisans', Labourers', and General Dwellings Company. The company, which catered for the cream of the working class, was then engaged in the development of a local housing estate. More than 80 per cent of its clients were teetotallers 'and all are active members of various co-operative societies'.[33]

The tenants' associations spoke for those sectors of the working class who were not only moderate and respectable, but aggressively self-reliant and proud of it. The Members for the City of Manchester, Thomas Bazley and Jacob Bright, both approved. And from the tenor of the chairman's remarks, delivered before a public meeting held at the Town Hall, 'a numerous attendance including many female householders', it is clear that these honourable gentlemen had not mistaken the character of their agitated constituents. The chairman subscribed fully to that 'shopkeeper radicalism' prevalent in the North. His views on municipal extravagance were virtually identical with those of the landlords with whom they were in conflict. The Manchester Town Hall and in particular the funds lavished upon the erection of the Chorlton Workhouse excited the deepest indignation. 'These buildings', he declared, 'were of a very costly character—more like palaces than workhouses; ... and further, when, as in Salford, the inmates were liberally supplied with gin and tobacco, and the guardians took an annual trip or two, with champagne and Madeira, the amount was still further augmented.' The meeting itself had been called to consider the progress so far made. The Hulme Tenants' Defence Association recognized the ultimate need to restore compounding but concentrated its efforts upon obtaining an interim settlement with the property-owners'

[32] *S.C. Poor Rates Assessment*, q. 2848.
[33] *Salford Weekly News*, 19 Dec. 1868 and 10 July 1869.

association. A conciliatory figure, Revd. A. Hall, had been prevailed upon to act as a mediator. The rival House Occupiers' Protection Association, by contrast, opposed negotiations and emphasized the political aspect of the struggle. It viewed the conflict as the unfinished business of the Reform Bill agitation. 'It was unwise to waste their steam in glozing [*sic*] over a wrong and leaving its cause unredressed', Mark Price, its leading spokesman, declared. Price, a prominent member of the National Reform Union, questioned the property-owners' faith. The 'first task', as he saw it, was 'to bring the landlords to their senses'. If his proposal to amalgamate the two tenants' associations were accepted, he was confident that the landlords would be 'knocked into a cocked hat' within 'a couple of months'. His proposal was rejected; the meeting broke up in uproar.[34] Negotiations with the property-owners continued.

The numerical strength of the individual tenants' associations remains unknown. This is unfortunate but it does not diminish the significance of their achievement. They had played an important role in organizing and voicing local opinion. Some landlords had, at first, been inclined to threaten dissenters with doubled rent or worse, but by the end of 1867 organized property-owners, unnerved by the strength of the opposition aroused, began to crumble. 'If the commotion that had been going on for three months after the passing of the [Reform] Bill had continued', said the secretary of the Hulme Property Owners' Association, 'I do not think there would have been a single owner that would not have been happy to go back to compounding.'[35] In the face of the unrelenting pressure of the tenants, the hostility of the local authority, and the reprobation of the local press, the landlords expressed a willingness to seek a negotiated settlement.[36] The attempt to throw the whole burden of the rates upon the tenants was forsaken. The landlords, Griffiths agreed, had been deflected by the combination of the tenants and the overseers.[37]

It was not an unqualified victory. The intention of the Reform Act was that no loss should fall upon the tenant in consequence of the abolition of compounding. This provision enabled an occupier

[34] *Manchester Examiner & Times*, 21 Jan. 1868; *Salford Weekly News*, 25 Jan. 1868.

[35] *Salford Weekly News*, 16 Nov. 1867; *S.C. Poor Rates Assessment*, q. 2911.

[36] *Manchester Examiner & Times*, 14 Dec. 1867 and 7, 8, and 31 Jan. 1868; *Salford Weekly News*, 28 Dec. 1867 and 11 Jan. 1868.

[37] *S.C. Poor Rates Assessment*, qq. 3029-30.

under a *subsisting tenancy* to deduct from the landlord's rent the full
rate that he himself paid. But this safeguard, as has already been
seen, was nullified by the expedient of creating a new tenancy. In
Manchester the property-owners now offered to take the average
yearly amount of rates for three years and reduce the rent so much
per week as would correspond to that average. However, the calculation was based on the assumption of composition with the result
that the tenant had to pay the difference between the full rate and
the compound rate; in effect, 30 per cent more of rates. The landlords
agreed to pay the two-thirds rate outstanding. The blow was softened
as a result of a private arrangement by which the landlord, in
Griffiths's phrase, undertook to act as a 'conduit pipe for the
conveyance of the rates to the overseers'.[38] This provisional settlement barely survived the year.

   The abolition of the compound householder had been undertaken
as a political expedient rather than as a measure beneficial in itself.
The new Liberal Government determined to bring the war between
owner and occupier to a swift conclusion. The Poor Rate Assessment
and Collection Act 1869, did not, however, restore the *status quo
ante*. Henceforth, the owner of a small property might be rated
instead of the occupier, either by agreement or by compulsory order
of the local authority. It applied to properties of a specific rateable
value: £20 in London, £13 in Liverpool, £10 in Manchester or
Birmingham, and £8 elsewhere. Owners who agreed to pay the
rates received a maximum rebate of 25 per cent: where the owner
was compulsorily rated, he received an allowance of only 15 per
cent, and then he was entitled to an additional 15 per cent abatement
if willing to pay the rates whether the property was occupied or
not.[39]

II

How extensive was compounding? No precise figures are readily
available. The best evidence suggests that it was less significant than
contemporaries imagined. In late-Victorian England and Wales
compounding accounted for an estimated 25 per cent of total rateable
value. Still, the number of tenants involved must have been considerable. Compounding, it was suggested, might even have been a

---

[38]   *S.C. Poor Rates Assessment*, qq. 2872-82, 3037.
[39]   32 & 33 Vict. c. 41. ss. 3-4.

factor in the chronic overcrowding that threatened the heart of empire.[40] Throughout the 1870s the ruthless hustling of the poor continued without respite. Unhoused by railway companies, street improvements and commercial development, the casual poor were chased from pillar to post by an army of sanitary inspectors armed with closing and demolition orders. For thirty years and more these victims of 'progress' had scurried from slum to slum—and all to no avail. By the end of the decade overcrowding seemed worse than ever: a crisis had been reached.

The meaning of that crisis, it is sometimes suggested, resides in the generation of a fruitful agitation that shattered parliament's habitual indifference and issued in significant legislation which prefigured the introduction of state-subsidized housing.[41] This questionable interpretation relies upon a non-existent synthesis between social reform and politics proper, the separation of which continued to impede progress in housing and other spheres. It is difficult to demonstrate a partisanship on the part of the parliamentary parties that outlasted the immediate hue and cry sparked by the publication of *The Bitter Cry of Outcast London* late in 1883. Chamberlain was quite unrepresentative of the bulk of Liberal opinion. 'His socialism repels me', wrote Gladstone, who also declared that he 'reserved his worst Billingsgate for those who would take private property for public use even though the use were the erection of healthy dwellings'.[42] Salisbury's intervention must, in view of his subsequent inaction, be regarded as a superb demonstration of that extraordinary cosmetic facility which constituted the essence of Tory social reform. The Housing of the Working Classes Act, 1890, the most tangible fruit of the Bitter Cry agitation, was a mere codificatory measure, and was understood as such.[43] There was no assumption of national responsibility and local administration excited few and bored many. ' "Society", deeply interested in Parliamentary politics', Sidney Low observed, 'has treated municipal

[40] On the extent of compounding, see Avner Offer, *Property and Politics, 1870-1914* (1981), p. 287; and for the suggestion that compounding encouraged overcrowding, *Report of the Urban Land Enquiry* (1914), p. 665.

[41] A. S. Whol, *The Eternal Slum*, (1977), Ch. ix.

[42] Gladstone to Granville, 9 Sept. 1885, Agatha Ramm ed., *The Political Correspondence of Mr Gladstone and Lord Granville*: 2 vols. (Oxford 1962), II, p. 393; G. W. E. Russell, 'The New Liberalism, A Response', *Nineteenth Century* (XXVI, 1889), p. 497.

[43] Eighth Special Report of US Commissioner of Labour, *The Housing of the Working People*, 53 Cong., 3rd Sess. (Washington, 1895), pp. 60-2.

affairs with well-bred contempt.'[44] Even in the Council chamber the fiction persisted that housing was a matter of administration not politics.[45] In no General Election before the Great War did housing reform figure except as a marginal issue.[46]

Social reformers were not unaware of the retardative effect of their political isolation.[47] But there were few, excepting Radical, Socialist, and the occasional disaffected backbencher, who would have had it otherwise. Shaftesbury himself regretted the appointment of the Royal Commission on Housing and, like most anxious contemporaries, constantly inveighed against precipitate action and the assumption of any rash commitment to state intervention.[48] It was a line of reasoning which reached an absurd apotheosis in the formation of the Society for the Promotion of the Gospel Amongst Landlords.[49] This stubborn defence of voluntarism, however, represented something more than the mindless bleatings of those unable to visualize the comfortable niche which the expansion of the bureaucracy would provide for their children and grandchildren.

Gareth Stedman Jones has suggested that the meaning of the housing crisis of the 1880s is best understood in relation to the situation of its middle-class critics and their attitudes towards the casual poor. The housing question in this context was symptomatic of the perceived breakdown of class relations in the capital, and the solutions proffered quite different in connotation from that unilinear *étatiste* progressivism that is supposed to have culminated in the creation of the 'welfare state'.[50] It was the reformatory rather than reform which remained the dominant strain in the social thought of the period. The dispersal of Booth's Class B, the residuum, upon which all future progress depended, was not in any case likely to be

[44] Sidney Low, *The Governance of England* (1904), p. 308.
[45] Cf. A. G. Boscowen to R. C. K. Ensor, 22 Apr. 1910 (R. C. K. Ensor Papers, Corpus Christi College, Oxford).
[46] Richard Price, *An Imperial War & the British Working Class* (1972) Ch. 3; A. K. Russell, *Liberal Landslide, The General Election of 1906* (Newton Abbot 1973 pp. 65, 83; Neal Blewett, *The Peers, the Parties and the People, The General Elections of 1910* (1972), Ch. xv.
[47] See, for example, Gilbert W. Child, 'Sanitary Legislation and the Homes of the Poor', *Contemporary Review* XXXII, (1878), p. 297.
[48] On Shaftesbury, see E. K. Abel, 'Canon Barnett and the first thirty years of Toynbee Hall' (University of London Unpublished Ph.D. thesis 1969) p. 32; 'The Mischief of State Aid', *Nineteenth Century* XXIV (1883); and see Stedman Jones *Outcast London*, pp. 227-30.
[49] On formation, see *Democrat*, 24 Apr. and 1 May 1886. This association appears to have led a lengthy, if uneventful existence: see *Labour Annual* (1895), p. 85.
[50] Stedman Jones, *Outcast London*, Parts II and III, esp. Ch. 18.

advanced by the provision of cheap accommodation in the central slum areas.[51]

At the end of the eighties housing reform had reached an impasse. The promise of serving both Mammon and Christ held out by commercial philanthropy was false. Mammon had won. Darkness descended. There had to be an alternative to subsidized housing: for the moment, though, most middle-class reformers were at a loss to imagine what it might be. 'It is far more easy to show the politician what difficulties and what dangers lie before him than to suggest any hopeful means of dealing with them...', wrote one of them. 'In short', he concluded, 'despair sets in when we look for such means.'[52] Socialism, however, had a longer way to march before it would become irresistible.

In the winter of 1881 the Democratic Federation announced that 'it had taken up the question of Fair Rents in London and intend to carry out a vigorous agitation for Rental and Sanitary Reform'.[53] The resolve to continue the campaign in support of municipal housing, launched in the previous year by the Manhood Suffrage League, marks a turning-point.[54] The men behind the initiative comprised that class-conscious coterie, the Soho O'Brienites, the men of '48, that extraordinary cadre of impoverished artisans and mechanics who upheld the cause of social revolution during the years of mid-Victorian stability: men such as John Sketchley, James and Charles Murray, William Townshend, Joseph Lane, and Frank Kitz, uncompromising land and currency reformers, republican and internationalist, admired by Marx; men whom Hyndman took pains to recruit and who formed the nucleus of the embryonic SDF.[55]

[51] Lettice Fisher, 'The Town Housing Problem', *Economic Journal*, XV (1905), p. 29.

[52] Frederick Greenwood, 'The Misery in Great Cities', *Nineteenth Century*, XXV (1889) pp. 747-8.

[53] *Labour Standard*, 24 Nov. 1881.

[54] On the opening of the campaign, see *Daily Chronicle*, 26 July 1880. In the next four months the *Chronicle* maintained extensive coverage, as did *House and Home*, a weekly journal which, by virtue of a special arrangement with the Club and Institute Union, had a wide circulation in the working men's clubs. The *West Central News*, a local Radical weekly, also provides regular reports. Another account is presented in Frank Kitz's not altogether reliable 'Recollections and Reflections', *Freedom*, Jan.–Aug. 1912.

[55] The world of the Soho O'Brienites is evoked by Stan Shipley, *Club Life and Socialism in Mid-Victorian London* (History Workshop Pamphlet, Oxford, 1971) and for a recent assessment of their activities in relation to the formation of the SDF, see W. E. Lincoln, 'Popular Radicalism and the Beginnings of the New Socialist Movement in Britain 1870-1885' (University of London Unpublished Ph.D. thesis, 1977, Chs. 5 and 6.

Herein is the source of that concern for housing reform, accorded priority in *Socialism Made Plain* (1883), which became a distinguishing feature thereafter. In the East End, where the agitation had been concentrated, a major rent strike was rumoured to be imminent.[56] Hyndman was convinced that the appointment of the Royal Commission on Housing was a triumphant recognition of the socialist presence.[57]

The Royal Commission heard a good deal of evidence of the growing unrest among working people which, in conjunction with the resurgence of agrarian radicalism in Ireland, aroused recurrent fears for the security of property on the mainland. The decade was punctuated by much loose talk of 'Plans of Campaign' and 'No Rent' strikes in the metropolis, in the main stump oratory of little consequence. The one attempt to organize tenants, undertaken by the Soho O'Brienites, was abandoned promptly because, as one of them explained, 'they found that they were becoming the persecutors of those they wished to benefit as when pressure was put on the landlords to improve their premises, they either evicted the tenants or put an extra amount on the rent'.[58]

The idea of the rent strike as an instrument of mass radicalization lingered, however. The fantastic vision of insurgent tenants poisoning landlords, hurling brickbats at bailiffs, clambering over the barricades and streaming forth from their slums to inaugurate the Co-operative Commonwealth seized the anarchist imagination.[59] It was a mirror image of that nightmare from which Booth rescued the middle classes at the end of the decade. These fringe elements developed an appropriate life style exemplified by Comrade Frederick Goulding, the Stratford anarchist, whose six evictions within two years were apparently considered a splendid recommendation. Kitz himself sadly acknowledged their derisory impact. After more than a generation of agitation he concluded that they

[56] *Labour News and Employment Advertiser.* 20 Oct. 1883; *Christian Socialist*, Nov. 1883.

[57] Hyndman to Helen Taylor, 29 Nov. 1884, (Mill-Taylor Papers, British Library of Political and Economic Science) *Housing Journal*, Jan. 1906.

[58] *Daily Chronicle*, 23 Nov. 1880.

[59] Speech of James Harragan, *Anarchist*, Dec. 1885; E. P. Thompson, *William Morris, Romantic to Revolutionary* (rev. edn. 1977) p. 589 *Commonweal*, 18 Oct. 1890; Sheila Rowbotham, 'Anarchism in Sheffield in the 1890's', in Pollard and Holmes, eds., *Essays on the Economic and Social History of South Yorkshire*, Ch. ix.

had had 'about as much effect upon the masses as trying to tickle an elephant with straw'.[60]

Rent strikes were not compromised by these antics. At the end of the 1890s the SDF was again ready to raise the standard on behalf of rack-rented tenants.[61] The growth of tenants' associations, however, represented more than a reaction against rising rents and over-crowding. Once again compounding bedevilled the matter.

III

The Poor Rate Assessment and Collection Act was not and could not be a final solution. The democratization of local government coupled with steeply rising rates led, in due course, to the inevitable renewal of the controversy. In the last years of Victoria's reign the growth of local expenditure was far more rapid than the growth of the rateable value of the country. In the years 1890-1900 rateable value in England and Wales increased by 16.7 per cent while expenditure rose by 47 per cent. In the following decade the growth of expenditure from the rates was more than twice as fast as the rise in assessable value. Moreover, the imposition after 1901 of new statutory duties, without any adequate matching relief from the central government, aggravated the plight of the local authorities, especially in the poorer areas.[62]

Although Disraeli's insistence upon the personal payment of rates as the basis of citizenship was a mere fiction—a high-sounding principle for the edification of a none too bright party rank and file—the guardians of property, casting around for some means of checking the alarming rise in municipal spending, were by the 1890s again ready to declare that compounding violated basic constitutional practice.[63] It was considered only right that those entitled to vote for the election of bodies charged with the raising and administration of public funds should be liable to personal payment of rates in order

[60] On Goulding, see *Freedom*, Oct. 1893 and *The Torch of Anarchy*, 1 Mar. 1896; also see Robert Barltrop, *The Monument, The Story of the Socialist Party of Great Britain* (1975), pp. 19-20. On derisory impact, see R. A. Woods, *English Social Movements* (1892) pp. 47-8. Quotation from *Voice of Labour*, 18 Jan. 1907.

[61] *Justice*, 2 Sept. 1899.

[62] On this, see *The Land: Report of the Urban Land Enquiry* (1914) pp. 506 and 610 ff.

[63] Spencer to Geo. C. Brodrick, 10 May 1891, David Duncan, ed., *Life and Letters of Herbert Spencer*, p. 304.

that they might appreciate directly the effect of economical or extravagant administration. However, critics maintained that in operational terms this was a rather abstract notion of political behaviour. Spokesmen for the Metropolitan Rate Collectors' Association stated that 'their experience at municipal elections leads them to the conclusion that the amount of interest taken depends almost entirely upon the activity of the local party organisations, and that personal interest without such influence would be practically nil'.[64] Mr Samuel Collier Potts, Treasurer for the Borough of Huddersfield, went further: 'I do not think that the direct payment of rates by the small occupiers would make much, if any, difference in their interest in local government. There are so many other matters affecting the health and convenience of residents and voters of much greater importance than the rates, which promote interest in the work of the Council, and I expect and believe this will increase rather than diminish in the future.'[65] Here was the crux of the matter. It was not the absence of interest in local affairs that animated the advocates of direct rating as much as the wrong kind of interest.[66] But they were not easily dissuaded. The assimilation of rates and rents, it was argued, deprived the occupant of compounded property of vital information as to that proportion of his rent which was due to the demands of the rating authority. If the rates rose his rent might be increased, but if it fell rents did not automatically follow suit. Since it was impossible to arrest, let alone reverse, the growth of local democracy, it was incumbent upon all public-spirited citizens to do their utmost to persuade working-class tenants to take a greater interest in their affairs.

The Poplar Borough Municipal Alliance was formed by a handful of such citizens. Its membership grew rapidly and within twelve months it claimed to represent nearly 40 per cent of the total rateable value of the borough. This spectacular progress represented a sharp reaction against the phenomenal rise in local taxation in recent years. Poplar was amongst the poorest districts in London. Yet it was also one of the early strongholds of the labour movement. George Lansbury, elected to the Board of Guardians in 1893, was

[64] 'Memorandum of the Metropolitan Rate Collectors' Association', para. 9, *R.C. Poor Laws*, app. vol. ix (PP 1910, XLIX) q. 93504.

[65] 'Replies from Mr Samuel Collier Potts', IV, app. xxvii, *R.C. Poor Laws*, app. vol. ix, p. 808.

[66] Cf. 'Replies by Miss Constance Bartlett', IV, app. xxiv, *R.C. Poor Laws*, app. vol. ix, p. 805.

later joined by other labour representatives who, although never a majority before 1914, were by their birth, training and commitment, able to dominate its proceedings. They had, moreover, established an extraordinary rapport with their constituents. It was their challenging policies on the humane administration of the workhouse and the generous provision of outdoor relief which precipitated the ratepayers' revolt,[67] that in the Spring of 1905 led to the formation of the Poplar Municipal Alliance.

The Municipal Alliance obtained the appointment of an inquiry conducted by J.S. Davy, Chief Inspector to the Local Government Board. His report was severely critical of the management of the Poplar Union.[68] In spite of this adverse and widely publicized document, the campaign mounted against 'socialism on the rates' did not commend itself to the electorate. Not one of the Municipal Alliance's seventeen nominees was returned in the ensuing Guardian elections. The Labour candidates, by contrast, did not forfeit public support.[69] In the winter of 1907/8 the defiant Guardians again dispensed outdoor relief with what was condemned as an outrageous liberality.[70] The Alliance redoubled its efforts. It wrested control over the Borough Council shortly afterwards.

The Poplar Municipal Alliance claimed to represent the community rather than a particular class or party. It appealed to those shopkeepers who had been hit by rising rates and reduced communal purchasing power but had not yet joined the mass exodus of small businessmen that was alleged to have taken place.[71] It also spoke on behalf of more substantial commercial interests. Its officials were in one way and another connected with the principal employers in the district, although spokesmen were understandably coy about the precise relation and refused to be drawn when challenged.[72] The large concerns in the locality were frightened and resentful at the seemingly irresistible march of municipal socialism, the resultant

[67] On this, see P. A. Ryan, 'Poplarism', in Pat Thane, ed. *Origins of Social Policy* (1978) Ch. 3.

[68] *Report to the President of the Local Government Board on the Poplar Union by J. S. Davy, Chief Inspector to the Board* (PP 1906, CIV)

[69] *15th Annual Report of the Poplar Labour League* (1907) p. 5; and see too George Haw, *From Workhouse to Westminister, The Life Story of Will Crooks M.P.* (1917), pp. 271-9.

[70] Gilbert Bartholomew, President, Poplar Municipal Alliance to Clerk, Poplar Board of Guardians, 30 July 1908 (Ensor Papers)

[71] *Transcript of Shorthand Notes*, (PP 1906, civ), pp. 229-30, 248.

[72] *Transcript of Shorthand Notes*, pp. 255-6.

depreciation in the capital value of property, and the raising of overhead costs to the point at which removal to a more favourable location could no longer be delayed. They mourned the successive extensions of the franchise. Nor were they alone in their grief. The Royal Commission on Local Taxation had earlier reluctantly abandoned an economically attractive scheme for the division of rates between owner and occupier accompanied by some extra-ordinary form of representation for the protection of large property owners: 'We do not, however, suppose that any effective scheme of this nature would be considered compatible with the increasingly democratic character of local self-government!'[73] R. V. Broadbank, Secretary of the Municipal Alliance dismissed all qualification. Unless the Legislature was willing to sanction some special protec-tion, limited liability companies were bound to resort to the creation of faggot votes.[74]

The Municipal Alliance, however, was more than a tool of local capitalists. Of its more than 2,000 members 60 per cent were said to be of 'the artisan class'.[75] The Alliance tried to project itself as a combination of independent citizens concerned with the efficient management of local affairs. It was quick to repudiate any charge of political bias.[76] In addition to the extravagant administration of the poor law, the Alliance denounced the compounding system. In Poplar where 85 per cent of properties were compounded, it was calculated that abolition would be equal to almost 1s. in the £ reduction of rates.[77] But the moral effects were incalculable. It was a fact of life that participation in local elections was often dis-appointingly small. In the Guardian elections of 1907, for example, less than one-third of the metropolitan electorate bothered to vote.[78] 'It has been alleged, and apparently with a great deal of truth', said

---

[73] 'Separate Report·on Urban Rating and Site Values', by Lord Balfour of Burleigh *et. al.*, *R.C. Local Taxation* (PP 1901, XXIV) p. 157.

[74] *R.C. Poor Laws*, app. vol. ix, qq. 91689-95, 91714-17, 91791-8.

[75] *Transcript of Shorthand Notes*, p. 247; *Estates Gazette* (19 May 1905), p. 911.

[76] The following indicates its notion of non-partisan politics: 'We said in our last issue that we are firmly anti-socialist. The reason for this is that as yet the Socialist Party's contribution of usefulness to the Borough is infinitesimal, and practically the whole of their proposals are contrary to the welfare of the people. The Alliance is so strongly non-political and so absolutely impartial, that any serious proposition advanced by even a Socialist, would receive support if there was any likelihood of beneficial results accruing to the Borough.' *Poplar Alliance Review*, 29 Oct. 1912.

[77] Memorandum of R. V. Broodbank, para. I, *R.C. Poor Laws*, app. vol. ix, qq. 91594, 91620.

[78] L.C.C., *London Statistics*, XVIII (1907/8), p. 27.

the Chief Inspector to the Local Government Board, 'that compounding ruins the electorate by concealing the fact that the labouring
classes pay any rates, and it gives them no interest whatever in the
fluctuations in the rates.'[79] The Poplar Municipal Alliance too held
that the anticipation of personal gain would provide the incentive to
turn out at the polls in droves. 'What I am striving at, and what our
association has been trying to get at', Broadbank explained, 'is to let
the man who pays his rent weekly know how the rates fluctuate. At
present it only fluctuates when the landlord puts on 6d or 1s a week.
What we want to do is to let him feel the penny, a sort of pin-prick ...
it is the pin-pricks which tell most.'[80] A model rent-card had been
devised for this purpose: 'It shows at a glance what your rents would
have been if the SOCIALIST PARTY had not PILED UP THE
RATES.'[81]

The Poplar Municipal Alliance was not the first of such bodies to
be established. But it was the most ambitious. It was extremely well
organized with committees in each of Poplar's fourteen wards.[82] In
addition to the publication of a monthly journal, the Alliance, in
courting the working-class vote, established its own labour bureau
as a token of Smilesianism in action. The bureau, it was claimed,
had provided work for 'well over' 800 men and boys.[83] It was an
example to others. In 1908 Mr Gilbert Bartholomew, its president
who also happened to be the head of Messrs Bryant and May,
chaired a meeting of some fifty ratepayers associations which in-
augurated the National Ratepayers' Association.[84] The Poplar
Borough Municipal Alliance was an aspect of a much broader
ratepayers' offensive which the London Municipal Society sought to
orchestrate.[85] Moreover, it was resilient. Lansbury was still fighting it
in the 1920s.[86]

The Poplar Municipal Alliance claimed the support of influential
persons. Octavia Hill, a resolute opponent of the compounding

[79] *R.C. Poor Laws*, app. vol. i (PP 1909, XXXIX) q. 2071.

[80] *R.C. Poor Laws*, app. vol. ix, qq. 91603, 91614.

[81] *Poplar's Local Municipal Review*, Oct. 1912; and for specimen rent-card, see
R.C. Poor Laws, app. vol. ix, app. IV (A), p. 527.

[82] *Estates Gazette* (3 Feb. 1906), p. 196.

[83] *Poplar's Local Municipal Review*, May 1911,

[84] *Estates Gazette* (28 Mar. 1908), p. 551.

[85] On this see K. Young, *Local Politics & The Rise of Party* (Leicester, 1975).

[86] See B. Keith-Lucas, 'Poplarism', *Public Law* (1962), pp. 52-80; 'Herbert
Morrison and Poplarism', *Public Law* (1973), pp. 11-31; and E. Briggs and A.
Deacon, 'the Creation of the Unemployment Assistance Board', *Policy and Politics*,
II, 1 (1973), pp. 43-62.

system, warmly approved. In 1895 Miss Hill, accompanied by Charles Loch of the COS, approached the model dwellings companies to try and arrange for a uniform reversion to direct rating. The companies were sympathetic but considered the administrative difficulties insuperable. The Royal Commission on the Poor Laws, which reviewed the problem some years later, took a different view. The compounding system, it declared, 'contravenes the whole theory on which the democratic form of government has been set up' and should therefore be phased out as soon as possible.[87]

Landlords too were uneasy, but they were concerned with percentages rather than principles. Their attitude towards compounding varied with circumstances but it was always determined by the calculation of personal advantage and where that conflicted with efficient administration so much the worse for the municipality.

Compounding affected the property market in three ways. First, it was thought to encourage jobbery in assessments. 'I am told', said J. S. Davy, 'that if the compounding limit is £20 you will find an abnormal number of houses rated at £19.10s.'[88] Second, as the Land Enquiry noted, the inflexible limits of rateable value produced 'excessive variations between the charges upon properties immediately above and just below the line, with the result that there is a tendency in erecting new houses to keep down the value to just below the compounding limit'.[89] In a period of inflated building costs these rigidities, it was suggested, severely constricted the supply of cheap accommodation. In Edwardian Birmingham, for example, it was shown that on small properties taken beyond the compound, it required a rent increase in excess of 11 per cent to give the same net return as was formerly obtained from the maximum rent chargeable under the old arrangement. If the limit were raised, however, owners' margins would be restored and builders supplied with sufficient incentive—i.e. something above the 5 per cent then availabe—to commence operations again. It meant that landlords need not rack-rent those properties that were just within the old compounding limit. At the same time it permitted a reduction in the rents of more expensive houses in order to bring them within the

---

[87] Octavia Hill, *Letters to My Fellow Workers* (1896), pp. 8-9; *Final Report of the Royal Commission on Local Taxation* (PP 1901, XXIV,) pp. 50-2; *Report of the Royal Commission on the Poor Laws and Relief of Distress* (PP 1909, XXXVIII), pp. 584-6.

[88] *R.C. Poor Laws*, app. vol. i. q. 2119

[89] *Report of Land Enquiry*, p. 665.

new limit. For example, a 10*s*. house could henceforth be let at 8*s*. 9*d*. and the landlord would still get the same return. It would thus bring a better class of accommodation within reach of the artisan, revive the ailing housing market, and in so doing obviate the need for greater municipal intervention.[90] There was one snag. The raising of the compounding limit amounted to a subsidy from the wealthier ratepayers. Finally, the distribution of benefit under the Poor Rate Assessment Act was thought to be too one-sided. Rebates, for example, were considerably in excess of the standard 5 per cent commission paid for the collection of rents.

Landlords, whose own margins were, in consequence of the upward spiral in local taxation, under very considerable pressure, were loath to forgo these preferential discounts. Any unilateral attempt at retrenchment on the part of the local authority was bound to encounter resistance.[91] Such intransigence underlines both the heterogeneity of the middle classes and the relative isolation of the small house-owner within that indeterminate stratum. It is significant that its principal officials, usually regarded as authorities on all matters pertaining to land and housing, could not, when testifying before an official enquiry, account for the number of ratepayers' associations affiliated to the United Property-Owners' and Rate-payers' Association of Great Britain.[92] Similarly, the Poplar Borough Municipal Alliance was not a landlords' association. Its audience consisted 'of the shopkeeper class and those who belong to them'. Of the few proprietors who were members, only a local dock company, which owned considerable residential property in the borough, bothered to issue its tenants with the Alliance rent card; local landlords and their agents considered it an irrelevance.[93]

In the expanding contest over the scope of compounding, property owners were in a strong position *vis-a-vis* the rating authority. In spite of the extensive redevelopment which took place in the generation following the passage of the Second Reform Bill, the sullen slums of urban Britain still scarred the landscape. Moreover, the crisis of 1868/9 had not been forgotten. Rate collectors were as reluctant as their predecessors had been to enter such districts and landlords knew it. The high rate of residential mobility amongst the

[90] For these calculations, see *Birmingham Housing Enquiry* qq. 1926-43, Statement of H. M. Grant (C) qq. 2602, 2808-14.

[91] See, for example, *Estates Gazette*, (30 Aug. 1902), p. 371.

[92] *R.C. Local Taxation* (PP. 1898, XLI) qq. 6686-8.

[93] *R.C. Poor Laws*, app. vol. ix, qq. 917373, 91746-8, 95824-7, 95877-83.

working classes in any case precluded outright abolition. This, indeed, was recognized by most reformers. J. S. Davy, for instance, readily confessed that under these circumstances he could see no means by which it could be accomplished.[94] Even the Poplar Municipal Alliance hesitated to advocate so drastic a course. The Alliance rent-card implied as much; it was in fact a compromise designed to create opinion in favour of reform, the shadow not the substance.[95] But it went against the grain to leave matters as they stood. Sir Samuel Provis, Permanent Secretary of the Local Government Board, and a member of the Royal Commission on the Poor Laws, grasped instinctively for an administrative solution. If the rating authority were to be placed on the same footing as the landlord and granted a summary means of distress, might it not be possible to abolish compounding and still recover the rates from the migratory classes? C. S. Loch and other Commissioners pursued this line with some enthusiasm. One Commissioner, however, found the asinine performance of his colleagues irritating and irrelevent. Lansbury, breaking a vexed silence, turned to the witness, a senior official of Poplar Borough Council:

And if all the obstacles to taking proceedings were swept away do you think the bulk of the people you have in your mind could pay the quarter's rate or the month's rate on the nail?—I am absolutely sure they could not.

Lansbury: That is the point of it, that we are airily discussing powers to compel people to do something which in your judgement they have not the means of doing?—That is so.[96]

[94] *R.C. Poor Laws*, app. vol. i. q. 2110.
[95] *R.C. Poor Laws*, app. vol. ix, q. 91600.
[96] *R.C. Poor Laws*, app. vol. ix. qq. 95941-52, 95977-6000.

6

Compounding and Conflict

The housing problem in London seemed as intractable as ever. Overcrowding declined somewhat in the last decades of the nineteenth century, but still it remained astonishingly high. It was aggravated as always by the failure to rehouse those displaced by the continuous redevelopment of the inner districts. Rents soared. At the turn of the century a sense of crisis was again apparent.

In East London signs of discontent were not wanting. In Barking the SDF, working in tandem with the local labour movement, was instrumental in the formation of a popular Rent and Ratepayers' League. The North West Ham Socialist Council countered the property owners' offensive through the agency of a broadly-based Anti-High Rents League. In the heart of the East End, where, in consequence of intensive immigration in the previous twenty years, rents had risen by a staggering 25 per cent, Jewish trade unionists were at the forefront of the campaign; Mile End Waste became the venue for a series of mass protest meetings. But it was their indoor meetings which were thought 'all the more remarkable considering that a charge of 2*d*. was made for admission', which, it was agreed, 'must be taken as evidence of the feeling which exists in East London on the subject'. At these often quite formidable gatherings there was no attempt to conceal the fury that had been aroused. 'Every now and again the audience would be seized with a fit of rage against the landlords and it almost seemed as if further proceedings would become impossible.' In the central districts too working men were active in the agitation.[1] Tenants across the river proved no exception. Their efforts are of more than passing interest. The formation of the Bermondsey Labour League in the wake of the Progressive victories in the County Council elections early in 1898, represented a new optimism amongst the hitherto fragmented Radical forces in the district. Frank Soutter, veteran of numerous

---

[1] *Justice*, 1 Oct. 1898; *West Ham Citizen*, 13 May 1899; *Reynolds's Newspaper*, 4 Dec. 1898; George Haw, *No Room to Live* (1899), p. 81.

campaigns, was its moving spirit and first secretary. Soutter, a colourful figure who had become something of a local celebrity, was born in North Lambeth in 1844. His father had been the manager of a Smithfield cigar manufacturing establishment. His mother came from a substantial family, proprietors of public houses and restauranteurs. But their untimely death left the 12-year-old lad orphaned and unprovided for. Shortly afterwards he was apprenticed to a carpenter, but later foresook the bench to become a successful shopkeeper.

A short, swarthy, powerfully-built man, endowed with what John Burns described as 'a bugle voice',[2] Soutter was drawn to politics like a moth to an incandescent lamp. He was, as T. P. O'Connor observed, 'a born agitator'.[3] Soutter first became seriously involved in working-class politics during his early twenties. A participant in the Hyde Park Reform Bill Riots, he joined the Workmen's Peace Society in 1870 and was elected to its executive three years later. A pronounced secularist and member of the Central Council of the National Sunday League, he was also for a short period editor of the *Free Sunday Advocate*, its monthly journal. His journalistic appetite was now whetted. At the beginning of the following decade he founded the *Radical*, a militant weekly which in retrospect may be considered a harbinger of the renascent artisanal Radicalism of the 1880s; a final efflorescence of a political tradition soon to be displaced by a new kind of Socialism with which Soutter remained temperamentally ill at ease.

In these years too he gained a certain notoriety arising out of the organization of a successful but often tumultuous campaign for the abolition of Church rates in Bermondsey. In 1889 the disorder which marked the struggle for the greater democratization of Vestry proceedings, in which Harry Quelch and himself were both involved, landed the pair of them in the dock.[4] These excesses, committed in order to vindicate the rights of the free-born Englishman, did not, however, commend him to an ungrateful municipal electorate. Moreover, an irritating maverick disposition made him a difficult colleague. Co-operation with Quelch proved short-lived. The local branch of the SDF was speedily alienated by his defiant progressivism,

---

[2] F. W. Soutter, *Fights for Freedom* (1925), p. 16.
[3] F. W. Soutter, *Recollections of a Labour Pioneer* (1923), p. 8.
[4] 'Police Court Proceedings in the trial of F. W. Soutter, H. Quelch, H. J. Glanville and J. Clarke for disturbance of the peace and damage to Bermondsey Town Hall, 1889' (MS, British Library of Political and Economic Science).

and its enduring enmity was not softened by the course of time. The Bermondsey Labour League did not evoke a positive response from that quarter.[5] There were also enemies on the right. Although himself a distinguished clubman, Soutter had somehow managed to fall foul of his confrères at the Bermondsey Gladstone Club which refused to extend customary facilities in order to help further the League's work.[6] No doctrinal matters appear to have been at issue. Indeed, the Bermondsey Labour League had tried to minimize friction, and from the outset cast its net as wide as possible. Its 'chief objects', ran an inaugural declaration, 'will be to stimulate and keep alive public opinion upon questions of public policy and the actions and resolve of the local governing bodies'.[7] There was little here to which any reasonable person might take exception, except perhaps its sheer vacuity. The outbreak of the Boer War and the attempt to mobilize a united opposition would soon provide the League with a more definite object to pursue.[8] Meanwhile the housing question absorbed its attentions.

Bermondsey at the beginning of the twentieth century was an overcrowded district which contained some of the worst concentrations of poverty in London. 'I know of no set of people in London who look quite so poor as those who do their marketing in Bermondsey New Road on Sunday morning', wrote Booth.[9] The principal source of employment was to be found in the Surrey Commercial Docks, in the wharves and warehouses which lined the river, and in the various branches of the leather trade. However, male-dominated industries such as these were in decline. Bermondsey's once famous tanneries were a thing of the past. 'The sites of the old tan yards are occupied by jam and pickle factories. Picklers have taken the place of fellmongers, and a leather warehouse has made room for the manufacture of baking powder.' Bermondsey's convenient location, plus the ready supply of cheap labour, made it an ideal centre for the biscuit, jam, and other manufacturers whose factories had transformed the skyline in the previous two decades. This invasion of the impoverished residential districts which made up inner South London was not at all uncongenial to the responsible citizens who governed these localities:

[5] Cf. correspondence of W. C. Portman, *Southwark Recorder*, 30 Apr. 1900.
[6] Soutter-Bell correspondence, *Southwark Recorder*, 3 Feb. 1900.
[7] *Southwark Recorder*, 12 Mar. 1898.   [8] Soutter, *Fights for Freedom*, pp. 210ff.
[9] Charles Booth, *Life and Labour of the People of London*, 17 vols. (1902), 3rd Ser., IV, pp. 101-2.

The erection of new factories has helped to push the better-off people out and the poorer people closer together. In some cases the factories have been in the gardens attached to larger houses. In other cases gardens have been absorbed for storage and stables. Borough Councillors who think only of rateable value and the increase of employment are said to be anxious to attract factories to Bermondsey by almost any means, regardless of the new difficulties they thereby create. Some would go so far as to tell any manufacturer who was contemplating coming in, 'We will not over assess you. We will shut our eyes to some of your machinery, we won't see it.'[10]

The continued expansion of industry and commerce at the expense of housing was seen by many as the solution to one of the most pressing questions of the day. The medical officer of health for Southwark looked to the not-too-distant future when, as a result of the march of industry coupled with the most stringent sanitary administration, all investment in small house property would have been rendered unremunerative. The housing problem would then have been solved; there would no longer be any workers to house![11]

Those who withstood this kind of devastation were immediately threatened by an even more formidable foe. The insane competition of the southern railway, in spite of working-class protests, destroyed the homes of an earlier generation.[12] No one cared. The policing of the token safeguards, introduced subsequently, remained lax; and so it was that, at the turn of the century, the inhabitants of the area were exposed to much the same anxieties as had been their forebears.

In 1897 the London and South Eastern Railway announced the need of a new loop line. It was intended to cut a swathe through one of the most populous districts of Bermondsey. Eviction awaited 900 people. Demolition proceeded without adequate provision having been made for those to be displaced. Alternative accommodation was situated two miles away and was of little value to those compelled to live close by their trade. The Home Office, alerted by an unusually vigilant vicar, became concerned. The company promptly entered into an agreement with the Guinness Trust to retain a number of its recently completed blocks at Snowfields, within spitting distance of

[10] 'Report by Constance Williams and Thomas Jones on the Effect of Outdoor Relief on Wages and the Conditions of Employment', *Royal Commission on Poor Laws*, app. vol. xvii (PP 1909, XLIII), pp. 15-16.

[11] *Annual Report of Medical Officer of Health for Southwark* (1903), pp. 6-7 and (1904), p. 6.

[12] *Report of Select Committee of House of Commons on Public Petitions* (1866), No. 907.

the clearances. But by not itself making good the deficit the LSER
had aggravated the crisis.[13]

Those unable to secure accommodation in the new dwellings had
a hard time of it. Rotherhithe was badly crowded. To the west, the
Lambeth Vestry was seeking to moderate the demands of the
London & South Western Railway to unhouse a further 2,000
people to facilitate extensions of Waterloo Station.[14] There was
nothing in Southwark where overcrowding was 'the Alpha and
Omega of local administration'.[15] Bermondsey seemed beseiged. In
addition to the intrusions of the railway company, people had to
contend with the clearances undertaken by the LCC in order to
widen the southern approaches to the new Tower Bridge, the
advances of the ubiquitous School Board, and the demolitions due
to the installation of public utilities. Rising rents aggravated overcrowding; in many instances the local authorities were compelled to
suspend enforcement of the sanitary laws for fear of making things
worse.[16]

The agitation began early in 1898. The opening shot, fired by
the outspoken Rector, Revd Henry Lewis, was initially directed
at the LSER. In May 1898 the *Parish Magazine* of St. Mary
Magdalen carried a critical account of the company's conduct, an
account which he subsequently repeated in the correspondence
columns of *The Times*. The inert vestry did not escape the attentions of this turbulent priest. Lewis was a new man to the district.
His second annual report, a sixty-four-page document, amounted
to a massive indictment of the Moderates who dominated local
affairs. It caused an uproar.[17] A tall thin man of about forty,
brown-haired, bespectacled, with small whiskers and moustache,
an altogether unimposing figure, and a dull speaker to boot, this
former Indian missionary had effectively set the campaign in
motion.

The clergy in South London were not noted for their commitment

[13] Cf. Lewis-Humphreys correspondence, *The Times*, 10, 12, 19 Apr. and 5 Mar.
1899; *Daily Chronicle*, 2 Nov. 1899; Charles Booth Notebooks, (B 275), fos. 67-9
(British Library of Political and Economic Science).

[14] *The Times*, 15 Feb. 1899.

[15] Booth, *Life and Labour*, 3rd Ser., IV, p. 54.

[16] *Board of Trade .... Changes in the Cost of Living of the Working Classes* (PP
1905, LXXXIV), p. 39; Booth, *Life and Labour*, 3rd. Ser. IV, pp. 89-90, 138.

[17] *South London Chronicle*, 25 Mar. and 8 Apr. 1899; 'Report of an interview with
Revd. Henry Lewis, St. Mary Magdalen, Bermondsey', 4 Dec. 1899 (Booth Notebooks B 275), fos. 53-7.

to the cause of Labour.[18] The Rector gained little support from his fellow clerics. The Vicar of the neighbouring parish of St. Anne's, 'the Belgravia of Bermondsey', told a confidant: 'Mr Lewis means well but has rather put his foot in it lately with his Vestry and other people.'[19] Others found the sensationalism offensive.[20] Non-conformists, by contrast, suspected that Lewis's histrionics were little more than a stunt to drum up support for a Church funds appeal.[21] Some clergymen, however, frowned at the very idea of rehousing the poor. Those admitted into the Guinness Trust dwellings at the behest of the railway company had turned Snowfields into 'a sink of abomination', so it was claimed.[22] Some parishioners too were outraged by their Rector's enthusiasm for the poor. 'A good clearance has been made of these vile paupers' wrote one of them. 'They ought not to marry and propagate the sordid species.' Lewis considered such sentiments barbaric.[23]

But this was not the sole critical voice to be raised. In the spring the presiding judge at Southwark County Court, alarmed at the fast-flowing stream of evictions coming before him, communicated his fears to the appropriate quarters, an unusual step for the occupant of so delicate a position.[24] This led to a conference convened in the summer of 1898 by R. K. Causton, Liberal MP for West Southwark, to which the principal local authorities sent representatives.[25] In the interval the Bermondsey Labour League established itself as a force not easily ignored. Its petitions, deputations and regular Sunday meetings at Star Corner, Bermondsey New Road, all served to impress its presence upon the community. Parochial prevarication drew the wrath of its impatient secretary. 'Judge Addison', he declared, 'might as well have been John the Baptist crying in the

---

[18] C. F. G. Masterman, 'The Problem of South London', in R. Mudie-Smith ed., *The Religious Life of London* (1904), pp. 215-16.

[19] 'Report of an interview with Revd. J. F. Benson Walsh, Vicar of St. Anne's, Bermondsey', 9 Jan. 1900 (Booth Notebooks B 279), fos. 55, 57.

[20] Report of an Interview with Revd. J. G. Curry, Rector of Holy Trinity, Southwark', 18 Oct. 1899 (Booth Notebooks B 275), f. 157.

[21] 'Report of an Interview with Mr H. Hall, Secretary of the Trustees of the United Methodist Free Church, Bermondsey', 23 Jan. 1900 (Booth Notebooks B 274), fos. 215-17.

[22] 'Report of an Interview with Revd. C. H. Bowden, Vicar of St. Paul's, Kipling Street', 15 Sept. 1899 (Booth Notebooks B 275) fos. 133-5.

[23] *A Third Dispatch from the Church Militant in Bermondsey, being the Parochial Report of Work Done...for1898-1899*, pp. 69-71.

[24] *Southwark Recorder*, 26 Mar. 1898.

[25] *Southwark Recorder*, 2 July 1898.

wilderness, for up to this moment neither the vestry, nor any of its committee, have given his letter so much as a moment's consideration'.[26] This was not strictly accurate. The Sanitary Committee, having examined the League's proposals, reported shortly afterwards that, under existing legislation, the Vestry was not empowered to embark upon a house-building programme; critics, it implied, must therefore look to the LCC for redress, a limp suggestion which few reformers were disposed to accept without equivocation.[27]

The agitation continued throughout the winter. In December a public meeting attended by several Labour luminaries, representatives from the LCC and spokesmen for the Radical working men's clubs, added its weight to the campaign; and as a further indication of the unity of progressive forces, it was proposed to amalgamate the Bermondsey Labour League with the nascent Workmen's Housing Council.[28] In April the following year the League resumed its regular weekly outdoor meetings. In addition to promoting the extension of cheap working men's trains' it had hitherto sought to persuade, or more accurately worry, the Bermondsey Vestry into adopting a more positive attitude towards its housing obligations. All the time the struggle for house space intensified. 'Houses difficult to get, and once lost impossible to get another', Booth was told.[29] Early in 1899 some ninety-three of its employees petitioned the Bermondsey Vestry to rescind the regulation compelling its workmen to live in the parish owing to the difficulties of obtaining decent accommodation.[30] Pressure for something more practical, some more immediate form of relief was becoming irresistible.

In the summer of 1899 Messrs Peak, Frean and Co., the largest employer in the area and the owners of considerable residential properties adjacent to their works, announced that, in view of soaring costs aggravated by the persistent and wilful neglect of the occupants, the company intended to discontinue payment of the water rate. Tenants were thus to be burdened with extra expense additional to the 1s.-a-week increased rent imposed in the previous year to cover the cost of sanitary improvements. The Bermondsey Labour League immediately took up the issue, challenging both the

[26] *Southwark Recorder*, 23 Apr. 1898.   [27] *Southwark Recorder*, 7 May 1898.
[28] *Reynolds's Newspaper*, 11 Dec. 1898; Minutes of the Workmen's Housing Council, 17 Dec. 1898.
[29] *Life and Labour*, 3rd. Ser. IV, p. 137.
[30] *South London Chronicle*, 11 Feb. 1899.

company's arithmetic as well as the justice of this latest demand. A company spokesman denied the charge that the rate increase was being used as a pretext to extract a new rent over and above the water rate. But the rebuttal did little to mollify the angry tenants who packed the several demonstrations which the League organized.[31] Moreover, the decision of the biscuit manufacturers, proprietors of upwards of one hundred multi-occupied houses, could scarcely fail to encourage the owners of lesser properties.

Soutter's noted secularism compelled Rector Lewis to decline any formal identification with the Labour League, although he remained in the forefront of the agitation, committed to its general principles, offering the League facilities and speaking from its platform.[32] And whatever their private reservations, the furore following Lewis's initial intervention, increasingly compelled other clergymen to adopt a sympathetic stance. Church schools, halls etc. were available for the asking. John Scott Lidgett, Methodist Warden of the Bermondsey Settlement, which had apparently made some impact upon Peak Frean's female employees,[33] was active after a fashion. The Warden, who was something of a trimmer, was certainly conscious of the landlord's sensibilities—he had once refused the chairmanship of the Board of Guardians in order not to offend them[34]—none the less 'felt bound to take a considerable part, not so much in protest against the landlords as in enforcing the immediate urgency of the Housing problem'.[35] Although he led a deputation to the company, Messrs. Peak Frean remained unrepentant.

The ill-concealed displeasure of the tenants, as yet marshalled behind the Labour League, teetered on the brink, threatening to dissolve in spontaneous violence. In East London similar elemental passions were poised to explode in a futile racism. 'Tenants were openly threatening to "put the landlord's light out".Some of them refused point blank to pay the extra rent and closed the doors and barricaded their windows against the collectors. To prevent distraint they distributed their furniture among neighbouring friends'. Antilandlordism was soon displaced by anti-semitism, however. The

[31]   *Southwark Recorder*, 17, 24 June and 22 July 1899.
[32]   Soutter, *Fights for Freedom*, p. 251.
[33]   W. F. Lofthouse, 'The Warden of the Bermondsey Settlement', in Rupert E. Davies, ed., *John Scott Lidgett, A Symposium* (1957), p. 62.
[34]   J. Scott Lidgett, *Reminiscences* (1928), p. 38; also see 'Report of an Interview with Mr H. V. Toynbee in special charge of the COS Committee at St. Olave's, Bermondsey', 19 July 1899 (Booth Notebooks B 273), f. 101.
[35]   *Eighth Annual Report of the Bermondsey Settlement* (1899), p. 42.

East London Observer, under the caption 'Rent Riots in Ernest Street', carried the following story:

The position in regard to Ernest Street, Stepney, is unique. So strong, indeed, is the local feeling, that at present a number of houses are empty because incoming tenants are seriously threatened if they take the houses at the higher rent their lives won't be worth many years purchase. Some of the houses are already wrecked; windows and doors are broken and burst; the surrounding population is in a general state of ferment, and the evictions which take place daily only tend to fan the flame. In essentials a Judenhetze prevails, and though we do not believe there is anything more than a local significance, it is, of course, quite obvious that such a feeling ought not to be encouraged, because although its beginning may be small, like a rivulet, its ending may be great.[36]

In Bermondsey, by contrast, the comparatively smaller, well-established, but still unstudied, Irish community—the Jews of Bermondsey, so to speak—appear to have played no peculiarly identifiable part in the campaign. Soutter, however, was conscious of the volatile mood within the locality. In nearby Lambeth violent resistance was expected to accompany the clearances caused by the improvement of Waterloo station. Those involved were truly desperate:

These latter are viewing the coming displacement with something more than mere alarm, as ejectment for them means in many cases loss of employment, and in that of a good few others possible starvation, as they cannot carry on their occupations elsewhere. The people about to be unhoused are specially indignant ... and they have been holding meetings lately at which they expressed their dissatisfaction with no uncertain voice. As they are not inclined to give in without a struggle, there is every probability that the aid of the police will have to be called in to effect their ejectment and the people of London may be treated very shortly to a repetition of the eviction scenes which outraged the whole of Ireland a few years ago.[37]

The formation of an energetic 'Watch Committee' checked the LSWR's attempts to evade the provision of suitable alternative

[36] Quotation from Haw, *No Room to Live*, p. 69. On housing and cognate matters relative to the genesis of anti-semitism in this period, see L. P. Gartner, *The Jewish Immigrant in England 1870-1914* (1960); J. A. Garrard, *The English and Immigration 1880-1910* (1971); B. Gainer, *The Alien Invasion* (1972); W. J. Fishman, *East End Jewish Radicals 1870-1914* (1975) and Colin Holmes, *Anti-Semitism in British Society 1876-1939* (1979).

[37] *Labour Leader*, 13 May 1899.

accommodation, and for the moment defused the crisis.[38] But the tension remained. 'The landlords of the metropolis', Soutter declared, 'had done more to stir up the people than all the reformers of London could do.'[39] But he was far from certain whether popular fury could be contained. A speech by W. C. Steadman extolling the benefits of controlled rents, for which Irish legislation provided a precedent, provoked a disturbingly jocular cry from an enthusiastic audience, 'Shoot the landlords.'[40] The speaker hastened to affirm his faith in the parliamentary road to progress. Soutter endorsed the sentiment. 'It must be remembered that they were not making war upon landlords in person', he remarked, 'but upon the system which allowed them to do such things.' Nothing, he agreed, 'would bring the landlords to their senses quicker than a "No Rent Manifesto", and then the Government would soon find out what was wrong'. Soutter, however, 'was not given to indulging in a spirit of despair. They were not forced into that position, and he wanted to see the victory over the landlords gained in a way marked by justice.'[41]

Frank Soutter, like most working-class reformers, possessed an undisguised contempt for the spurious epicurian disposition of the populace: its coarse, vulgar, and sometimes brutalizing amusements were exasperating distractions which furrowed the brow of political activists everywhere. A founder member of the Sunday Shakespeare Society, he was, like Tom Mann, Frederick Rogers, and other contemporaries, possessed of a voracious appetite for the finest literature. A life-long abstainer, Soutter too was a devotee of self-improvement, though not, of course, a slavish adherent to the bland destructive egotism which it often engendered. He had, in John Burns's phrase 'a touch of the Puritan in him'.[42] They were, indeed, kindred spirits. The moral elevation of the masses to which Radical, Secularist, and Socialist were alike committed, waited upon the growth of a mature rationalism. This desirable state was, of course, to be nurtured within an ordered structure. The proletarian cosmos was conceived above all as an organized phenomenon. The world of labour was finite and associational. Spasmodic violence directed at landlords, bailiffs, or policemen, threats and intimidation of rent collectors, the destruction of property, the mere registration of protest, anonymous and anarchic, indulgent private acts, the

---

[38] 'Report of an Interview with Miss Cons', 19 Dec. 1899 (Booth Notebooks B 273), f. 149.
[39] *Southwark Recorder*, 8 July 1899.   [40] *Southwark Recorder*, 1 July 1899.
[41] *Southwark Recorder*, 29 July 1899.   [42] Soutter, *Fights for Freedom*, p. 16.

unlettered graffiti of the impoverished—these and such alien ephemera would not reduce rents nor provide decent housing. But equally, in the absence of some immediate relief, the prospects for a sustained campaign were limited. Already families were being broken up and forced into the workhouse for want of room to live.

The outcry provoked by Messrs Peek, Frean and Co. underlined the irrelevance of the Bermondsey Labour League's pro-Boer stance and questioned its somewhat indeterminate ecumenicalism. The tenants' deteriorating situation indicated the need for greater acuity. C. H. Chapman, a member of the ILP, provided the first intimation of new thinking. In a letter published in the local newspaper, he emphasized the centrality of the rent issue. 'The agitation now started can be made the biggest and most effective which has taken place in London for years. We have now reached a point when something must be done, and that quickly.' It was no longer enough to press for long-term municipal housing programmes:

A reform such as this will unfortunately, take some years to accomplish, but in the meantime something in the direction of lowering present high rents may be carried out if there is sufficient determination on the part of those who are suffering from the evil. In order to thoroughly organise an attempt to lower Bermondsey rents, I would suggest the formation of a Tenants Defence League.[43]

In North London tenants had already embarked upon such a course. The Tottenham Working Men's Housing League was formed to bring the protection of the law to the harassed occupants of the area.[44] Membership reached 800 following an early victory on the Coleraine Park Estate which resulted in a negotiated reduction, a halving of the 1*s.*-a-week increase that had first been announced.[45] Its influence was quickly felt in the neighbouring districts. A spokesman for the nearly 500-strong Cheshunt Working Men's Housing League told an early meeting he would 'like to see bigger joints to carve in the houses of the working classes and more room to carve them in'.[46] The campaign was also taken up by the 450 members of the newly formed Edmonton Housing League.[47]

The secretary of the Workmen's National Housing Council viewed the activities of these affiliates with satisfaction. Proprietors had

[43] *Southwark Recorder*, 24 June 1899.   [44] *Labour Leader*, 13 May 1899.
[45] *Housing Journal*, Aug. 1901 and June 1902.
[46] *Housing Journal*, June 1901 and May 1903.
[47] *Housing Journal*, Nov. 1901.

assured him that statutory rent control would provoke the fiercest resistance. 'Courts for the settlement of Fair Rents in towns', declared the *Estates Gazette*, 'will not come in this country until common-sense, like political economy, has been banished to Jupiter and Saturn.'[48] Yet, if tenants could only be so mobilized and the Rubicon crossed, a dramatic transformation in the agitation might be swiftly affected and victory assured. It was this belief which earlier led him to outline a programme, described by the *Daily News* as 'a plan of campaign which recalls the balmy days of the Irish agitation', for a co-ordinated series of rent strikes which would force Westminster to concede.[49] The solid trade unionists who composed the executive of the Housing Council were not convinced. Their caution is readily understandable.

The difficulties entailed in the organization of a rent strike were formidable. First, the landlord differed from all other creditors in the possession of a summary right to distrain upon the goods of defaulting tenants as well as the power to terminate a tenancy at will and evict the occupant thereafter. Beyond the proper fulfilment of contractual duties, the law recognized no further obligations whatsoever. Octavia Hill knew what she was about when describing the position as 'a tremendous despotism'.[50] It is true that moral sanctions did exist which could, under certain circumstances, be brought to bear upon the aggressive exercise of unbridled avarice as, for example, occurred in Salford during the post-Reform Bill agitation. But the outcome was always uncertain. Even where roused, public opinion could not shake the resolve of a really determined proprietor. The obduracy of the British coal-owner is in this respect too well known. And, moreover, while such sympathy might be forthcoming in a one-off campaign for the redress of a specific act of injustice, it was not likely to be readily extended to the kind of campaign such as Knee envisaged.

Second, the home as an arena for self-expression was not to be lightly hazarded upon the vagaries of a rent strike, and an entanglement with an unfamiliar judicial process. Investigators in Lancashire during the inter-war years discovered innumerable poor middle-aged women, often war widows, living in abject poverty, with little education, few skills, and nothing to look forward to—nothing that

---

[48] *Estates Gazette* (19 May 1899), p. 849.
[49] Minutes of Workmen's Housing Council, 4 Dec. 1899; *Daily News*, 5 Dec. 1899.
[50] *Royal Commission on Housing of the Working Classes* (PP 1884-5, XXX), q. 8967.

is, except the silent joys and personal pleasures of domestic privacy. These people, it was noted, held on to their 'few possessions with grim determination': 'Even if all their belongings are only worth a few shillings, their present home is the only home they know ... Their few pieces of property are of far greater value to them than an outsider can readily understand ... Many.of them have experienced their only happiness in making their single rooms "a bit of a home".'[51] Nearly a century earlier Mayhew had found the same inner directed sentiment amongst the poorest inhabitants of the vilest slums. Indeed, the literature is replete with reference to these, the 'quiet uncomplaining poor'—exceptions, no doubt, but visible and apparently growing in number throughout the century. Sir Robert Ensor may have exaggerated in describing *Home Sweet Home* as 'a second National Anthem'[52] but the cult of home is a factor which cannot be cursorily dismissed when considering working-class reluctance to engage in rent strikes. The refusal to do so was not, however, a matter of calculation: ideology, Dr Althusser reminds us, is the 'lived' relation between men and their world. Allied to a sombre Lassalean pessimism was an awful immobilizing fixation upon the dominant rights of private property. 'This law of rent', declared one socialist, 'which takes to itself automatically every rise in wages, every municipal improvement, though that may also involve an increase in rates, every social betterment of whatever description, is the modern Franken-stein. It is far more of an iron law than ever Ricardo's law of wages was. For you can strike against industrial conditions; but a rent strike at once involves a thousand laws which safeguard private property.'[53]

Even the miners, who as tenants were in some respects better placed than most, drew back from such a confrontation, although rent strikes in mining communities were not unknown.[54] There had been intermittent attempts to obtain redress, but it was not until after the brutal ejectments of striking railwaymen at Hamilton and Motherwell in 1891 coming hard on the heels of the violent scenes at Silkworth in the previous year that trade unionists began to campaign with greater determination for an amendment preventing the eviction of the tenants of company housing during an

[51] Pilgrim Trust, *Men Without Work* (Cambridge, 1938), p. 251.
[52] R. C. K. Ensor, *England 1870-1914* (Oxford, 1936), p. 169.
[53] *Labour Leader*, 24 June 1904.
[54] P. Beirne, *Fair Rent and Legal Fiction* (1977), p. 220, note 10.

industrial dispute.[55] In this instance, however, tenure formed part of the relations of production, and the Home Office refused to countenance such alterations as might prejudicially affect the employers' position. In the words of an anonymous scribe:

The proposal constitutes a fresh departure from the principle of freedom of contract; and it is possible that the Bill might have the effect of discouraging the excellent work which railway companies and other large employers of labour are doing in the way of providing comfortable houses for their workpeople. This proposal might also, if it became law, operate very considerably to the disadvantage of an employer of fresh hands if he were unable to provide them with accommodation; and would clearly therefore put a powerful weapon in the hands of the strikers.[56]

The failure of relatively powerful associations of workers—the Scottish Trade Union Congress or the Miners' Federation of Great Britain—did not encourage isolated groups of tenants to willingly engage the growing combinations of property-owners.

Rent strikes, which do not of course exhaust the purposes of combination amongst tenants, were regarded as a last resort. Tenants in general appear to have removed quietly when presented with a rent increase that overstrained their slender resources or, if possible, sought a corresponding wage increase. The desire to moderate inflationary wage demands was not the least of the factors which eventually led to the introduction of rent control. Hitherto, the tenant's decision was dictated by a combination of factors—the nature of his or her occupation, the state of trade, and the character of the local housing market. It was when conditions militated against removal, often during an upswing in the building cycle when all choice, however limited, was temporarily constricted, that latent antagonisms came to the fore. These episodic outbursts, it will be seen, were not the prelude to continuous organization: on the contrary, they were indicative of the desperation to which the participants were reduced.[57]

Meanwhile, the Bermondsey Labour League had become embroiled in a bruising campaign to forestall further evictions occasioned by the decision to proceed with the construction of a new electric

[55] 'Evictions in Trade Disputes' (PRO HO. 45/10537/154025); *Annual Reports of Scottish Trade Union Congress* (1898-1900).
[56] 'Memorandum on Workmen's Houses Tenure Bill, 1900', (PRO HO. 45/10557/165795).
[57] Cf. S. Pankhurst, *The Suffragette Movement* (1931), p. 529.

power generator. The struggle with the local authority absorbed its energies during the first six months of 1900 in the course of which Soutter succeeded in alienating 'Progressive reactionists', former supporters such as William Stevenson of the Builders' Labourers' Union, as well as the management of the Gladstone Working Men's Club. The campaign failed. Radical forces remained weak and divided. Tenants were left to shift for themselves. The Bermondsey Labour League lingered awhile, an inconsequential political zombie. The forces of reincarnation, however, had not yet lost their magic.

I

Ever since the passage of the Poor Rate Assessment and Collection Act, 1869, there had been a steady decline in the amount of rebate which the metropolitan local authorities were willing to allow. But this downward movement was constantly impeded; for the minimum compulsory allowance (15 per cent) established a threshold below which owners refused to compound when the arrangement was optional and the rebate discretionary. As the Statistical Officer of the LCC remarked: 'Since they cannot be rated compulsorily without a rebate of 15 per cent being allowed (without agreement to pay full or empty) they are naturally slow to accept a smaller rebate *with* such agreement.'[58] In spite of the reduction in the scale of abatements, none of the rating authorities, except Lewisham and Islington, had found it possible to forgo compounding in its entirety. At the same time the inexorable pressure of rising rates made the search for further economies ever pressing. However, it was in the poorest districts where this pressure was most intense that compounding was most extensive.[59] It provided landlords with a powerful source of leverage.

In Southwark where the compounding allowance amounted to £8,000 per annum,[60] the new Borough Council that took office following the reorganization of metropolitan local government, determined to continue the work of its predecessor. In 1898 the

[58] 'Memorandum on the Practice of Compounding for Rates in the Administrative County of London', by Edgar Harper, *Departmental Committee on House-Letting in Scotland* (PP 1908, XLVII), app. I, p. 275.

[59] On this, see 'Memorandum of Metropolitan Rate Collectors' Association' and Appendix No. XIII (A) & (B), *R.C. Poor Laws* app. vol. IX, qq. 93519-24, 93540-51; also Harper, Memorandum, pp. 274-6.

[60] *South London Chronicle*, 29 June 1901.

discount had been reduced from 25 to 15 per cent.[61] In May 1901 landlords were informed that the allowance was henceforth reduced by a further 2½ per cent. This proved unacceptable. There followed nothing less than a 'landlords' strike.[62]

The militants were drawn from amongst the most prominent property owners in the locality: the Peabody and Guinness Trustees; the Industrial Dwellings Company; Messrs Sutton and Dudley, proprietors of upwards of 4,000 pairs of tenements; Edward Yates, the largest builder in South London;[63] and James Pullen, one of the biggest and harshest of landlords.[64] Together they accounted for almost half the total rateable value of the borough. The local authority was left to try and recover the rates as best it could from more than 5,000 occupiers.

Southwark Borough Council's Rating Committee picked up the gauntlet and prepared to give battle. It sought to enlist the support of the tenants. A circular issued with the demand note explained that the reversion to direct rating was forced upon the Council by the greed of the landlords who accepted 10 per cent in Camberwell but refused 12½ per cent in Southwark which, taken in conjuction with the additional 15 per cent deduction for repairs, insurance, and maintenance allowed in the assessment of rateable value, was more than adequate to cover all contingencies. The circular also made the important point that, where in some cases landlords had reduced the rent, the reduction was insufficient because it was calculated upon the compound rate rather than the full rate which the tenant was compelled to pay without any discount. It was alleged that in consequence of the new arrangements and the pretext it provided for raising rents, landlords were making an extra 20 per cent out of their tenants.[65] The situation was reminiscent of the crisis which followed the passage of the Reform Bill nearly forty years earlier.

[61] Harper, Memorandum, p. 275.

[62] *South London Chronicle*, 4 May 1901.

[63] On Yates's building operations, see H. J. Dyos, *Victorian Suburb, A Study of the Growth of Camberwell* (Leicester, 1973), pp. 127-35.

[64] The local vicar gave the following character: 'He had the poorest opinion of Pullen. Rents were high all round, but this man is the worst screw, and very rough, boorish and ignorant. The very worst landlord that the poor can have to deal with is, the Rector thought, a self-made man who is also ignorant, and of this class Pullen appears to be a horrid example'. 'Report of an Interview with the Rev. Canon Palmer, Rector of St. Mary, Newington', 23 Jan. 1900 (Booth Notebooks B 275), fos. 195-7. Cf. James Pullen, obit., *South London Chronicle*, 10 Aug. 1901.

[65] *South London Chronicle*, 18 May 1901; George Haw, *Britain's Homes* (1902), p. 162.

Organized resistance centred in the first instance on three streets intersected by the Old Kent Road at its southern approach. In the summer of 1901 the occupants of the 150 properties in Cornbury Street and Comus Place were summonsed for six months' rates and ordered to pay within seven days. The tenants were stunned. None had the slightest intimation of the reversion to direct rating. The landlord was determined to exploit the situation to the full. Enquiries on the part of the occupants elicited nowt but 'a coarse rejoinder'. Tenants were henceforth to be compelled to pay the rates as well as the old rent. In nearby Marcia Road, adjacent to the Bricklayers' Arms, Edward Yates, owner of upwards of forty properties, remained obdurate. Injustice was, in this case, aggravated by the introduction of differential assessments in consequence of the London Government Act, 1899. One side of the street was thereby transferred to Bermondsey; the other remained within the jurisdiction of St. George the Martyr where assessments were 2s. in the £ lower.[66]

Notwithstanding the ravages of urban redevelopment, the district formed part of an area in which, according to Booth, 'there is said to be a love of home not often found; an almost romantic attachment of the respectable poor to their little courts, not easily to be reproduced'.[67] The character of the occupants is not inconsistent with this judgement. A memorial submitted to Yates bearing the signatures of all but two of his seventy-six tenants declared it 'very hard that good old tenants like most of us have been' should be so ill-treated. Soutter described them as 'decent, sober, industrious working people'.[68] Marcia Road, on the basis of Booth's classification of London streets by colour, was inhabited by the comfortable working classes; the tenants of the remaining streets, though not so well-off, were not of the most wretched slum-dwellers.

On the evening of Monday 15 July 1901 a protest meeting of weekly tenants was held at the corner of Surrey Square, Old Kent Road. It attracted a large audience, estimated at 1,000 persons. The proceedings were orderly, Mr F. W. Soutter who, in the words of a dextrous reporter, 'is ever in the forefront of such battles, put the case of the tenants in an exhaustive speech'. The meeting adjourned at 10.30 having unanimously resolved upon the formation of a

[66] *Southwark Recorder*, 20 July 1900.
[67] *Life and Labour*, 1st Ser., I, p. 263; also R. A. Bray, 'The Boy and the Family' in E. J. Urwick, ed., *Studies of Boy Life in Our Cities* (1904), p. 29.
[68] *Southwark Recorder*, 3, 31 Aug. 1901.

tenant's protection league.[69] In addition to open air agitation, the Bermondsey Tenants' Protection League engaged a solicitor to provide paid up members with free legal assistance to resist the extortionate demands of landlords and rent collectors. A committee was appointed to meet every Thursday from 8.30 to 10.15 p.m. at the 'Help Myself Coffee Palace', Old Kent Road, to enrol members, receive the fixed twopence weekly subscription, and to review their complaints. Tenants were instructed to ignore any verbal alteration in the tenancy upon which the landlord might insist, and on no account to enter into any written agreement without prior consultation. The subscription card also carried the following advice:

When the landlord becomes a defaulter to the parish, and refuses to pay the rates, the law does not require the tenant to find the money to help the landlord out of the difficulty. When the rate collector calls upon the tenant to pay the rates, the tenants should at once cease paying rent and pay the rates instead. Then give the landlord his rate receipts instead of cash. If he refuses to accept them, or abuses you for paying the rates, or in any other way seeks to intimidate you by unlawful threats report the matter at once to the officers of the Tenants' Protection League.

The idea was to bring an action against the landlord for breach of contract and violation of the law.[70] But it was not easy to overcome the deeply-rooted inhibition against any kind of involvement with the judicial process. Members needed encouragement. 'The most prudent tenant', Soutter declared, 'was he who was the boldest.'[71] Dr Cooper, Bermondsey's Progressive representative at Spring Gardens, offered a variant. He 'advised tenants who were put upon by their landlords to refuse fresh terms, and to make them go to the full length of the law'. Tenants, he argued, 'should not agree to new and extortionate terms, but should allow the landlord to get process against them. It would take him six weeks to get them out during which time he could not get a farthing of rent, and if all adopted this

[69]   *Southwark Recorder*, 20 July 1901.
[70]   *Southwark Recorder*, 27 July 1901. The Peabody Trust moved quickly to close the loophole. Tenants on its Blackfriars Road Estate, Southwark, were required to sign an agreement creating a fresh tenancy by which they undertook to pay the rates to the local authorities, and not to deduct the amount from the rent. The owners who had not made such an arrangement were quickest to accept the 15 per cent allowance when the Borough Council later climbed down: 'Housing Question and the Rates', *The Times*, 2 Apr. 1902.
[71]   *Southwark Recorder*, 17 Aug. 1901.

method the landlords would soon find it did not pay.'[72] But the former approach prevailed.

'There never was a league started by a few working men, without any capital, which in so short a time has proved so successful.'[73] Such was the expression reported a few weeks after the inaugural meeting. The first public demonstration drew a very considerable audience: 'Splendid order was maintained, and all present appeared to be in sympathy with the League.'[74] It was, like most subsequent meetings, a resounding success. In a matter of days subscriptions from almost 1,000 people were said to be pouring in.[75] In the course of the next fourteen months or so spectacular advances were registered. A West Southwark Tenants' Protection League, led by Dr Massie, a general practitioner, and S. W. Pascall, the noted local confectioner and a leading Liberal luminary, was formed early in August. At its peak it had branches at Brentford, Vauxhall, Peckham, and Dulwich.[76] The enlarged central committee attracted increasing support from local notables—borough and county councillors, guardians, clergymen, the political secretary of the North Camberwell Working Men's Club, and Dr T. J. Macnamara, the local Liberal MP.[77]

Contact was made quickly with the relatively superior but equally hard pressed tenants of the commercial dwellings companies who probably constituted the chief source of popular support. The Sutton and Dudley's Buildings, Walworth, provided more than 100 recruits. Support was also forthcoming from 'several hundred of Guinness Trust tenants'. Amongst the 420 tenants of the Peabody Buildings, Blackfriars Road, there was said to be 'a widespread feeling of disgust and annoyance prevailing throughout the buildings'. The Governors did not doubt it. For his 'admirable services ... under the very trying circumstances connected with the foregoing matter' the Superintendent was rewarded with a £10 gratuity.[78] The Superintendent of the Southwark Street buildings, too, received an additional three guineas for 'extra services during the change of rents'.[79] The original militants had not been displaced, however. James

[72] *Southwark Recorder*, 27 July 1901.   [73] *Southwark Recorder*, 31 Aug. 1901.
[74] *Southwark Recorder*, 27 July 1901.   [75] *Southwark Recorder*, 3 Aug. 1901.
[76] *Southwark Recorder*, 29 Nov. 1902.
[77] *Southwark Recorder*, 12 Oct. 1901.
[78] *Southwark Recorder*, 17 Aug. 1901; Minutes of Board of Governors, 23 July 1901 (Peabody Trust MSS, London).
[79] Minutes of Board of Governors, 3 Feb. 1902 (Peabody Trust MSS).

Binham of Marcia Road, Bermondsey, 'an old trade unionist who had been engaged in many conflicts with the masters', an indefatigable campaigner across South London, exemplified the energy and resource which many of his equally humble neighbours brought to the cause.[80]

The Bermondsey and West Southwark Tenants' Protection Leagues were, within a few weeks, described as having 'already assumed somewhat gigantic proportions'. The *Southwark Recorder*, a sympathetic newspaper which reported their proceedings *in extenso*, was confident that victory was at hand in view of 'the vast interests disturbed by the even mild revolt of tenants against their landlords which at present exists'.[81] In fact, the Borough Council did not concede until quite late in the year. In the interval the tenants had conducted a campaign which, if not an unqualified triumph, was not without its moments.

In Cornbury Street and Comus Place the crisis which had precipitated the formation of the Bermondsey Tenants' Protection League quickly moved to a denouement. On the morning of 17 July 1901 the brokers' men accompanied by the local rate-collector, made their appearance. 'About thirty of the tenants, by withdrawing inside and shutting both doors and windows managed to prevent the brokers entering.' Those who were taken unawares had their homes entered, an inventory made, and 3s. cost charged to the tenant.[82] Eighty-four warrants were issued. Eight tenants, who were threatened with immediate distraint in order to encourage the others, promptly paid up.

Councillor Frederick Redman, chairman of the Rating Committee—the very same body which at the outset had appealed for the support of the tenants against the landlords—expressed confidence in the conduct of the brokers. The collector, too, he declared, had 'behaved with propriety and consideration for the unfortunate people concerned'. This statement was issued to the Press as a rebuttal of the allegations of unlawful behaviour which Soutter, when invited before the Committee, was unable to substantiate, so it was claimed.[83] Neither the Mayor nor the Borough Council, who were also approached, showed any inclination to question the collective wisdom of Councillor Redman and his colleagues. Soutter, however, was not disposed to withdraw: on the contrary, in the

[80] *Southwark Recorder*, 17 Aug. 1901.   [81] *Southwark Recorder*, 17 Aug. 1901.
[82] *Southwark Recorder*, 27 July 1901.   [83] *Southwark Recorder*, 17 Aug. 1901.

course of the following five months the Tenants' Protection League and its lawyers produced incontrovertible evidence that local brokers customarily acted in defiance of the law in the execution of their duties.

On 13 August 1901 William Bishop, occupant of three rooms in Forest Road, Bermondsey, an exemplary tenant, received the following communication: 'Sir, please take notice you will be ejected from your rooms if not gone at once. Do not make any mistake about it: it will be done.—A & H Lott. To a bad lodger.' Two days later, during Mr Bishop's absence, the brokers' men arrived and, with the connivance of the landlord, proceeded, in the words of counsel for the complainant, to 'tear out the furniture in a most ruthless way'.[84] Forcible entry and the commission of malicious damage was, in fact, frequent. Spokesmen for the Tenants' Protection League could cite numerous similar cases. So indeed could local missionaries. The redress of such grievances had long formed part of the staple of their work.[85] Moreover, the broker customarily extorted a hefty 6s. 'storage fee' for the return of those goods which, during the course of unlawful sequestration, had not been broken, stolen, or lost. Messrs A. & H. Lott of Trinity Street, Borough, an experienced firm of certificated bailiffs, were amongst the most notorious offenders. This well-known and much respected partnership, who often acted on behalf of the police court and the County Court, should, the Tenants' Protection League decided, be made to serve as an example; a warning to others against the commission of further outrages, and an advertisement for the power which tenants, when united, could exert. The League's resources were mobilized for a protracted legal battle and several prosecutions were brought before the magistrate.

Mr Alfred Lott, the senior partner, scorned the puny efforts of his lilliputian adversaries. In conversation with the three plaintiffs after one of the numerous police court hearings, Mr Lott, Soutter recalled, 'thought fit to intrude his presence in our midst, and in his most characteristic style say "Ah! you will want more 'twopences' than you will ever get to smash me" '. This 'impertinent remark', he supposed, was a 'vulgar sneer' at the inadequacy of the League's meagre finances.[86] Lott had unwittingly touched an exposed nerve.

[84] *Southwark Recorder*, 31 Aug. 1901.
[85] W. L. Vyvyan, *Charterhouse in Southwark, Some Account of the Charterhouse Mission* (n.d.), p. 7.
[86] *Southwark Recorder*, 14 Dec. 1901.

The League's Honourable Secretary, in fact, became somewhat reticent whenever critics demanded the publication of an annual balance sheet.[87] But on this occasion the harsh and overbearing defendant had underestimated the strength of the opposition: funds were sufficient, the tenants determined; retribution was nigh. Before the end of the year this would-be Goliath—champion of the broking fraternity—had been humbled, his certificate withdrawn, and his conduct held up to public execration by one of His Majesty's County Court Judges. Thus emboldened, the tenants girded their loins and went forth to give battle to the Philistine hosts lurking in the hinterland. In Deptford and Camberwell the enemy had been engaged; in Dulwich the Tenants' Protection League scored a notable victory.[88] It is not without significance that the disgraced Lott, whose certificate was later restored, should have been treated to a public dinner by some fifty tradesmen and others; a ritualized though none the less provocative affirmation of the bonds uniting the *petit-bourgeois* creditor classes of South London whose authority had been so rudely challenged in the recent past.[89]

Although legal defence work was vital to encourage tenants to continue the resistance, the League's absorption in litigation to some extent reflects the impasse which had quickly been reached in the campaign for the restoration of compounding. Neither the owners nor the local authority had, notwithstanding the numerous protest meetings and several appeals addressed to them, evinced any desire to compromise. The obduracy of the Peabody Trust in particular excited the greatest indignation. Its apparent alignment with rapacious landlords such as Pullen or Yates seemed inexplicable. The Trust was in fact experiencing acute difficulties.

In spite of its preferential status (the Peabody Donation Fund enjoyed complete exemption from the income tax and from inhabited house duty where weekly rentals were not in excess of 7s. and 6d.), the Trust found it hard to reconcile its obligations as a

[87] See letter of 'A Subscriber', *Southwark Recorder*, 1 Feb. 1902. It might be added that, whatever its finances, the League was apparently able to sustain quite substantial losses. At one point it had two cases in the County Court: '...in one we were defeated on a technicality, and in the other, the defendent, rather than face the consequences of his illegal acts, cut his throat on a South Western train and the case was struck out, the joint result to us being a loss of £21'. Soutter to Fred Knee, *Housing Journal*, May 1903.

[88] There are extensive reports of the agitation conducted by the Dulwich Branch of the Tenants' Protection League in the *Dulwich & Peckham Post* for 1902.

[89] Cf. letter of Soutter, *Southwark Recorder*, 3 Jan. 1903.

charitable housing agency with the reproduction of the profits vital for the progressive extension of its operations. In 1898 the Governors had tried to offset the loss in income from the reduced compounding allowance by raising rents.[90] But this simple expedient could not be repeated indefinitely, not without having to forsake the attempt (or even the pretence) of providing decent accommodation for the respectable poor. Meanwhile the advance in the cost of wages and materials was relentless. The unresolved dilemma was obvious from the low return on capital which in 1901 reached its nadir, being fractionally less than 2½ per cent. The Governors had no option but to stand firm against the local authorities in Southwark and elsewhere.[91]

To the tenants their attitude seemed incomprehensible; for the Governors accepted the lower allowances offered by the Camberwell Borough Council but refused the higher award in Southwark. When challenged the Trustees seemed unable to offer a satisfactory answer.[92] Some became convinced that this so-called charitable Donation was being misused. The fact that its governing board was graced by the Rt. Hon. Walter Long, Conservative President of the Local Government Board, seemed, to the Radical Secretary of the Tenants' Protection League, to constitute evidence of a prima-facie case of maladministration. Soutter, outraged and perplexed, tried to commit the League to a campaign for a parliamentary inquiry into its management.[93]

The struggle between the local authority and the owners thus continued, and all the while, as Soutter put it in an address to the Prime Minister, the occupants continued to be 'mowed down by each of the combatants in a most ruthless manner'. The Salisbury administration had no interest in such matters.[94] Sir Henry Campbell-Bannerman, however, received a private deputation and listened sympathetically for more than one hour and forty minutes while the League's spokesmen explained their predicament. The Leader of the Opposition promised to circulate their grievances amongst his colleagues.[95] This was tactful—but that was all.

The victory, when finally it came, proved something of an anti-climax. In November 1901 the Borough Council, faced with a mounting deficit, at last climbed down. But the terms of surrender

---

[90] *Daily Chronicle*, 1 Apr. 1899.   [91] *The Times*, 2 Apr. 1902.
[92] *Daily Chronicle*, 2 Sept. 1901.   [93] *Southwark Recorder*, 17 Aug. and 12 Oct. 1901.
[94] *Southwark Recorder*, 24 Aug. 1901.   [95] *Southwark Recorder*, 17 Aug. 1901.

brought little solace to those who had already lost their homes. Nothing, moreover, could really compensate for the anxieties generated in the previous six months. The triumphal cup was in any case dashed from the lips even before its sweetness could be savoured. Early in the spring of 1902 private and corporate landlords were reported to be taking advantage of the reversion to compounding and again raising rents.[96]

The Peabody Trust remained intransigent. Encouraged by the crumbling resolve of the Southwark Borough Council, it refused to revert to the old arrangement unless the discount was raised by a further 2½ per cent. This the local authority refused.[97] Elsewhere too the Governors determined upon a hard line; and they were not alone. The Artisans', Labourers', and General Dwellings Company, which withdrew rather than accept the reduced allowances on its Noel Park and Queens Park estates, spoke for many: 'We did not take it because if we did so from Paddington, we should have to take it from Marylebone, Battersea, and half a dozen other places...'[98] This determined display was sufficient to bring the authorities in Westminster and St. Pancras into line and cuts in the compound allowance were promptly restored. The Peabody Trust also adopted a general rule to refuse to enter into compounding agreements with any local authority where the discount was less than 15 per cent. In addition, it began to seek from the local authorities concessions comparable to those granted by the Board of Inland Revenue.[99]

Its confidence was not shared by all corporate landlords. 'I may here explain that the Peabody Trust has been able to enforce direct payment of rates on the part of the tenants largely owing to the lowness of the rents charged', the Secretary to the Donation Fund told the Royal Commission on the Poor Laws. 'Where owners exact full rents, the occupiers leave the buildings rather than submit to the annoyance of saving up and paying direct to the rate collector.'[100]

[96] Correspondence of W. Edwards and S. W. Pascall, *Southwark Recorder*, 22 Mar. and 5 Apr. 1902; and Haw, *Britain's Homes*, p. 163.
[97] *R. C. Poor Laws*, app. vol. ix, p. 816.
[98] Artisans', Labourers' and General Dwellings Company, *Annual Report* (1905), p. 16.
[99] See F. B. Crouch, Secretary to Peabody Donation Fund, 'Additional Memoradum Regarding Assessments upon Low Rates Dwellings and the Direct Payment of Rates by Occupiers', app. No. XXXIII (B), *R.C. Poor Laws*, app. vol. ix, p. 814.
[100] 'Replies by F. B. Crouch', app. No. XXXIII, *R.C. Poor Laws*, app. vol. ix, p. 814.

This is precisely what happened. At Queens Park there was some talk of an organized rent strike amongst the occupants which the Workmen's National Housing Council tried to encourage[101] but nothing came of it; most tenants preferred to vote with their feet when circumstances permitted.[102] Octavia Hill, who had been impressed by the resolve of the Peabody Trust to the point of herself introducing direct rating on the extensive South London estates which she managed on behalf of the Ecclesiastical Commissioners, later found that many tenants preferred a less spartan regime and removed to the new LCC dwellings which became available a few years after.[103] In Islington, where the Borough Council had earlier abolished compounding, the loss by empties rose steadily until, in the case of the Improved Industrial Dwellings Company, the percentage ranged from 20 to 36. The restoration of compounding in this case was to the mutual benefit of both sides.[104]

Peabody tenants, however, were less prone to register passively their dissatisfaction. At Herne Hill, a new twelve-block estate, consumer resistance was considerable; successive petitions against high rents had to be conceded, and finally, direct rating restored.[105] At Whitecross Street and Clerkenwell Buildings, Finsbury, they organized and intervened successfully in the struggle between the Borough Council and the Governors. Assessments were, in consequence, reduced and tenants relieved of the liability of paying rates direct.[106] But, claimed the Secretary of the Peabody Fund, 'the most striking instance' of the political impact of direct rating was the action of the 433 tenants of one estate, in 1903, who organized the return of six candidates pledged to obtain an acceptable discount from the local authority in order to secure the reversion to the payment of rates and rents combined. 'Unfortunately', he added,

---

[101] *Housing Journal*, Oct. 1901.

[102] See London County Council, Report by the Housing Manager to the Housing of the Working Classes Committee: Norbury Estate, 17 Feb. 1909 (R. C. K. Ensor Papers [Unsorted], Corpus Christi College, Oxford).

[103] Octavia Hill, *Letters to My Fellow Workers* (1906), p. 6.

[104] 'Statement as to Compounding by Arthur Moore, Secretary of the Improved Dwellings Company', app. No. XXXVII; also see 'Replies by Thomas Wilkinson, Secretary to East End Dwellings Company', app. XLI, *R.C. Poor Laws*, app. vol. ix, pp. 823, 825-6.

[105] Minutes of Board of Governors, 24 July 1902, 10 June 1904, 2 Dec. 1904 and 17 Feb. 1905 (Peabody Trust MSS).

[106] For a succinct account of this episode, see F. B. Crouch, 'Special Report Concerning Finsbury Assessments', app. No. XXXIII (D), *R.C. Poor Laws*, app. vol. ix, pp. 820-1.

'no sooner have the tenants been allowed to revert to the payment of rates with their rents than they have entirely relapsed into their previous state of indifference.'[107]

Peabody tenants on the Blackfriars Road Estate, Southwark, were, as has already been seen, altogether less fortunate. With the exception of the Peabody Governors, nearly all landlords had accepted the return to compounding at 15 per cent. The Tenants' Protection League appeared a spent force. Rumours of its imminent demise abounded. Soutter tried to scotch them. There was much unfinished business, he insisted. In order to consolidate the achievements so far gained it was necessary to advance on a broad front. Some form of socialized housing remained the key target. The League resumed the housing agitation which, ever since the collapse of the Bermondsey Labour League, had remained of secondary importance.

On 12 February 1902 Bermondsey Town Hall was packed to capacity. A housing conference, attended by delegates representing all sections of metropolitan labour, borough councils, and boards of guardians, convened by the League, indicated the switch in emphasis.[108] It was resolved that a deputation should wait upon the London Members of Parliament, and a few weeks later that resolution was given effect.

The Serjeant-at-Arms was startled by the 300 irate delegates who arrived at St. Stephens in pursuit of the elected representatives of the Metropolis. There was no place in Sir Charles Barry's neo-Gothic enthusiasm for such eventualities. In due course the deputies were ushered into the Grand Committee Room of the House of Commons. It quickly lost its grandeur. Deputies were compelled to sit on the floor, an unconventional posture in that august building, but one considered preferable to their continued disconsolate meanderings through its stately corridors. The twenty-one Unionist Members, who several weeks earlier had voted against the proposals of organized labour as embodied in Dr Macnamara's amendment to the Address, were the immediate object of attention. One by one they hastened to reassure the incredulous deputation—'all expressing great sympathy with the working classes amidst derisive comments from the audience'. Dr Macnamara, Radical Member of

---

[107] 'Replies by F. B. Crouch', app. No. XXXIII, *R.C. Poor Laws*, app. vol. ix, p. 814.

[108] *Southwark Recorder*, 15 Feb. 1902.

Camberwell and the parliamentary spokesman for the Workmen's National Housing Council, whose own apostasy still lay in the future, appeared 'to be taken aback by the militant tone of the delegates'.[109] It was an impressive display of invective but whether it was politically astute was open to doubt. Knee, for one, censured the 'excessively bitter style of attack' and the neglect of substantive matters of housing policy. 'The feeling present in the minds of those addressed, as well as many of the deputation themselves', he wrote, 'was that it was only "a Radical dodge".' Soutter, like so many of that generation, seemed preoccupied with the mere registration of protest. 'It is only right to say', Knee concluded, 'that the Workmen's National Housing Council Executive suspected the move from the very first, but as the Tenant's Defence League was an affiliated body, they could not well ignore them. We regret the throwing away of a splendid opportunity.'[110]

The Tenants' Protection League, in consequence of the temerity and resource of its dashing secretary, continued to hog the headlines nevertheless. In a move designed to attract the maximum publicity, embarrass the Government, even perhaps jolt it from its shameful complacency, Soutter decided to appeal direct to Edward VII who, as Prince of Wales, had been a member of the Royal Commission on Housing nearly twenty years earlier. In April 1903 His Majesty received several photographs of Bermondsey slums accompanied by a supplicatory note in the hand of this loyal subject.[111] On Good Friday, Soutter escorted a gentleman of the Press on a tour of these districts. It made good copy but failed to arrest the loss of momentum; the League was in decline. These divisive ostentatious gestures were incapable of reviving its flagging spirits. The Tenants' Protection League, like the proverbial old soldier, simply faded away. Nevertheless, valuable experience had been gained. Tenants had learnt that it was possible to organize. The knowledge thus gained was later to be put to advantage.[112]

[109] *Daily News*, 5 Mar. 1902.
[110] *Housing Journal*, Apr. 1902.
[111] *Daily News*, 8 Apr. 1903.
[112] Dan Rider, one of the League's most active supporters, later founded the War Rents League that played an important part in the agitation for rent control and in the subsequent campaign to defend and consolidate the protection gained in 1915: see Dan Rider, *Ten Years Adventures Amongst Landlords and Tenants* (1927).

7

Rents Agitation, 1912–1914

The final building boom of the uncontrolled economy collapsed at the same time as the last liberal Government took office. There was no connection. Demand had slackened some years earlier. Landlords were nevertheless to hold Mr Lloyd George responsible for the hard times that had overtaken them. This was to confuse symptom and cause.[1] The crisis of the Edwardian property market was, in short, the product of imperialism and social reform reacting upon an archaic system of local finance that struck at small house property with disproportionate severity. It was not simply a question of guns or butter; social tensions in Britain did not admit of any such choice. Somehow provision had to be made for both guns and butter. Real property bore much of the burden in the form of failing demand, increased rates and depreciating values. Even before the advent of rent control contemporaries feared that the condition of the private rented sector was terminal rather than cyclical.[2] In Scotland, where its protracted death-rattle was to be so painfully audible in the years ahead, the decade after 1901 witnessed a more than 20 per cent reduction in the number employed in the construction industry.[3] In Glasgow values plummeted. The decline, however, was not quite as catastrophic as Table 4 at first suggests.

The inflation of the mid-seventies represents a period of intense speculation in rents, while the nadir of 1911/12 refers to proprietors who, for one reason and another, were forced to sell up. The fourteen years' purchase obtained at the turn of the century was generally considered a fair and attractive price.[4] Recovery was

---

[1] H. W. Richardson and D. H. Aldcroft, *Building in the British Economy between the Wars* (1968), pp. 27-32 provides a summary of the various explanations of pre-war cyclical movements in building.

[2] On the crisis of the Edwardian property market, see Avner Offer, *Property and Politics 1870-1914* (Cambridge, 1981), Chs. xvii-xviii.

[3] *Royal Commission on Housing of the Industrial Population of Scotland: Minutes of Evidence*, 4 vols. (Edinburgh, 1921), qq. 2282-3.

[4] *R. C. Housing in Scotland*, qq. 38092-4.

Table 4: Property Values in Glasgow

Year	Number of Transactions	Total Price Realised	Average Years' Purchase of Rental
		£	
1872	75	177,540	14.3
1876	73	234,295	17.0
1881	58	148,292	13.5
1886	67	140,935	12.8
1891	132	338.069	13.0
1896	192	580.695	14.1
1901	111	415.660	14.9
1906	41	100,400	13.0
1907	40	84.085	12.1
1908	33	61,705	12.20
1909	21	46,971	11.77
1910	24	54,917	11.22
1911	18	24,626	9.75
1912	20	34,895	9.50
1913	12	14,145	10.19

Source: App. No. CXXXII, *R. C. Housing in Scotland*, IV, p. 156.

retarded by severe industrial depression, soaring local taxation, and the uncertainties created by the Finance Act, 1910. Above all, the flow of cheap capital, which in previous years offset rising building costs, had dried up,[5] although rents did not rise in proportion. On the contrary the persistently high level of empties intensified competition for occupants.[6] New building was thus impossible. William Fraser, a recognized authority in these matters, reckoned that the net return on invested capital was not in excess of 3½ per cent and frequently less.[7] The dramatic slump in turnover registered the want of confidence in this once secure investment. On the eve of the Great War business was virtually at a standstill.

In England and Wales too the property market was in the doldrums. In the Edwardian period turnover and values slumped by 40 per cent.[8] The industrial boom of 1913 signified the return of

[5] Cf. *Scottish Land: Report of the Scottish Land Enquiry Committee* (1914), pp. 388-90.

[6] William Fraser, 'Fluctuations of the Building Trade and Glasgow's House Accommodation', *Proceedings of the Royal Philosophical Society of Glasgow* (1908), p. 20.

[7] *R. C. Housing in Scotland*, qq. 38182-5.

[8] See the comprehensive discussion in Offer, *Property and Politics*, Chs. vii, xvii-xviii.

prosperity. In Scotland, where rents had emained stationary for nearly ten years, memories were stirred of a bygone era when rents were high and markets buoyant, a profitable age to which investors hoped soon to return. At the beginning of 1914 landlords had 'reasonable expectations' of being able to increase their rents 'to some extent nearer to their original level', i.e. the level obtained fifteen years earlier.[9] English landlords too hoped to recover lost ground; and in the last two years of peace there was, in the words of the President of the National Association of Property Owners, 'a slight improvement' in that direction.[10] But following a period of declining real wages such adjustments were bound to generate friction. Tension was heightened by the failure of the incremental approach to housing reform to keep pace with rising expectations. At the annual conference of the Workmen's National Housing Council in 1913 the call for an accelerator in the form of a rent strike was again voiced.[11] The resort to direct action which characterized the industrial unrest of these years found a parallel in the housing reform movement. The idea was first canvassed by George Lansbury, editor of the *Daily Herald*. 'It is time, high time, that we abandoned the gross and childish delusion that wretched slum dwellers are in some mysterious way benefited by the erection of Garden Cities for the artistic middle class and well-to-do artisans', he declared:

The question arises however, whether mere denunciation of overcrowding and its evils, with occasional appeals to Parliament and local bodies, is adequate. Has not the time come to think seriously of other steps? Has not the time come for organising a strike against paying rents to slum landlords? … As regards tenants who are living under conditions so flagrant, the case is not quite so clear. Still we are of the opinion that the formation of Tenant Societies to resist the exactions of landlords by all possible means might wring great benefits from that selfish class, even as Trade Unions have extorted concessions from grasping employers ….

Such an organisation, powerfully directed, might make history, and will do more to expedite the cause of Housing Reform than all the tedious and futile debates of our descredited Parliament.[12]

---

[9] 'Memorial of Incorporated Society of Law Agents in Scotland, Jan. 1918' (PRO Reco. 1/644).

[10] Departmental Committee on the Operation of the Rent Acts: MS Minutes of Evidence, 1 Mar. 1920, p. 45 (PRO HLG. 41/2).

[11] *Daily Citizen*, 1 Apr. 1913. On incremental approach, see P. Wilding, 'Towards Exchequer Subsidies for Housing 1906-1914', *Social and Economic Administration* VI (1972).

[12] *Daily Herald*, 10 May 1912.

Trouble was brewing.

I

On 18 March 1913 the Wolverhampton and District Property Owners Association resolved to raise weekly rents from the end of the month. A differential increase in order to retain the benefits of compounding was to be imposed: those for houses let at 5s. a week were to be raised by 3d. and for houses at 5s. 3d. by 6d. per week.[13]

Wolverhampton, like other industrial centres, had suffered by the long years of depression. The property market had suffered worse than most. According to an analysis by the Board of Trade, rents had fallen by three per cent in the past seven years while remaining stable in most other cities.[14] These were years when the supply of accommodation was well in excess of demand, years in which the better-off and more discriminating wage-earner enjoyed an unusually wide choice of residence. 'I found the secretary of the Trades Council living in a very good six-roomed house at 6s. a week', an investigator observed. 'He said it was exceptional, but inquiry hardly confirmed that'.[15] In this cramped, grimy, insanitary city the typical working class home consisted of the two-storied terraced house containing four or five rooms.[16] The four-roomed houses were built in blocks of from six to forty, divided at intervals by narrow passageways that ended in a small backyard shared by several or more tenants. The front door opened directly into the sitting-room. The more modern five-roomed houses contained a kitchen and scullery and a sitting room on the lower floor and three bedrooms upstairs. In this class a small number of dwellings were distinguished by the addition of small forecourts, low bays, and a back garden. But during a period in which the cost of living outstripped the rise in wages such properties were reserved for the sole occupation of the families of the most abstemious working men.

The decision to increase rents was sparked by the return to prosperity in the previous year. As industry regained its momentum the number of unoccupied houses fell drastically. In mid-1913 those

[13] *Express & Star*, 19 Mar. 1913.
[14] *Report on an enquiry by the Board of Trade into Working Class Rents, Housing, Retail Prices and Standard Rates of Wages in the U.K.* (PP 1913, LXVI), p. 260.
[15] Arthur Shadwell, *Industrial Efficiency*, 2 vols. (1906), I, p. 154.
[16] For a dense but brief analysis, see G. J. Barnsby, *A History of Housing in Wolverhampton 1750-1975* (Wolverhampton, n.d.), Ch. i.

seeking a home were limited to 180 reasonably decent houses.[17] By the end of the year there were only fifty vacant houses and overcrowding was chronic.[18] As the number of empties dropped tension rose.

The Wolverhampton Property Owners' Association was a relatively well-organized body with considerable experience of local administration. Its interests were well protected by several vigilant representatives on the Borough Council who had successfully minimized municipal expenditure and resisted costly sanitary improvements to their properties unless undertaken at the ratepayers' expense.[19] Organized labour, by contrast, was still in its infancy. In the previous decade Labour had entered municipal politics and transformed local contests which had once been exclusively issue-oriented affairs. Housing and sanitary reform, although prominent aspects of the working-class programme, did not have much of an impact on the less than one fifth of the population who were eligible to vote at local elections.[20] The property-owners' association anticipated no difficulty in imposing the new rents. In this they were mistaken.

The proposal to raise rents was greeted with a hail of protest. The local newspaper was deluged by angry correspondents. Political differences were cast aside. Liberal, Labour, and Conservative working men pondered the possibilities of a rent strike.[21] On 2 April the Trades Council convened a public meeting to consider the matter. There was 'a numerous attendance and considerable enthusiasm was manifested'. It was agreed to form a Tenants' Defence League. The meeting rejected entirely the view that housing was just another commodity to be regulated by the vagaries of uncontrolled market forces. There was an emotional and moral investment on the part of the tenants which demanded recognition. Landlords were going to be compelled to justify the use of their property. The unity and determination of the tenants was evident in the election of a twelve-man organizing committee to which the Labour Councillor, James Whittaker, President of the Trades Council, and

[17] *Express & Star*, 7 June 1913.
[18] *Report of Urban Land Enquiry* (1914), pp. 69-70.
[19] G. W. Jones, *Borough Politics, A Study of the Wolverhampton Borough Council 1888-1964* (1969), pp. 131-2.
[20] Jones, *Borough Politics*, pp. 34, 359-61, 363.
[21] See correspondence, *Express & Star*, 20, 22, 24, 25, 26, 31 Mar. and 1, 7, 8, 9, 13, 27, 29, and 30 Apr. 1913.

Mr S. Belcher, a noted Tariff Reformer, were appointed chairman and secretary respectively. Those present then pledged themselves to refuse payment of the increased demand. The community was startled more perhaps by the novelty than by the virulence of the protest. The Tory *Express & Star* viewed matters with a curious combination of sympathy and cynicism. Although tenants were said to be 'up in arms', the struggle was conceived more as an entertaining spectacle than an issue of vital importance. Its account of the inaugural meeting of the Tenants' Protection League concluded on a bemused note: 'At any rate, there is the prospect of some fun, and we shall await developments with a degree of interest.'[22]

The tenants, however, meant business. A negotiated settlement was at first sought. The Tenants' Defence League preceded its approach to the property-owners by a number of protest meetings designed to impress the doubters within and without its ranks. At one such meeting members reaffirmed their determination to resist 'with the demonstrativeness of French Revolutionists'.[23] Wolverhampton's councillors refused to expose themselves to this kind of pressure and in view of their past neglect and the Mayor's much publicized admission that 500 houses were suitable for immediate demolition, the refusal to accept the invitation which had been extended was not at all unwise. Further indications of the restive mood were no doubt conveyed to their employers by the rent collectors whose presence served as a flashpoint for tenant anger. In a street visited by one of their number, the tenants were said to be not only prone to refuse to tender the new rent but 'to assemble in the road and threaten to roll him in the gutter'.[24] In face of the growing outcry the property-owners agreed to meet the representatives of the Tenants' Defence League.   The tenants appeared to have scored a moral victory: landlords were for the first time having to account for their actions. This delusion was to some extent fostered by Revd J. A. Shaw, a well-meaning but naïve supporter of the Tenants' Defence League. In this he was not alone. The belief that justice would triumph over power by the superiority of unarmed Virtue was common to most of the League's leadership. It even affected veterans such as James Walsh, the treasurer, who, before leaving London many years earlier, had been an executive member of the Workmen's National Housing Council and a representative

[22] *Express & Star*, 3 Apr. 1913.   [23] *Express & Star*, 14 Apr. 1913.
[24] *Express & Star*, 12 Apr. 1913.

at ministerial deputations and official inquiries. The property-owners appear to have been more concerned to probe the strength of the opposition rather than offer concessions.

Landlord and tenant met without conferring. Lest this meeting be taken as a sign of weakness, the property-owners, though forewarned of its composition, decided suddenly to take exception to the two wives in the deputation who were occupants rather than tenants.[25] This untoward display of virility failed to impress. A second meeting was arranged shortly afterwards. Its purpose was by no means clear. The landlords insisted that they were not in conference but assembled only for a formal exchange of statements on their respective positions. However, it did throw some light on the situation. The spokesman of the property-owners stated that 80 per cent of the 9,000 tenants who had been notified had paid the new rents. The tenants disputed this figure. But whether greater or smaller, the numbers involved were clearly far from negligible. Walsh thought that the stiff approach of the landlords reflected uncertainties within their own ranks and it does seem to have been the case that the Property Owners' Association was still undecided as to an appropriate course. Certainly, the proprietors had so far shown remarkable restraint. Their chairman confessed 'that where the tenants were working with the League, they were passed by'; action was contemplated 'where the tenant said he would neither pay the——rent nor leave the——house', to which Walsh replied: 'the two kinds of tenants really meant the same thing. Some did not express themselves as well as others'. But the meeting broke up without any progress having been made. The landlords promised a considered response to tenant grievances at a future meeting.[26]

At the end of April the proprietors resolved unanimously that 'this association is satisfied that the increase suggested by them is both reasonable and justifiable, and that its members therefore call upon the tenants to carry out the terms of the notice'. At the same time they did express a willingness to seek a negotiated reduction in the assessment on those 2,000 properties upon which a 6*d*. increase had been imposed, and if successful, would 'willingly ease their tenants in a corresponding manner'. But in the meantime the increase had to be paid.[27]

The sparring was over and the Tenants' Defence League knew it.

[25] *Express & Star*, 19 Apr. 1913.   [26] *Express & Star*, 25 Apr. 1913.
[27] *Express & Star*, 1 May 1913.

At a public meeting held on the following day a manifesto outlining a plan of campaign was received with acclamation. Tenants were urged to tender their rents minus the increase in the presence of a witness. This exemplary document also contained a number of piquant questions designed to expose slum landlordism in its moral and legal aspects.[28] Lansbury, searching for a response to his earlier clarion call, was elated:

There are welcome signs throughout the country of an impending strike against rent.

Rent strikes were worked out and successfully carried out in Ireland to an extent little known in this country, and although the rent strike suggested in some parts of England is not of so drastic a nature, there is no knowing to what such steps will lead, and therefore we welcome the first appearance in England of anything like a war against the House Bosses.[29]

Those closer to events were altogether less confident. The unshakeable resolve of the landlords exposed the weakness of the tenants. One rent striker hoped the manifesto would rally support, though he already sensed defeat. 'Had there been absolute unanimity on the part of the tenants in resisting these demands, it is questionable whether there would have been any rent question to discuss now ... I do not hesitate to say it is because some tenants in a moment of weakness, as a result of being bluffed by the landlord, have given way and paid the advances that has weakened the case for those who have so far resisted.' How many tenants, he wondered, 'have stuck to their pledge with bulldog tenacity or have sneaked like little poodle dogs and quietly paid'.[30] Before the month was out, the answer was forthcoming. What was described as 'an echo of the Wolverhampton Tenants's War' faded into obscurity in the County Court.

A saucy tenant could be a tiresome sort. But if the rent was paid on time and the house not vandalized, the occupant's waspish tongue might be dismissed with a shrug. A rent-striking tenant who refused to curb his tongue, however, represented a deliberate challenge which no landlord could long ignore. Oliver Elie Howe was one such tenant. According to counsel for the plaintiff, this railway porter had had the temerity to remark to his landlord: 'You will see who will be the top dog at the finish. I am not going to stand any of your humbug and shall not come out.' Eight weeks after the said

[28] *Express & Star*, 2 May 1913.   [29] *Daily Herald*, 19 May 1913.
[30] *Express & Star*, 3 May 1913.

words were alleged to have been uttered, Mr Howe stood in the Wolverhampton County Court facing an action for possession.

The action had been brought on behalf of the Property Owners' Association; the defendant was represented by a solicitor retained by the Tenants' Defence League. *Brotherton* v. *Howe* was widely regarded as a test case. Its outcome determined the course of the rent strike. Other than on a technicality there could be no defence. The plaintiff was awarded possession in five days with costs. He was amazed at the leniency of the judgement. His Honour tried to soothe the proprietor's ruffled feelings. 'If there had been an assertion that the landlord had no right to raise the rent because it was uneconomical he should have given the order forthwith.'[31] In not challenging this right, counsel for the defendant had probably prevented the summary eviction of his client, but at the same time he had obscured the whole point of the exercise. Once the campaign moved into the court room, the cause was lost.

The rent strike collapsed amidst a certain amount of recrimination. The Tenants' Defence League resumed the labour campaign for municipal housing. But although the Borough Council proved more than usually amenable to their scheme, it does not appear to have aroused any great enthusiasm amongst the defeated tenants. 'When', asked an embittered and disillusioned worker, 'are we to see any good results from the Tenants' Defence League? I thought by now we should have been delivered from all our troubles. Has there been more slumping than work?'[32] What, asked another, was the point of appealing to a Town Council which, by their own admission, was dominated by slum landlords and others who cared nowt for the people?[33] The fact was acknowledged that there was no other course available, or if there was, the tenants' leaders were unaware of it.[34]

It has been suggested that the long term electoral gains of this abortive campaign far outweighed the immediate aftermath of despair, that the rent strike played a significant part in helping to define and demonstrate the independence of Labour and its meaningful articulation of the problems of the Wolverhampton wage-earner. The same authority later suggests, however, that it was the extension of the franchise and expansion of the working-class electorate after 1918 that was the decisive factor in the subsequent

[31] *Express & Star*, 26 May 1913.   [32] *Express & Star*, 4 June 1913.
[33] *Express & Star*, 7 June 1913.   [34] *Express & Star*, 9 June 1913.

growth of the Labour vote.[35] The two kinds of explanation are not mutually incompatible, although it is the latter which is the more susceptible of proof. What is clear, though, is that Wolverhampton tenants had not recovered sufficient morale to play a signficant part in the agitation for rent control in 1914/15. The renewed confidence brought about by the passage of the Rent Act, 1915, led to a speedy revival. The following year the Trades Council's Housing Committee was again active on the tenants' behalf.[36]

II

The Wolverhampton rent strike was not an isolated incident. The campaign had attracted a good deal of attention. The *Midlands County Express*, a weekly paper which circulated widely throughout the region, carried fairly extensive accounts of the strike. The idea was in the air. The events at Wolverhampton helped focus attention upon the insecurities which increasingly affected even the most respectable of working-class tenants. As early as the spring of 1912 organized resistance had in fact been canvassed in Coventry. The objects of the proposed association were to fight, both in the courts and on the streets, 'the ever-encroaching power of Landlordism'. Provision, in the form of a weekly allowance, was to be made to all who, in consequence, 'may be sent to his Majesty's pleasure'.[37] The following year the Coventry branch of the Amalgamated Society of Engineers was threatening to adopt some such plan unless there was a halt to the growing number of evictions in the town.[38] But it was in the Metropolis of the Midlands where collective resistance first occurred.

Erdington was once a quiet, prosperous suburb, a part of Birmingham much favoured by teachers, clerks, superior artisans, shop assistants, and travellers. In April 1913 its calm was shattered by one of the largest landlords who raised the rents on nearly 200 houses by 1s. a week. This latest imposition proved too much. Rents which nine months earlier had commanded a substantial house of 7s. 6d., had since been advanced to 9s., and there were cases cited of 10s. a week being demanded for houses formerly let at 8s. The total

[35] Jones, *Borough Politics*, pp. 48-9, 51-2. Cf. p. 58.
[36] J. Whittaker to A. Henderson, 2 Mar. 1916 (War Emergency Workers' National Committee Papers, Labour Party Archives).
[37] *Daily Herald*, 12 May 1912.
[38] *Birmingham Gazette*, 26 Nov. 1913.

cessation of suburban building in preceding years and the constant growth of population had combined to create a near perfect monopoly situation. In 1914 a vacant house was almost as rare as a precious stone.[39] At the end of May 1913 the *Birmingham Gazette* reported the demise of the Wolverhampton rent strike. The following week its readers learned of the formation of the Erdington Tenants' Defence League.[40]

The action of the Erdington tenants highlighted the marked distinction between inner Birmingham and its periphery. The vacation of the central areas and concurrent expansion of the suburbs had, in the course of two generations, quite transformed the city. This continuous outward migration affected 'the more temperate and self-respecting [amongst] the working class, men earning good and regular wages, ... leading wholesome and orderly lives'. Those who remained—'the idle, careless and uncleanly, who live in wilful or ignorant resistance to sanitary regulations'—served to neutralize the effects of costly administrative improvements.[41] The separation of the working class and 'the poor' had assumed a fixed geographical dimension. On the eve of the Great War, Birmingham possessed 43,000 back-to-back houses which provided accommodation for 200,000 people. These were distributed throughout the central districts of the city, residual areas inhabited by low-paid workers which, like all slums, were characterized by the highest mortality and morbidity rates.[42]

Official intervention served to aggravate the situation. Rather than adopt an expensive programme of central urban redevelopment the Housing Committee had, under threat of demolition, sought to coerce owners into maintaining their properties in a proper state of repair. This policy, the Special Housing Enquiry of 1914 noted, 'has often been contemptuously referred to as a policy of "patching"!' The contempt was well merited. In short, it was disastrous. The expense of improving short-lease property was prohibitive. It 'generated a good deal of friction and a sense of injustice among owners', the Special Enquiry concluded, 'and in an increasing degree they have preferred to demolish their property or leave it derelict

[39] Corporation of Birmingham, *Report of Special Housing Enquiry* (Birmingham, 1914), pp. 12, 251.
[40] *Birmingham Gazette*, 2 June 1913.
[41] C. A. Vince, *History of the Corporation of Birmingham* 4 vols. (Birmingham, 1902), III, p. 128.
[42] *Annual Report of Medical Officer of Health for Birmingham* (1918), Maps. 1-7.

rather than comply with the drastic requirements of the Housing Committee'.[43] The resultant diminution in the supply of cheap accommodation intensified overcrowding and, in due course, encouraged rent-raising. Those 'respectable and industrious' families who could not escape such areas were reduced to an impotent rage. The poor settled accounts in a traditional manner. The central districts, according to the Special Enquiry, were peopled by 'tenants who are the bane of all landlords, who produce false rent books and false references, who systematically avoid payment of their rents and who by filthy habits and destructive propensities not only damage the houses in which they live, but lower the whole tone of their neighbourhoods'.[44] The very thought of having to return to such districts acted as a powerful radicalizing agent.

The Birmingham artisan never took to flats. The dominant aspiration was to live in a spacious home in the suburbs.[45] Owner-occupation was probably of secondary importance: quality was what mattered. 'The generality of people in our neighbourhood', said one of the Erdington tenants, 'desire to live in a comfortable house, an eight-roomed house, with a small garden. That is their ambition. They don't want to live in the City and Slum neighbourhoods.'[46] The sort of accommodation to which the speaker was accustomed consisted of four rooms (including a kitchen and scullery) downstairs, and four above: 'A front bedroom, middle bedroom, bath room and small room at the back, what you might call a lumber room, as the case may be, but it is used as a bedroom in our neighbourhood.'[47] Those who formed the Tenants' Defence League had achieved such a standard of comfort. The prospect of losing it and of being forced back into the slums was unbearable.[48]

The members of the Tenants' Defence League were under no illusion as to their precarious situation. An attempt on the part of some neighbours to organize a similar resistance was crushed without difficulty.[49] The search for a safe haven was uppermost in their thoughts. 'It is not so much the present increase in rents', said one of

[43] *Birmingham Housing Enquiry*, pp. 4-5, 11.
[44] *Birmingham Housing Enquiry*, p. 2.
[45] *Birmingham Housing Enquiry*, qq. 3126-7; Anthony Sutcliffe, 'A Century of Flats in Birmingham, 1875-1975', in *idem*, ed., *Multi-Storey Living: The British Working Class Experience* (1974), pp. 184-5, 187-8.
[46] *Birmingham Housing Enquiry*, q. 3155.
[47] *Birmingham Housing Enquiry*, qq. 3107-9.
[48] *Birmingham Housing Enquiry*, q. 3162.
[49] *Birmingham Housing Enquiry*, qq. 31304-5.

them. 'We have no guarantee that we shall not have a further increase. There is an uncomfortable feeling that we are in the landlords hands. What we want is security of tenure.'[50] Salvation lay in some form of socialized housing. Although their experience of the local authority was not exactly encouraging—the Town Council had ignored their petition and local councillors declined support[51]— cost rent municipal housing was thought to offer the best chance of retaining some degree of control over an increasingly unstable environment. Municipal housing, it was agreed, was 'the only line of defence'.[52] The principle of public accountability, enshrined in the notion of local self-government, in theory provided the council house tenant with a source of leverage and protection denied the occupant of privately rented accommodation.[53] It was this aspect which, in the eyes of the tenants, ensured the superiority of council housing over garden city or co-partnership schemes of suburban development. Owner-occupation was no longer considered a realistic ambition.[54]

The sense of foreboding common amongst the Erdington tenants was in no sense a figment of overwrought imaginations. Rent-raising was pretty general across the city. The secretary of the Birmingham and District Property Owners' Association estimated that by 1914 only 50 per cent of properties had recovered their 1900 position on rents.[55] The attempt to recover the outstanding arrears ensured Birmingham's vanguard position in the coming struggle for rent control.

III

On 28 February 1913 the Leeds and District Property Owners' Association resolved upon a general rent increase.[56] Within three months tenants in Holbeck, East Leeds, and Harehills had received notification of the new rents together with an inventory itemizing

[50] *Birmingham Housing Enquiry*, q. 3172.
[51] Statement of Walter Field, *Birmingham Housing Enquiry*, p. 251.
[52] *Birmingham Housing Enquiry*, q. 3151; *Erdington News*, 7 June 1913.
[53] *Birmingham Housing Enquiry*, qq. 3115-19, 3123-5, 3152-3.
[54] *Birmingham Gazette*, 26 Dec. 1913; *Birmingham Housing Enquiry*, qq. 3139-42, 3149-50. Cf. Minutes of Birmingham Trades Council (Housing Sub-Committee), 20 Mar. 1919.
[55] Departmental Committee on the Operation of the Rent Acts: MS Minutes of Evidence, 5 Mar. 1920, pp. 15-16 (PRO HLG. 41/4).
[56] *Leeds Weekly Citizen*, 7 Mar. 1913.

the elements of rising costs by way of explanation. The tenants scrutinized the document with some care and concluded that it was nothing less than an impertinent fiction. The logic of market forces was deemed insufficient justification for the new rents. Resistance commenced at Holbeck where sixty-four tenants, encouraged by the local Labour paper, the *Leeds Weekly Citizen*, banded together in defiance of the new demand.[57]

It was not the first time that tenants in Leeds had organized to resist the demands of their landlords. In 1904 shopkeepers and stallholders united to form a Market Tenants' Association and withheld rent in protest against the excessive charges and unreasonable regulations imposed by the Corporation.[58] This successful action, however, exerted no lasting influence upon the tenants of residential properties. It was Lansbury's intervention which revived interest in the idea. In a significant contribution, John W. Lake, secretary of the East Leeds Labour Party, tried to theorize the comparative advantages of this mode of struggle. Industrial action, a vital part of the workers' armoury, did not, Lake suggested, afford complete protection. The rent strike promised to improve traditional defences and minimize the privations which their use entailed:

We want a strike that week by week will add to our income while it lasts. One that will take away wealth from the idle classes and transfer it to the workers, one in which all may join, in a strike that we can hope will last for ever that will not mean the kiddies going without boots and food, but one that will mean more boots and food, and at the same time cut at the very roots of the Capitalist System.

The rent strike, he argued, fulfilled these conditions. If assured of sufficient support the strikers would be invulnerable to the assaults of even the State's most powerful servants. He was confident that police and army would shrink from the execution of such onerous duties. The risk of blacklegging too was minimal. 'The most wooden-headed Liberal or Tory working man living next door to a free-renter would quickly join the strike.' But Lake went further. 'Rent, interest and profit are the chains that bind our class in servitude', he declared, 'and the first of these is rent.' The impact of a successful rent strike was, therefore, incalculable: the demise of capitalism seemed imminent.[59] The ejectment of an East Leeds

[57] *Leeds Weekly Citizen*, 6 June 1913.
[58] *Leeds & Yorkshire Mercury*, 27 July and 11 Aug. 1904.
[59] *Daily Herald*, 5 June 1912.

Labour Party activist for the sole reason of having allowed her front room to be used as a committee-room during the municipal elections of 1912, may well have given an added impetus to the circulation of these naive sentiments.[60] Anti-capitalist rhetoric proved sadly deficient in the coming struggle.

In Bradford, too, such ideas were in the air. There, the upswing in the business cycle was beginning to be reflected in rising property values. 'The statement was often made a few years ago that there was 5,000 empty dwellings in Bradford', ran one report '... Now indeed, the complaint is that there is a dearth of houses which come within the means of the working and lower middle classes. It would probably be quite true to say that at no time in the past ten years has property been so well occupied in Bradford as it is today.'[61] The local labour movement had for almost a generation been campaigning for municipal housing. The local authority could not ignore the agitation, but tempered its response so that progress gave minimal offence to proprietors. The improvement of property—notably the replacement of privies by water-closets—would, it was hoped, obviate the need for more extensive forms of municipal intervention. In some areas the local authority possessed the confidence to make such improvements at the landlord's expense. Not so Bradford, where the cost of conversion was subsidized by a generous grant from the public purse. As an added incentive, water rates were abolished on those properties where improvements had been undertaken. Tenants were to foot the bill. On 16 April 1913 the Bradford Property Owners' Association met and resolved to raise rents. The president of the Association explained: 'The tenants had previously been too well treated, and they must be brought to realise that, since they had a share in the benefits of municipal activity, they must also bear some of the expenses.'[62] The following week an indignant trade council discussed the matter. 'The property owners', said one member, 'were blaming the Labour members for the increase in rates, which had been brought about chiefly by subsidies to the property owners.' The call for some form of organized resistance was generally approved.[63] Two days later it was reported that the advice was being acted upon 'to a limited extent' in the Bradford Moor District.[64] A 'vigorously worded' circular calling for

[60] *Leeds Weekly Citizen*, 10 Jan. 1913.   [61] *Yorkshire Observer*, 26 Apr. 1913.
[62] *Yorkshire Observer*, 17 Apr. 1913.
[63] *Yorkshire Observer*, 25 Apr. 1913.   [64] *Yorkshire Observer*, 26 Apr. 1913.

widespread rent strikes was subsequently issued jointly by the Trades Council, the ILP, and the Workers' Municipal Federation.[65] But neither it nor subsequent protest meetings appear to have evoked a positive response from the tenants.

At their quarterly meeting, the Property Owners' Association was informed that the decision to raise rents 'had been generally carried out ... and ... that the increase in rent had been the means of bringing home to many householders an idea of the public expenditure of the city'. The absence of opposition encouraged them to go further. It was resolved to approach the Corporation with a view to securing the reversion to direct rating since the compounding system was held to have become unprofitable. There was no attempt to disguise the fact that further increases were imminent.[66] Labour returned to the Council chamber to continue the campaign for municipal housing.

The abortive rent strike in Bradford was not without a sobering effect in Leeds. John Lake's enthusiasm for this particular form of direct action was not shared by his colleagues. His attempt to commit the Leeds Labour Representation Committee to a no-rent campaign produced a rather desultory discussion.[67] The Labour Party was constitutionally, and perhaps temperamentally, ill-prepared for such innovation.[68] It was finally agreed that the Labour Group be given a free hand to decide upon an appropriate course. The Housing Question was to be the dominant issue in the forthcoming municipal elections.[69] Meanwhile, the sixty-four rent-striking tenants at Holbeck were left to their own devices. Landlords openly boasted of their determination to exploit the growing scarcity to the utmost.[70] Opposition remained muted until the end of the year.

In the interval the housing crisis became more acute. A census of unoccupied houses conducted by the City Engineer in September 1913 indicated its dimensions. Empties were fast becoming negligible. In spite of the existence of 2,395 vacant dwellings, there was a severe shortage of decent accommodation. Analysis of the distribution and rents of these properties disclosed that nearly 70 per cent were concentrated in the congested central areas of the city.[71] These

[65] *Yorkshire Observer*, 5 May 1913; *Labour Leader*, 8 May 1913.
[66] *Estates Gazette* (21 June 1913), p. 1051.   [67] *Leeds Weekly Citizen*, 6 June 1913.
[68] Cf. Minutes of Leeds Labour Representation Committee, 12 Feb. 1914.
[69] Minutes of Leeds Labour Representation Committee, 18 Sept. 1913.
[70] *Estates Gazette* (12 July 1913), p. 77; *Yorkshire Post*, 7 July 1913.
[71] See maps, *Leeds Weekly Citizen*, 8 May 1914.

inferior properties were such that no self-respecting artisan would willingly occupy. Whereas such persons generally rented houses at 5–10*s*. a week, no less than 1,919 of the total number of unoccupied dwellings were let at a rental below 4*s*. These were considered 'too narrow and cramped for family life, ... the type of houses that possess a revolting closet for every three or four cottages; that have ugly factory walls within a few feet of the only door.' Many contained the living room in the basement.[72] Property-owners readily confessed that hitherto such residences had been impossible to let:

I admit, [said one of the largest estate agents], that there is a famine in certain districts where the houses are all good sculleries and small throughs. The respectable working classes will no longer live in dwellings with cellar kitchens, and consequently there is always a good demand for the class of houses I have mentioned.

In the poorer districts, however, there are hundreds of houses to let. The neighbourhoods may not be all that is desirable, the dwellings themselves are not exactly the sort you would find in a model village. Still, they are there, and so long as they remain empty it is not correct to say there is a house famine.[73]

Organized resistance began in the better-off areas.

Christmas 1913 was spoilt by the landlords. The increase in the rates that was expected to follow the settlement of the Corporation Strike provided the pretext for a renewed burst of rent-raising. The New Year was blighted before it begun. In the third week of December, Tom Paylor, the veteran Socialist, drew attention to the forthcoming increases and called for the creation of a tenants' defence league.[74] The annual review of the real estate market confirmed the need of such a formation. In spite of the labour disturbances, the improvement in the position of residential property, evident at the beginning of the year, had remained unimpaired,

... and therefore, we may expect to find that, owing to the pressure of demand, rents will increase until they reach nearer the level of former years when builders built with confidence, and investors were willing buyers. In our opinion the working classes will then appreciate the increase of rates, for landlords will be able to add them to the rent, in a way that, for some years, they have not been able to do in consequence of the number of empty houses.

[72] *Leeds Weekly Citizen*, 19 Dec. 1913.
[73] *Yorkshire Evening Post*, 29 Jan. 1914.
[74] *Leeds Weekly Citizen*, 19 Dec. 1913.

The report concluded on an optimistic note: it predicted 'a decidedly better time' for the owners of working-class property, but urged 'the utmost caution' to those thinking of investing in middle-class housing where consumer resistance, improved transport facilities and fashionable caprice created uncertainties.[75]

Early in 1914 tenants in Burley received notice of an average weekly increase of about 6*d*. Several occupants refused to pay, and organized a petition bearing 300 to 400 signatures, asking for a reconsideration of the matter. The landlord declined to negotiate. The three ringleaders, residents of the same street, were then served with a week's notice. Others, deceived by an artful rent collector, promptly paid-up. However, Fred Patchett, one of the victimized trio, refused to submit without a struggle. Notwithstanding the inclement season he managed to organize a large demonstration in the neighbourhood—'a splendid crowd'—and in so doing rallied support for further resistance. 'There were seven circles in hell, so Dante said, and he would see them right in the middle of the seventh before he would pay this exorbitant demand.' Other residents spoke with less eloquence but equal determination. Although not present in an official capacity, R. M. Lancaster of the Trades Council offered encouragement. The trades council had, some weeks earlier, decided to take the initiative. A conference to consider the matter was to be convened the following week-end. The tenants would not fight alone. A collection of a guinea was taken. The tenants resolved to meet again the following week.[76]

There was a large attendance of trade unionists at the special meeting at the Leeds Trades Hall on Saturday 17 January. The president of the Trades Council occupied the chair. Conference seemed determined to check the property-owners' offensive. The militant tone of the proceedings owed something to the bitterness unleashed by the Corporation Strike which was then in its closing stages.[77] Mr B. Sullivan, of the Clothiers' Union, vowed to 'make the landlords of Leeds sorry for their policy during the past few years'. 'If we are determined', he added, 'they can do nothing in the matter. You will not find university students and middle class residents as strike breakers to pay rent for your little houses.' John

[75] *Leeds Weekly Citizen*, 2 Jan. 1914.

[76] Minutes of Leeds Trades Council, 31 Dec. 1913; *Leeds Weekly Citizen*, 16 Jan. 1914.

[77] On this, see J. E. Williams, 'The Leeds Corporation Strike in 1913', in Asa Briggs and John Saville, ed., *Essays in Labour History, 1886-1923* (1971), pp. 70-95.

Lake's customary optimism was shared by Mr Owen Conellan who told the cheering delegates: 'We will fight, if need be, until the flames of Hades freeze, and after that we will continue the way on the ice.' The stirring language indicated the absence of any considered policy. Although keen to brandish the mailed fist, prudence compelled consideration of the kinds of preparation which might have to be made to protect the dependents of defiant tenants during the bread-winners term of imprisonment! A delegate from the Armley and Wortley branch of the BSP urged caution: 'In the law of landlord and tenant', he said, 'the landlord had it every time.' He suggested that a committee be appointed to bring before an adjourned meeting a comprehensive plan of campaign. It was also resolved to ask the landlords to receive a deputation to negotiate a settlement.[78] A Tenants' Defence League had, at any rate been formed, in spite of the uncertainties which characterized its birth.

The next two months saw the growth of extensive support throughout the city. Branches were established in Burley, West Hunslet, Harehills; in the less prosperous districts—Wortley, Holbeck, and East Leeds, and in the central North East Ward. At the end of January 'the whole city' was said to be 'up in arms'. Steps had been taken to obtain 'the best legal advice'; Burley landlords were said to have capitulated.[79] Women were in the vanguard. 'The women, it is said, are marching about the streets brandishing pokers, rolling pins, and toasting forks, to show that they intend to protect their homes.'[80] Open-air meetings drew attendances said to number in the hundreds, and on one occasion at least 2,000 people were thought to have been in attendance.[81] However, the actual number of rent-strikers remained a subject of contention. The secretary of the Property Owners' Association, which controlled 30,000 tenancies, stated that there were only six objectors among the 10,000 who had so far been notified of the higher rents.[82] Sylvia Pankhurst, who had adopted the slogan 'No Vote, No Rent' in furtherance of the suffragette campaign, claimed that there were 1,000 families on strike against the landlords.[83] Claim and counter-claim were advanced as to the solidarity of the tenants.[84] The concern to undermine

[78] *Leeds Weekly Citizen*, 23 Jan. 1914.
[79] *Leeds Weekly Citizen*, 30 Jan. 1914 and 6 Feb 1914; Minutes of Leeds Trades Council, 28 Jan. 1914.
[80] *Woman's Dreadnought*, 8 Mar. 1914.   [81] *Leeds Weekly Citizen*, 23 Jan. 1914.
[82] *Leeds Weekly Citizen*, 20 Feb. 1914.   [83] *Woman's Dreadnought*, 8 Mar. 1914.
[84] Cf. *Yorkshire Evening Post*, 9 Feb. 1914 and *Leeds Weekly Citizen*, 20 Feb. 1914.

its support was taken by the Tenants' Defence League as positive proof that the campaign was beginning to bite. None the less, such allegations did create a sense of unease. Repeated canvasses were undertaken for mutual reassurance. In Burley where 'hundreds of notices to quit' had been served at the beginning of February,[85] the poll disclosed a sharp decline in support. Burley was the stronghold of the movement, but by the fifth week there were only 150-60 of the original 280-90 tenants who were still on strike. Patchett tried to apply a Darwinian gloss:

Those of the tenants who have paid the increase have done so because they have been intimidated, threatened and bullied by these shining lights of the Nonconformist movement. Men who, I have no doubt, cheerfully do the knee drill on Sunday, and the rest of the week worship the commercial Gods of Rent, Interest and Profit, and have about as much regard for the tenants' welfare as a cat has for its ancestry.

But we have left to us in the fight men and women of sterner stuff than those who have paid.

The militants took heart from reports that similar resistance was in progress in Liverpool, Glasgow, and Edmonton. But at the same time, a solicitor was retained to represent their interests in the Leeds County Court where, it was already acknowledged, the outcome of the strike would be decided.[86]

It had been hoped to avoid litigation. However, negotiations proved abortive. In Burley the property-owners promised no victimization but refused to rescind the increased rents. The terms were rejected.[87] The dictatorial manner adopted in the course of negotiation seemed to add insult to injury. 'Deputations who waited upon them', said one irate tenant, 'were told to go home and enjoy their Irish stew, and if they could not pay the increased rents to get into the slums.'[88] The shadow of the slums indeed hung heavy over the strikers. Many said they would die rather than occupy one of the vacant houses in the city centre. 'Some of them', Fred Patchett told one meeting, 'are in such a condition that the cats won't court in the basement (Laughter). I would not be paid 10*s*. a week to live in one of them.'[89] Those under notice to quit were all eminently respectable. In Burley all had long been resident in the area, and none were

[85] *Leeds Weekly Citizen*, 6 Feb. 1914.
[86] *Yorkshire Factory Times*, 12 Feb. 1914; *Leeds Weekly Citizen*, 13 Feb. 1914.
[87] *Leeds Weekly Citizen*, 30 Jan. 1914.
[88] *Leeds Weekly Citizen*, 27 Feb. 1914.   [89] *Yorkshire Factory Times*, 5 Feb. 1914.

previously in arrears. It was thought fit to remind the landlords that they were 'a superior class of tenants.... People who throughout their lives had been held down by toil, had paid regularly for twelve and even twenty years, and now were to be rewarded by the demand for an extra sixpence.'[90] Tenants felt they were being treated in a manner more appropriate to the lumpenproletariat. 'The ejectment laws', one of them declared, 'were passed solely for the purpose of dealing with undesirable tenants of criminal tendencies who annoyed neighbours and depreciated property.'[91] They were encouraged in this belief by inept legal advisers who elevated respectability to a point of law. It was the opinion of their solicitors that:

the statute in question was never intended to be used to assist landlords to coerce their tenants into submission to an increase of rent at a time when they have to choose between acquiescence in a demand, however unreasonable, on the one hand or ejectment on the other, but that the object of the legislation in question was to deal with recalcitrant and undesirable tenants, and that, in practice, it has in the past been used only to provide an inexpensive machinery for getting rid of this class of tenant.[92]

Not everyone shared this optimism. From the outset the *Leeds Weekly Citizen* had tried to direct the campaign towards the continuing struggle for municipal housing. It had few illusions as to the outcome of a direct clash with the local property owners. 'The landlords are also to a large extent lawlords', ran one editorial. 'They therefore become a small but very formidable company to resist.' The tenants' spirited defiance was admirable: 'They will find the real remedy, however, in other directions.'[93] The Tenants' Defence League had not in fact neglected the housing dimension and both the Corporation and the Local Government Board had been petitioned to this end. The *Citizen's* intransigent tone, however, pulled the tenants in one direction while its formal proposals pushed them in another. In this it reflected the indecision of the local labour movement.[94] The adjourned conference to formulate a plan of campaign had still to be reconvened when, early in March, the critical test cases were taken before Judge Greenhow in the Leeds County Court. The proceedings aroused considerable interest. The Tenants' Defence League was accused by the plaintiff of endeavouring 'to make the whole relationship between landlord and

[90] *Leeds Weekly Citizen*, 30 Jan. 1914.   [91] *Leeds Weekly Citizen*, 27 Feb. 1914.
[92] *Leeds Weekly Citizen*, 6 Feb. 1914.   [93] *Leeds Weekly Citizen*, 23 Jan. 1914.
[94] Minutes of Leeds Trades Council, 11 Feb. 1914.

tenant into one of class against class'. The Property Owners' Association was charged with operating 'a system of terrorism'. His Honour sympathized with the tenants but found for the landlords: possession orders were postponed for one month.[95]

The strike collapsed. The Tenants' Defence League tried to secure the best terms possible for the few who still held out and were threatened with eviction.[96] The flag was finally hauled down a month later when the campaign for municipal housing met with a decisive rebuff from the Corporation.[97] Mopping-up was all that remained; five days before the outbreak of war the Trades Council heard an appeal on behalf of tenants who were still being victimised for their activities in the previous winter.[98] Leeds played no part in the subsequent agitation for rent control.[99]

[95] *Yorkshire Post*, 26 Mar. 1914; *Leeds Weekly Citizen*, 6 Mar. 1914; *Yorkshire Factory Times*, 5 Mar. 1914.

[96] *Leeds Weekly Citizen*, 6 and 13 Mar. 1914.

[97] *Leeds Weekly Citizen*, 8 May 1914.

[98] Minutes of Leeds Trades Council, 29 July 1914.

[99] A week before the introduction of the Rent Bill in the House of Commons, it was proposed that the labour movement 'take up the whole matter at once'. Minutes of Leeds Labour Representation Committee, 17 Nov. 1915.

8

Scotland
The Missive Question

Socialism in Scotland had experienced a slow and rather erratic growth since the banner was first raised in Glasgow in 1884. The preserve of a handful of enthusiasts, its expansion aroused little interest in the city until the turn of the century. The formation of a Citizens' Union in 1902 in response to the growing politicization of local administration was indicative of the stealthy advance of the Workers' Municipal Election Committee in the seven years since its foundation.[1] Clydeside was still far from 'Red' but the challenge of socialism could no longer be discounted.[2] The Labour Party would not capture outright control of the Corporation until the early 1930s, but long before then it had made its presence felt at George Square. From the outset housing reform constituted an important plank in its programme. Indeed, its eventual triumph in both parliamentary and municipal contests derived to a considerable degree from the vigorous prosecution of the housing campaign in the years preceeding.[3] So much is relatively familiar. The focus of existing research, however, conceals much that is of interest and relevance to the student of tenants' associations.

The function of the Municipal Housing Commission, appointed in 1902, was not to resolve the mounting crisis but to curb the seemingly boundless ambitions of the City Improvement Trust. In this it gave satisfaction.[4] Throughout 1902 the city was absorbed by the outcry against the proposed extension of the Trust's borrowing powers. In

[1] For an outline account of these developments, see W. H. Marwick, *A Short History of Labour in Scotland* (Edinburgh, 1967), pp. 68 ff.

[2] Cf. 'Sunday Socialism in Glasgow', *Glasgow Herald*, 9 Oct. 1907.

[3] R. K. Middlemas, *The Clydesiders* (1965), p. 19 and passim; Iain Maclean, 'The Labour Movement in Clydeside Politics 1914-1924' (University of Oxford Unpublished D. Phil. thesis, 1971), Ch. xiii.

[4] *Glasgow Herald*, 14 July 1904. On the operation of the Improvement Trust, see C. M. Allan, 'The Genesis of British Urban Redevelopment with special reference to Glasgow', *Economic History Review* 2nd. Ser. XVIII (1965), pp. 598-613.

the summer the labour movement mounted one of the most impressive prewar demonstrations seen in Glasgow. It was said that 20,000 people had joined together to signify their support for municipal housing and protest against the Taff Vale decision.[5] Although Lord Provost Chisholm's surprising defeat in the municipal elections in November was commonly ascribed to the strength of feeling which the Trust aroused, the setback experienced by the municipal reformers was far from complete. Labour candidates were returned in seven of the thirteen wards in which contests took place; the Citizens' Union was easily trounced.[6] There was mileage in housing reform.

The report of the Municipal Housing Commission, published in 1904, signified the intellectual bankruptcy of this, the most advanced municipality. After an exhaustive inquiry, it was concluded that nothing beyond the continuation of current policies was required. However, there was one major recommendation. In the previous year the Citizens' Union modified its root-and-branch opposition to municipal enterprise. A spokesman told the annual meeting that, 'it was the duty of the city to give every possible encouragement to private enterprise to overtake the housing question, reserving and restricting themselves to dealing with the lowest section of the poor, who required to be looked after just in the same way as criminals and lunatics or such like (Applause)'.[7] The Municipal Commission accepted this advice, almost to the letter.[8] Thereafter progress depended upon the persistence and imagination of the Glasgow Labour Party: its refusal to bow before the shibboleths of vulgar political economy and its Single Tax or marginalist variants.

Housing reform continued to receive priority in the programme of the Workers' Municipal Election Committee.[9] This politically broadly-based body at first represented all sections of the labour and socialist movements. But it was weakened by the defection of the SDF and the Irish Nationalists. The loss of the latter proved fatal and, as Dr Maclean has shown convincingly, did much to retard the growth of the Labour vote.[10] It was absorbed by the

[5] *Glasgow Herald*, 22 Sept. 1902.

[6] *Glasgow Herald*, 5 Nov. 1902.

[7] *Glasgow Herald*, 4 Feb. 1903.

[8] *Report and Recommendations of Glasgow Municipal Commission on the Housing of the Poor* (Glasgow, 1904), para. xiii.

[9] *Forward*, 24 Aug. 1907.

[10] Maclean, 'The Labour Movement in Clydeside Politics', Ch. xiv.

Glasgow Labour Party which, since its formation in 1908, consistently harried the local authority: its failure to adopt a positive building programme, the lavish use of compensation that rewarded rather than penalized slum-owners; and the inadequate enforcement of public health and sanitary regulations.[11] But the financial dimension of the housing question had not been satisfactorily resolved. Working-class housing reformers foresaw and did not flinch from the astronomical expense that was required for the realization of their programme. 'It would run into hundreds of millions, if not thousands of millions', Wheatley told the Royal Commisson on Housing.[12] Parliament alone could sanction expenditure of this magnitude, and the Glasgow Labour Party was in the vanguard of those calling for interest-free loans to the local authorities.[13] Hitherto, however, the Scottish labour movement had looked to the land reformers who had been so influential in its formative stages, for the principal source of finance.[14] Until 1913 progress in Glasgow waited on the maturation of opinion in Westminster. In that year Councillor Wheatley unfolded a bold and politically attractive scheme which at once become a source of controversy both within and beyond the labour movement.

Briefly, Wheatley proposed to finance the construction of low-density suburban housing out of the surplus profits of the tramway system. Wheatley argued that, having eliminated the crippling interest charges on the capital cost, his cottages could be self-financing at the wonderfully low annual rental of £8. [15] Orthodoxy demanded that such funds be devoted to rate relief. This was predictable. But Wheatley's proposals also drew the wrath of the unorthodox. Geddes, for example, thought it misconceived.[16] The Glasgow Fabian Society too was opposed.

The indirect use of subsidies in this manner, it was suggested, was inefficient, unjust, and at variance with the 'national minimum' to which its members were, of course, committed. The housing scheme was roundly condemned as a form of 'municipal philanthrophy' that

[11] *Forward*, 29 Mar. 1913.

[12] *Royal Commission on the Housing of the Industrial Population of Scotland, Minutes of Evidence*, 4 Vols. HMSO, (Edinburgh, 1921), q. 22594.

[13] *R.C. Housing in Scotland*, q. 22535.

[14] On the influence of land reformers upon the housing policy of the Workers' Municipal Election Committee, see Memorandum and evidence of John Ferguson, *R.C. Local Taxation* (PP 1899, XXXVI), app. xxii, qq. 16821-985.

[15] John Wheatley, *£8 Cottages for Glasgow Workers* (Glasgow, 1913).

[16] Patrick Geddes, *Cities in Evolution* (1915), p. 158.

was best left to the Liberals and Tories.[17] Sidney Webb was invited to adjudicate. 'Economic rent', he argued, ought to be devoted to an object of common good; and the housing scheme, designed for the private advantage of the few, did not come within that category. Webb's contribution received a respectful airing in *Forward*—and was promptly discarded.[18]

Within the ILP there was a long-standing aversion to the traditional tenement.[19] It was not so much the form of provision as the prospect of immediate action that was so compelling. The tramway surplus was sufficient to provide 1,000 houses per annum. When taxed with the discrepancy between the rate of construction and the outstanding requirements (there were 10,000 uninhabitable houses in need of immediate closure), Bailie James Steward replied that it was better than the inaction or vagaries of the critics: 'the prospect of getting 1,000 decent houses a year or something like that, seems to us like paradise'.[20] Wheatley made much the same point. 'We simply put before you that which we think would be the beginning of a drastic housing reform', he told a sceptical Royal Commission, 'But how it would develop is beyond our power to estimate at present. Certainly it would have a revolutionary effect on the whole basis of the housing question.'[21]

It was with the generation of this 'revolutionary effect' that the housing reformers were most concerned. The truth of the matter was that the £8 cottage scheme was a vote-winner. Wheatley asserted that the use of the tramway surplus was a key issue in the municipal elections of 1913 and that almost every candidate who voted for rate reductions lost their seats. 'Among the working class generally, the feeling is very strongly against it being put to a reduction of the rates.'[22] The 50,000 copies of Wheatley's pamphlet that were distributed during the election were thought to have brought about a result that was considered 'exceedingly satisfactory'.[23] On the eve of war the Labour Party had seventeen councillors, and was still growing. If the £8 cottage scheme would not solve the housing problem, it would certainly help to accelerate the election of those

[17] Correspondence of William Gillies, *Forward*, 18 Oct. and 1 Nov. 1913.
[18] *Forward*, 13 Dec. 1913.
[19] On this, see evidence of Joseph Burgess, *GMC*, pp. 254 ff.
[20] *R.C. Housing in Scotland*, q. 22615.
[21] *R.C. Housing in Scotland*, q. 22620.
[22] *R.C. Housing in Scotland*, q. 22542.
[23] *Forward*, 27 June 1914.

who, more than any one else, were determined to do so; and that was sufficient justification. The campaign continued. A Housing Committee convened by Andrew M'Bride was established to provide co-ordination. Its members included Wheatley and James Stewart, who had 'in large measure' conceived the scheme.[24] It was further agreed that a petition bearing 100,000 signatures should be organized and ready for presentation to the Town Council in time for the local elections of November 1914.[25] The initial results seemed encouraging.

In Glasgow where landlord tenant relations were always tense, it was understood that any scheme which did not hold out the prospect of greater protection against extortionate rents would not arouse popular enthusiasm. Although precise data are not readily available, it has already been shown that sequestration and eviction was a serious problem for working-class tenants in industrial Scotland. 'Rachmanism' was a fact long before the term was coined. But it was also suggested that it was the poor, rather than the respectable tradesmen who formed the backbone of the labour movement, who were most prone to be evicted. In Glasgow high rents rather than security of tenure provided the greater cause for concern. The formation of a local fair rent court, which had earlier been approved by the Trades Council on recommendation of the Workers' Municipal Election Committee,[26] became an important plank in the Labour Party's platform. In 1913 a motion to this effect, introduced by Councillor Hugh Lyon, was lost in the Town Council by a single vote.[27] However, the Glasgow Labour Party was not the sole source of tenant initiative.

II

The origins of the peculiarly restrictive house-letting system in Scotland are obscure. In pre-industrial Britain houses appear to have been let by the year, rent being paid half-yearly or on the four quarter days. It was a convenient form of tenure in a relatively stable population where 'cottage economy' was practised widely. But with the advent of industrial capitalism, the transformation of urban land values, disappearance of gardens, and the emergence of a highly mobile labour force, English landlords and tenants found

---

[24] *Forward*, 8 Nov. 1913.   [25] *Forward*, 10 Jan. 1914.
[26] *Glasgow Herald*, 15 Oct. 1903.   [27] *Glasgow Herald*, 25 Apr. 1913.

the weekly let a more suitable arrangement. In Scotland, however, where industrialization came later, the use of short lets did not become widespread except in old and inferior properties, chiefly one-roomed apartments. In Glasgow these formed an ever diminishing fraction of the city's housing stock.[28] The very worst of them, rented at less than £5 per annum, and let by the month or week, housed a transitory population whose vicious and destructive propensities were, it was claimed, a principal cause of the cessation in the building of that type of property. Others by contrast emphasized rising building costs and a general loss of confidence amongst builders arising out of the expectation of extensive municipal intervention.[29] Whatever the reason, it is clear that an increasing number of working people were occupying houses of a higher rental. Of dwellings between £5 and £10, 60 to 90 per cent were on yearly lets. Above £10 practically all houses were let by the year, and, with the exception of company housing, about 80 per cent of all working-class houses in Scotland were so let, rents being paid monthly, quarterly or half-yearly.[30]

A second peculiarity of the Scottish system was the insistence that yearly tenants enter into a written agreement or 'missive'. In England and Wales removals took place all the year round; in Scotland removal terms had, ever since the late seventeenth century, been limited by statute. The system was less than satisfactory. In 1881, and again five years later, Parliament was forced to intervene. Under the Terms Removal Act, 1886 removal terms were restricted to Whit Sunday (defined as 28 May) and Martinmas. But in practice removals in urban areas were, as heretofore, confined to Whit Sunday. Term day was in consequence characterized by inordinate expense, apprehension, and congestion. The building trades suffered a brief spell of intensive work followed by a corresponding period of idleness; removal vans were at a premium; workmen were everywhere and nowhere. Tradesmen worked furiously in the course of the preceding month in order to make new houses ready for the incoming tenants: masons, joiners, plasterers, plumbers, and painters vied for space in which to complete their allotted tasks; work was

[28] John Butt, 'Working Class Housing in Glasgow, 1815-1914', in S. D. Chapman, ed., *The History of Working Class Housing* (Newton Abbot), p. 71.

[29] *Report of Glasgow Municipal Commission on the Housing of the Poor* (Glasgow, 1904), p. 15.

[30] *Report of Departmental Committee on House-Letting in Scotland* (PP 1907, XXXVI), p. 3.

scamped; chaos reigned supreme. In the older (often insanitary) properties essential repairs were not to be had until after the new tenant had taken up occupation. 'It is quite common for people to bundle all their furniture into one room, and live themselves like pigs almost for six weeks because they cannot get their walls whitened and cleaned' said one irate working man.[31]. Moreover, as a result of the annual scramble for the best houses and the most reliable tenants, the period of the occupier's liability had been so extended that in effect the *yearly* tenant found him or herself bound for *sixteen* months.

The stampede began early in the year. In January the factors enquired whether sitting tenants were to retake their houses from 28 May, and insisted upon a reply on or before 2 February. In the absence of such reply, the factor reserved the right to relet at will. Working-class wives appeared panic-stricken. 'When the letting season comes on, said the President of the Glasgow Trades Council, 'there seems to be a fever among the women.'[32] There was no time to lose. People feared to be left out in the cold; they were told they must take or want.[33] The advantage rested almost exclusively with the landlords. It not only minimized the cost of administration, but also reduced competition and thereby held down maintenance costs. Scottish landlords, unlike their English counterparts, had less often to repair and decorate their properties in order to satisfy the fastidious artisan who was otherwise the most desirable of tenants.[34]

Reform was also discouraged by the peculiarities of Scottish rating and valuation.[35] When compared with the English system, Scots practice was far more restrictive in the scope of compounding and considerably less generous in the abatements permitted. Furthermore, local taxation in Scotland was not based upon 'rateable value' with the result that in England assessments were levied upon roughly two thirds of the sum paid by the tenant to the landlord instead of the full amount as in Scotland. It was not the only disincentive, however.

Short lets implied the demise of annual rate collections and a corresponding extension of compounding. Scottish property owners

[31] *Departmental Committee on House-Letting in Scotland, Minutes of Evidence* (PP 1908, XLVII), q. 1614.
[32] *House-Letting in Scotland* (1908), q. 1589.
[33] *Glasgow Herald*, 30 Jan. 1894.
[34] SRO DD. 6/547-8; *House-Letting in Scotland* (1908), q. 1351.
[35] On this, see *House-Letting in Scotland* (1907), pp. 4-6.

were opposed to both. Landlords would become liable for the rates of defaulters. The personal payment of rates, it was also argued, fostered the growth of popular civic pride whereas indirect payment was calculated to increase 'irresponsible voting' and to intensify pre-existent antagonisms between landlord and tenant. Experience showed that tenants tended erroneously to assimilate rates and rents and thereafter to regard increased weekly payments brought about through municipal extravagance as yet another attempt on the part of unscrupulous landlords to extort higher rents. An official of the Glasgow Landlords' Association claimed that, if compounding became widespread, 'there would be a good deal of odium cast on the landlord and it would be made use of at the municipal elections of Parish Council elections.'[36] Moreover, it would enfranchise defaulters and those exempt from payment on grounds of poverty who previously were automatically disqualified as voters.

The growing predominance of the two and three-roomed apartments in Glasgow meant that working people were occupying better accommodation than their predecessors; it also meant that classes hitherto unaffected by the restrictive house-letting system were progressively coming within its ambit. It is a minor irony that in Glasgow of all places there persisted, in the guise of an archaic form of house tenure, one of those artificial obstacles to the perfect mobility of labour condemned repeatedly by Adam Smith and his disciples; and one moreover, that was not to be finally removed until after the Great War. The difficulty was particularly acute on Clydeside. Compared with Edinburgh, Aberdeen, or Dundee, the industries in and around Glasgow were so situated that change of employment frequently entailed a change of residence. Especially was this true of shipbuilding, in which technological innovation and the application of 'hustling methods' to the labour process led to an improvement in the rapidity of job-completion.[37] In the words of the Departmental Committee of 1906: 'The same class, therefore, who formerly got monthly lets for the cheaper houses are now compelled to take yearly lets, although their employment remains as shifting as before.'[38] The Committee reckoned that the 'great majority' of occupations in and around the Clyde district necessitated frequent removal, although this is difficult to measure with any

[36] *House-Letting in Scotland* (1908), qq. 1085, 1087, 1089.
[37] *House-Letting in Scotland* (1908), q. 3772.
[38] *House-Letting in Scotland* (1907), p. 14.

accuracy. The numbers affected by the proposed conversion of yearly lets is, however, more certain. In 1905/6 they numbered some 124,265 tenancies or more than 70 per cent of all tenancies in Glasgow.[39]

Where removal between terms was unavoidable the tenant might be faced with the prospect of having to pay double rent—the balance of rent for the premises left and the rent of the premises taken. Not surprisingly the heavy outlay deterred all but the bravest or most desperate. Although a source of continuous complaint amongst tenants, the Departmental Committee found only 2-3 per cent of removals between terms and concluded that the monetary loss to the working class was therefore slight. However, the more usual course in this situation was for the outgoing tenant to obtain another occupant; and for the privilege of subletting the factor charged a 'relatively substantial' 5 per cent on either the whole or the unpaid rent.[40] When a substitute could not be found, always difficult when there were a large number of empties on the market, the outgoing tenant faced real privation. But the comparative infrequency of removal between terms does not exhaust the matter. Rather than move house and home, the bread-winner was often compelled to deny himself the company of family and friends and take lodgings or, where possible, to endure the expense and delay of commuting to and from the outlying districts. In either case it implied extra expenditure which few could afford. To what extent the house-letting system depressed living standards cannot be adequately assessed, but there must have been many who refused better employment because of it.

The absence of freedom of contract with respect to the duration of tenure together with the compulsion to contract four months before the term of entry, known collectively as 'the missive system', involved considerable hardship. 'That expression', an official inquiry observed, 'has become a familiar one in recent years in connection with municipal and parliamentary contests especially in Glasgow and the Clyde district.'[41] The reform of the house-letting system rather than housing provision or high rents provided the background against which the earliest tenants' associations emerged.

The Scottish Federation of Tenants' Association was formed in

[39] *House-Letting in Scotland* (1907), pp. 3, 13.
[40] *House-Letting in Scotland* (1907), pp. 13-14.
[41] *House-Letting in Scotland* (1907), p. 6.

the autumn of 1912.[42] The twenty-three delegates who attended the inaugural meeting represented affiliates drawn from the West of Scotland. These were small but by no means negligible bodies. Paisley Tenants' Defence Association, for example, had an annual income of £73; Clydebank Tenants' Association possessed £57.[43] With its 622 subscribers, Paisley Tenants' Defence Association had a membership slightly in excess of the Pollokshaws Tenants' Defence League. Both were dwarfed by the 1,000-strong Clydebank Association.[44] These formalities are not the sole criterion of their representativeness. In 1906 the secretary of the Glasgow Tenants' Protective Association which had been formed five years earlier, explained: 'Our paying membership is over a thousand, but we get people at public meetings to come and support us, and unanimously pass resolutions by the thousand'. These working-class tenants were 'quite unanimous—red hot'.[45]

The Scottish Federation of Tenants' Associations represented the culmination of almost thirty years of intermittent agitation for the reform of the house-letting system. Hitherto tenants' associations came and went with bewildering rapidity. Indeed, the very frequency of their sporadic efforts was sufficient to undermine the credibility of the organizers. 'These weekly annuals, the Tenants' Defence Associations, are in evidence again', a socialist critic remarked in 1895, 'but their fleeting display is too short-lived to raise even hope.'[46] A few formed at the turn of the century managed to maintain a continuous existence, but in the main it proved exceedingly difficult to consolidate membership once the initial enthusiasm had subsided. 'The difficulty in getting associations of that kind', said Hugh Lyon, President of the Glasgow Tenants' Protective Association, 'is that it is only one grievance that has an effect on people, and it affects them acutely at one time of the year, when they sign the missive, but that is the only time you can get enthusiasm raised. Of course it is affecting them all the year round, but it is when they come to sign the missive that they feel it. So it is diffiuclt to keep them up against it.'[47] But the issue would not die. 'I cannot

[42] *Justice*, 12 Oct. 1912.

[43] *Paisley & Renfrewshire Gazette*, 20 Feb. 1915; *Clydebank & Renfrew Press*, 5 Feb. 1915.

[44] *House-Letting in Scotland* (1908), q. 561; *Pollokshaws News*, 14 June 1912; *Clydebank & Renfrew Press*, 13 Feb. 1914.

[45] *House-Letting in Scotland* (1908), qq. 3576-8, 3580.

[46] *Clarion*, 9 Feb. 1895.

[47] *House-Letting in Scotland* (1908), q. 3717.

recollect the time when it has not been before us', said George
Carson, Secretary of the Glasgow Trades Council. 'It has always
been a standing question in Glasgow.'[48] Carson's intervention was
symptomatic of the close association between the organized tenants
and the labour movement. They were kith and kin. Although it was
not a primary interest, the tenants' associations often campaigned
for municipal housing in addition to a more generalized concern for
their members welfare.[49] In 1888 the Glasgow Trades Council had
itself sponsored one of the earliest of the several associations that
were formed in these years. Fifteen years later it again took the lead
in the formation of the Glasgow Tenants' Protective Associations.[50]
In Paisley too it was the Trades Council which took the initiative
that resulted in the foundation of a tenants' association.[51] This
intimacy was at times considered unhealthy. Some trade unionists
felt that union business was neglected by officials who devoted too
much attention to the tenants' movement.[52] But on the whole it was
an amicable relation. The Scottish Trades Union Congress supported
the reform of the missive system.[53]

In the fifteen years which preceded the appointment of the Departmental Committee on House-Letting in Scotland, 1906, amending
legislation had been proposed and rejected on at least nine separate
occasions.[54] This snail-like pace represents something more than
Westminster's traditional indifference to Scottish affairs. The reformers were, in the first place, weak and divided. Overwhelmed by
its mounting complexities and depressed by the intransigence of the
Glasgow Landlords' Association, A. D. Provand quit the campaign
after four years. At a conference of trade unionists convened early
in 1894, Provand announced his intention to introduce a bill for the
abolition of hypothec on the grounds that it was this extraordinary
form of protection which preserved the system of yearly tenures.[55]
It was a transparently fallacious argument. Alexander Cross,

---

[48] *House-Letting in Scotland* (1908), qq. 1513, 1522.
[49] See, for example, *Clydebank & Renfrew Press*, 11 Mar. 1899; *House-Letting in
Scotland* (1908), qq. 582, 588.
[50] *House-Letting in Scotland* (1908), q. 1513; Minutes of Glasgow Trades Council,
4, 25 Mar. and 13 May 1903; *Glasgow Herald*, 11 and 12 June 1903.
[51] *House-Letting in Scotland* (1908), q. 560.
[52] Angela Tuckett, *The Scottish Carter, The History of the Scottish Horse and
Motormens' Association, 1898-1914* (1967), p. 85.
[53] *Report of Second Annual Scottish Trades Union Congress* (1898), p. 42.
[54] *House-Letting in Scotland* (1907), pp. 21-2.
[55] *House-Letting in Scotland* (1908), qq. 747, 758-63, 774-5. See too letter of
Provand, *Glasgow Herald*, 30 Nov. 1906.

Unionist Member for Bridgeton, who led the campaign thereafter, was also too easily convinced that anything beyond the reduction of the missive term was impractical. The Convention of Burghs too, supported reform of the missive system but not the introduction of compounding.[56] The labour movement, however, continued to demand outright abolition. The Glasgow Trades Council supported the principle but not the detail of Cross's numerous initiatives; at ministerial meetings these differences were apparent.[57] Moreover, in spite of long years of co-operation, Cross was never fully able to persuade the labour people that his sympathies were other than instrumental in determination.[58] Indeed, the bipartisan character of the campaign constituted a principal cause of retardation. Campaigns of this nature are not necessarily advanced when separated from the ritual passions aroused by inter-party rivalry. The struggle for the reform of the missive system, like the history of housing reform, can be read in this light. After fifteen years there was scarcely a Member for an industrial borough who did not subscribe to reform.[59] However, its position on the parliamentary agenda had not, in consequence, been rendered any the less problematical.

The reformers were confronted by adversaries who were no less tenacious and a good deal more resourceful. The opposition was led by the Glasgow Landlords' Association to which organized property owners throughout industrial Scotland looked for strength and guidance. Several (often contradictory) forms of vilification were employed to undermine the tenant's position. The agitation was at first dismissed as the work of 'a very small but noisy section who had stirred up the matter in this city and elsewhere'.[60] This unrepresentative and fanatical minority, it transpired, was hell-bent upon the abrogation of all freedom of contract and the indefinite extension of municipal socialism. In view of the fact that their ranks included Glasgow's Conservative and Liberal Unionist MPs, this argument was difficult to sustain. The Departmental Committee rejected it out of hand.[61] On reflection, the troublesome minority was found to reside amongst the disgruntled Sassenachs who, it was suggested,

---

[56] 'Memorandum by the Parliamentary Committee of the Convention of Royal Burghs on the House-Letting and Rating Bill', (SRO DD. 6/540 File 9343/237).
[57] *Glasgow Herald*, 1 Nov. 1893; *House-Letting in Scotland* (1908), q. 1633.
[58] Cf. *Glasgow Herald*, 30 Sept. 1909.
[59] *House-Letting in Scotland* (1908), qq. 1649-52.
[60] *Glasgow Herald*, 26 Apr. 1894.
[61] *House-Letting in Scotland* (1907), p. 4.

exercised a disruptive influence on the otherwise pliant Scots working man. This too was without foundation. It was the case that migrant English workers participated in the campaign. They had 'naturally drifted into it', the President of the Glasgow Tenants' Protective Association explained, 'because they feel it, perhaps, in a different degree from what the Scotsman does. They look upon it as a perfect outrage.'[62] But he firmly denied any suggestion that the English were the instigators. His opinion was backed up by officials from other tenants' associations, and the Departmental Committee was unable to refute it.[63] This attempt to exacerbate nationalist sentiment, if that is what it was, fell flat. There were, however, other forms of differentiation within the working class which could be exploited.

Short lets entailed extra administration and therefore higher rents; they also had a dangerous levelling tendency. The occupants of weekly and monthly lets were drawn from the semi-criminal elements, drunks, casual labourers, brothel-keepers, and so forth— noxious persons from whom the respectable tradesman shrank in horror and disgust. George Carson of the Glasgow Trades Council, himself a sheet-metal worker, explained: 'I would say that the best of people live in yearly houses. There is a certain amount of stigma attached to a monthly house at present, and our people are generally above that.'[64] 'It is the yearly tenants that are agitating for reform, and the most respectable among them', said the secretary of the Paisley Tenants' Association.[65] The social basis of such bodies was evident in their perfunctory interest in the plight of the evicted and in their readiness to concede the landlords' claim to a summary right of ejectment. The Glasgow Association, for example, approved of summary proceedings against objectionable tenants.[66] The Glasgow Trades Council thought that the 48 hours' notice, for which most landlords campaigned, was too short a period, but it did not challenge the power to evict. 'We are not here to defend bad tenants', Carson told the Departmental Committee.[67] Landlords regarded these prejudices as a useful source of leverage. Amongst

[62]   *House-Letting in Scotland* (1908), q. 3587.
[63]   *House-Letting in Scotland* (1907), p. 4.
[64]   *House-Letting in Scotland* (1908), q. 1530.
[65]   *House-Letting in Scotland* (1908), q. 649.
[66]   *House-Letting in Scotland* (1908), q. 3751.
[67]   *House-Letting in Scotland* (1908), qq. 1659-62; and see too Tenants' Defence Associations of Scotland, *Explanatory Notes on the House-Letting and Rating (Scotland) Act, 1911*, by Alexander Cross (Glasgow, 1912), p. 27.

those who gave evidence before the Departmental Committee were three working men, who, it was claimed, had been specifically briefed for this purpose.[68]

Although landlord and tenants were the principal contestants, the local authority could not stand aside from the struggle. In February 1903 Glasgow Corporation threw its weight behind the tenants movement. The Town Council resolved to employ its powers to secure an amendment to the law. The Corporation furnished evidence of its new resolve six months later with the abolition of missives on its own substantial properties.[69] However, it was a marriage of convenience: neither partner had much affection for the other.

The local authority was concerned to reduce extensive rate leakage. In 1905/6, an exceptionally good year, the irrecoverable assessment on rents of £4-10 in Glasgow amounted to 24 per cent. Above that level losses were negligible. Nearly 20,000 people were in consequence disfranchized, three quarters of them for non-payment of rates; the remainder were paupers or had been granted exemption.[70] In the previous seven years the annual loss on such rentals averaged 22 per cent. It was suggested that these losses could be substantially reduced if, following English practice, liability for the rates was transferred to the owners. Tenants would be better able and more willing to pay when rates were collected in small weekly instalments alongside the rent. Hitherto the annual collection of rates in the winter, when work was scarce and incomes depleted, acted as a positive inducement to seek exemption or, worse, to do a moonlight flit. English experience suggested that landlords became zealous rate collectors and that compounding was the cheapest and most efficient means of recovery. When pressed, spokesmen for the tenants' associations expressed a preference for this system, although their substantial members as a rule experienced little difficulty in meeting the assessor's annual precept (£2 on a £10 rental). It was in fact a secondary concern: for them the abolition of the missive lay at the heart of the matter. For its realization they were even willing to embrace those disreputable elements who had been disqualified for non-payment of rates. The Glasgow Tenants' Association, said Mr Baillie, its President, was 'all in favour of bringing these people on to the roll, and making them respectable whether they will or no'.[71]

[68] *Forward*, 2 Feb. 1907.
[69] *Glasgow Herald*, 6 Apr. 1904.
[70] *House-Letting in Scotland* (1907), p. 12.
[71] *House-Letting in Scotland* (1908), q. 3737.

The missive question figured prominently in industrial Scotland during the General Election of 1906, and all candidates were pledged to work for reform if returned.[72] These expectations were not disappointed. Representations from Scottish Members elicited a favourable response from the new Lord Advocate. His senior colleague, the Secretary of State for Scotland, was at first more luke-warm and refused to take over Cross's new bill.[73] But before long he relented, influenced, no doubt, by the growing campaign in its support that was sweeping across Scotland. 'I am inundated with resolutions from associations, trade and co-operative societies, in favour of the Bill', Cross wrote the Executive of the Paisley Tenants' Defence League. 'Many of these have sent copies to the Prime Minister and Scotch Secretary and have done much to educate public opinion.' His hyperactive correspondents were gratified, having themselves inspired the bulk of the petitions and resolutions with which the House of Commons was deluged.[74] In November, 1906, the Secretary for Scotland agreed to the formation of a departmental inquiry. An all-party group of twenty-three back-benchers met soon after and appointed a small steering committee to supervise the preparation of evidence.[75]

The seven-man departmental committee met under the chairmanship of Lord Guthrie, an eminent Scots lawyer. Its members also included Thomas Binnie, an authority on all matters pertaining to the sale and management of property, and John T. Howden of the Carpenters' and Joiners' Union, a distinguished trade unionist soon to be elected President of Glasgow Trades Council. Its report, published in August the following year, tried to strike a balance between the competing interests. It thus coupled a shortening of the period for the retaking of houses with the provision of adequate remuneration for landlords charged with the collection of rates together with an indemnity against defaulting tenants. And as an added boon the committee recommended that henceforth empty properties should not be rated. Similarly, the abolition of urban hypothec to the extent of £10 was offset by a recommendation in favour of the summary eviction of non-paying tenants after 48 hours' notice. Finally, it recommended that legislation should be adoptive rather than compulsory.[76]

[72] *Clydebank & Renfrew Press*, 20 July 1906.
[73] *Glasgow Herald*, 25 May and 26 June 1906.
[74] *Paisley Observer*, 25 May 1906.   [75] *Glasgow Herald*, 22 Nov. 1906.
[76] *House-Letting in Scotland* (1907), pp. 22-4.

The tenants' associations welcomed the report. The Government was urged to proceed with its own legislation or to grant facilities for the new measure put forward on behalf of the all-party group.[77] The Glasgow Trades Council, however, withheld support: it continued to press for amending legislation along the lines set out in Howden's Minority Report which argued for compulsory legislation, for the outright abolition of the missive system, and for statutory protection against the eviction during trades disputes for the tenants of company housing.[78]

The property owners by contrast found the Guthrie proposals unacceptable. But the writing was on the wall. The Glasgow Land-lords' Association renewed its call for a voluntary solution—a stale exercise in public relations which fooled no one. As a further token of its desire for an equitable settlement, the Landlords' Association went to the length of actually drafting fresh legislation. 'But', the annual meeting was informed, 'it was an actual fact, though it would scarcely be believed, that they could not get a single member of Parliament to interest himself in the bill or to introduce it into the House of Commons.' In addition, the directors had been engaged in intensive lobbying. 'The work', said the chairman, 'had undoubtedly been heavy, but it was absolutely necessary, ... and had not been without effect in quarters where a telling effect was needed.'[79] On publication of the Guthrie report, the Secretary of the Landlords' Association predicted 'a troubled and protracted' struggle ahead.[80] This proved to be the case. The campaign made no progress in Parliament until the case for reform was finally embodied in a Government measure in the spring of 1909.

The House Letting and Rating Bill met with an untimely death. Opposition to compounding in principle had all but been abandoned. 'The real point at issue', said the Surveyors' Institution, 'is in fixing the scale of allowances.' The proposed scale 'is not only inequitable but so low that, so far as Glasgow is concerned, it would mean a very serious loss to all owners of small houses'.[81] The measure was killed in the House of Lords. Lord Camperdown, who strongly dis-

[77] *Glasgow Herald*, 10 Feb. 1908.

[78] *Glasgow Herald*, 14 May 1908 and 24 June 1909; Memorandum by Joseph Dobbie and John T. Howden, *House-Letting in Scotland* (1907), p. 26.

[79] *Glasgow Herald*, 22 Jan. 1909.

[80] *Glasgow Herald*, 16 Nov. 1907.

[81] 'House Letting & Rating (Scotland) Bill, 1909', Memorandum by the Council of the Surveyors' Institution, *Scottish Supplement to Professional Notes*, XV (1908-9), pp. 43-6.

approved of the enfranchisement of non-ratepaying tenants, not only deleted the compounding provisions, but inserted a new clause which would have diminished Glasgow Corporation's rating powers. The Corporation pressed for the bill to be withdrawn; the Government was willing to oblige. Reform was postponed and the Glasgow Landlords' Asociation elated. The House of Lords, said its secretary, was the repository of 'truest statesmanship'. The tenants' associations already looked to the next General Election for redress.[82] Ministers were not perhaps displeased with the outcome. The struggle for the 'People's Budget' was beginning to move towards a climax, and any extra evidence of the Lords' disregard of the popular will would not come amiss.[83]

The House Letting and Rating Bill, reintroduced two years later, passed through both chambers without serious obstruction. But there was no jubilation on the Clyde.

III

The pre-existent division of rates between occupiers and owners gave rise to an endless source of friction, and landlords were wary of changes which threatened to accentuate these mutual antipathies. Tenants felt that they paid everything and the landlords nothing; that landlords in arrears received preferential treatment by the authorities while occupiers were sold up; that owners were absolved of costs on overdue taxes while tenants had to make prompt payment. These animosities were intensified by a Provisional Order submitted to parliament in 1909. This proposed to double the cost of the stair-lighting rate which was levied exclusively upon the occupiers, who were also called upon to pay the lion's share for the lighting of private streets. And the more it was scrutinized the more oppressive the division of local taxation appeared to be. Something had to be done. The Hutchesontown Branch of the ILP gave the lead. At a public protest meeting, George Barnes, the principal speaker, was mandated to oppose the measure in the House.[84] The offending clause was subsequently withdrawn, but resentment flared up again the following year when the Corporation renewed the affair.[85]

The operation of the House Letting and Rating Act which came

[82] *Glasgow Herald*, 2 Oct. 1909.   [83] Cf. *Glasgow Herald*, 4 Oct. 1909.
[84] *Forward*, 23 Jan. 1909.   [85] *Forward*, 19 Feb. 1910.

into force early in 1912, did nothing to relieve the tension. Tenants were convinced that it was the pretext for a concerted attempt at rent raising.[86] Defective arrangements for the combined collection of rates and rents acted as a positive incentive for landlords to overcharge the rates and pocket the extra. Property owners had always argued that the extra expense of more frequent collections and removals would, notwithstanding the commission obtained from the local authorities, inevitably result in higher rents, which, because of the abolition of hypothec, would henceforth have to be paid in advance. The attempt to impose these terms encountered immediate resistance.

In March 1912 the Scottish Council of the BSP issued a manifesto calling for the formation of tenants' defence associations in every town and city. These were encouraged to work closely with the local Housing Councils that were also to be set up to concentrate upon the campaign for state subsidized housing.[87] A united stand was essential. 'The landlords could not do without the tenants. They could not evict everybody', Alexander Cross assured one meeting.[88] George Pollock, a member of the BSP, and Secretary of the Pollokshaws Tenants' Defence Association, urged the people to stand shoulder to shoulder. The Pollokshaws Tenants' Association had, moreover, retained a legal adviser and promised to pay the removal costs of any victimized tenant over and above fighting the case. 'If they dare to eject anyone, the members of the association will put forth every effort to see that no-one else is mean enough to take the house, and by organising outdoor meetings and demonstrations the particular factor will have a hot time of it'. If necessary, the tenants were willing to go beyond peaceful means to obtain redress.[89] In Hamilton, where rents were being raised, the House Letting and Rating Act was said to be 'a very vexed question'.[90] In Cambuslang 2,000 tenants attended the demonstration organised by the Tenants' Defence Association to protest against excessive rents.[91] In Dundee tenants began to organize for the first time.[92] Confidence rose in Galashiels following an early success by the newly-formed Tenants'

[86]   Robert Lemmon, Secretary of Greenock and District Trades & Labour Council, to Secretary of State for Scotland, 17 Feb. 1912 (SRO DD. 6/550 File 23080/13).

[87]   *Justice*, 2 Mar. 1912.   [88]   *Greenock Herald*, 2 Mar. 1912.

[89]   *Pollokshaws News*, 14 June 1912.

[90]   *R.C. Housing in Scotland*, q. 1447.

[91]   Owen Coyle, Chairman of Cambuslang Tenants' Defence Association, to Thomas McKinnon Wood, 19 Apr. 1912, (SRO DD. 6/550 File 23080/35).

[92]   *Justice*, 9 Mar. 1912.

Association.[93] In Greenock the hitherto moribund association experienced a remarkable revival. Similar enthusiasm had been
aroused there twelve years earlier 'but in a short time no-one
seemed to care a tu'penny ticket whether the organisation lived or
died, and die it did before it had shaken off its baby clothes'. The
new body, however, seemed more firmly rooted: 'For one thing, it
has over £50 at its back, and that', a local commentator remarked,
'is something not to be sneezed at.' The new executive included
members chosen from each of the influential municipal Ward Committees and appeared to have 'something strong about it'.[94] In
Paisley too there were signs of growing militancy. After failing to
persuade the factors' association to moderate their demands, delegates of the Trades and Labour Council, the Tenants' Protective
Association, and the Co-operative Societies agreed to convene a
protest meeting to formulate a line of resistance.[95] In the event, an
overflow meeting had to be hastily improvised in order to accommodate the estimated 6,000 persons who attended. Paisley tenants
like those in other districts resolved to refuse forehand rents and
agreed not to commit themselves to new missives where increased
rents were demanded.[96] In Edinburgh, the fear of mass disfranchise-
ment due to irregularities in the arrangements for the collection of
rates, was an added source of disquiet.[97]

The position of tenants previously exempted from paying rates
had been rendered uncertain by the new legislation.[98] Lawyers were
divided in their opinions as to the legality of continued relief.
Glasgow Corporation, under pressure from the Labour Party,
decided to continue relief pending an authoritative directive,
whereas Paisley Town Council thought it prudent to suspend further
exemptions. The confusion was aggravated by the contradictory
advice emanating from the Scottish Departments. In the House of
Commons Barnes had, at the instance of the Paisley Tenants'
Association, elicited a favourable opinion from the Secretary for
Scotland which appeared to put the matter beyond dispute. But

[93] See evidence of Thos. Nisbet Railston, Secretary of Galashiels Tenants'
Association, *R.C. Housing in Scotland*.

[94] *Greenock Herald*, 18 May 1912.

[95] *Paisley & Renfrewshire Gazette*, 9 Mar. 1912.

[96] *Paisley & Renfrewshire Gazette*, 23 Mar. 1912.

[97] Robert Walker, Secretary of Leith Trades & Labour Council, to Secretary of
State for Scotland, 3 July 1913 (SRO DD. 6/550 File 23080/115).

[98] See 'Memorandum on House-Letting & Rating Act, 1911: Exemption from
Rates on Grounds of Poverty' (SRO DD. 6/554 File 23080/125).

shortly afterwards a circular issued by the Scottish Local Government Board virtually prohibited the practice. In these circumstances, the tenants affected were advised to tender the rent only until the local authorities could be prevailed upon to make suitable arrangements. Paisley Corporation, after considerable delay, finally gave way to the joint pressure of the organized tenants and the labour movement, restored the old system of relief, and prepared to await the consequences.[99]

In Glasgow too the House Letting and Rating Act was described as 'the burning question' among working people.[100] A survey conducted by the City Assessor disclosed substantial rent increases well in excess of any additional administrative costs necessitated by the new legislation.[101] In Govan and Partick discontent was particularly acute. When these districts were annexed to Glasgow in 1912, it was understood that the water rate would be reduced from 10*d*. to 4½*d*. in the £. Landlords, however, refused to pass on the reduction. It meant that a £10 rental was overcharged 3*s*. 9*d*. per annum, and a £20 rental 7*s*. 6*d*. The same kind of sharp practice was applied to the stair-lighting rate. The better off people with rentals above the compound limit therefore gained from annexation while the poorer sorts suffered. When they inhabited the same tenement the sense of injustice was magnified. The Govan Tenants' Defence Association responded vigorously; demonstrations were organized and the assistance of the Secretary of State sought after. McKinnon Wood was not, however, disposed to intervene.[102]

Some idea of the extent of the excess charges imposed was made public in 1914 by a report of a Special Committee which had been appointed by the Corporation at the insistence of the Glasgow Labour Party. Complaints were asked for, and 2,000 sent in at random. Analysis disclosed that tenants had been overcharged by £478 9*s*. 3*d*. The returns showed that on average 1*s*. 6*d*. had been impropertly appropriated in 1913, and 2*s*. 6*d*. in 1914. On the strength of these calculations, the Secretary of State was advised that 'there is surprisingly little foundation for the allegation that the

[99] *Paisley & Renfrewshire Gazette*, 18 Jan. 1913.

[100] *R.C. Housing in Scotland*, q. 22655.

[101] 'Memorandum by City Assessor, Glasgow', 30 Mar. 1912. (SRO DD. 6/546 File 23080/26).

[102] *Forward*, 12 Apr. 1913; D. T. Holmes MP to McKinnon Wood, 8 May 1913 (SRO DD. 6/551 File 23080/106); David Wardley, Secretary of Govan Branch ILP, to McKinnon Wood, 26 May 1913 (SRO DD. 6/551 File 23080/108).

landlords have made the Act a cloak for screwing up rents'. The sums involved were, indeed, small. Popular indignation, however, was fuelled by the fear that these increases foreshadowed a systematic campaign to raise rents across the city.[103]

The distribution of the excess charges is of the greatest significance. Of the total amount overcharged, £357 had been taken from tenants in 500 houses in the Fairfield Ward of Govan. Of the 483 schedules sent in from this quarter, it was proved that the correct charge was made in only sixteen cases. It has already been noted that the missive question was most keenly felt among workers engaged in shipbuilding. In Govan and Partick, the centres of shipbuilding in Glasgow, elections were won and lost on the issue.[104] Here the outcry which followed the passage of the House Letting Act and which led to the formation of the Govan Tenants' Defence Association, did not fade away.[105] The burning resentment thus engendered in part explains why these districts were to be the storm centres in the rent strikes of 1915.

The legal position in regard to these and other excess charges was uncertain. It could only be resolved through litigation. Those who formed the Scottish Federation of Tenants' Associations hoped to husband their resources in order to test the meaning of the new act in the highest court in the land.[106] The first test case taken at Clydebank, however, did not inspire confidence: the tenants lost.[107] Yet in retrospect something of value had been gained. The case for the tenants was conducted by one D. D. Cormack, an astute Dumbarton solicitor, later described by an official inquiry as 'an ingenious legal adviser', who led the resistance at Clydebank in the post-war years with distinction.[108] Those such as John Maclean who were most active in the foundation of the Scottish Federation of Tenants' Associations viewed a successful test case as a primary but not ultimate object of the campaign. No Scottish Socialist, and least of all a member of the BSP, could be indifferent to the housing question. Maclean's principal interest in the agitation centred on its possibilities as an agent of mass radicalization and precipitant of a

[103] Minute initialled R.L., 14 Feb. 1914 (SRO DD. 6/556 File 23080/124); *Forward*, 7 Feb. 1914.

[104] *House-Letting in Scotland* (1908), qq. 3817-18.

[105] *Report of the Departmental Committee on Increases in the Rental of Small Dwelling Houses in Industrial Districts in Scotland* (PP 1914-16, XXXV), qq. 795-802.

[106] *Pollokshaws News*, 4 Oct. 1912.

[107] *Clydebank & Renfrew Press*, 1 May 1914.

[108] *Report of the Committee on the Rent Restriction Acts* (PP 1924-5, XV), p. 15.

revolutionary general strike and in this he remained consistent to the end.[109] But the BSP did not enjoy the field to itself. Patrick Dollan too was aware of the significance of the mounting unrest amongst the tenants, and like Maclean he called for direct action in place of resolutions in favour of fair rent courts. In this respect, he argued, the energetic campaign conducted by the Govan Tenants' Defence Association, commendable though it was, did not go far enough. Nothing short of an immediate rent strike would suffice:

This is a splendid chance for the Govan and Partick Labour parties. Let them organise a *combined refusal* to pay the extra charges imposed by property owners on poor tenants. Let them draft a manifesto stating that the people will not pay the 'extras', and let them canvas signatures for the manifesto. This manifesto could be a sort of tenants' covenant, the signing of which would entitle a tenant to the protection of his fellow tenants should the landlord attempt harsh measures.

It is a glorious opportunity for a tenants' rebellion, which if properly organized, should mean the return of a Labour member for every vacant seat in Govan and Partick at the November elections ... A well-organized agitation will secure concessions for the tenants and at the same time create opinion in favour of Municipal Housing.[110]

Two years later this advice was acted upon: the Glasgow Labour Party placed itself at the head of the agitation and reaped a deserved electoral reward.

But on the eve of war the issues raised by the missive question had not been settled to the tenants' satisfaction. The suspicion and anger aroused by fraudulent and rapacious proprietors had quite transformed the question: the search for protection against further impositions had become *the* dominant consideration.[111] The formation of fair rent courts to settle these increasinlgy bitter disputes, was fast becoming the least drastic form of intervention. Galashiels Tenants' Association, for example, pressed for an amendment to fix rents for a twelve-month period during which time increases would be prohibited.[112] However, the Secretary of State for Scotland whose protection had repeatedly been sought after, declined to intervene. Proposals advanced by the Scottish TUC to safeguard the position of tenants and indigent occupiers were summarily dismissed as senseless dreams.[113]

[109] Nan Maclean, *John Maclean* (1973), p. 104.
[110] *Forward*, 14 June 1913. [111] See correspondence in SRO DD. 6/551.
[112] Thos. N. Railston to McKinnon Wood, 11 Dec. 1913 (SRO DD. 6/550 File 23080/121).
[113] See SRO DD. 6/554 File 23080/125.

9

Retrospect

The evanescent character of Victorian and Edwardian tenants' agitations should not obscure certain points of interest. The rent strike crystallized the latent antagonisms between landlord and tenant. In challenging the basis of rent determination tenants were forced to probe the rationale of an oppressive system. But although quick to embrace the principle of socialized housing, their militancy was framed in the language and concepts of a pre-socialist tradition. Tenants were above all concerned with justice and fair dealing. Thus rents were defined as excessive not only in relation to income, but also with a view to the quality of the accommodation provided. 'The houses are not worth the money asked for', said one tenant. 'Some of them had been put up in a hurry, and reminded him of the sort of houses where you saw the foundations being dug out in the morning and the tenants being evicted for arrears of rent in the evening.'[1] 'Six-and-six a week, and it is not worthy of a dog lying in it', exclaimed another.[2] The market was deemed incompatible with that concern for natural justice by which all social intercourse ought to be regulated. 'The average Bradford landlord has become blind to the existence of his tenant as a human being', one correspondent remarked. 'His only concern seems to be to draw his rent and shirk as much as possible his responsibilities with regard to his own property.'[3] Such complaints were legion.

No less outrageous was the exploitation of vital necessities. Landlords and economists might talk of an imbalance between supply and demand; tenants spoke of the 'House Famine'. If the sanctions of the crowd were rarely applied, the same demand for consumer-protection which had once animated their riotous forebears still struck a responsive chord amongst the working-class tenants of our period. 'In olden times there was a bread famine and a man locked up his corn in order to make more out of it; when people were

[1] *Leeds Weekly Citizen*, 13 Feb. 1913.   [2] *Express & Star*, 3 Apr. 1913.
[3] *Yorkshire Observer*, 24 Apr. 1913.

reduced to extremity his place used to be burned down' said John Benn addressing a meeting organised by the Bermondsey Labour League. 'He thought that the man who took advantage of a house famine was just as guilty.'[4] The ideals of the 'moral economy' were freely invoked by the tenants. They form a recurrent motif which found programmatic expression in the demand for fair rent courts as voiced by the Workmen's National Housing Council and the Glasgow Labour Party. Neither, however, got far beyond an outline of the machinery of the proposed tribunals. A 'fair rent' remained an ambiguously flexible concept, but one affected by the status and expectations of the militants.

From its inception the Labour Party pitched its appeal at 'skilled and organised labour'.[5] It was a recognition not only of material realities, but also of the fact that the active supporters of socialism were most likely to be drawn from the more affluent sectors of the working classes, those in regular employment. Those who participated in the various tenants' associations were not of the labouring poor. The Paisley Tenants' Protective Association, it is true, claimed 'members down to the ·lowest working class', but in this it was exceptional.[6] Those who campaigned against the missive system were drawn overwhelmingly from the élite of the labour movement. 'It is noticeable that it is not the monthly tenants who are agitating for a change of the law' the Departmental Committee observed. 'It is yearly tenants, who are prepared to take the risk not only of higher rents, but of any loss of social status.'[7] In Govan and Partick, as was noted earlier, it was the skilled workers who were quick to organize resistance to the rent increases that accompanied the operation of the House Letting Act. In Glasgow the slum-dwelling population took no part in the rent strikes of 1915.[8] The same pattern of recruitment characterized tenants' movements in England and Wales. The following petition, bearing almost 150 signatures, and drawn up by a committee of disaffected tenants in Tottenham, was typical of the status and sentiments of those who were reluctantly engaged in the growing struggle:

[4] *Southwark Recorder*, 29 July 1899.
[5] 'Report of a Policy Committee', Minutes and Papers of Labour Representation Committee, I, ff. 1-3.
[6] *Departmental Committee on House-Letting in Scotland, Minutes of Evidence* (PP 1908, XLVII), q. 561.
[7] *Report of Departmental Committee on House-Letting in Scotland* (PP 1907, XXXVI), p. 13.
[8] *Report of the Departmental Committee on Increases in the Rental of Small Dwelling Houses in Industrial Districts in Scotland* (PP 1914-16, XXXV), q. 586.

We the undersigned tenants of Clonmel, Lismore and Alton Roads, view with regret the proposed increase of 1*s.* per week in our rents, and respectfully ask that the rent remain at 9*s.* 6*d.* as before. A shilling per week increase, we contend, is very excessive, and as most of us are very old tenants we consider ourselves to have been very badly treated in receiving such short notice. We are compelled, by family reasons, to remain in the neighbourhood, and this increase of rent, coupled with the increasing cost of living, would be keenly felt by us all. Your tenants are mainly business men, postal servants, mechanics, railway servants and other professions, who are endeavouring to maintain their families and bring them up as respectable citizens. We would deem it a favour if you would receive a deputation to discuss the matter at your earliest convenience. The raising of existing rents constitute a grave danger of the tenants subletting, and this is undesirabe, as it would tend to lower the respectability of the roads.[9]

People such as these were not accustomed to the threat of eviction for non-payment of rent and had little sympathy for those who were compelled habitually to resort to moonlight flits and other devious stratagems. 'We are not here to defend people on that point at all' said an indignant George Carson before an official enquiry.[10] The very idea, indeed: 'The law of ejectment', said a Leeds rent striker, 'was never framed for a trustworthy class of tenant. It was framed for those who, when they had no chips to light their fires with, chopped the doors up.'[11] Soutter too would 'not plead for the tenant who did not and would not pay his rent. He had not done so in the past and would not do so now, but he would advocate most urgently the cause of those who did their best to live decently and pay their way. These should have proper protection.'[12] None questioned the landlord's right to evict unwanted tenants. The virtual complete neglect of the problem of security of tenure in the Rent Restriction Act, 1915 was to some extent a reflection of the biases of these eminently respectable militants.

Indeed, the comparative infrequency of organized action on the part of working-class tenants owed something to the relative affluence of this privileged stratum. It was also perhaps a reflection of an emergent privatized life style which, it has been suggested, became a characteristic feature of working-class culture in late Victorian

[9] *Tottenham & Edmonton Weekly Herald*, 5 June 1914.
[10] *House-Letting in Scotland* (1908), q. 3749.
[11] *Yorkshire Factory Times*, 5 Feb. 1914.
[12] *Southwark Recorder*, 31 Aug. 1901.

Britain.[13] John Elliot, organizing secretary of the Paisley branch of the Scottish Carters' Association, was convinced that it was the 'mock respectability' of the tenants which encouraged landlords to increase rents.[14] 'Had we not been damned with too much respectability', said the *Scottish Typographical Journal* during the great struggle of 1915, 'resistance would probably have been made ere now to such extortions.'[15] In a situation in which the landlord enjoyed a virtual monopoly, solace in status differentiation proved an inadequate protection once negotiations had failed. With their backs to the wall, and believing in the justice of their cause, respectable working-class tenants had no option—other than removal to the slums or paying up—but to stand and fight.

Tenants in Edwardian England entered upon a rent strike with nothing beyond the certainty of their own convictions. There was no coherent strategy. Revd. J. A. Shaw told the Wolverhampton re-sisters that 'no magistrate would sign an order for a tenant's eviction in such a case, for public opinion would be too strong against that'.[16] The campaign surged forward on a wave of indignation. Its organization and direction was hastily improvised. The want of fore-thought proved fatal. The labour movement was quick to offer support but, since no adequate preparations had been made, its intervention was of limited value. Lansbury's vision was obscured by the rhetoric of direct action. The theory of the rent strike advanced by John Lake, the Leeds socialist, expressed little more than his own pronounced anti-capitalist enthusiasms. The *Daily Herald*'s attempts to generate widespread support for the idea foundered on the absence of a workable strategy. The Irish example, so freely invoked, offered at best a vicarious satisfaction rather than a blueprint for action. No labour leader seriously advocated the application of those forms of protest which brought rent control to the countryside in Ireland and Scotland. Indeed, the Parliamentary Labour Party had yet to commit itself to the principle of subsidized housing, although municipal housing was a mainstay of all local labour movements.[17] Progress here, however, was to be determined

[13] Gareth Stedman Jones, 'Working Class Culture and Working Class Politics in London, 1870-1900: Notes on the Remaking of a Working Class', *Journal of Social History*, VII (1974), pp. 485-9. In spite of its title this article generalises beyond the metropolitan experience: see p. 498.

[14] *Paisley & Renfrewshire Gazette*, 23 Mar. 1912.

[15] *Scottish Typographical Journal*, Oct. 1915.   [16] *Express & Star*, 12 Apr. 1913.

[17] Francis Johnson, 'Labour Municipal Programmes', *Socialist Review* (Feb. 1912), pp. 446-52.

in the polling booth. The tenants' agitation was useful in directing attention towards the inevitability of these policies. In Leeds and Wolverhampton élitist prejudice together with a want of imagination did nothing to arrest the drift into the county court.

The scope for alternative action was admittedly limited. The campaigns which enjoyed a modicum of success were those in which the tenants eschewed litigation and instead relied upon the force of an aroused public opinion to shame their adversaries into moderating their claims. This too was a difficult course to pursue. After six months continuous agitation, membership of the Edmonton Tenants' Defence League had reached 950 and was still growing although there was no indication that local landlords were at all influenced by its well-publicized activities; at least there was no slackening in the pace of rent-raising.[18] But beyond the campaign for municipal housing, the tenants refused to go. Tenants in Edmonton hesitated to withhold rent until after the commencement of hostilities. In Birmingham too the Tenants' Defence League, as we have seen, kept well clear of the courts. On the outbreak of war it had not suffered a decisive defeat and thus escaped that demoralization which appears to have disabled tenants in Leeds and Wolverhampton in 1915.

But in the main rent strikes were born of desperation rather than misjudgement. However, associated action was not dependent upon direct conflict with the landlords in this fashion. In the 1890s the Woolwich and Plumstead Tenants' Defence League intervened with some success in the administration of 'Kentish London'. At the beginning of that decade the still expanding Mansion House Council was seeking to involve working men in sanitary reform, annexing branches to the working men's clubs and other interested labour institutions. But in Woolwich its services were rendered superfluous. Working men required little guidance in these matters. J. W. Horsley, the Progressive clergyman, who had been elected to the Board of Works with working-class support, reported that the 'Local Committee does not meet frequently as a new and most vigorous body called the Tenants' Defence League, does a grand work in searching out all insanitary defects and forwarding them to me'. The Tenants' Defence League worked in unison with the local labour movement, contesting local elections and exposing slum-owners, a strategy with which local Fabians were quick to identify—'landlordism being

[18]　*Tottenham & Edmonton Weekly Herald*, 12 June 1914.

easier to attack than capitalism where the only large industry is the Government work'.[19]

The Woolwhich Tenants' Defence League was eclipsed at the turn of the century by the emergence of a united and exceptionally well-organized Labour Party machine. The Bermondsey Tenants' Defence League was wound up under altogether less happy circumstances. The resolution of the compounding issue deprived the League of its *raison d'être* in spite of an attempt to transform itself into a proletarian variant of the 'poor man's lawyer'. On Clydeside by contrast disenchantment with the House Letting Act after the long years of campaigning had a radicalizing effect which had not run its course when war broke out.

[19] Mansion House Council on the Dwellings of the Poor, *Annual Report* (1890), p. 21; *Fabian News*, July 1891; *London*, 30 Aug. 1894, p. 556.

PART 3

Rent War, 1914–1918

Political science would now regard the private ownership of urban dwelling houses to be let to tenants as an obsolete device. I do not know any competent economist who would not agree to this in principle.

Sidney Webb, 5 Nov. 1918. Committee on Increase of Rent Act: Minutes of 8th Meeting, (Doc. 69), PRO Reco. 1/645.

10

Rent Strikes, 1915

The politicization of the Housing Question has never been adequately explained. The introduction of rent control during the First World War, the decisive step in this process, was not a peculiarly British phenomenon. All the principal belligerents were compelled to intervene in the management of the economy and, where necessary, to subordinate market forces to the efficient prosecution of the war. The war, then, created the conditions which made rent control possible. In each country, however, the specific form of control was determined by a unique conjuncture. In Britain investigation has until recently been largely confined to the Whitehall end, centring upon the immediate economic pressures and administrative forces that shaped the Housing and Town Planning Act, 1919.[1] The presence of the working class has received some acknowledgment to be sure; but the activities of working people have been ignored. The following chapters will seek to redress the balance.

The social and political impact of the war upon the working classes remains problematical. In regard to housing reform, however, it did not denote a sharp discontinuity. What had altered was not the aspiration but the intensity of the demand for improved housing. It reflected a heightened consciousness of social injustice. The perception of unequal sacrifice gave rise to a deep resentment against 'the Prussian at home'. Patriotism, that disturbingly irrational sentiment, anathema to Hobson and other exponents of progressive opinion, generated a radical egalitarianism which circumscribed but did not diminish class conflict. It was a force with which politicians of all persuasions had to come to terms.

[1] On this, see Marian Bowley, *Housing and the State 1919-1944* (1945); Paul Barton Johnson, *Land Fit for Heroes, The Planning of British Reconstruction, 1916-1919* (Chicago, 1968); Bentley B. Gilbert, *British Social Policy, 1914-1939* (1970); J. R. Jordan, 'Homes for Heroes: Housing Problems at the end of the First World War' (University of Kent Unpublished MA thesis, 1971); Paul Wilding, 'The Housing and Town Planning Act, 1919: A Study in the making of Social Policy', *Journal of Social Policy*, IV (1973).

Little thought had been devoted to the formulation of a national housing programme until after the establishment of the first Reconstruction Committee in the spring of 1916. In the main, policy was determined by the logistics of arms production, and as such it was the responsibility of the Ministry of Munitions:

Its primary interest in housing was to secure and increase output, the welfare or social side of the question was but the means to an end; the permanent interests both of the State which provided the house and the workman who lived in it were subordinated to the needs of the moment. This attitude coloured the policy of the Ministry during the war.[2]

Working people saw the issue in different terms. The failure of social reform, it has been suggested, derived to a considerable degree from an inability to appreciate those terms and to plan accordingly.[3] Although never formally a part of the decision-making process, Labour's role was anything but negligible. Housing reform could not be divorced from the reality of the class struggle, and during the war that struggle was fought principally upon the question of rent determination.

Its first fruits, the Rent Act, 1915, represented a major advance in the campaign for state-subsidized housing. It is arguably the case, however, that the war retarded rather than hastened this development. Before the war, it has been noted, the desirability of public subsidies in the sphere of social administration had gained widespread recognition. Amongst Lloyd George's talented entourage application was considered a matter of detail and timing. The ever-restless Winston Churchill, for instance, who viewed the prospect with perfect equanimity, '... spoke enthusiastically of the day when the working classes would live in fine blocks of dwellings with central cooking and heating, swimming baths, etc., subsidised by the State or municipality'.[4] On this reading, the ideas of these housing reformers were far less Victorian than was once supposed.[5] But, whatever its fascination, a crystal ball cannot offer a definitive resolution of the question. The Rent Act, 1915, removed all un-

---

[2] *History of the Ministry of Munitions*, 12 vols. (1920-4), part V, vol. 3 (hereafter cited as *HMM*, V, 3). p. 2.

[3] Philip Abrams, 'The Failure of Social Reform, 1918-1920', *Past & Present*, No. 24 (1963), pp. 43-64.

[4] Paul Wilding, 'Towards Exchequer Subsidies for Housing 1906-1914', *Social & Economic Administration*, VI (1972), pp. 3-18. Quotation from Lord Riddell, *More Pages from My Diary 1908-1914* (1934), p. 22.

[5] Cf. Bowley, *Housing and the State*, pp. 2-3.

certainties. Henceforth the State would have to intervene in the provision of working-class housing. It was not an unqualified success, but it remains a major achievement worthy of more than the cursory attention so far received.

The fight for rent control was not a uniform movement. The fiercest struggles occurred in the key centres of armament production. No national tenants' federation emerged. Co-ordination, in so far as it existed, came from the War Emergency Workers' National Committee.[6] Once alerted, the Committee provided programmatic form and continuous departmental contact for the various associations of tenants that were formed in these years. The relation was anything but 'democratic centralist' in character. The National Labour Housing Association (formerly the Workmen's National Housing Council), denied official representation in order to restrict membership to manageable proportions, had to make do with informal contacts.[7] The War Rents League, another associate, was out of sympathy with the militant Clydesiders. 'The Scottish policy', its secretary recalled 'was an attack upon private landlords, whilst ours was a defence of all landlords against unscrupulous ones. Our policy has led to agreement and conciliation, whist theirs has engendered open conflict, much to the disadvantage of all tenants throughout the kingdom'.[8] The self-confident Clydesiders, however, were themselves suspicious of the Committee's moderation. The South Wales miners, too, were often inclined to keep the Committee posted and pursue an independent approach to Whitehall.[9] Responding to events, tenants confronted the State united in their separate identities. The diversity of opinion was at times confusing; official advisers, bewildered by the variation, looked to the Committee for guidance having previously been 'unable to obtain any considered expression of Labour views'.[10] The tenants' growing

[6] On the formation and activities of this important organization, see Royden Harrison, 'The War Emergency Workers' National Committee, 1914-1920', in Asa Briggs and John Saville, ed., *Essays in Labour History 1886-1923* (1971), pp. 211-59 and J. M. Winter, *Socialism and the Challenge of War: Ideas and Politics in Britain 1912-1918* (1974), Ch. vii.

[7] J. S. Middleton to J. S. Whybrew, Secretary of the National Labour Housing Association, 26 Mar. 1915, (War Emergency Workers' National Committee Papers, Labour Party Archives).

[8] Dan Rider, *Ten years Adventures Amongst Landlords and Tenants* (1927), p. 64.

[9] J. S. Middleton to W. Harris, District Organiser of South Wales Miners' Federation, 27 Nov. 1917 (WNC Papers).

[10] W. G. Wallace, Secretary to Committee on the Increase of Rent & Mortgage Interest (War Restrictions) Acts, to J. S. Middleton, 26 July 1918 (WNC Papers).

confidence was certainly enhanced by an awareness of their statutory rights which the Committee did much to promote, but where undertaken, the resort to direct action owed little to Sidney Webb and his colleagues. The Workers' National Committee led from behind.[11]

Trouble had long been expected. The outbreak of war was bound to involve a certain amount of disruption. The military had prepared for 'vast numbers of ignorant, underfed, and discontented unemployed, together with the alien and criminal population' who, while the troops embarked for France during the opening and critical stages of mobilization, might threaten the heart of empire and the safety of the realm.[12] Nobody gave a second thought to the loyal and respectable working-class tenant. Mr Lloyd George was emphatic that his condition gave no cause for concern. 'There is not a decent, self-respecting landlord in the kingdom', he told the House of Commons, 'who would sell up an honest working man who paid his rent regularly because, owing to the troubles of the time, he had been unable to earn any wages'.[13] Too many proprietors, it is to be feared, were not self-respecting.

The Housing Question was not to be allowed to remain in cold storage for the duration. Signs of widespread discontent were immediately apparent as landlords and hire purchase firms competed for possession of working-class homes. The labour movement was alive to the problem. At its first executive meeting, the Workers' National Committee considered the issue. The Cabinet responded to its representations with the Courts Emergency Powers Act which prohibited the levying of distress before a court appearance, and gave magistrates discretionary powers to refuse orders for possession in cases of hardship arising out of the war.[14] The *Daily Citizen*, which considered the measure likely 'to alleviate more private misery during the war than even the National Relief Fund', was elated. 'It might well be called the Poor Man's Home Protection Bill'.[15] But any deterrent effect the act might have possessed was vitiated by the almost deafening silence with which it was received

[11] Harrison, 'War Emergency Workers' National Committee, 1914-1920', pp. 233-4.

[12] 'Memorandum by the Director of Military Training on the Measures required for the Protection of the Capital in Time of War', 11 Dec. 1908, (PRO WO. 32/5270).

[13] *HC Deb*. 5s. lxvi (1914), 229.

[14] War Emergency Workers' National Committee, 'Points on the Committee and its work, 5 Aug. to 2 Nov. 1914, by J. S. Middleton', 6 Nov. 1914 (WNC Papers).

[15] *Daily Citizen*, 28 Aug. 1914.

in the national press.[16] Neither was the Government noticeably enthusiastic about publicizing its provisions. The responsibility for informing tenants of their rights fell almost exclusively upon the labour movement.

The Workers' National Committee was particularly well-suited for the task. The overworked secretary of the Workmen's National Housing Council, who represented the London Trades Council on the Committee, quickly drafted an explanatory leaflet; the Labour press did its bit.[17] But having broached the legal thicket, it was apparent that professional guidance was required if the Committee was not to lose its way in the undergrowth. In this respect, it was fortified by the accession of H. H. Slesser, the distinguished barrister, who offered his services gratuitously in September 1914.[18] Slesser improved upon the work already begun. The Workers' National Committee was thus set to become the most important tenants' advisory centre.

However, housing reform remained the higher priority. The comparative neglect of the problem of rising rents was shaped by the Committee's *raison d'être*, the prevention and relief of distress. Here the commitment to full employment and the secondary importance accorded inflation[19] enhanced the role of house-building, a view doubtlessly encouraged by Fred Knee who was, as ever, eager to spend the £4 m. reserved for this purpose under the Housing Act, 1914.

Ever since Burns's transfer from the Local Government Board, the most constructive move of his long tenure at that post, the outlook had brightened. Herbert Samuel, his successor, quickly appointed Knee and Webb to an advisory Committee on Urban Housing to consider schemes under the new legislation. But before the year was out it had been disbanded and nothing achieved.[20] As early as September it was evident that, in the absence of remedial action, progress would be sabotaged by galloping inflation. 'Complaints'. Middleton informed an anxious correspondent, 'have been

[16] Cf. J. S. Middleton to C. Gaunt, Secretary of Burton-on-Trent Labour Representation Committee, 21 Dec. 1914 (WNC Papers).

[17] Workmen's National Housing Council, Leaflet No. 18, *Housing and the War* (1914); Fred Knee to J. S. Middleton, 18 Aug. 1914 (WNC Papers); *Labour Leader*, 22 Sept. 1914.

[18] H. H. Slesser to Arthur Henderson, 10 Sept. 1914 (WNC Papers).

[19] Winter, *Socialism and the Challenge of War*, p. 192.

[20] *44th Annual Report of the Local Government Board*, Part II (PP 1916, XII), p. 6.

received from all over the country that housing and other building schemes are being held up on account of the high prices of material'.[21] Ministers were urged to intervene[22]—and intervene they did. In the autumn the Chancellor's axe fell: belts were to be tightened and local authorities to curb all unnecessary expenditure; municipal housing was shelved. The Committee's protests were to no avail. The application of the act was to be limited only to those areas where unemployment was abnormally severe. It remained a dead letter.[23] In the event, house building was determined by the problems of labour supply for arms production.

It had been hoped that a more intensive use of the housing stock would suffice. In some areas officials of the local Labour Exchange prepared a register of vacant accommodation to cope with the influx of new workers. It was a useful but temporary expedient. In Newcastle, where lodgings had still to be found for the extra 8,000 to 9,000 workers who were soon to arrive, congestion was acute by the end of 1914. Disaster was narrowly averted owing to the sharp rise in empties along the coast caused by the fear of enemy naval raids, and by the troops exchanging their billets for canvas.[24] Early in the new year, the manager of the Barrow Labour Exchange informed London that workers were quitting the area owing to the absence of accommodation. Vickers, who were suffering severe labour leakage problems, stepped in with an eleventh-hour press campaign designed to ferret out further sources of accommodaton. This too brought a temporary reprieve, but, the General Manager warned, 'unless some serious attempt is made to grapple with the question, it would not be possible to import to Barrow-in-Furness, the large number of men which the firm require'.[25] The same desperate improvisation took place in all the major engineering centres.

[21] J. S. Middleton to C. R. King, Secretary of Luton Branch of Amalgamated Society of Carpenters & Joiners, 16 Sept. 1914 (WNC Papers); and for a general survey, see War Emergency Workers' National Committee, 'Report on Municipal Housing Schemes, 1914' (WNC Papers).

[22] J. S. Middleton to Herbert Samuel, 9 Sept. 1914 (WNC Papers).

[23] 'Deputation by the War Emergency Committee to the Rt. Hon. David Lloyd George MP (Chancellor of the Exchequer), The Treasury', 6 Oct. 1914: shorthand notes (WNC Papers); 'State Assistance for Housing', Memorandum by the Housing Department, Local Government Board, May 1917 (PRO Reco. 1/568).

[24] 'First Report on the Operation of the Munitions of War Department, 4 May 1915' (Beveridge Collection on Munitions, British Library of Political and Economic Science I, f. 188). On the subsequent deterioration of conditions, see *Report to the Housing Committee by the Medical Officer of Health upon the Shortage of Houses in Newcastle* (Dec. 1917), pp. 4-7 (PRO Reco. 1/484).

[25] A. Rawson to William Beveridge, 14 Jan. 1915 (Beveridge Collection on Munitions, I, fos. 74-5).

Until the formation of the Ministry of Munitions in June 1915, responsibility for housing was spread amongst some half-dozen departments. Perhaps the most conspicuous feature of Government policy in the first ten months of war was the absence of co-ordination. It was less that problems were unforeseen but rather that they were only seen in part. In consequence action remained fragmentary and inadequate. The rapid deterioration of conditions at Woolwich, where the numbers employed at the Arsenal rose from 10,866 in August 1914 to more than 44,000 in October, and where a further 20,000 were expected shortly, registered with the authorities by the end of the year. An inter-departmental conference reviewed the situation early in 1915 and agreed to proceed with the erection of more than 1,000 houses and flats—the Well Hall Estate.[26]

The Ministry of Munitions, staffed by men of 'push and go', quickly established a special housing section. Its work was to be constantly impeded by the fragmentation of central government. War or no war, the Treasury, the Office of Works, the Public Works Loan Board, and the Local Government Board all had to give their approval before any scheme could be sanctioned.[27] The latter, never noted for its dynamism at the best of times, was at first inclined to drag its feet.[28] Operations did not really get under way until 1916. In due course, the Ministry of Munitions became a substantial landlord in its own right, and was involved in the provision of both temporary and permanent accommodation for nearly 20,000 people.[29] It was an impressive achievement.[30] But such action was exceptional.

The uncertainties of the situation, the need of retrenchment, the collapse of the building industry—all conspired to limit the scope of intervention. The spread rather than the concentration of contracts

[26]   *HMM*, V, 1, pp. 1, 23.   [27]   *HMM*, V, 1, pp. 3-6.

[28]   Christopher Addison, *Four and a Half Years*, 2 vols. (1934), I, p. 132.

[29]   On statistics of provision, see *Report of Committee of Public Accounts* (PP 1917-18, III), app. No. 12, p. 220 and *HMM*, V, 1, pp. 79-82.

[30]   Though not, one might add, quite the unqualified triumph which the Official History wished to suggest. On being shown the relevant draft section of the History of the Ministry of Munitions, the civil servant in charge of the Housing Department remarked: 'In fact my main criticism of it would be that it creates an impression that things went on in a more orderly and logical manner than they really did. No Report could reproduce the atmosphere of living absolutely from hand to mouth with which we were all familiar, nor could it indicate the difficulties of drawing up a proper housing programme when one was liable to learn after a scheme was well on its way that the factory it was intended to serve was going to be built at Lancaster instead of Sheffield. These things are perhaps better left to the memory or the imagination.' R. V. Vernon to G. I. H. Lloyd, 22 Oct. 1920 (PRO Mun. 5/330). See too Humbert Wolfe, *Labour Supply and Regulation* (Oxford, 1923), p. 19.

coupled with the improvement in transit facilities might, it was hoped, encourage a more efficient utilization of scarce house space, and at the same time obviate the need for more expensive forms of provision.[31] This approach was embodied in a proposed amendment to the Defence of the Realm Act empowering Ministers to billet civilian workers compulsorily, if need be. But in 1915 this was considered too extreme, and for the time being more cautious counsel prevailed. The amendment was limited to the acquisition of unoccupied premises, and in some districts this power was 'very freely exercised'.[32] All sorts of buildings were thus turned into temporary accommodation, but there was never a chance that the new Ministry could mobilize resources sufficient to contain the mounting crisis with which it was confronted.

The improvement in the quality of the Worker's National Committee's advisory service which followed upon Slesser's arrival was not matched by a corresponding improvement in the Committee's judgement. The inherent caution of the professional barrister perhaps unwittingly inhibited a more realistic appraisal of the situation. The Courts Emergency Powers Act, designed as part of the machinery for the relief of distress, gave no express protection against profiteering in house rents. Yet with the unimpaired market mentality with which Britain went to war, no great foresight was required to anticipate such an eventuality. In the last year of peace there were indications of an upswing in the building cycle. One indicator was rising rents. So long as 'business as usual' remained the order of the day, prudence suggested the need for careful surveillance. Here the Committee's dependence upon the state bureaucracy may be of some significance. Although the Workers' National Committee was formally denied access, it is difficult to believe that its members respected the confidentiality of the official 'intelligence' reports to which many of them were privy (by virtue of appointment to various governmental committees), especially the Webbs. One consequence of this discreet pragmatism, Dr Winter suggests, was that 'the factual basis of the War Emergency Committee's policy dealing with the producer was formidable indeed'.[33]

[31] *HMM*, I, 3, pp. 4-5, 58; Wolfe, *Labour Supply and Regulation*, pp. 57-64.

[32] *HMM*, I, 2, pp. 60-1; 'Secret Weekly Report of the Labour Department', 18 Dec. 1915 (PRO Mun. 2/27).

[33] On formal denial of access, see Ernest Laws, Secretary of Local Government Board Intelligence Department, to J. S. Middleton, 10 Sept. 1914 (WNC Papers). On Sidney Webb's alleged indiscretion, S. G. Hobson, *Pilgrim to the Left* (1938), p. 76, Quotation from Winter, *Socialism and the Challenge of War*, p. 193.

The same source also furnished considerable material on the position of the consumer as tenant which was of an inferior order. Digested uncritically, this least intelligent 'intelligence' might have confirmed Slesser's belief in the elasticity of the Courts Emergency Powers Act. Although attention had been drawn to the problem of inflated rents in 1914,[34] Slesser's curiosity was not evidently fully aroused. As late as October, the following year, he was still of the opinion that faith in the courts was not misplaced, although the Workers' National Committee no longer shared his optimism.[35] In spite of the Committee's promising start, the initiative passed to the tenants.

Although no official evaluation was undertaken, the adequacy of the Courts Emergency Powers Act remained unquestioned. Defects were brushed aside: if anything, the measure was too protective. Shortly before the outbreak of war, an 'intelligence' unit was established at the Local Government Board to monitor fluctuations in unemployment and distress. The bulk of its weekly reports comprised collations of material culled from several central and local government agencies.[36] The material collected on arrears of rent was the least satisfactory. Incomplete returns submitted by the LCC and the commercial dwellings companies were supplemented by the impressions of estate agents and 'lady' rent collectors. No information was taken from beyond the metropolitan county boundary.

On the outbreak of war increased rents were, of course, to be expected. Much of the resultant hardship was mitigated by the landlords' considerate action. Numerous instances of their patriotism were cited. Not only were tenants not being evicted for non-payment of rent, but in many areas rents were actually being reduced.[37] However, when the numbers in arrrears remained constant while the level of empties dropped and employment improved, some explanation beyond unavoidable distress was required. The favourite was that the tenants had misunderstood the moratorium on debt

[34] W. Wilmott of Hitchin, Herts., to J. S. Middleton, 29 Oct. 1914; J. S. Middleton to W. J. Smithson of Holbeach, Lincs., 4 Dec. 1914 (WNC Papers).

[35] Minutes of War Emergency Workers' National Committee, 14 Oct. 1915 (WNC Papers).

[36] Copies of these reports are available at the Public Record Office or at the London School of Economics identifiable as S. & B. Webb, Reports and Papers on the Relief of Distress 5 vols. (1914-15).

[37] On reflection, however, proprietors were thought to have been rather less generous: 'The small landlords', it was noted, 'probably allowed very few arrears even at the beginning of the war.' 'Report of the Intelligence Department of the Local Government Board', May 1915 (PRO T. 172/198).

which formed part of the emergency legislation introduced to stabilize the currency and prevent the commercial collapse which the ill-considered actions of panic-stricken investors might otherwise have induced.[38] Now, so far from misunderstanding the moratorium, working people were only too aware of its class bias.[39] The restriction of the moratorium to commercial transactions and debts above £5 constituted a form of discrimination which did nothing to sweeten proletarian tempers. 'When', wrote a 'Clyde Workman' from Fairfield, Govan, 'we know that in Germany and France a moratorium on house rents during the war is now law this fact has exasperated us more than anything else.'[40]

The authorities in Whitehall, however, interpreted the growth of arrears as a confirmation of the fundamental dishonesty of the working classes. Summarizing the position in mid-September 1914, an official wrote: 'From the many reports in the Boroughs the impression is gained that there is a certain amount of non-payment of rent not due to inability but unwillingness to pay.'[41] The demoralizing effect of anything which even faintly resembled security of tenure was thus laid bare. How else could the behaviour of the Bermondsey dockers be explained except that 'as rent books have to be produced by applicants for relief, it is suggested that arrears of rent is sometimes accumulated on purpose'.[42] By the fifth week of hostilities the conviction was firmly established that unwillingness rather than inability to pay constituted the crux of the problem. Relief scales were in consequence fixed without regard to rent. 'There is no doubt a general impression that landlords will not or cannot successfully press for rent, and that evictions will not be sanctioned.'[43] The situation was serious. Already in some districts tenants offered their landlords calculated defiance 'trading on the fact that magistrates will not sign eviction orders'.[44] The largest of London's landlords moved swiftly to counter this delusion. The

[38] 'Report of Intelligence Department of LGB', 25 Jan. 1915 (PRO T. 172/193). Popular misconceptions were not apparently a metropolitan phenomenon: see *Glasgow Citizen*, 13 Aug. 1914.

[39] See, for example, *Yorkshire Factory Times*, 27 Aug. 1915.

[40] *Sunday Chronicle*, 7 Mar. 1915.

[41] 'Report of Intelligence Department of LGB', 19 Sept. 1914 (PRO T. 172/167).

[42] 'Report of Intelligence Department of LGB', 5 Sept. 1914 (PRO T. 172/165).

[43] K. D. Brown, *John Burns* (1977), p. 182; Harrison, 'War Emergency Workers', National Committee, 1914-1920', p. 233. Quotation from 'Report of Intelligence Department of LGB', 12 Sept. 1914 (PRO T. 172/166).

[44] 'Report of Intelligence Department of LGB', 26 Sept. 1914 (PRO T. 172/168).

LCC, encouraged by the salutary effect produced by the reception of notice to quit amongst a pilot sample, promptly served notice on a further 56 of its 384 tenants in arrears on the Boundary Street Estate.[45] But, it was feared, such exemplary action was exceptional. Landlords were their own worst enemies. 'It is probable that there is still a tendency to be easy with tenants and that very few are evicted', it was noted somewhat reprovingly early in the new year.[46] The Intelligence Department of the Local Government Board never ceased to lament the unfortunate reception of the moratorium. 'Arrears of rent in the Industrial Dwellings have never recovered from the tenants' impression of the meaning of the "moratorium" at the beginning of the war', it reported as late as May 1915.[47] The rent problem resolved itself into coaxing payment from cunningly obstreperous tenants.

The Courts Emergency Powers Act was framed on the twin assumptions that landlords respected at least the letter of the law, and that magistrates understood its meaning. Both were open to doubt. In Manchester County Court, Judge Mellor KC took the occasion of the annual renewal of certificates to warn bailiffs that he was not unaware of the 'subtle and ingenious' forms of evasion that were being practised.[48] The Liverpool police, prompted by organized labour, considered it prudent to remind proprietors of the need to observe due process in ejectment proceedings.[49] There were, of course, flagrant violations of the law, but surely few were as crude as the Warrington landlord who, in order to obtain vacant possession, threatened to remove the doors of the disputed property, or the Reading landlord who 'dragged a partially dressed soldier's wife from her bedroom landing to the street and there beat her upon the head with an umbrella', an action for which he was fined £10.[50]

In addition to evasion and intimidation, tenants had to contend with the prejudices of the local bench. The quality of the protection afforded by the act, it was felt, varied with the type of court and the

[45] Laurence Gomme, Clerk of the Council, to Susan Lawrence, 21 Nov. 1914 (WNC Papers).
[46] 'Report of Intelligence Department of LGB', 9 Jan. 1915 (PRO T. 172/192).
[47] 'Report of Intelligence Department of LGB', May 1915 (PRO T. 172/198).
[48] *Manchester Evening News*, 29 Jan. 1915.
[49] S. Higenbottam, Secretary of Liverpool Workers' Vigilance Committee, to J. S. Middleton, 26 Oct. 1914 (WNC Papers).
[50] Mrs Westwood to J. S. Middleton, 14 Oct. 1914 (WNC Papers); *Daily Sketch*, 30 Sept. 1915.

mood of the presiding magistrate.[51] In Glasgow 200 cases a day were being heard. In some courts decisions were given at anything between 60 and 100 per hour.[52] This was hardly a pretence of justice. Tenants had little faith in the new law: a court appearance involved the loss of time and money for working men and disruption of the household for women encumbered with children. It was a degrading ordeal from which the tenant, at best, gained a temporary reprieve.[53]

'All the other Bills which we have passed, or could pass, pale into insignificance compared with this drastic and most comprehensive document', said one anxious Member on the Second Reading of the Courts Emergency Powers Bill. Its contents, he added, 'shocked me immeasurably'.[54] There were many landlords who were no less stupified. But in this instance familiarity bred delight rather than contempt. So much so that, even before the end of hostilities, proprietors were ready to step forth gingerly brandishing Britannia's shield and trident. 'I think property owners all over the country can claim credit that they received this measure with a true vision of national patriotism, and no opposition worth mentioning was directed against it', declared the Secretary of Birmingham Property Owners' Association.[55] The more frequent intervention of the courts in the settlement of disputes was found to be of considerable benefit in that tenants were inclined to comply with the usual Court order and repay arrears in regular instalments. The Registrar of Birmingham County Court, in a letter to one of the national dailies, cited the opinion of 'one of the most experienced rent bailiffs' in that strife-torn city to the effect that the Courts Emergency Powers Act was 'undoubtedly the best device for collecting rent that had yet been invented.'[56]

Disquiet as to the working of the act was voiced in Parliament on several occasions during 1915. W. C. Anderson who drew attention to its shortcomings in February, elicited a depressingly bland response from Front Bench spokesmen.[57] Two months later Mackenna, questioned on rising rents in Glasgow and other centres, was insistent

[51] Cf. J. Austin Smith, Secretary of Burton-on-Trent ILP Branch, to J. S. Middleton, 22 June 1915 (WNC Papers).

[52] *Glasgow Herald*, 11 Dec. 1914.

[53] Statistics on ejectments for the fortnight following the introduction of the act are reported in *Glasgow Herald*, 13 Nov. 1914.

[54] *HC Deb*. 5s. lxvi (1914), 228.

[55] A. J. Wilson, *War Time and Other Legislation affecting Property Owners* (Birmingham, 1918), p. 14.

[56] *The Times*, 21 May 1919.   [57] *HC Deb*. 5s. lxx (1914-15), 232-44.

that the act afforded sufficient protection.[58] The Government appeared impervious to the seriousness of the situation when Anderson again raised the question six weeks later.[59] On 24 June Walter Long, President of the Local Government Board, brusquely dismissed the very idea of rent control. 'I cannot imagine a more controversial question', he told the House.[60] Five months later he rose to introduce the Rent Restriction Bill. The 'demise of political economy' which Barnes too readily applauded[61] had not, however, been won without a struggle.

The origins of rent control in Britain remain obscure. In spite of recent discoveries, the legend that the Rent Act, 1915 was passed in response to the near revolutionary activities of Glaswegian tenants still finds its way into the text-books.[62] No evidence is brought forward in support of this contention; indeed, none can be. The myth that the Clyde Workers Committee led the rent strikes of 1915 was effectively demolished some time ago.[63] How then can we explain the introduction of this momentous piece of legislation? One student has argued for the primacy of Lloyd George and the resolution of inter-departmental rivalries in favour of the Ministry of Munitions as *the* vital factor in its genesis.[64] But in the absence of adequate documentation owing to the non-preservation of the essential Cabinet records, this plausible but improbable thesis remains unproven. Another scholar has suggested that the act was the result of the intervention of the Parliamentary Labour Party primed by the Workers' National Committee. This argument, however, relies upon an inference based upon significant absences in the archives of the Workers' National Committee.[65] It too remains not proven. From a quite different perspective Dr Clinton also directs attention from the struggles in Glasgow. The passing of the Rent Act, he suggests, owed something to the working-class agitation outside Scotland.[66] In this he is surely correct.

The first rent strikes began within weeks of the declaration of

[58] *HC Deb*. 5s. lxxi (1915), 828-9.   [59] *HC Deb*. 5s. lxxiii (1915), 655.
[60] *HC Deb*. 5s. lxxiii (1915), 1326.   [61] *HC Deb*. 5s. lxxvi (1915), 749.
[62] See, for example, John Burnett, *A Social History of Housing 1815-1970* (Newton Abbot, 1978), p. 217.
[63] James Hinton, *The First Shop Stewards' Movement* (1973), pp. 125-7.
[64] Iain Maclean, 'The Labour Movement in Clydeside Politics 1914-1924' (University of Oxford Unpublished D. Phil. thesis, 1971), p. 34.
[65] Winter, *Socialism and the Challenge of War*, p. 204.
[66] Alan Clinton, *The Trade Union Rank and File: Trades Councils in Britain 1900-1940* (Manchester, 1977), pp. 39-40.

war.[67] Not long after, London property owners appealed to the Commissioner of Police to curb the activities of the Shoreditch Trades Council whose members, it was alleged, were 'flagrantly inciting breaches of the law and of the peace'. The Trades Council's offence consisted in its efforts to organize a rent strike. Public meetings had been held and resolutions passed demanding the suspension of rent payments during the war. Volunteers had also been enrolled to resist the bailiffs.[68] Support came from unexpected quarters. From a recruiting platform the Mayor of Bethnal Green censured rapacious landlords. In his worship's opinion 'it was an abomination to Bethnal Green for landlords to increase rents during a time of distress'.[69] In Hammersmith there was said to be 'exceptional difficulty' in collecting rents.[70] In Camberwell the Labour Party encouraged tenants to resist excessive demands.[71] Keeping a clear rent book, as Table 5 suggests, was becoming increasingly difficult.[72] The National Administrative Council of the ILP advised affiliates that prevention of distress for rent be accorded priority in their work on local relief committees.[73] In Woolwich the call for a rent strike become more clamant towards the end of the year.[74] Work on the Well Hall Estate began shortly afterwards.

Unrest in England and Wales grew in volume throughout 1915. The willingness to resort to direct action proved contagious. Burton-on-Trent branch of the ILP, following the example of tenants in Govan, Edinburgh and Luton, was thus encouraged to go ahead and organize a similar resistance in its own district.[75] In some coalfields too miners withheld rent.[76] Manchester Trades Council, however, resisted local pressure for a rent strike.[77] Instead, the Trades Council, following publication of a systematic investigation

[67]   *Daily Citizen*, 19 Aug. 1914.
[68]   *Property Owners' Journal*, Sept. 1914.
[69]   *Hackney & Kingsland Gazette*, 21 Sept. 1914. The authorities, however, were told that, despite the alarming rise in arrears in the borough, 'leniency is being shown all round'. 'Report of Intelligence Department of LGB', 12 Sept. 1914 (PRO T. 172/166).
[70]   'Report of Intelligence Department of LGB', 10 Oct. 1914 (PRO T. 172/170).
[71]   Clinton, *Trade Union Rank and File*, p. 39.
[72]   'Report of Intelligence Department of LGB', 5 Dec. 1914 (PRO T. 172/177).
[73]   *Labour Leader*, 17 Dec. 1914.
[74]   *Woolwich Pioneer*, 20 Nov. and 4 Dec. 1914.
[75]   See enclosure, Francis Johnson to J. S. Middleton, 16 June 1915 (WNC Papers).
[76]   J. Wansworth, General Secretary of Barnsley Miners' Union, to F. W. Jowett, 4 Oct. 1915 (WNC Papers).
[77]   *Manchester Evening News*, 14 Sept. 1915.

Table 5: Arrears in London for week ending 28 Nov. 1913–14

Housing Agency	1913 (per cent)	1914 (per cent)
Peabody Trust	1	4
Improved Industrial Dwellings Co.	4	5
LCC	10	17
Artisan, Labourers' & General Dwellings Co.	10	17
East End Dwellings Co.	12	19
Four Per Cent Industrial Dwellings Co.	8	19

Source: 'Report of Intelligence Department of LGB', 5 Dec. 1914 (PRO T.172/177)

into the increase in house rents, undertaken on behalf of the Workers' National Committee, sponsored the formation of a Tenants' Defence League to agitate for the introduction of a Fair Rent Court.[78] Elsewhere munition workers, supported by their employers, urged the authorities to take action in order to prevent 'the systematic exploitation of the workers'.[79] The Minister of Munitions, concerned at the continued labour wastage in the metal trades due to the want of accommodation, agreed to examine the problem.

Before his investigation was completed it had already been established that the provisions of the Courts Emergency Powers Act afforded insufficient protection to munitions workers against the raising of rents.[80] Subsequent inquiries, although based upon a full examination of conditions in the major centres of production, completely misread the situation. 'On the whole', it was concluded, 'they do not indicate an improper or unfair attitude on the part of landlords, and in all the areas the rises in rents have been due as much to normal economic causes as to the rapacity of landlords.' Profiteering was, indeed, a source of considerable tension in the work-force but, the Minister was informed, this was due to working-class avarice: 'In many cases tenants are principally to blame for the rise in rents by demanding unconscionably high lodging rates from imported workmen.' Although some protest meetings had been

[78] Manchester & Salford Trades & Labour Council, *Report on Increase of House Rents in Manchester and Salford since the commencement of the War* (Manchester, 1915); *Manchester Evening News*, 20 Oct. 1915; *Manchester Guardian*, 27 Oct. 1915.
[79] *The Times*, 18 Sept. 1915.
[80] 'Secret Weekly Report of Labour Department', 25 Sept. 1915 (PRO Mun. 2/27).

organized there was, with one exception, 'no marked industrial unrest' in the fourteen areas inspected. The one exception was Birmingham where, said the report, 'serious trouble is anticipated unless matters are speedily improved'.[81]

The Rent Act of 1915 represented, to a degree which hitherto has not been appreciated, the culmination of the pre-war struggle between landlord and tenant that was analysed in the previous chapter. In Birmingham where the call for a rent strike had been voiced earlier in the year,[82] the dispute between landlord and tenant continued to be bedevilled by the compounding issue. The Trades Council sought to enlist the support of the Assessment Committee in curbing illicit rent increases.[83] The collection of evidence was, however, an arduous and protracted task; and tenants were impatient.

At the beginning of October 130 of 'the best class of tenants' in the Lozells district combined to refuse the new rents. The following week they were joined by tenants in Witton. A round robin, signed by most of the 50 tenants affected, was promptly dispatched to the owner. It was accompanied by a typewritten letter which gave notice of their unshakeable resolve and bore the legend 'The Awakening'. The Aston and Handsworth Tenants' Association, which had been formed six months earlier, was active in the agitation. But the action was not confined to one or two districts. In both Saltley and Erdington action 'which may easily assume large proportions' was rumoured to be imminent. 'Something drastic must be done' said Councillor Jeseph Kesterton, Secretary of the Birmingham Trades Council.[84] But nothing was, and the agitation spread.

'My Council', he complained, 'is inundated with cases of extortionate increases in rents of working class houses ... In all parts of the City there is a system of extortion which is intolerable.'[85] At Lozells the chairman of the striking tenants advised the women, who were particularly active in the campaign, to 'keep their temper' and not molest the agent while he made his weekly round.[86] The local constabulary thought it prudent to maintain a 'low profile' during his visits. But their presence was superfluous: the women

[81] 'Secret Weekly Report of Labour Department', 23 Oct. 1915 (PRO Mun. 2/27).
[82] *Birmingham Gazette*, 15 Feb. 1915.
[83] *Birmingham Gazette*, 8-11 Sept. 1915.
[84] *Aston News*, 9 and 16 Nov. 1915.
[85] Joseph Kesterton to J. S. Middleton, 2 Nov. 1915 (WNC Papers).
[86] *Handsworth Herald*, 30 Oct. 1915.

and children confined themselves to nothing more than verbal abuse. Indeed, in spite of the extreme provocation there was remarkably little violence in Birmingham or any other city. There was certainly nothing which even faintly resembled the spontaneous rioting directed at aliens and others in the previous spring. But in that tumultuous episode the labour movement had not been engaged.

In neighbouring Tamworth the Trades Council took the lead in organizing the tenants' campaign.[87] In West Bromwich County Court Mr Norman Birkett conducted the defence on behalf of some 32 rent-striking tenants from the Smethwick area.[88] Yet the everpresent fear of eviction was proving less and less of a deterrent. In Halford Road, Aston, for example, fourteen tenants who had been visited by the Aston and Handsworth Tenants' Association were reported to have joined the resistance—'but in fear and trembling as they know the law is on the side of the landlord, who has served notices and threatened ejectment.'[89] Amongst the Lozells rent-strikers the prospect of civil proceedings did not seem to cause undue alarm. 'The landlord', said one of them, 'is not the only person who has seen the lawyers; we know perfectly well where we stand and are prepared to await eventualities.'[90] There was not long to wait. In the second week of November the Clerk to the Birmingham Assessment Committee was ordered to London to seek the arbitration of Mr Lloyd George himself. The Minister ordered that rents be reduced.[91] 'The victory of the tenants', wrote *The Times*'s correspondent, 'was celebrated with much rejoicing flags and banners being stretched across the streets from house to house.'[92] But the time had passed when the dramatic intervention of a Minister of the Crown or a favourable ruling in the courts could have stilled the agitation. Working people, said the Secretary of the Aston and Handsworth Tenants' Association, 'were not out for litigation, but for legislation'. Nothing less than pre-war rents would suffice.[93]

London too was affected by the rising tide of tenant militancy. In Poplar and Dulwich rent strikes broke out; Bermondsey tenants prepared 'to offer the most stubborn resistance'.[94] In Edmonton where three concurrent rent strikes affecting 1,000 tenants were in progress, landlords, said one report, 'are being "strafed" by the

[87] *Birmingham Gazette*, 12 Nov. 1915.   [88] *Evening Despatch*, 22 Oct. 1915.
[89] J. Kesterton, 'Raising of Rents', Nov. 1915 (WNC Papers).
[90] *Evening Despatch*, 1 Nov. 1915.   [91] *Birmingham Gazette*, 13 Nov. 1915.
[92] *The Times*, 16 Nov. 1915.   [93] *Handsworth Herald*, 13 Nov. 1915.
[94] *New Statesman*, 13 Nov. 1915; *The Times*, 11 Nov. 1915.

tenants of their own country ... in a manner that, probably, only the Germans could express themselves towards this nation'.[95] Out of the successful resistance of some 350 Tooting tenants there emerged the War Rents League.[96]

Reports of demonstrations and further rent strikes in London and elsewhere grew in volume throughout the autumn. The Workers' National Committee, having completed extensive inquiries, warned the Prime Minister of the adverse effects upon morale, recruitment, and industrial production unless the continuous rise in rents was promptly checked.[97] The outcry could no longer be ignored and without doubt the decision to intervene was influenced by the 'considerable agitation in London and other parts of England'.[98] Nevertheless, it was the campaign on Clydeside that was decisive in shaping the measure that finally emerged.

On Clydeside the friction between landlord and tenant had not been smoothed out by the House Letting and Rating Act, 1911, and underlay much of the hostility that would soon erupt.[99] It was fuelled by the indiscriminate eviction of servicemen's dependents for non-payment of rent, in spite of an undertaking by the Glasgow Houseowners' Association that no such actions would be sanctioned.[100] There was in fact an alarming increase in the number of ejectments during the first month of hostilities, as is shown in Table 6. The civic authorities in Glasgow, unlike the Whitehall-based Intelligence Department of the Local Government Board or the parsimonious National Relief Fund, had few illusions as to the vulnerability of servicemen's families. A special relief fund, raised by voluntary subscription and administered by the Soldiers' and Sailors' Families Association, was set up to mitigate hardship as

[95] *The Times*, 9 Nov. 1915; *Tottenham & Edmonton Weekly Herald*, 22 Oct. 1915.

[96] *Daily Sketch*, 9 and 11 Nov. 1915; Rider, *Ten Years Adventures*, pp. 30 ff.

[97] J. S. Middleton to H. H. Asquith, 18 Oct. 1915 (WNC Papers).

[98] 'Increase of Rents on Workmen's Dwellings', Memorandum by T. McKinnon Wood, 17 Nov. 1915 (PRO Cab. 37/137/29). See too 'Rent Raising', Memorandum by H. W. Law, 18 Oct. 1915 (Christopher Addison Papers, Box 63, Bodleian Library, Oxford).

[99] 'It seems', an observer remarked in the autumn of 1915, as the rent strikes gathered pace, 'as if the smouldering feud between landlord and tenant which is as old as the housing system, will be fanned into open hostility by the present troubles.' *Govan Press*, 1 Oct. 1915; also see *Report of Departmental Committee on Increase in the Rental of Small Dwellings in the Industrial Districts of Scotland* (PP 1914-16, XXXV), p. 7 and W. Robinson, Secretary of Renfrew Trades & Labour Council, to McKinnon Wood, 19 Apr. 1915 (SRO DD. 6/551 File 23080/142).

[100] *Forward*, 22 and 29 Aug. 1914; also see *Weekly Record & Mail*, 30 Oct. 1915.

Table 6: Comparison of Numbers Evicted for Arrears of Rent in Glasgow, August and September 1913–1914

Year	1913	1914
No. of Citations	3148	3763
No. of Evictions	484	738

Source: *Glasgow Herald*, 11 Sept. 1914.

best it could. Response was good but not good enough. Moreover, the labour movement, excluded from meaningful participation, remained resentful and suspicious.[101] The Lord Provost's Fund, as it was called, did useful work but failed to arrest the growth of the agitation. The plight of the servicemen's family and the rapacity of the landlord infused the ideology of the moral economy with a new patriotic thrust and bite which Glasgow's working-class housing reformers were not slow to exploit.

The eviction of servicemen's dependents was the most emotive issue. But the predicament of the civilian work-force was no less explosive. The shortage of accommodation, apparent from 1912 onwards, was aggravated by the tremendous influx of munitions workers into the Clyde Valley. By the spring of 1915 the region was saturated. Landlords seemed determined to exploit the situation to the utmost. On 14 January 1915 the Glasgow Houseowners' Association called for a co-ordinated upward movement in rents. Early in February a joint insurance scheme designed to create a monopoly was rumoured to be in circulation amongst the factors. The proposed fund was to be financed out of a general 10 per cent increase in rents, a fourth of which was to be paid as a premium against losses on empties.[102] The widespread fear that some such plan would sooner or later materialize was later officially recognized as an important factor in the generation of popular unrest in the district.[103]

Discontent advanced quickly. Early in the new year the rising ground swell became more clearly defined as organized grass-roots opinion prepared for the reopening of Parliament. An indication of the subsequent pattern of events came in February with the first of a series of protest meetings organized by Clydebank Trades Council

[101] 'Interview of Deputation from Glasgow Workers' War Emergency Committee with Glasgow Division Soldiers' and Sailors' Families Association', 30 Apr. 1915 (WNC Papers); *The Times*, 12, 13, and 21 Apr. 1915.

[102] *Forward*, 13 Feb. 1915.

[103] *Report on Increase in Rentals of Small Dwellings*, p. 7.

outside the factory gates. Scottish MPs and the Government were soon apprised of the problem; resolutions demanding some form of rent control began to issue in profusion from the industrial communities of the West of Scotland.[104]

Table 7: Vacant Accommodation on Clydeside, May 1915

Place	No. House Unoccupied	Per Cent
Glasgow	8,122	4.7
Partick	158	0.9
Govan	333	1.6
Greenock	31	0.2
Paisley	348	1.8
Barrhead	36	1.3
Clydebank	—	—

Source: *Report on Increase in Rentals of Small Dwellings*, p. 4.

But attention remained fixed on Glasgow. Here the creative role of the ILP, the dominant force on the Glasgow Labour Party Housing Committee, was critical.[105] From the inception of the crisis, working-class housing reformers in Glasgow refused to regard the conflict with the landlords as a discrete or war-related difficulty. There was never any pretence that it was other than part of the continuing struggle for state-aided housing.[106] The repudiation of Fair Rents Courts in favour of pre-war rents also grew out of enmity and mistrust engendered in earlier struggles.

The new year found the Glasgow Labour Party in a confident mood. The £8 Cottage Scheme remained at the forefront of its programme. On 4 January 1915, some 420 delegates representing 207 separate organisations, assembled in St. Mungo's Hall for what was described as 'one of the most successful Conferences ever held for a specific Socialist purpose'.[107] Nevertheless the Town Council continued to withhold approval. The euphoria aroused by the St. Mungo's conference quickly evaporated. Property-owners were encouraged by the Town Clerk's declaration that the proposed

[104] Circular letter of War Emergency Glasgow Workers' National Committee enclosed in Ben Shaw to J. S. Middleton, 25 Feb. 1915 (WNC Papers); *Clydebank & Renfrew Press*, 5, 12, and 19 Feb. 1915; *Coatbridge Gazette*, 20 Feb. 1915; *Paisley & Renfrewshire Gazette*, 20 Feb. 1915; *Cambuslang Advertiser*, 6 Mar. 1915.
[105] Cf. Walter Kendall, *The Revolutionary Movement in Britain, 1900-1921* (1969), p. 115.
[106] *Report on Increase in Rentals of Small Dwellings*, p. 7.
[107] *Forward*, 9 Jan. 1915.

method of financing the Socialist housing programme was *ultra vires*. Upon him Councillor Wheatley vented his spleen: 'The Town Clerk for the moment stands between this horde of blood suckers and the rage of an awakened working class. And they don't understand that not even a Town Clerk can save them.'[108] Bluster aside, Wheatley as yet probably possessed no real conception either of the depth of this 'rage' or what direction it might assume. At this juncture there were few signs of disenchantment with the formal democratic process. 'Everybody is asking what the Labour Party will do now', Johnston wrote, and though confident that it would do something to retrieve the situation, he considered 'the most feasible approach' consisted in pressing the Corporation to seek parliamentary approval for the necessary financial powers.[109]

The Labour Party's campaign against rising rents also made little progress. By the end of 1914 the inadequacies of the Courts Emergency Powers Act had been fully exposed. On 16 February Barnes raised the subject with the Prime Minister at Question Time. Asquith, however, felt that the situation had been exaggerated and suggested that further information be submitted to the Secretary for Scotland for consideration. The Glasgow Labour Party took up the challenge and began to prepare a dossier on the extent of rent-raising.[110] The following month the question of a fair rent court was again raised at the Town Council. After a certain amount of prevarication, it was agreed to petition parliament for an inquiry.[111] But in this Glasgow acted alone: the Convention of Burghs would have no truck with such tribunals.[112] The Scottish Office, too, was less than enthusiastic. 'It is difficult to see what good an enquiry could do', the Minister was advised, 'and an enquiry by Govt [sic] might raise hopes of intervention by legislation which would be disappointed ...'[113] Meanwhile the Labour Party began to attend to rising food prices. M'Bride's attempt to arrange for the reception of a deputation of the Women's Housing Association was again spurned by the Town Council. Frustrated at every turn, the Labour Group was reduced to outright obstruction.[114]

On 29 April 1915 Barnes presented the Glasgow Labour Party Housing Committee's evidence to Mckinnon Wood. The Minister

108 *Forward*, 13 Feb. 1915.   109 *Forward*, 27 Feb. 1915.
110 *Forward*, 20 Feb. 1915.   111 *Forward*, 13 Mar. 1915.
112 *Scotsman*, 7 Apr. 1915.
113 Minute initialled R. L., 24 Mar. 1915 (SRO DD. 6/551 File 23080/136).
114 *Forward*, 7 Apr. 1915.

was not impressed. On the basis of the information supplied, Barnes claimed that 170-200 petitions were being taken daily in the Glasgow Sheriff Courts. Official figures disclosed that the daily average in the previous quarter was less than a tenth of this figure. During that period there had been a substantial reduction in the number of evictions compared with the same quarter in the previous year. Moreover, there was no evidence that soldier's dependants constituted a sizeable proportion of those affected. The Corporation's request for a governmental inquiry was also turned down.[115] Once again the Clydesiders had drawn a blank. However, the negligent briefing of a dull-witted champion had to some extent undermined their case. Barnes had made an elementary error in formulating his question. Had he demanded aggregate figures on the number of petitions since the outbreak of war as the basis for comparison with the corresponding period in the previous year the result might have been different. Moreover, the comparative reduction in the first quarter of 1915 still left 6,441 petitions for eviction which had in fact been granted in the Glasgow courts.[116] This was outrageous.

The matter could not rest there. Arthur Henderson was approached and the Labour Party requested to move a resolution calling for the suspension of further increases for the duration. The Labour Party, which to date had not played a distinguished part in the campaign against rising rents, was not disposed to exert itself on behalf of the Clyde workers. Dan Rider, Secretary of the War Rents League, who had also tried to arouse interest in the plight of tenants in the metropolis, had a similar experience. 'The majority of Labour Members', he recalled, 'were too enthusiastic about enrolling recruits and preserving Trade Union conditions to give much thought to this growing grievance.' Henderson was reluctant to divide the House without a more substantial case to offer and, after consultation with Barnes, advised the presentation of further evidence.[117]

At this juncture the 'rage' of which Wheatley had spoken earlier suddenly materialized. The manifest determination of the Govan tenants to resist fresh exactions came at a fortunate time for the Glasgow Labour Party. The resort to direct action was framed in terms of the timidity of the Parliamentary Labour Party. 'I think after this experience', M'Bride wrote,

[115] *HC Deb.* 5s. lxxi (1915), 844-5.
[116] *HC Deb.* 5s. lxxi (1915), 859-60.
[117] *Forward*, 4 June 1915; Rider, *Ten Years Adventures*, p. 23.

it will be clear to the minds of most of us that we need not depend on the Labour Party in the House of Commons for support to any proposal that would betray a want of fidelity in His Majesty's Government.

Under these circumstances, it would seem that, unless the people themselves take vigorous steps to show the Government that they are not going to permit this landlord robbery, the Government will do nothing to save the people.[118]

The new departure, however, offered the Glasgow housing reformers the prospect of a release from their impotent meanderings through the corridors of power, locally and nationally. Tenant intransigence gave the Glasgow Labour Party inspiration and the opportunity to telescope the housing and rent struggles into a united campaign. At the same time, it served to disguise its less than masterly handling of those grievances in Parliament. The tenants provided the lead, the Committee the leadership.

It was not entirely fortuitous that the rent strikes commenced in Govan, the most militant area before the war and the highest rented since.[119] On 23 April 1915 Messrs. Neilson, house factors, announced further increases in the rents of their extensive Govan properties to take effect from the end of the May term. This, the tenants complained, was the fourth increase in the area since its incorporation into Glasgow in 1912, and the second since the declaration of war. The landlord refused to reconsider. The tenants went on rent strike. In mid-May the Govan branch of the Women's Housing Association intervened. A public meeting was convened at which the women 'declared war' on the new demands. A plan of campaign was worked out in concert with the Govan Labour Representation Committee and the Glasgow Labour Party Housing Committee. It was decided to tender the old rent but withhold the increase. The tenants of the 250 houses involved were canvassed by local militants 'with the result that practically every man and woman signed the petition of protest against the increase' although 'a small minority' immediately retracted, and it later transpired that only 120 tenants actually resorted to strike action. The factor was informed of their decision but refused to accept the old rents. A week later, however, he changed his mind.

[118] *Forward*, 4 June 1915.

[119] On the distribution of rent increases, see *Report on Increase in Rentals of Small Dwellings*, p. 5. The remainder of this and the following paragraph is based on *Forward*, 4 and 12 June 1915; *Labour Leader*, 14 Oct. and 25 Nov. 1915; *Glasgow Citizen*, 26 Aug. 1915; and *Weekly Record & Mail*, 19 June 1915.

In that time the tenants had exposed the landlord as a scoundrel and in so doing enlisted the support of some major industrialists. Govan was a trade union stronghold. All the rent strikers were trade unionists and more than half employed on Government work. The Govan Tenants' Defence Committee, dominated by newly active women, at once began a series of open-air demonstrations outside the shipyards. Clydeside industrialists, having barely recovered from the February engineers strike were in no mood to provoke further dislocation in order to gratify the landlords. Land and Capital rarely achieved any real harmony of interest. While both were concerned with the defence of private property, the concrete forms of that property and its exploitation were not of necessity mutually beneficial. But they were not polarities and at times might be combined. The needs of a stable labour force frequently entailed investment in working-class housing on the part of industrial enterprise. In ship-building, a migratory trade with a labour force moving freely between the Tyne, the Clyde, and Northern Ireland, such needs became more urgent during periods of expansion when the size of order books might depend upon the availability of decent accommodation. One of the attractions of Belfast, for example, was said to be its superior housing relative to other shipbuilding centres. Clydeside shipbuilders were certainly aware of this: some offered generous financial assist-ance to the local authority for slum clearance and replacement housing while others were substantial proprietors in their own right.[120] Housing provision for these companies was best considered as part of fixed capital costs. Economic rents were demanded, but the returns were hardly the vital source of profit. Neilson's claim to be an agent for Messrs Harland and Wolff who, it was alleged, had requested accom-modation for 100 to 150 new workers, was a sheer fabrication. The Managing Director, approached by the Tenants' Defence Committee, rebutted the charge in no uncertain terms: 'We are pleased to hear that the tenants of the Govan district propose refusing to pay these increased rents, and we sympathise entirely with them. We trust that the legislature will intervene to annul all the increases which have recently taken place and to prevent any further increases, as it seems to us there is absolutely no justification for them.'

[120]   On housing in Belfast, see Cornelius O'Leary and Ian Budge, *Belfast: Approach to Crisis, A Study of Belfast Politics, 1613-1970* (1973), pp. 108-9; on financial aid to local authority, Thomas Ferguson, *Scottish Social Welfare, 1864-1914* (Edinburgh, 1958), pp. 141-2; on company housing, *Clydebank & Renfrew Press*, 30 Dec. 1904, 8 and 15 May 1915; and *Report of the Committee on the Rent Restrictions Acts* (PP 1924-25, XV), p. 18.

Fairfield's put out a statement to the effect that none of their employees would be allowed to occupy the house of any person victimized for refusing the higher rents. Stephen & Sons of Linthouse announced that the rents on their extensive properties had not been raised.[121] The industrial implications of the campaign were confirmed by the willingness of the newly-established Armaments Committee to investigate the situation.[122] The industrialists in general remained sympathetic towards the tenants; Beardmore's were even thought to have exerted pressure on their behalf as the struggle moved towards its climax later in the year. The factor, isolated and disgraced, appeared to have given way. After a mere seven days the Glasgow Labour Party Housing Committee was 'pleased to announce that the Factor, beaten to his knees, has accepted the rents at the old figure', and that thus encouraged, preparations were in progress for the extension of the campaign.

On Tuesday 8 June 1915, Michael M'Hugh was summonsed to appear at 10 a.m. at the Summary Ejectment Court to answer a petition for his eviction. Mr M'Hugh, a resident of Shettleston and a father of seven, was unable to attend. He was in fact lying in a Rouen hospital recovering from a severe wound. His two eldest sons were also not available: one, already possessed of two wound stripes, was on sick leave; the other was undergoing preparatory training for the trenches. Two of his five younger children were seriously ill. Five weeks arrears, less than 20*s.*, were outstanding. The Shettleston branch of the Miners' Union to which Mr M'Hugh subscribed, had expressed a willingness to settle the debt within the month. Mrs M'Hugh appeared in her husband's absence. She had received the usual dependant's allowance. She was given 48 hours' notice to quit.

In the normal course of events, a case such as this would have passed without comment. In wartime Glasgow it raised the fiercest of passions. It became something of a minor *cause célèbre*. 'In the long line of cruel, crushing, insulting treatment to which the Capitalist Class have subjected the working class', Wheatley thundered,

[121] English industrialists were apparently less generous. On Tyneside substantial increases had, in some instances, been imposed on the rents of company housing: North East Coast Armaments Committee, Minutes of Executive Committee, 17 June 1915 (PRO Mun. 5/9).

[122] The Glasgow & West of Scotland Armaments Committee, composed of representatives of employers, trade unions and government, was established in April 1915 to advise on the improvement of productivity. It possessed no powers of compulsion and under pressure its prestige and authority collapsed. It was wound up four months later: see *HMM* I, 3, pp. 141-8.

'nothing could be found to compare with their conduct in refusing the commonest shelter to the helpless children of the forgiving souls who in this crisis have placed their lives at the nation's service.'[123] The Glasgow Labour Party Committee tried to defend tenants as best it could. Rosslyn Mitchell and the two other solicitors whom Dollan had engaged,[124] had worked hard. But their industry notwithstanding, the numbers in need of legal aid were overwhelming. Nevertheless, a Labour Councillor was generally available to advise the defendant. Wheatley, who had attended court with Mrs M'Hugh, was acutely conscious of the stress and anguish to which poor people were regularly subjected. This is encapsulated in the cold fury which informed his description of these outrageous proceedings:

About 100 persons, mostly women, were huddled together in the corner of the courtroom, near the door which they had entered. They formed a heap of human misery ... In another corner of the room, a cheery little factor's clerkess sat chattering to some budding factor. Her neat, blue costume, with etceteras to match, provided sufficient contrast to set one thinking of the health and beauty and joy of which the very poor had been robbed ... And yet they seemed to feel that they were the criminals, and that the factors and lawyers present for the purpose of torturing them further, were the respectable people. When we had all risen and honoured the arrival of the wigged representatives of the law of the ruling class, business began. An official with a loud voice called the cases, and if the defender was present— about one in five—she went forward nervously, and was rushed through the following dialogue:—

    'Are you Mrs.————————?'
'Yes'
'Is this a monthly house?'
'Yes'
'Are you behind with your rent?'
'Yes'
'Where is your husband?'
'In the Army'
'Do you receive the usual allowance?'
'Yes'
'48 hours notice to leave the house'.

Not a word of explanation or defence listened to. The women were almost without exception soldiers' wives. During these proceedings, the sheriff, a well-fed, carefully groomed person, strutted backward and forward on his platform ...[125]

[123] *Forward*, 12 June 1915.   [124] *Glasgow Herald*, 12 Dec. 1914.
[125] *Forward*, 12 June 1915.

The following evening Wheatley addressed a crowd of between 3,000 and 4,000 people outside the M'Hughs' home. The pledge was unanimous; eviction would be prevented. The crowd was dominated by indignant women. Wheatley encouraged their participation. He said 'this was pre-eminently a fight for a poor woman and that poor women should undertake it'. The audience was in accord. At the break-up of the meeting 500 women made for the ILP rooms and offered themselves as pickets.

Their rising temper was in evidence the following day:

On the Thursday there was intense excitement. Women pickets were everywhere armed with all sorts of weapons; children would not go to school and a flag flew bravely from Mrs M'Hugh's house as a signal. Crowds paraded the street in front of the Factor's office, which was guarded by police, who are understood to have advised the non-execution of the warrant. The Factor's effigy was publicly burned and a raid made out to his house, but came back at once upon hearing that the Factor was ill. At night however, a huge crowd again marched to his house and smashed his windows.[126]

One James M'Kenna displayed insufficient concern for the factor's property. 'The accused', said the report, 'who was a ringleader in the demonstration, used most obscene language and behaved in a threatening manner, kicking and smashing the door of the factor's house'. His conduct, the report concluded, 'almost constituted a riot'. M'Kenna was sentenced to thirty days' imprisonment or a £5 fine.[127]

On the same day Wheatley succeeded in raising the matter in debate at the Town Hall, but his motion calling upon the Government to suspend the ejectment of servicemen's families was lost by twelve votes. *Forward*'s bold headline stigmatized the dirty dozen as 'A Black List of Dubious Patriots Who Would not Oppose Eviction'. Wheatley himself may well have been disturbed by the tumultuous spontaneity in the locality. The next day he tried to lower the collective temper, first by vaguely suggesting a demonstration outside the Armaments Committee office for which no subsequent preparation was made; and then by wiring Kitchener in London. Britain's warlord replied the following day. Separation allowances could not be raised, and as for special protection against eviction, his telegram concluded: 'no action feasible by War Office'. Wheatley was not exactly surprised. An earlier inquiry by the Govan tenants had elicited the same response. The menacing crowd, however, had long since dispersed. But Mrs M'Hugh was not evicted.

[126] *Forward*, 19 June 1915.   [127] *Weekly Record & Mail*, 19 June 1915.

The success at Govan and Shettleston proved contagious. Shortly afterwards tenants in three streets in the Richmond Park district decided that they too had had enough. On 22 June they held a public meeting and agreed to fight the factors in the same manner as had the Govan tenants.[128] A month later tenants of one street in West Partick decided to follow suit.[129]

At this stage the inertia of the Government appears to have stiffened the landlord's resolve to continue the struggle. In response to the furore unleashed by M'Bride's Housing Committee, the Board of Trade and the Scottish Office late in June had requested Glasgow Corporation to prepare a statement on the increase in house rentals. M'Bride was elated. 'We think it has now been clearly established that women can organise and defeat the factors and we are confident, with a little effort on the part of the tenants, the Government will be compelled to intervene.'[130] The Town Clerk's report appeared to justify his optimism. It disclosed excessive increases in some areas and unjustified increases in those districts annexed to Glasgow three years earlier.[131] But if the indecision of the central authorities was a source of encouragement to some landlords, mounting financial pressures were in any case tending towards an intensification of the crisis.

The insatiable thirst for money which the Government had acquired with the war was not without repercussions on the housing crisis. The issue of the second War Loan in June at once threatened the existing supply of housing finance and immediately provoked an acceleration in the pace of rent raising.[132] The rate of interest was the single most important determinant of the profitability of residential property. More than 90 per cent of house property in Glasgow was mortgaged or held on bond. The general rule was for the landlord to mortgage two-thirds of the value of his property in the expectation of a net return of anything beyond 6-7 per cent on the remaining third. A slight rise in bond rate necessarily led to a disproportionate reduction in profit margins. A rise in bond rate by half a per cent required a corresponding increase in rent of from 4-5 per cent to maintain former levels of net rent. In pre-war years it was customary for bond rate to be 1 per cent above current rate on Consols.[133]

128   *Forward*, 26 June 1915.   129   *Forward*, 26 Aug. 1915.
130   *Forward*, 26 June 1915.   131   *Forward*, 18 Sept. 1915.
132   *British Labour Statistics: Historical Abstract 1886-1968* (HMSO, 1971), p. 166.
133   On housing finance in Glasgow, see A. K. Cairncross, *Home and Foreign Investment 1870-1913* (Cambridge, 1953), pp. 34-6.

The issue of the first 3½ per-cent War Loan reduced the bond-holders' return by half a per cent above the Government rate. The second issue at 4½ per-cent implied a return of half a per cent below that rate. The prospect of widespread foreclosures appeared imminent as bondholders began to transfer their funds into the more lucrative War Loan. Others, anticipating further issues, demanded 5 per cent on their bonds. To prevent a slump in property values the Glasgow Faculty of Procurators, the authority in these matters, resolved upon a 4½-per-cent bond rate to take effect from 11 November.[134] Glaswegian landlords had already seen the writing on the wall. On 15 July they met and resolved to raise rents yet again.[135]

The property owners' offensive gathered momentum during the summer. But it quickly brought diminishing returns. Once again Messrs Neilson led the attack. The Govan 'victory', celebrated in *Forward* at the beginning of June, was more apparent than real. The announcement was calculated to rally fresh support; and as such it typified a style of campaigning which influenced the eventual outcome of the struggle, but one which also constitutes a source of confusion for the unwary. The Govan 'victory' was hardly an unqualified success. In fact the new demands had not been withdrawn. A personal intervention from the proprietor, ostensibly designed to facilitate negotiations, only seemed to aggravate the situation.[136] The factor eventually turned to the courts for a resolution of the difficulty. His two victims, however, were not well-chosen. In one case the old rent had been accepted which invalidated notice to quit as a fresh tenancy had not in consequence been created. In the second case the factor withdrew the action on learning that the defendant was a mother of nine whose husband was at the Front.[137]

But at Partick he had better luck and appeared to have broken the solidarity of the tenants after three weeks through a simple deception which left one tenant with the impression that the others had paid up. Thereafter the strike quickly disintegrated as the remainder, fearful of selective proceedings, all followed suit. By the third week of August the strike was over. Neilson's renewed confidence was evident from the relish with which two ringleaders were victimized.[138]

However, within weeks fresh strikes broke out in blocks hitherto

---

[134] *Report on Increase in the Rental of Small Dwellings*, p. 6.
[135] *Glasgow News*, 16 July 1915.   [136] Cf. *Forward*, 19 June and 10 July 1915.
[137] *Glasgow Citizen*, 26 Aug. 1915.   [138] *Forward*, 18 Sept. 1915.

unaffected. The first incident involved 130-40 tenants 'of the respectable working class', occupying houses 'of a very good class including several three-apartment dwellings', who also agreed to tender the old rent minus the increase. Daniel Nicholson, the factor, personally returned their remittances. On arrival 'he was followed by a very large and hostile crowd, who booed and hissed him and he was liberally spattered with pease meal'. The timely intervention of the police ensured that nothing more untoward came to pass.[139] A few days later, according to one source, the number of rent strikers was estimated at close on 500. But in the opinion of the 'special Commissioner' of one of the popular Glasgow weeklies, the number of rent strikers in Partick—'the real hot-bed of dissatisfaction at present'—had remained stationary.[140]

Rent strikes, however, were now becoming more widespread. Tenants at Dennistoun, Ibrox, Bellahouston, and Parkhead had decided to join the resistance. The situation at Parkhead was of considerable significance. On 25 August 300 tenants united to fight the factor.[141] Their action struck a responsive chord at Parkhead Forge where the depth of feeling amongst the rank and file caught some shop stewards unawares.[142] On 3 October Kirkwood informed the Town Clerk that the shop stewards, supported by a general meeting at Parkhead Forge, regarded the housing situation as intolerable and would consider the continued eviction of rent strikers 'as an attack on the working classes which called for the most vigorous and extreme reply and one which might have disastrous consequences'.[143]

Four days later 800-1,000 rent strikers, drawn mainly from Partick, although representing five different districts in all, set out to march to the town centre. By the time they converged on St. Enoch Square at noon, their ranks, swollen with sympathizers, had increased threefold.[144] Four and five deep, they then marched in procession to the City Chambers. The crowd consisted 'of nearly all women and children of the respectable working class'. Although their banners suggested the presence of soldiers' dependants, it was felt that

---

[139] *Glasgow News*, 29 Sept. 1915; *Weekly Record & Mail*, 9 Oct. 1915.

[140] *Govan Press*, 1 Oct. 1915. Cf. *Weekly Record & Mail*, 16 Oct. 1915.

[141] *Glasgow Eastern Argus*, 28 Aug. 1915.

[142] David Kirkwood, *My Life of Revolt*, (1935), p. 122.   [143] *Forward*, 9 Oct. 1915.

[144] This and the following paragraph are based on *Glasgow Herald*, 8 Oct. 1915; *Glasgow Citizen*, 7 Oct. 1915; *Glasgow News*, 8 Oct. 1915; *Daily Sketch*, 9, 10, 12, and 13 Oct. 1915; *Manchester Guardian*, 8 Oct. 1915.

'probably the majority of those present were from the families of munitions workers'. The demonstration, ostensibly in support of a deputation from the Women's Housing Association, had been carefully marshalled by the Glasgow Labour Party Housing Committee, and the striking effect of women and children 'of a very orderly description' was not lost on the media. The element of stage management, however, does nothing to diminish the representative character of the demonstration. The rent strikers beyond dispute expressed the sentiments of the working classes in the city. 'The demonstrators', it was observed, 'received a great ovation from their neighbours as they set out, and in one case—that of Partick—the strikers passed through long rows of cheering spectators who lined the streets.'

Nevertheless, the deputation made little more than a partial impression on the town council. Although unwilling to muster the two-thirds majority necessary to suspend standing orders to permit immediate debate, the councillors discreetly referred a recommendation from the City Improvements Committee proposing to raise rents on Corporation tenancies. More important to the rent strikers was the extensive and highly favourable coverage, especially in the national dailies. The extension to housing of the moral opprobrium associated with profiteering had become a critical feature of the campaign. The effect of women and children demonstrating with placards branding the landlord as 'the Hun at Home' was electric. The projection of the campaign as a parallel of the military struggle captured popular imagination in a way in which all the tedious tales of mean streets and the turgid details of housing schemes, however meritorious, had never been able to do. The *Daily Sketch* invited its readers to forward their own grievances in support of its campaign for some form of rent restriction. The *Manchester Guardian* warned the authorities: 'The sympathy of the Glasgow dockyard and factory workers, who have come in latter years to realise the extent to which their city is landlord-ridden, will be warmly with threatened tenants, and wider trouble may result from any tactless handling of the grievances.' It too expressed support for some form of control.

The Government was disturbed. Four days later Mckinnon Wood, Secretary for Scotland, and Robert Munroe, the Lord Advocate, were dispatched to confer secretly with the rent strikers. The tenants were represented by James Steward and Andrew M'Bride, and the meeting lasted more than an hour. Ministers did not commit themselves but Dollan felt that, at last, the tenants 'had got the Government on the hop'.[145] Shortly afterwards Lloyd George, in a written reply, informed the House that he was aware 'that the unpatriotic course adopted by certain landlords in taking advantage of the national need to extort increased rents in munitions areas is aggravating labour unrest in certain districts', and warned of the Government's resolve to intervene should the investigations, in progress within his department, warrant such a course. McKinnon Wood also announced the appointment of 'a small and impartial committee to inquire into this matter promptly and rapidly'.[146]

The Government's response was generally well received. McKinnon Wood's inquiry, said the *Glasgow Herald*, was 'eminently desirable'. 'The matter has now developed so far that some attempt must be made to restore, if not complete harmony, at any rate some sort of working arrangement between landlord and tenant.' At the same time it insisted that, if proposed, intervention be limited to the specific problems arising out of the efficient prosecution of the war. 'That consideration we think bars off interference with the operation of economic conditions in relation to property which is not used by munitions workers.'[147] The exclusion of servicemen's dependants and the working population at large was totally unacceptable to the tenants' leaders.[148]

From the tone of Lloyd George's statement it was evident that some form of restriction was imminent. In the absence of any reliable indication as to the degree of control contemplated, Scottish landlords took fright and began to intensify their campaign. Daniel Nicholson of Partick was again in the vanguard. Rosslyn Mitchell's skills notwithstanding, Nicholson had obtained eviction orders against all but one of his ten victims.[149] Respect for the law was by now wearing thin. On Saturday 13 October more than 1,000 tenants assembled to prevent enforcement of the warrants. After a five hour vigil, the Sheriff's Officer conceded.[150]

Resistance spread. Govan Central, Craighton, Govanhill, Kinning Park, Fossilpark, Polmadic, Maryhill, Woodside, Garngad, Anderston, and Overnewton had, within a fortnight of Lloyd George's statement, come within the ambit of the strike movement.

[145] *Forward*, 16 Oct. 1915.   [146] *HC Deb*. 5s. lxxiv (1915), 1285, 1576.
[147] *Glasgow Herald*, 14 Oct. 1915.   [148] *Glasgow Herald*, 15 Oct. 1915.
[149] *Daily Record & Mail*, 13 Oct. 1915.   [150] *Daily Record & Mail*, 18 Oct. 1915.

'Consequently', Dollan remarked, 'one may assume with safety that tenants are on strike in every working-class area of the city and that the number of strikers is certainly not less than 15,000'.[151] Historians have tended to share this assumption—an assumption for which, it is suggested, there is no evidence whatsoever.[152]

Patrick Dollan, a future Lord Provost of Glasgow and a senior figure in labour politics, was at this time a flamboyant journalist who wrote extensively for the Labour Press. He was the tenants' chief publicist. The myth that the rent strike was well-nigh universal almost certainly emanates from his pen. Dollan's influential reporting was, of course, part of the campaign for rent restriction. In his concern to impress the gravity of the crisis upon the authorities he was not above inflating the extent of mass support. His claims must be treated with caution. In his analysis of the distribution of the strike movement, for example, Dollan frequently made no clear distinction between an isolated street or group of streets, a block or two or a whole district. His figures on the growth of the movement are equally suspect. In the issue of the *Labour Leader* for 2 October 1915 he estimated the number on rent strike as no less than 10,000. But, writing in the *Herald* four days later, the number of strikers had been halved. However, by 23 October the number had again climbed to 10,000 and the following week *Forward* claimed 15,000.[153] On 13 November Dollan, writing in the *Herald*, put the number of rent strikers at 30,000; the following week he changed his mind and in *Forward* revised the figure downwards by some 5,000.[154] In effect Dollan appears to have plucked a nicely rounded figure out of the air as the mood took him. The Glasgow Labour Party Housing Committee simply did not possess the administrative machinery to monitor fluctuations of this amplitude. Such an exercise would have taxed the resources of professional bureaucrats to the utmost. It was well beyond the capacities of the Clydesiders.[155] Although sometimes projected as the Carnot of the tenants' movement. M'Bride,

[151] *Forward*, 30 Oct. 1915.
[152] Cf. Hinton, *First Shop Stewards' Movement*, p. 126; H. McShane and J. Smith, *Harry McShane, No Mean Fighter* (1978), p. 75; Joseph Melling, 'Clydeside Housing and the Evolution of State Rent Control, 1900-1939', in Joseph Melling, ed., *Housing, Social Policy and the State* (1980), p. 149.
[153] *Forward*, 23 and 30 Oct. 1915.   [154] *Forward*, 20 Nov. 1915.
[155] It is not without significance that the Glasgow Labour Party Housing Association should have been unable to prepare meaningful statistics on the extent of rent increases in the city: see evidence of Andrew M'Bride, *Report on the Increase in Rentals of Small Dwellings*, qq. 578-718.

according to the Secretary of the Scottish Labour Party, was not the most competent of administrators. 'An attempt is being made by the Glasgow Labour Party Housing Committee to regularise the Organisation', he wrote early in November: 'Mr M'Bride's methods have hitherto been very individualistic, though always carried out in good humour; but slackness, friction and something of secession have occurred in two or three Districts through individuals emulating his methods and becoming independent leaders in their own districts.'[156]

The Glasgow Labour Party Housing Committee and the contemporary historian share one thing in common: neither can accurately assess the numerical extent of participation in the rent strikes of 1915. Newspaper accounts other than those filed by Dollan suggest that the numbers involved may not have exceeded 2,000, and propably were a good deal less.[157] This does nothing to diminish the achievement of the Glasgow tenants or their leaders: on the contrary, it is a tribute to the skilful extemporization that was to carry the campaign from fair rents to pre-war rents.

McKinnon Wood's promised inquiry opened in an atmosphere of rising tension late in October. Neither Lord Hunter, the chairman, nor his colleague, W. R. Scott, inspired much confidence amongst the tenants' representatives. Lord Hunter, a High Court Judge and former Liberal MP for Govan, had recently given a verdict which was felt to have encouraged bondholders to increase interest rates. Professor Scott was an economist at Glasgow University not noted for his labour sympathies.[158] It was felt that, at best, the inquiry might provide 'some splendid propaganda material'. 'It may be that the tenants will be fobbed off with a Fair Rent Court, or some such jocular remedy', Dollan remarked, 'but the propaganda has been made, and now thousands of people who never knew before about the economics of housing are now sitting up *thinking*.'[159] At the same time it was hoped that something more tangible might yet be obtained.

The Hunter Committee, which also took evidence from Rutherglen, Aberdeen and Dundee, reported within two weeks of its appointment. In that fortnight doubts as to the comparative merits

[156] Ben Shaw to J. S. Middleton, 10 Nov. 1915 (WNC Papers).
[157] This 'guesstimate' is based on an examination of the Glasgow local press. It is, however, impossible to differentiate intent to withhold rent from those who went on rent strike.
[158] *Forward*, 23 Oct. 1915.   [159] *Forward*, 6 Nov. 1915.

of Fair Rent Courts hardened into a firm conviction that pre-war rents alone would provide tenants a wholesome protection against proprietors adept at manipulating the law to their own advantage. The furious round of rent-raising coincident with the opening of the official inquiry was adduced as further evidence of the devious strategy pursued by their adversaries. These increases, said Dollan, were 'a cunning endeavour to get the Commissioners to inquire not into the reasonableness of the increases already imposed during the war, but into those increases they are now seeking to impose'. 'From enquiries which I have made', he wrote, 'I learn that the tip has been passed round for the factors to increase rents now, as further increases are likely to be prevented during the war. Indeed, the factors are even prepared to forgo further increases except such as are rendered necessary by increased rates, if the present increases are allowed to stand.'[160]

In this poisonous atmosphere the quest for absolute security became the paramount consideration. Old slogans were abandoned. 'There can be no fair rental with private enterprise meeting the needs of the people', M'Bride told the Hunter Committee.[161] The mere fact that the House Owners' and Factors' Association had in private indicated its support for a Fair Rent Court was sufficient to discredit the proposal.[162] Nothing was to be left to chance—or the lawyers.

The Clydesiders' unilateral action was the source of some embarrassment in London where the Workers' National Committee, in conjunction with other groups, was busily lobbying Ministers on behalf of fair rent tribunals. The usually unflappable Middleton was quite put out by their inconsiderate militancy. 'I am bound to say that it is most unfortunate that the Glasgow people should play "ducks and drakes" with their Municipal Programme when such an excellent opportunity arises to realise it.' He added: 'I am afraid we are too far committed now to go back on the principle of Fair Rent Courts.'[163] Six days after this letter was written Glasgow witnessed one of the most momentous demonstrations in modern British social history.

---

[160] *Daily Record & Mail*, 23 Oct. 1915; *Forward*, 30 Oct. 1915.
[161] *Report on the Increase in Rentals of Small Dwellings*, q. 597.
[162] Ben Shaw to J. S. Middleton, 10 Nov. 1915 (WNC Papers). In England and Wales too organised property owners were reconciled to the introduction of such tribunals: see 'Rent Raising', Memorandum by H. W. Law, 18 Oct. 1915 (Addison Papers, Box 63).
[163] J. S. Middleton to Ben Shaw, 11 Nov. 1915 (WNC Papers).

In spite of the unseemly haste with which it was compelled to operate, the investigations undertaken by the Hunter Committee were sufficient to confirm the upward trend in house rentals. In Glasgow it disclosed an average increase of 6 per cent since the outbreak of war. The Committee was above all concerned to assess the differential impact of these increases upon working-class incomes, for the critical factor in the agitation lay in the likely response of those in the metal trades engaged on vital war work. On this aspect there seemed to be few grounds for concern. 'The proportion of wages which most munitions workers are asked to pay in extra rent by reason of these increases cannot, on the average, be called excessive', it concluded. Real hardship was confined to those workers whose wages had either declined or remained stationary. Amongst these grades 'the dread of further increases ... appears to be a matter of the very greatest anxiety ...'[164] These fears were not without foundation. Edwin Evans, President of the National Federation of Property Owners Associations, who had himself been instrumental in securing the withdrawal of at least 3,000 notices, later confessed that the trend of rent raising 'was quite sufficient to show what might have happened if there had been no restriction'.[165] However, it was amongst the better-paid workers, resident in the Govan-Finneston district, where rent increases were highest and most concentrated, and where the operation of the House Letting Act continued to generate most friction, that tension reached ignition point.

The situation at Partick was particularly acute. Having failed to evict his defiant tenants, Daniel Nicholson, the factor, applied to the Small Debt Court for an order for the arrestment of the wages of some eighteen tenants, including Andrew Hood, editor of the *Partick Gazette*, who also happened to be the chairman of the Partick Tenants' Defence Association. The rent strikers greeted this latest move with another of those displays of solidarity which had by now become a commonplace in the Glasgow area. Partick tenants were joined by others from Scotstown and Whiteinch in a demonstration outside the factor's office.[166] Of far greater

[164] *Report on the Increase in Rentals of Small Dwellings*, pp. 5, 7.

[165] 'Remedies for Rent Raising' (Addison Papers, Box 63). Quotation from Departmental Committee on the Operation of the Rent Restriction Acts: MS Minutes of Evidence, 1 Mar. 1920, p. 45 (PRO HLG 41/2); and see to Frank Hunt, 'The Position on the Expiration of the Rent Restriction Act in 1923', *Journal of the Surveyors' Institution*, I (1921), pp. 122-3.

[166] *Glasgow Evening News*, 15 Nov. 1915.

importance was the response from the shop floor and the shipyards.

The Partick Tenants' Defence Association was largely composed of munitions workers. All but two of those summonsed for arrestment of wages were shipyard workers.[167] Such persons were not unable to afford the higher rents. It was the rampant profiteering, Hood explained, to which they took exception: 'So far as Partick is concerned it is largely a fight on principle'.[168] And patience was exhausted. The first indication of a possible fusion between the nascent unofficial shop-floor movement and the tenants' agitation had been evident at Parkhead Forge at the beginning of October. In the same month threats of a general strike against continued evictions had been voiced by shipyard workers at Fairfields, Govan.[169] This convergent tendency became more pronounced in the weeks that followed. Unofficial Vigilance Committees, apparently the precursors of the Clyde Workers' Committee, which had been formed amongst some engineering workers, had, according to Councillor Dollan, established contact with the rent strike movement.[170] In the shipyards it was these Vigilance Committees which took the decision to strike on 17 November, the day on which Nicholson's application was due to be heard. In the days preceeding the hearing, official overtures were made to both sides. On 16 November the Munitions Board informed the Vigilance Committees that the proposed strike had been rendered superfluous as the factor had given an undertaking 'to make a statement in court which he hoped will settle the matter'. That evening Nicholson informed the tenants that, in deference to the wishes of the authorities, the application would be adjourned for three weeks on condition that, in the interval, they continued to tender the old rent.[171]

The outright rejection of the truce thus offered highlighted the tenants' growing confidence, a confidence which their erstwhile leaders did not, perhaps, share in full. The Glasgow Labour Party, having before the war established its credentials as the most dynamic force for housing reform naturally assumed the leadership of the agitation once the rent strike began in the spring. M'Bride and associates, acutely conscious and fearful of the oppressive powers of

[167] *Report on the Increase in Rentals of Small Dwellings*, q. 961; *Glasgow Evening News*, 15 Nov. 1915.

[168] *Report on the Increase in the Rentals of Small Dwellings*, qq. 1013-14, 1041-3.

[169] *HMM*, IV, 2, p. 55.

[170] On Vigilance Committees, see Hinton, *First Shop Stewards' Movement*, pp. 104 ff; for Dollan's report, see *Herald*, 13 Nov. 1915.

[171] *Glasgow Citizen*, 17 Nov. 1915.

the state in wartime, had, notwithstanding their uncompromising language and escalating demands, conducted the subsequent campaign with great circumspection.[172] The style and form of tenant militancy had been carefully contrived to dramatize and register the state of popular feeling without recourse to methods calculated to invite state repression. The Women's Housing Association was given considerable exposure and took the lead in the guarded approaches to the industrial workers while M'Bride's Housing Committee remained discreetly in the background.[173] It was hoped that the threat of industrial disruption would suffice. No explicit call for industrial action was issued on behalf of the tenants. A circular that was distributed throughout the shipyards by the Govan Tenants' Defence Association appealed for support of a non-specific nature.[174] Similarly, Dollan in his articles drew attention to the probable consequences of official inaction without ever going so far as to encourage a cessation of work. Where, as at Parkhead or Fairfields, a preference for strike action had been expressed, it was not in response to a request from the Glasgow Labour Party Housing Committee, although it must be said that the relation between the Vigilance Committees and the local Labour Party remains unclear. This ultra-cautious approach probably was not necessary. Even if feasible, it is difficult to see on what grounds a prosecution might have been secured.[175]

The growing involvement of the authorities indicated concession rather than repression. Lloyd George's earlier statement in the House, the appointment of the Hunter Committee, and the desperate official initiatives to delay a ruling on Nicholson's application for arrestment—together constituted unmistakable evidence that legislation was imminent. Indeed, within the Ministry of Munitions amending legislation had been under consideration since the beginning of October. Rent control had become a matter of detail

---

[172] On ILP attitudes towards the state at this time, see Terence Brotherstone, 'The Suppression of *Forward*', *Journal of Scottish Labour History Society*, I (1969). Such apprehensions were not confined to Clydeside. The self-censorship of the *New Statesman* in regard to the rent strikes is a case in point: see *New Statesman*, 20 Nov. 1915; and see too Andrew Boyd, Organiser of Northampton Building Trades Federation, to J. S. Middleton, 14 Dec. 1914 (WNC Papers).

[173] On the role of women, see Sean Damer, 'State, Class and Housing: Glasgow 1885-1919', in Melling, ed., *Housing, Social Policy and the State*, p. 104.

[174] Cf. *Weekly Record & Mail*, 28 Aug. 1915.

[175] Incitement to strike became a punishable offence on 30 Nov.: 'History of the Legal Department', Memorandum by J. C. Miles, 2 Feb. 1917 (PRO Mun. 5/353).

rather than principle. The number of rent strikes was immaterial: 'Even if cases of increased rents are not so numerous as is alleged in the newspapers the existence of a comparatively small number of them causes a quite disproportionate amount of agitation and discontent which should be removed.'[176] The delay in bringing forward the planned legislation proved fatal. What might have passed as an act of benign statesmanship some months earlier, was now perceived as a sign of weakness and vacillation. Firm action at this juncture might ensure that the minimal concessions embodied in the Rent Bill known to be in preparation might be made into something more substantial.

On 17 November crowds of striking workmen appeared on the outskirts of the city and marched in procession to the County Court Buildings headed by an improvised band 'including tin whistles, "hooters", and a dilapidated big drum'.[177] Extra police had been drafted into town in case of trouble though in the event, the crowd— estimated at anything between 4,000 and 15,000—was generally good-humoured. 'Their presence on the principal thoroughfares, nevertheless attracted a great deal of public attention, and when the vicinity of the Court House was reached there was much cheering and shouting, interspersed, it must be confessed, with many caustic remarks as to the legitimacy of their proceedings.' The crowd consisted principally of shipyard workers who had struck work 'to see that justice was done'. Their mood is perhaps best encapsulated in the following stanzas of a song composed by James Maxton for such occasions:

> To hell with the sheriff
> To hell with the crew
> To hell with Lloyd George
> and Henderson too
>
> I don't like the factor
> His rent I won't pay
> Three cheers for John Wheatley
> I'm striking today

[176] *HMM*, IV, 2, p. 104. Quotation from 'Remedies for Rent Raising' (Addison Papers, Box 63).

[177] This and the following three paragraphs are based on *Forward*, 20 and 27 Nov. 1915; *Glasgow Herald*, 18 Nov. 1915; *Weekly Record & Mail*, 20 Nov. 1915 and *Labour Leader*, 18 Nov. 1915.

> To hell with the landlord
> I'm not one to grouse
> But to hell with him
> And his bloody old house[178]

A fourteen-strong deputation was selected to interview Sheriff Lee, the presiding judge, who, in spite of the delicate legal position, agreed to see the men in chambers before taking the case. The Press, with the exception of *Forward* and *Vanguard*, complied with the request and withheld publication of these unusual proceedings. The Workers' spokesmen adopted a fiercely intransigent line. Representatives of the engineers explained that it was only with the greatest difficulty that they were able to persuade the rank and file to forgo a personal appearance at the Court House; others emphasized their inability to control the consequences of an adverse decision. One worker spoke bluntly: 'We have left our work and are determined not to go back unless you give a decision in favour of the tenants. It might look like coercion and we are sorry, but we are anxious to avoid serious trouble. If you decide in favour of the tenants it will be an indication to the Government to move in our favour.' Sheriff Lee then returned to his court, but only to order an adjournment.

Tension mounted. Outside the court a certain amount of scuffling broke out. As each minute passed the determination to force the issue hardened. What had began as a one-day stoppage was suddenly transformed into an indefinite general strike until satisfaction be obtained. A resolution to this effect, moved by John Maclean, was telegraphed to the Prime Minister in London. Whether Sheriff Lee too had contacted the authorities during the adjournment, as *Forward* alleged, remains uncertain. At any event, on resumption of proceedings Nicholson was persuaded to drop the case.

The tenants were jubilant. In Partick, where the Women's Housing Association had been particularly active, there was much enthusiasm: 'two hundred women celebrating the victory by indulging in a "cup of tea"'.[179] It boosted working class confidence everywhere. At Rugby disturbances were expected; at Birmingham industrial action was threatened.[180] At the beginning of the month

---

[178] The complete song is reproduced in Fenner Brockway, *Towards Tomorrow*, (1977), p. 38.

[179] *Glasgow Evening News*, 18 Nov. 1915.

[180] 'Secret Weekly Report of the Labour Department', 20 Nov. 1915 (PRO Mun. 2/27); and see correspondence of Frank Evans, District Secretary of ASE, *Birmingham Daily Mail*, 25 Nov. 1915.

the secretary of the Birmingham Trades Council thought that a 7½ per cent ceiling on rent increases, though not desirable, 'would be tolerable'.[181] Ministers too hoped to avoid universal rent control based on pre-war rents.[182] But time was tight. Fair Rent Courts had to be abandoned. The inevitable delay in the introduction of such controversial tribunals, the Cabinet was informed, would provoke further unrest. McKinnon Wood added: 'I think my colleagues will appreciate the fact that these courts once established would be difficult to abolish after the restoration of peace.'[183] The intention to restrict the measure to selected areas prescribed by Order in Council was also discarded.[184] Until legislation was brought forward Clydeside remained unsettled. One thousand men were still on strike when, on 25 November, Walter Long rose in the House to introduce the Rent Restriction Bill.[185]

[181] J. Kesterton to J. S. Middleton, 2 Nov. 1915 (WNC Papers).

[182] 'Increase of Rents and Mortgage Interest', Memorandum and Draft Bill by Walter Long, 23 Nov. 1915 (PRO Cab. 37/138/3).

[183] 'Increase of Rents on Workmen's Dwellings', Memorandum by T. McKinnon Wood, 17 Nov. 1915 (PRO Cab. 37/137/29).

[184] This was at the insistence of the Labour Party prompted by the Workers' National Committee: see J. S. Middleton to Charles Duncan MP, Secretary of the Parliamentary Labour Party, 29 Nov. 1915, and Minutes of War Emergency Workers' National Committee, 2 and 16 Dec. 1915 (WNC Papers).

[185] 'Secret Weekly Report of the Labour Department', 27 Nov. 1915 (PRO Mun. 2/27).

11

The Impact of War

The rent strikes of 1915 have sometimes been portrayed as little more than the prelude to the 'dilution' struggle; the continuing conflict between landlord and tenants has been forgotten.[1] Hitherto no attempt has been made to assess the operation of wartime rent controls, to explain the continuous growth of tenant militancy, nor to relate that remarkable upsurge to the genesis of socialized housing in Britain. This chapter will seek to repair the omission.

I

The thrust of the 1915 campaign was directed towards the abolition of profiteering in house rents. On this the Rent Restrictions Act appeared to give satisfaction. Rents of working-class dwellings were fixed at pre-war levels; evictions in England and Wales became negligible, at least in those sensitive munitions districts for which information is readily available.[2] In Sheffield, for example, the number of orders for ejectment made in the magistrates' court dropped from an average of 40 to 4 per week after the introduction of rent control.[3] Yet apprehension was not allayed. Interviewed by officials on behalf of the Ministry of Munitions early in 1918, Kesterton of the Birmingham Trades Council was reported to have taken 'a most violent attitude on this question and said that evictions must be stopped at all costs'.[4]

In industrial Scotland, where the Rent Act had little or no effect upon the internecine warfare between landlord and tenant,[5] the urgent need for extra accommodation remained a potent source of

---

[1] Cf. S. Pankhurst, *The Home Front* (1932), p. 262.

[2] See 'Reports of Central Billeting Board' (PRO Mun. 5/97).

[3] 'Central Billeting Board, Report on Sheffield', 12-15 Dec. 1917 (PRO Mun. 5/97).

[4] 'Central Billeting Board, Report on Birmingham', 28-9 Jan. 1918 (PRO Mun. 5/97).

[5] See *Civil Judicial Statistics for Scotland* (1917-21).

unrest. 'We are convinced', wrote the anxious peripatetic officials quoted above, 'that serious industrial trouble will result if some immediate steps are not taken, and we were continually faced with the unanswerable question of whether the Government wished the Clyde workers to resort to extreme steps before dealing with a problem which was universally admitted to be a matter of the most extreme and desperate urgency.' The visitors concluded that the immediate provision of between 2,000 and 3,000 houses 'would be more to allay industrial unrest on the Clyde than any other action'.[6] The Rent Restrictions Act, 1915, restored the peace without bringing the agitation to an end.

Framed in the interests of a working-class élite whose members did not habitually swell the eviction lists, it provided some protection against excessive rent increases but ignored the problem of security of tenure. In consequence, persons purchasing houses were in a position to obtain possession for their own occupation or for the occupation of an employee; no provision was made for the outgoing tenant. The scope for abuse was considerable: 'the possession of sufficient means to buy a house', wrote one trade unionist, 'makes the position of the poor almost intolerable'.[7] The demand for the outright suspension of ejectments during the war, voiced by the York Labour Party at the beginning of 1916, was to become more widespread.[8] The Act also made no provision for the substantial number of lodgers who flooded into the munitions districts. It was a fatal defect and, in view of the Ministry's involvement in its drafting, a curious one.[9]

The want of adequate data precludes a definitive assessment of the impact of these movements of population upon the housing problem. The impression, however, is that the improvement in the health of civilian workers was not accompanied by a corresponding improvement in their housing conditions.[10] There was, of course, considerable regional variation. Clydeside remained one of the very

[6] 'Central Billeting Board, Report on the Clyde', 12-16 Nov. 1917 (PRO Mun. 5/97).
[7] On the sale of houses and eviction of occupants, see *HMM*, V, 5, pp. 29-30. Quotation from W. Harris to J. S. Middleton, 20 Nov. 1917 (WNC Papers).
[8] A. V. Iredale to J. S. Middleton, 3 Jan. 1916 (WNC Papers).
[9] Cf. 'Secret Weekly Report of Labour Department', 18 Dec. 1915 (PRO Mun. 2/27).
[10] On the relationship of overcrowding and disease, see Thomas McKeowen and C. R. Lowe, *An Introduction to Social Medicine* (Oxford, 1966), pp. 162-7. On improvement in the health of the population, see J. M. Winter, 'The Impact of the First World War on Civilian Health', *Economic History Review*, 2nd Ser. XXX (1977).

worst black spots. Although scarcely credible, lodgers were in many cases taken into single-roomed apartments. 'The conditions resulting from such a state of things', an official visitation observed, 'can be better imagined than described.'[11] The position in industrial Ayrshire was hardly better. The eviction of two colliers and their families, former employees of Messrs William Baird at Dreghorn, was in these circumstances considered provocative. The company's action, wrote the secretary of the North Ayrshire Labour Party 'is causing intense irritation among the miners in the district and may if the matter is not rectified, lead to serious trouble'. Bairds reconsidered without further ado.[12] In Ardrossan and Salcoats, where the continuous extension of plant and machinery at the expense of housing had brought about a long-threatened crisis, some forty families, supported by local trade unionists, refused to surrender possession unless the authorities were willing to provide alternative accommodation and requisition the substantial but under-used 'holiday' houses that lined the coast.[13]

Statistics provided by the medical officer of health for Barrow-in-Furness disclosed a continuous increase in the extent of overcrowding. In 1914 there was on average 5.6 persons per house; in 1917 each house contained 6.5 persons.[14] In Lincoln too the shortage of accommodation was such that twenty men, employed by Messrs Rushton & Co., were literally compelled to sleep on the job—on sacks in the messroom floor, a form of repose which 'created great dissatisfaction in the works'.[15] The position on Tyneside was equally desperate. Not so Birmingham where, it was claimed, there was a perfect correspondence between inward and outward migration.[16] Too many workmen, however, *felt* that conditions had deteriorated and with the Corporation acknowledging the immediate need of

[11] 'Central Billeting Board, Report on the Clyde', 12-16 Nov. 1917 (PRO Mun. 5/97).
[12] Quotation from J. S. Campbell to J. S. Middleton, 22 Dec. 1916; and see enclosure in Campbell to Middleton, 18 Jan. 1917 (WNC Papers).
[13] On the housing crisis in this part of industrial Ayrshire, see 'Report rethreatened evictions by Messrs Nobels Explosive Co. Ltd., Ayrshire' (PRO Mun. 3/431); *Ardrossan & Salcoats Herald*, 4 and 18 May 1917; also correspondence of Androssan Branch of National Union of Railwaymen, 3 May 1917 and John Bromley, General Secretary of ASLEF, to Ministry of Munitions, 8 May 1917 (PRO, Mun. 3/432).
[14] 'Central Billeting Board, Report on Barrow-in-Furness', 19 July 1917 (PRO Mun. 5/97).
[15] 'Central Billeting Board, Report on Lincoln', 26 Oct. 1917 (PRO Mun. 5/97).
[16] 'Central Billeting Board, Report on Birmingham', 28-9, Jan. 1918 (PRO Mun. 5/97).

50,000 homes who could blame them? Birmingham remained one of the most militant districts.

Levels of overcrowding were often affected by exogenous factors: in Barrow, Coventry and Birkenhead poor communications with the outlying districts encouraged concentration around the principal source of employment.[17] In some instances, however, considerations of status and position were a sufficient dispersant. Messrs Barclay Curle & Co. of Whiteinch, Glasgow found that 'their better class of workmen' preferred to live a half-mile to one mile from their works and only the lowest class of labourer actually lived at the gates'.[18] This kind of differentiation, said Sir George Carter, actually inhibited the supply of additional accommodation. Messrs Cammell Laird, of which he was the managing director, would willingly have made provision but for the fact that 'the various trades would not mix, i.e. rivetters would not live in the same hostel with joiners'.[19]

The perception of the character of the prospective lodger was also a factor of some importance. In the west end of Sheffield, for example, there was increasing resistance to the newcomers and 'many complaints were being received that the munitions workers now being brought into Sheffield were of such a rough type that they could not be readily accommodated in billets'.[20] Elsewhere, landladies refused to accept lodgers without an indemnity against defaulters, and on Tyneside the Admiralty obtained a special grant for this purpose.[21] In some districts this want of confidence was said to be 'a great difficulty'.[22] In Morecambe, where the problem was particularly acute, the attempt to deduct arrears from wages embittered relations and had to be abandoned, ostensibly on grounds of an insufficiency of administrative personnel. Here, as in other seaside resorts, the irritating practice of turning out munitions workers during the summer season in order to take in visitors at higher rates, did nothing to sweeten tempers.[23] In Coventry, by

[17] On this see *HMM*, V, 5, pp. 47-8, 51-2.

[18] 'Central Billeting Board, Report on the Clyde', 12-16 Nov. 1917 (PRO Mun. 5/97).

[19] 'Central Billeting Board, Report on Liverpool, Birkenhead, Bootle and Wallasey', 6-9 Feb. 1918 (PRO Mun. 5/97).

[20] 'Central Billeting Board, Report on Sheffield', 12-15 Dec. 1917 (PRO Mun. 5/97).

[21] 'Central Billeting Board, Report on the Tyne', 7-11 Jan. 1918 (PRO Mun. 5/97).

[22] 'Central Billeting Board, Report on Ealing', 18 May 1917, (PRO Mun. 5/97).

[23] 'Central Billeting Board, Reports on Bognor, Littlehampton and Morcambe', July-Aug. 1917 (PRO Mun. 5/97).

contrast, the boot was on the other foot; 'Many complaints had been received about the lodgings particularly from girls of a superior class who stated that their beds were let in daytime to men'.[24]

The form of provision also influenced overcrowding. It was often the case that migrant munitions workers considered the relative freedom of cramped uncomfortable lodgings in the most congested quarters preferable to the spartan regime applied in the hostels managed on behalf of the authorities and large employers of labour. Coventry work-girls complained that one such hostel resembled a compound for black labour! The Benbow Hotel, built by Messrs Beardmore at Dalmuir, though it contained 386 bedrooms and served good inexpensive meals, was unpopular: 'The men object to the Hostel, as they think it savours of a model lodging house.' In one of the most crowded parts of Port Glasgow there stood a workmen's home with 100 vacant beds.[25]

Freedom such as this was expensive. The chance to exact fabulous rents was irresistable. 'Key money', often between £5 and £10, was almost universal. In many areas those with lodgings to let, formally, and sometimes brazenly, banded together in an organized system of extortion.[26] Working people were not immune. The opportunity for personal enrichment was simply too good to pass up.[27] In Barrow, a town in which working-class home-ownership was unusually common, proprietors went so far as to lodge a formal protest against the erection of additional accommodation that might depreciate the value of their dwellings and deprive them of a useful income from lodgers.[28] In that town, too, working-class landlords were no less prone to eject unwanted tenants. 'This is not a question of the aristocracy turning out democracy', said a local magistrate, 'it is the working man turning out the working man every time: it is always the same thing.'[29] The same was true of working-class Woolwich. 'The sale of houses to munitions workers who like comfort has been increasing' said a by no means unsympathetic observer. 'They have

[24] 'Central Billeting Board, Report on Coventry', 3 Oct. 1917 (PRO Mun. 5/97).

[25] *HMM*, V, 5, pp. 16, 39; 'Central Billeting Board, Report on the Clyde', 12-16 Nov. 1917 (PRO Mun. 5/97).

[26] 'Central Billeting Board, Report on Lancaster', 27 Sept. 1917 (PRO Mun. 5/97); *HMM*, V, 5, pp. 34-5.

[27] *HMM*, V, 5, pp. 34-5.

[28] *HMM*, V, 5, p. 49. Cf. correspondence of 'Yet Another Trade Unionist', *North Western Daily Mail*, 7 Sept. 1917.

[29] 'Minutes of Proceedings of a Conference on the Making of Ejectment Warrants at Barrow', 7 Sept. 1917 (PRO Mun. 5/97).

shown much selfishness in not considering those they try to turn out.'[30] The labour movement, it should be added, did not countenance such conduct; indeed, it was in the forefront of the campaign for the extension of the Rent Act.

The relaxation of the much-resented Munitions of War Act cast an oblique light on these intractable difficulties. The reduction in tension on the shop floor brought about by the abolition of the 'leaving certificate' in the autumn of 1917 was offset by the irritation caused by the housing shortage. The absence of accommodation continued to impede the supply of labour and in spite of the assumption of compulsory billeting powers, leakage remained a source of constant complaint.

The Billeting of Civilians Bill became law early in the spring of 1917. It provided for the formation (under the guidance of the Ministry of Munitions) of a Central Billeting Board drawn from representatives of the principal Government departments. Where investigation disclosed the need for action, the Board was empowered to appoint a voluntary local committee comprised of representative civic dignitaries, trade union officials etc. assisted by two salaried executive officers, whose principal function was to fix the rates to be paid for board and lodging, basing their calculations upon the market value of comparable accommodation in the area.[31]

The new legislation was not well received. The *Labour Leader* considered it 'an outrage on all the British working classes have held most dear'.[32] The element of compulsion was most offensive. Cowes Trades Council threatened strike action against its application; the Board was informed that, on the Isle of Wight, compulsion was 'entirely out of the question, the whole of the Committee are dead against it'.[33] Even the conciliatory Sheffield Trades Council thought that the Billeting Act would have to be applied 'with the greatest caution and only on a voluntary basis'.[34] Coventry householders, acting in defiance of the law, refused to co-operate with local officials in the preparation of a census of accommodation.[35]

[30] 'Instances of House Grabbing of which the War Rents League has full particulars' (WNC Papers).

[31] On this, *HMM*, V, 5, pp. 35-7.

[32] *Labour Leader*, 26 Apr. 1917. Cf. *New Witness*, 26 Apr. 1917, and *Woman's Dreadnought*, 28 Apr. 1917.

[33] E. L. Webb to R. H. Crooke, Secretary Central Billeting Board, 23 Aug. 1917 (PRO Mun. 5/97).

[34] 'Central Billeting Board, Report on Sheffield', 12-15 Dec. 1917 (PRO Mun. 5/97).   [35] Cf. *Midland Daily Telegraph*, 18 Mar. 1918.

Its class bias was particularly objectionable. In Bedford, for instance, it was thought that 'a considerable amount of additional accommodation could be found for civilian billeting purposes if the whole town was systematically dealt with, but there were a large number of ladies, pensioned Officers etc., living in Bedford who could not very well be asked to take in munitions workers'.[36] The Mayor of Hereford said that 'the better class of residents would be extremely apprehensive at such a system being introduced, and that property would depreciate in consequence'; members of the Advisory Committee on Women's War Employment 'laid great emphasis upon the servant difficulty in Hereford. It was pointed out that servants would not stay if asked to wait on munitions workers.'[37] The canvass undertaken on behalf of the Board at Coventry excluded the 250 'large residential houses' situated chiefly in the Kenilworth Road.[38] The sanctity of working-class homes alone, it seemed, was no longer inviolate. 'This question', wrote the official historians of the Ministry of Munitions, 'indeed, presented particular difficulties to the Board, for it was found that the scarcity of domestic service, combined with the food shortage, made it in practice impossible to call upon occupiers of better-class houses, who had not been in the habit of accepting lodgers, to provide accommodation for munitions workers.'[39]

The intervention of the Central Billeting Board in Barrow aroused suspicion. Its investigations confirmed what was already common knowledge, namely, that the better off elements of the community—civic dignitaries and the like—who spoke loudest of the need for patriotic self-sacrifice, were also those who were the least willing to lodge munitions workers in their own homes; and as in other centres there was considerable resentment at the unequal burden the working classes were compelled to shoulder. 'The Local Labour Advisory Board', the authorities in London were informed, 'showed some distrust or even antagonism towards the proposal to billet in the town, and pressed for equal treatment all round.'[40] However, working people were determined that, if unavoidable,

---

[36] 'Central Billeting Board, Report on Bedford', 11 Dec. 1917 (PRO Mun. 5/97).

[37] 'Central Billeting Board, Report on Hereford', 22-3 Aug. 1917 (PRO Mun. 5/97).

[38] 'Central Billeting Board, Report on Coventry', 3 Oct. and 1 Nov. 1917 (PRO Mun. 5/97).

[39] *HMM*, V, 5, p. 38; and see too 'Memorandum on the History and Work of the Central Billeting Board, Prepared by the Secretary to the Board', p. 15 (PRO Mun. 5/352).

[40] 'Central Billeting Board, Report on Barrow', 19 July 1917 (PRO Mun. 5/97).

coercion would be administered in an equitable manner. 'Labour is strongly represented on this [Local Billeting] Committee', a local columnist observed, 'and it is no secret that the Labour members are looking to villadom to mitigate the overcrowding in the artisan quarters.'[41] At the same time it was feared that, should billeting prove successful, an extensive housing scheme wrung from the Ministry might be axed.

The decision to employ compulsion, provoked by the continued resistance of Barrow's more substantial citizens, brought these fears to light.[42] Resolutions passed at six different meetings of Vickers' workers condemned it as 'a hypocritical way out of a legitimate demand for working-class houses'.[43] Serious disorder was predicted if the decision was implemented.[44] Labour members of the Local Billeting Committee promptly resigned in order, so it was said, to placate the active and influential Shop Stewards' Committee.[45] But at Lincoln, where 'extremists' of this sort were unknown, the Trades Council was also convinced that the Billeting Act would prejudice a much-needed housing scheme, and warned that its application 'will meet with strong opposition from the labour organizations'.[46]

The fact that compulsion was not in the event anywhere applied did nothing to diminish the resentment which had been aroused. The Civilian Billeting Bill fed the unrest coincident with its passage. Underlying the wave of strikes which convulsed the country in the spring of 1917 was a combination of grievances of which poor housing was not the least important.[47] Moreover, it was not civilian morale alone which was affected thereby. The contrast between an orgiastically vile Home Front and the men in the trenches, that enduring image of the Great War, needs to be set against the unsettling effect which the knowledge of deprivation at home produced upon the troops in France. In addition to apprehension caused by food shortages, there was a certain discontent arising out

---

[41] *North Western Daily Mail*, 1 Sept. 1917; and see too *Barrow Guardian*, 15 Sept. 1917.

[42] 'Central Billeting Board, Minutes of 9th Meeting', 22 Oct. 1917 (PRO Mun. 5/97).

[43] 'Billeting of Civilians Act, 1917: Barrow-in-Furness Local Committee', Minutes of Meeting, 24 Oct. 1917 (PRO Mun. 5/97).

[44] M. H. Picken, Executive Officer, Barrow, to R. H. Crooke, 29 Oct. 1917 (PRO Mun. 5/97).

[45] Cf. W. H. Sergent, Clerk to Barrow Local Billeting Committee, to R. H. Crooke, 26 Oct. 1917 (PRO Mun. 5/97).

[46] 'Central Billeting Board, Report on Lincoln', 26 Oct. 1917 (PRO Mun. 5/97).

[47] See *Reports of Commission of Enquiry into Industrial Unrest* (PP 1917-18, XV).

of the evasion of the Rent Act.[48] 'Chaplains with the troops at the front started sending me distressing letters from the wives of soldiers in their regiments, containing notices to quit', Dan Rider recalled. 'They said the men were distracted, and had come to them for advice, and they asked me to look into the matter.' Rider found intimidation and harassment to be widespread. 'The chaplains', he wrote, 'did not spare themselves on the men's behalf. Several wrote me stinging letters asking what these landlords were up to, as their men were beside themselves upon receipt of such letters from home, and they were threatening to return to England and finish off the landlords, and then come back to Flanders and polish off the Germans.' In some cases, he added, these anxieties 'almost led to mutiny'.[49] The demand for further protection became irresistible.

II

The agitation began at Barrow. In November 1916 Vickers informed the Ministry of Munitions that 'The congestion in housing is now at breaking point.'[50] The 600 houses built since the outbreak of war were insufficient to accommodate an ever-expanding population which rose from 75,368 at the end of 1914 to 79,206 in 1915 and was still growing, having reached 85,179 by the close of 1916. The introduction of dilution at this point led to a strike which, in the words of the official historians, 'emphasised so strongly the necessity for providing accommodation for imported labour, more particularly female, that an order temporarily prohibited the importation of more women into Barrow until proper housing could be provided'.

The labour movement was not indifferent. The shortage evident before the war continued to engage its attentions. However, the abnormal conditions and the resultant uncertainties had an immobilizing effect on the Corporation; a scheme brought forward by the Labour Party in the spring of 915 was narrowly defeated.[51] The agitation was renewed the following year.[52]

---

[48]   A third of the 200-odd individual complaints of eviction following a transfer of ownership received by the Local Government Board between Sept. 1916 and Apr. 1918 were from servicemen's dependents: Walter T. Jerrad, Assistant Secretary to Local Government Board, to W. G. Wallace, 6 May 1918 (PRO Reco. 1/644).

[49]   On unrest in the military, see David Englander and James Osborne, 'Jack, Tommy and Henry Dubb: The Armed Forces and the Working Class', *Historical Journal*, XXI (1978). Quotation from Rider, *Ten Years Adventures*, pp. 95-6, 99.

[50]   On housing conditions in Barrow, see *HMM*, V, 5, pp.44 ff.

[51]   *Barrow Guardian*, 6 Feb., 6 Mar. and 29 May 1915.

[52]   *Barrow Guardian*, 9 Dec. 1916.

The Ministry of Munitions had, in the wake of the anti-dilution strike, prepared a scheme for 250 permanent houses for eventual purchase by the local authority. Negotiations were protracted, and before the first brick was laid matters came to a head. The scheme was abandoned and 'merged in a more extensive one undertaken as a result of popular feeling'.[53]

The Commission on Industrial Unrest, set up in the aftermath of the May strikes, visited Barrow early in the summer of 1917. The situation in the town was by then extremely grave. Although eviction was not a problem of any statistical significance—in the 18 months since the passing of the Rent Restrictions Act 42 orders had been made out of a total of 88 cases entered—the fears which it aroused were real enough and of the utmost importance.[54] The difficulties of securing accommodation and the exorbitant cost of lodgings had, in conjunction with industrial fatigue and growing food shortages, combined to produce a state of considerable tension. It found expression in a marked resentment directed at the several hundred Belgian refugees who had been set to work at Vickers, and who, in several cases, had purchased houses and applied for warrants to evict the sitting tenant. 'That is a very sore point', a local magistrate told the Minister of Munitions. 'As sure as you and I are here there will be Satan's own row if Belgian people are allowed to buy houses and the working classes in Barrow-in-Furness are turned out into the streets. There will be a riot, I feel sure'.[55] The presence of the Commission provided an opportunity to short-circuit both the Corporation and the Ministry. The hearings lasted two days. Although the bulk of the evidence was taken in camera, the Commissioners, on request, allowed representatives of the Trades Council and Shop Stewards' Committee to be heard in public.[56] The subsequent publicity transformed the agitation.

Six weeks elapsed before the Commissioners' report was published. In the interval the unrest gathered momentum. The civic authorities sensed the ugly mood and were alarmed. The Board of Guardians

[53] *HMM*, V, 5, p. 46.

[54] *Commission on Industrial Unrest* (North Western Area), p. 33; 'Central Billeting Board, Report on Barrow-in-Furness', 7 Sept. 1917 (PRO Mun. 5/97).

[55] 'Minutes of Proceedings at a Conference on the Making of Ejectment Warrants at Barrow', 7 Sept. 1917 (PRO Mun. 5/97); and for anti-alien sentiment in this connection, see correspondence of 'A Handy Man', *Barrow Guardian*, 10 July 1915 and 'An English Trade Unionist', *North Western Daily Mail*, 1 Sept. 1917.

[56] *North Western Daily Mail*, 11 July 1917; *Barrow Guardian* 14 July 1917.

called for a crash programme of temporary accommodation to meet the emergency. Councillor Ellison, however, leader of the eight-strong Labour Group on the Town Council, demanded 1,000 houses and warned that 'if they did not get those houses by peaceful methods of persuasion, they would get them—make no mistake about that.'[57] The Ministry required evidence of the need for the enlarged scheme. A bureau set up at Labour Party headquarters sought to provide it; nearly 1,000 applications were received.[58]

The magistrates too were uneasy. The want of discretion in the administration of justice undermined respect for the law and brought on a crisis of conscience. 'We acknowledge that the Magistrates and County Court are called upon to deal with very difficult matters', said the Commission on Industrial Unrest, 'and these Courts are being brought into disrepute, not so much by the decisions they had to give as by the law which shackles them in making decisions which are sensible and humane'.[59]

Some Justices were on the point of resignation. The Bench felt 'compelled to question the moral right of the law to turn many people out of their houses'.[60] The extent of demoralization may be gauged from the tone of the following resolution forwarded in conjunction with one of several requests for an interview with the authorities in London:

That, the Justices gravely fear that, unless some steps are taken to give the Justices power to refuse ejectment warrants, and to ameliorate the sufferings of a very large number of the working classes, industrial unrest is likely to ensue, with a possible accompaniment of strikes and rioting; the Justices, therefore, desire to impress upon His Majesty's Government the extreme urgency of the matter.[61]

This was sent to the Ministry of Munitions. In this instance, however, the 'Men of push and go' neither pushed hard enough nor went far enough.

The report of the Commission on Industrial Unrest was released on 27 August. It made, from the standpoint of the working-class housing reformers, an excellent fourpenceworth of reading matter. The Commission, in an extraordinary censure upon bureaucratic

[57] *North Western Daily Mail*, 31 July 1917.
[58] *Barrow Guardian*, 1 Sept. 1917.
[59] *Commission on Industrial Unrest*, p. 33.
[60] *Barrow Guardian*, 25 Aug. 1917.
[61] 'Minutes of Proceedings of a Conference' etc. (PRO Mun. 5/97).

procrastination and ineptitude, described the position at Barrow as 'a crying scandal', one which constituted 'a terrible indictment ... against the Rulers and Governors'.[62] The lid was off. The *Manchester Guardian* promptly dispatched its 'Special Commissioner' to the town. His report, coupled with a blistering leader, castigated the Government and the local authority. 'For such a paper to call attention to it', a local columnist remarked, 'means that the condition which obtains in Barrow has become a national question which has got to be answered by the Government'.[63] At a meeting of the Board of Guardians shortly afterwards it transpired that earlier resolutions addressed to the Ministry had received nothing beyond a routine acknowledgement; and, as had been foreseen, the position had deteriorated to the point where civil disturbance seemed unavoidable.

In order to surmount the opposition of a reluctant magistracy and adverse country court, an appeal on behalf of the prospective Belgian owners had been taken to the High Court and an order obtained for the ejectment of several sitting tenants in Byron Street, Hindpool. Those to be displaced had nowhere to go but the workhouse. The Guardians were livid. 'It was a vicious state of things', said Councillor Basterfield of the ILP. 'Hindpool was flaming, and if the Government did not take action immediately something would happen'. That something, he conjectured, would take the form of a strike in the shipyards. He himself was prepared to use 'physical force' and go to gaol if need be. His fellow Guardians were no less anxious. A telegram, sent to the Government protesting against official inaction, demanded that the ejectments in Barrow be suspended for the duration.[64] 'This Government lethargy', declared the Conservative *North Western Daily Mail*, 'is getting unbearable'. It too foretold 'trouble' and 'serious consequences'.[65]

Barrow Trades and Labour Council was no less apprehensive, and, possibly in order to contain unofficial action, decided to hold a mass protest meeting on Sunday 9 September, preparatory to seeking a personal interview with Mr Churchill. The magistrates' nerves almost reached breaking-point on learning that the Shop Stewards' Committee contemplated a more forceful intervention. But, however

[62] *Commission on Industrial Unrest*, p. 31.
[63] *Barrow Guardian*, 1 Sept. 1917.
[64] *North Western Daily Mail*, 29 Aug. 1917; *Barrow Guardian* 1 and 8 Sept. 1917.
[65] *North Western Daily Mail*, 1 Sept. 1917.

belatedly, the new Minister of Munitions had at last grasped the tiller and the possibility of suspending ejectments was under consideration.[66] Two days before the proposed demonstration, which in the event passed off without incident,[67] Dr J. H. Thomas JP and Mr S. E. Major, Clerk to the Barrow Justices, were summoned to London to discuss the matter.[68]

Dr Thomas, a general practitioner of more than forty years' standing, was peculiarly well qualified to assess the popular mood. 'I have been chairman of the Football Club, Chairman of the Athletic Club, Sports Judge and things of that kind', he said, 'so that I am fairly well in touch with the working classes—not in the Primitive Methodists style—I do not know much about the working classes from that point of view.' But then that point of view was not germane to the matter in hand. He continued:

I saw the chairman of the Labour Party yesterday and he told me there was a meeting of the Shop Stewards on Sunday. You know that these gentlemen are very busy. The Shop Stewards are the people who made the row in the last strike—it was not their Leaders. They say they are going to send a deputation to see you again on Tuesday: that they wish to do it and they are going to do it. They are very assertive in the matter. I told them and my Clerk told them that perhaps you did not wish to see them, but they said you would have to see them.

Unless allowed greater latitude in refusing orders for possession, the magistrates intended to take unilateral action. 'I am afraid that if the law is not altered', said Dr Thomas, 'the Justices will do something on their own and not make the Orders.' The Minister did not doubt it. A senior official, he explained, had already been posted to Barrow with instructions to draw up a scheme for the erection of up to 1,000 temporary and permanent houses. Materials and labour were to be mobilized forthwith. Nothing would be allowed to impede the progress of the scheme. But in the meantime something had to be done to prevent the explosion that was certain to follow upon the continued eviction of innocent working people. This, said Dr Thomas, was the crux of the matter.

Mr Churchill was in a delicate position. It was for the moment inexpedient to proceed by Order in Council under the Defence of

[66] 'Munitions Council Daily Reports', 4 Sept. 1917 (PRO Mun. 1/1).
[67] *North Western Daily Mail*, 10 Sept. 1917.
[68] The following account is drawn from 'Minutes of Proceedings of a Conference' etc. (PRO Mun. 5/97).

the Realm Act since parliament was not then in session and in consequence sanction could not be obtained for the necessary emendation of the law. Under the Rent Restrictions Act, however, persons applying for possession had to satisfy the court that the premises were 'reasonably required' by the landlord for the occupation of himself or an employee. Much depended upon the meaning of 'reasonably'. Unfortunately in *Sharp* v. *Wakefield*, 1916, this had been interpreted in such a restricted manner as to preclude the exercise of any discretionary power on the part of the magistrates. Mr Churchill, briefed by the Treasury Solicitors, proposed an alternative interpretation. In short, the Bench was told to ignore *Sharp* v. *Wakefield* and play for time. Even if challenged in the High Court, the Minister was confident that additional accommodation would be available long before the lawyers stopped talking. Tenants should be encouraged to resist any such action; the Ministry would foot the bill. 'After all', said Mr Churchill, 'we are at war and we cannot have a disturbance in a great centre of this kind.' The following day the Press Bureau announced that work on the housing front was to begin immediately.

The severity of the crisis revealed by the Commission on Industrial Unrest was such that responsibility could not longer be localized within the Ministry of Munitions. The Commission recommended the appointment of a dynamic and exceptionally able figure armed with plenary powers to coerce even the Treasury if need be in order to expedite matters. But the War Cabinet appointed the prosaic George Barnes as its chief trouble-shooter.[69] In spite of subsequent Herculean efforts the new dwellings at Barrow could not be ready for occupation until the new year. In the meantime those who had been evicted were promptly rehoused in unoccupied premises requisitioned under the Defence of the Realm Act; for the rest Ministers looked to the Central Billeting Board to ease congestion in the town.[70]

On 29 September 1917 Regulation 2A(2) of the Defence of the Realm Act came into effect.[71] It empowered the Minister of Munitions to schedule districts in which munitions work was carried out

[69] *Commission on Industrial Unrest*, p. 31; War Cabinet Minute 232 (16), 13 Sept. 1917 (PRO Cab. 23/4).
[70] 'Inadequacy of Housing Accommodation at Barrow', Memorandum by George Barnes, 26 Sept. 1917 (PRO Cab. 24/27 GT 2130).
[71] Text reprinted as appendix to Minutes of War Emergency Workers' National Committee, 25 Oct. 1917 (WNC Papers).

'special areas' in which the ejectment of munitions workers, who observed their conditions of tenancy properly, was henceforth prohibited without the Minister's approval. Shortly afterwards, Barrow and the surrounding district was declared a special area.

A week before it came into force, Mr Churchill, in a correspondence concerning the proposed deputation, informed the secretary of the Barrow Trades Council of his intention to invoke the new Regulation as soon as possible.[72] The effect of this premature announcement, in conjunction with the impolitic reticence of the magistrates who, ever since their return from London, had kept a still tongue, now became evident, 'Why on earth the magistrates decided to keep mum on the subject, which is of such great interest, cannot be conceived', said the *North Western Daily Mail*. 'By their reticence the magistrates have allowed another body to step in and take the credit for having these ejectments stopped. It matters little, of course who gets the credit....'[73] But it did matter. Workers could hardly fail to be encouraged by such signal success. The events in Barrow could not be viewed in isolation: concessions granted under pressure in one district were bound to generate demands for equal protection elsewhere.[74]

Workers in Coventry were first to respond. The scramble for labour amongst covetous employers in that town had been so intense that, where provided at the company's expense, accommodation was managed as a form of tied housing. Messrs White & Poppé, employers of upwards of 8,000 workers, were amongst the most notorious proprietors in this respect, ejecting automatically those who had left their employ. 'We discussed with them the general question of applying the Order prohibiting evictions in Coventry', said the investigators in their report to the Central Billeting Board, 'and it was evident that they viewed the suggestion with some alarm.' The secretary of the Coventry Branch of the Ironfounders' Society, a member of the Local Labour Advisory Board, and 'a man of great influence among Coventry workers', considered that these evictions, together with the multiple evasions of the Rent Act were a matter of the utmost urgency. 'There was great dissatisfaction at Coventry and he thought that if evictions continued the results would be serious.' The Chief Investigation Officer of the Ministry of

---

[72] *North Western Daily Mail*, 22 Sept. 1917.
[73] *North Western Daily Mail*, 29 Sept. 1917.
[74] Cf. J. S. Middleton to Christopher Addison, 30 Oct. 1917 (WNC Papers).

Munitions at Birmingham concurred. He suggested that the whole of the district including Birmingham, Dudley, Wolerhampton, Leamington, Warwick, Nuneaton, and Rugby should be declared a special area.[75] The pressure for further extension would soon become difficult to resist, but for the moment the Regulation was limited to Coventry.

Newcastle workers were no less interested in the new Regulation.[76] Mr James, Chief Investigation Officer for the Ministry for the North East, was of the opinion that, while the scarcity of lodgings gave some cause for complaint, 'the principal agitation was on the question of evictions'. 'His own view', he added, 'was that the whole Tyne area from South Shields to Newcastle should be declared a special area but he admitted that the evidence brought forward to support this was not very strong.' The principal evidence, however, was political rather than statistical. It was the activities of groups such as the Wallsend Munition Workers' Housing Association rather than the length of the eviction list that was the dominant consideration. This Housing Association, formed 'owing to the dissatisfaction among the better class of workmen' with the slothful local authority, was said to be 'an extremely active representative body and appears to reflect the opinions of the more moderate section of the Labour Party in the district'. It was this association which had first raised the question of evictions and the demand that Wallsend 'should be declared a special area as at Barrow-in-Furness'.[77]

In Birkenhead too the question 'excited considerable interest'. Cammell Lairds, the Corporation, and the tenants were all united in supporting the demand for the application of Regulation 2A(2) to the district. Yet, as the Town Clerk observed, 'the difficulty was more apparent than real, and that the number of evictions, except for non-payment of rent or misconduct, was not large'. The observation was correct; in the previous two years only half of the eighty applications for possession had been granted. Nevertheless, it was considered prudent to recommend that Birkenhead be scheduled a special area.[78]

[75] 'Central Billeting Board, Report on Coventry', 31 Oct. and 1 Nov. 1917 (PRO Mun. 5/97).

[76] E. Gibbins, Organiser Newcastle Labour Representation Committee, to J. S. Middleton, 11 Oct. 1917 (WNC Papers).

[77] 'Central Billeting Board, Report on the Tyne', 7-11 Jan. 1918 (PRO Mun. 5/97).

[78] 'Central Billeting Board, Report on Liverpool', etc., 6-9 Feb. 1918 (PRO Mun. 5/97).

Workington tenants proved no less obstinate in pressing their claims. In the three years after the passing of the Rent Act, magistrates in this overcrowded steel-making town granted a mere twenty-eight of the seventy applications for possession which came before them. Few of these involved ejectment consequent upon a change of ownership. The vast majority of orders were given against tenants in arrears.[79] And yet in March 1918 this was said to be *the* issue of the moment. When interviewed, officials of the Trades Council, the Workington Tenants' Defence League and the Labour Party 'took a very violent attitude on the question'; twenty-two resolutions calling for the enforcement of the Regulation had been passed. 'They also threatened that if this were not done, their members would insist upon drastic action being taken and they thought it most probable that a strike would ensue.'

Although there was nothing in the conduct of local estate agents that could be held to have been improper, 'the unusual anxiety of the Workington property owners to sell their property on as advantageous terms as possible' had, it was observed, 'produced an impression of a conspiracy to compel working people to purchase their homes or quit'. 'What they chiefly complained of was, not the number of actual evictions, but the uncertainty under which working men tenants laboured, ie they never knew when their houses might be bought over their heads and they would have to find another house.' Although only nine such cases had occurred in the past three years, tenants remained apprehensive. Neither the statistics on ejectments with which they were furnished nor the fact that the Regulation demanded would not afford any protection to those in arrears, affected their determination to press for its enforcement. 'The position seems to be that the local Labour leaders, taking their cue from Barrow-in-Furness, have applied for Workington to be declared a 'special area' without any adequate knowledge of what their application involves', said the Board's investigators, in view of which it was concluded that 'the agitation of the Labour Party is based on sentimental grounds'. But such sentiment had to be appeased. The situation, said despondent officials, 'is very similar to that in Erith, where no real grounds for making the Regulation were disclosed, but the agitation has reached such a stage, combined with such an amount of misconception, that the best course will probably

---

[79] This and the following paragraph are based upon 'Central Billeting Board, Report on Workington', 14 Mar. 1918 (PRO Mun. 5/97).

be to follow the Erith precedent, and declare Workington to be a special area...'

The extraordinarily high level of evictions in Glasgow meant inevitably that the demand for further protection would be echoed loudly in the Clyde Valley.[80] The reverberations of the success at Barrow, however, were not confined to the problems posed by insecure tenures. In industrial Scotland the want of housing remained the dominant cause of unrest, especially in the outlying centres of heavy industry—in Airdrie, Coatbridge, Hamilton, Motherwell, Wishaw, and the Middle Ward of Lanarkshire; all desperately crowded communities in which representatives of the coalminers and the iron and steel workers were influential figures. A deputation from these various authorities, irked at the apparent neglect of previous representations, who attended the Scottish Local Government Board in October, 1917, 'expressed the hope that it might not be necessary for the Clyde and Lanarkshire workers to carry their agitation to the same extent as had been done at Barrow, in order to obtain consideration of their claim'. A further deputation waited upon the Board shortly afterwards 'and their attitude was threatening in the extreme'.[81]

Neither was the campaign initiated at Barrow limited to the solution of the particular problems of munitions workers. The Trades Council in that isolated town had, on the contrary, been amongst the first to call for an extension of the Regulation so as to embrace all workers rather than those engaged on war production alone.[82] Dollan, too, was quick to demand universal protection.[83] The agitation which had begun in the North West culminated in the Increase of Rent and Mortgage Interest (Amendment) Act, 1918.

III

'Looking at this now', Dan Rider wrote of the first Rent Act, 'we see how feeble was the protection afforded to the tenant.'[84] The War Rents League, under his capable guidance, was to play an

---

[80] *Herald*, 1 Sept. 1917. The Scottish Office, anticipating popular response, had strongly pressed for the universal application of the Regulation in its preparatory stages: (PRO T. 172/481).

[81] 'Central Billeting Board, Report on the Clyde', 12-16 Nov. 1917 (PRO Mun. 5/97).

[82] J. H. Brown, Secretary of Barrow Trades Council, to J. S. Middleton, 16 Oct. 1917 (WNC Papers).

[83] *Herald*, 20 Oct. 1917.   [84] Rider, *Ten Years Adventures*, p. 70.

important part in the subsequent campaign to strengthen its provisions. Formed almost casually in the summer 1915, the League comprised a self-appointed committee of tenants, dominated by the Bohemian circle in which its principal spokesman and progenitor moved—a coterie of minor artists, sculptors and men of letters under the chairmanship of Robert Steele, an authority on Bacon.[85] In spite of its dilettante character, this modest and unobtrusive committee, which also included one of Rider's cronies from the long-defunct Bermondsey Tenants' Protection League, proved a serious, astonishingly tenacious, and well-disciplined body which in the course of the next nine years met almost every day. Yet the League remained something of a mystery. Operating on a shoe-string budget, without mass support, and with no political affiliations, it possessed no permanent offices, published no journal and eschewed the glittering subscription list and self-laudatory annual reports issued by the great (and not so great) philanthropic institutions. Rivals were suspicious. The War Rents League, according to J. S. Whybrew of the National Labour Housing Association, was a fiction, a vehicle designed to further the ambitions of its secretary.[86] Its presumed influence was, however, rewarded by representation upon the first of the interminable official inquiries into the operation of the Rent Act.

From its inception the War Rents League was dependent upon the drive and initiative of its indefatigable secretary and his ability to attract the support of public-spirited citizens, especially lawyers and journalists willing to offer their services, as well as men of good-will ready with those vital small donations upon which it was reliant. Rider's commitment was total: 'Nothing else on earth mattered, everything must give way to this one end ... I bought a copy of the Annual County Court Practice and made myself acquainted with its thousand and more pages, paying particular attention to those bearing upon landlord and tenant ... and even carried "Woodfall's Landlord and Tenant" nightly to bed with me!'[87] Through the unfailing efforts of this small businessman turned solicitor's clerk[88] nationwide contacts were established. The War

[85] On the formation of the War Rents League, see Rider, *Ten Years Adventures*, Ch. iv.

[86] Onslow Committee on Rent Restriction Acts: MS Minutes of Evidence, p. 93 (PRO HLG. 41/24).   [87] Rider, *Ten Years Adventures*, p. 90.

[88] Cf. Rider, *Ten Years Adventures*, p. 103 and Report of Committee on Operation of the Rent Acts: MS Minutes of Evidence, 8 Mar. 1920, p. 40 (PRO HLG. 41/5).

Rents League was able to furnish valuable information to the Workers' National Committee and other interested parties. Counsel was provided on the at least 270 occasions that the League chose to contest or initiate an action.[89] At the same time numerous disputes were settled amicably following its discreet intervention.

The scope for this kind of voluntary endeavour was related to the *laissez-faire* attitude of the central authorities. The Local Government Board proved an indifferent watch-dog.[90] The policing of the emergency legislation and correction of its manifold defects devolved upon the labour movement. The Workers' National Committee and its affiliates consistently exposed abuses and sought redress both in the courts and through the introduction of amending legislation.

The shortcomings of the first Rent Act were quickly apparent. Some indeed had been foreseen. W. C. Anderson, during the Committee stage of the Bill, had withdrawn an amendment designed to establish the indisputable right of the tenant to deduct or recover excess charges on standard rent (i.e. the rent fixed on 3 August 1914), after assurances were given that the Bill already contained such provision.[91] Although given in good faith, these assurances were worthless.

'Cases have already come to our notice of landlords absolutely refusing to obey the Act, and threatening the tenants with dismissal if they are insistent', wrote the secretary of the Newcastle Labour Representation Committee shortly after the new legislation came into force.[92] 'Many of the working class are still being terrified into paying increased rents imposed during the war', an indignant Birmingham Trades Council observed.[93] Complaints such as this were to grow in volume and fuelled the unrest that marked the latter stages of the war. Trades Councils and the various sections of the labour movement everywhere squared up to these outrageous in-

[89] Committee on Increase of Rent Act etc: MS minutes of 6th Meeting, 18 Sept. 1918, p. 5 (PRO Reco. 1/645).

[90] On the persistent attempts of the Board to avoid the assumption of departmental responsibility, see 'Minute re Proposed Committee on Amendemnt of Increase of Rent etc. Acts' (PRO Reco. 1/585); 'Increase of Rent and Mortgage Interest (Restrictions) Bill', Memorandum by the President of the Local Government Board, 13 Mar 1919 (PRO Cab. 24/76 GT 6977); also War Cabinet Minute 545 (2), 17 Mar. 1919 (PRO Cab. 23/9).

[91] *HC Deb.* 5s. lxxvi (1915), 1514.

[92] W. Grainger to J. S. Middleton, 26 Jan. 1916 (WNC Papers).

[93] Minutes of Birmingham Trades Council, 2 Mar. 1916.

fringements of the law.[94] 'We have a number of cases being discovered almost every day', a South Wales correspondent informed the Workers' National Committee, 'but we have also scored some victory's [*sic*].'[95] The miners of that region, however, had to contend with more than the illegal exactions of the landlords. Time and again their cause was compromised by the prejudice of the local magistrates. In November 1916 a deputation representing thirteen local Trades Councils waited upon the President of the Local Government Board. Monmouthshire tenants, they complained, were denied protection under the Rent Act in consequence of the misconduct of the local Bench. Too many magistrates, it was alleged, were house-owners or estate agents and prone to allow personal and class interests to influence their decisions. The Minister undertook to investigate.[96] Whatever the outcome, the complaint persisted.[97]

The class bias of the judiciary represented a major obstacle towards the attainment of justice. The recruitment and training of an élite legal profession which identified the preservation of the rights of property with the welfare of the citizen was a source of some confusion. Lawyers, judges and magistrates were inevitably perplexed by the revolutionary alteration in the relations of landlord and tenant embodied in the legislation of 1915, a departure which seemed at variance with the habits and assumptions of a lifetime. 'During the first six months of 1916', Dan Rider wrote, 'pandemonium reigned':

The Judges and the Registrars of the Courts seemed to be in a daze, and to be afraid to administer the Act of the Parliament in favour of the tenants in whose interests it was passed. Some of them said it had to be interpreted strictly, and this was found to mean strictly against the tenant. From the number of appeals for help that I received, I could see that the Rent Act was being turned into a formidable weapon of intimidation against tenants. Hearing of the way they were being treated in the Courts, tenants were in dread of legal proceedings ... They had only protection in theory, but not in practice.

[94] See, for example, E. Robinson, Secretary of Grimsby Trades Council, to J. S. Middleton, 5 Feb. 1916; G. Carruthers, Secretary of Maryport and District Trades Council, to J. S. Middleton, 2 Feb. 1916; John McGilliveray, Secretary of Newton-Mearns Vigilance Committee, to J. S. Middleton, 31 Mar. 1917; Minutes of War Emergency Workers' National Committee, 5 Nov. 1917 (WNC Papers).
[95] W. Harris to J. S. Middleton, 17 Feb. 1917 (WNC Papers).
[96] Proceedings of deputation reprinted as appendix to Minutes of War Emergency Workers' National Committee, 30 Nov. 1916 (WNC Papers).
[97] Arthur Seabury, Secretary of Warrington Trades Council, to J. S. Middleton, 29 Sept. 1917 (WNC Papers).

The bewildered resistance of the leaders of the profession set an example that was not without effect upon their subordinates. 'In my experience', Rider recalled, 'with but one exception, Deputy Judges seem to be so timid and self-conscious that they are afraid to show they are human beings, in case this might re-act against their reputation as lawyers. Possession orders were being granted for the flimsiest of reasons.' Solicitors too, who of course obtained a good deal of business from property-owners, were less than keen on the new legislation. 'It was with some difficulty that I could get them to present the tenants' cases with any enthusiasm.'[98]

The administration of justice in the County Courts gradually improved and was certainly far superior to proceedings in the lower courts where the additional safeguards against summary eviction, embodied in the Rules issued by the Lord Chancellor defining the procedure to be followed in connection with the Rent Act, did not affect applications for possession made under the Small Tenements Recovery Act. This curious anomaly effectively deprived the poorest tenants of any real protection.[99] Magistrates, accustomed to dealing summarily with 'the destructive classes' under the act of 1838, found it extraordinarily difficult to master their prejudices and adjust to the new conditions. Rider noted the difficulty:

Before the war these were chiefly people who did not pay their rates; people who were a fearful nuisance, who got drunk, who were disorderly and knocked the places about. They were brought up to the Court by summons, they had no defence and they were simply turned out at twenty-one days notice. Now the misfortune is, I think, this, that these Magistrates and those Justices have got so much in the habit of saying "Yes, three weeks", that they continue to say it now, and they do not recognise there is an Act to help the tenant at all. If a tenant says anything about it they simply say "your case is decided": they hardly allow a man to speak.[100]

Tenants in search of justice were compelled to seek redress in the more expensive County Courts 'as the Police Court decisions are often given at the present time without any consideration of the Act at all'.[101]

[98] Rider, *Ten Years Adventures*, pp. 83, 87-8.
[99] 'Memorandum of Suggestions upon Points arising for the decision of the Committee submitted by Dan Rider' (Document 58), Commitee on Increase of Rent Act (PRO Reco. 1/646).
[100] Departmental Committee on the Operation of the Rent Act: MS Minutes of Evidence, 8 Mar. 1920, p. 41 (PRO HLG. 41/5).
[101] 'Reports of Rents Sub-Committee on the Increase of Rent etc. Amending Bill' (WNC Papers).

The additional expenditure consequent upon such flagrant mal-practice strained the always slender resources of local labour movements. The sheer expense of any kind of remedy was without doubt a major deterrent. The absence of any penalty against the contravention of the Rent Act encouraged landlords to attempt to extort illegal increases. Confronted by a refusal to pay the excess charge, the landlord might then apply for an ejectment order. Even if this was refused, costs could not be obtained for legal assistance or loss of wages.[102] However, if the tenant was *not* represented in court, the order was granted automatically. The mere threat of proceedings was generally sufficient to compel compliance. The Workers' National Committee, having examined the matter, concluded that 'unless a penalty is imposed there is no defence of the tenants against unscrupulous landlords'.[103]

Evasion of the Rent Act, however widespread it may in practice have been, is not easily measured. A small but perceptible increase in house rents, registered on the official cost of living index in mid-1918, does not distinguish permissible increases due to rising rates.[104] In some key centres, however, there is incontrovertible evidence of significant evasion. A survey undertaken by the Birmingham Assessment Committee eighteen months after the introduction of rent control disclosed a widespread determination to act in defiance of the law. Of the 152,769 working-class dwellings canvassed in the parish of Birmingham, it was found that rents had been increased on 60,755 weekly properties, upon which rates were then raised accordingly.[105] Evictions too, though not large relative to the size of the population, had not ceased.[106] Neither had the

---

[102] On the position with respect to costs, see Charles Howard, Laycock & Co., Solicitors, to William Mellor, 28 Sept. 1917 (WNC Papers).

[103] 'Memorandum on Amendments to the Courts (Emergency) Powers Bill with the object of amending the Rent & Mortgage Interest (War Restrictions) Act, 1915' (WNC Papers).

[104] *British Labour Statistics: Historical Abstract* (HMSO, 1971), p. 167.

[105] *Local Government Journal*, 28 Apr. 1917.

[106] *Evictions in Birmingham*

	1915	1916	1917
No. of applications	866	714	411
warrants granted	834	648	338
warrants issued	423	246	133
warrants executed	418	240	125

Source: Central Billeting Board, Report on Birmingham, 28-9 Jan. 1918 (PRO Mun. 5/97)

agitation to which they had given rise. In May 1916 a further step towards more systematic organization was taken with the formation of the Birmingham and District Tenants' Federation, a non-political body, whose lineage is directly traceable to the spontaneous upsurge of the previous year. In the aftermath of the passage of the Rent Act there had been a continuous expansion of tenants' associations, so that by the time of its formation the Federation represented some twelve or thirteen districts in all.[107] In addition to tenants' defence work, the Federation saw itself as the nucleus of a burgeoning grass-roots housing reform movement—'not in the Town Planning sense, but the practical housing without exploitation of usury and vagabondage'. 'We want a happy and contented people enjoying their home life without let or hindrance', its secretary informed the Workers' National Committee. 'Your efforts are glorious in this direction and by the creation of assns. [*sic*] we are educating the people into application and the acceptance of responsibility which brings inspiration and loyal service to each other.'[108] In this noble task the Federation had, from the outset, looked to the Birmingham Trades Council for support.

The Trades Council had earlier determined to force a decision on the vexed and confusing question brought about by the conflicting judgements concerning the tenants' right to deduct excess charges on standard rent from future payment.[109] In the celebrated case of *Sharp* v. *Chant*, heard in Birmingham County Court in May, 1916, this right was upheld, and reaffirmed on appeal to the Divisional Courts six months later. Kesterton was elated. 'I have a letter from our lawyer today saying he does not think they will appeal', he wrote to Middleton immediately afterwards. 'I am not shouting yet till I am quite sure—then we shall advertise our achievement'.[110] The opportunity for so doing, however, was denied; upon a further appeal by the landlords to the Court of Appeal, the verdict was reversed and such deductions rendered illegal.[111]

The national bearings of the case together with the overwhelming expense of continued litigation compelled the Trades Council to

[107] *Town Crier*, 17 Oct. 1919.

[108] William Ellis to J. S. Middleton, 27 Apr. 1918 (WNC Papers).

[109] See appendix to Minutes of War Emergency Workers' National Committee, 9 Nov. 1916.

[110] J. Kesterton to J. S. Middleton, 23 Nov. 1916 (WNC Papers).

[111] See Times Law Reports, reprinted as appendix to Minutes of War Emergency Workers' National Committee, 15 Mar. 1917 (WNC Papers).

relinquish control over these proceedings. A special appeal fund was launched by the Workers' National Committee and preparations made for a final appeal to the House of Lords. The situation created by the adverse decision of the Court of Appeal was ludicrous. It drove a coach and four through the Rent Act and legitimized that which parliament had expressly intended to prohibit. Landlords henceforth could defy the act with impunity. If allowed to stand it threatened to destroy all the progress made since 1915. Landlords immediately set about recovering the deductions previously made. The Workers' National Committee was alarmed by the speed of the counter-attack:

How far reaching this decision is may be gauged from the fact that corres-pondence which has reached the Party Office since the decision was given, indicates that in Hull, for instance, the amount of deductions made exceeds in the aggregate over £1,500. In many other districts the same must apply. In South Wales, for instance, where agitation regarding the administration of the Act has been particularly widespread, tenants will be intimidated by the landlords as the result of this decision into refunding the deductions they have already made and which are essentially illegal charges made by landlords in direct contravention of the Act.[112]

As the verdict froze on the Master of the Rolls' lips, Birmingham tenants were compelled under duress to make similar restitution.[113] The decision was roundly condemned. 'The feeling here', wrote the secretary of the Tenants' Federation, 'is, however innocent the Court of Appeal mind is: their decision is in effect wicked: making the working of the Act remunerative, appealing to the cupidity and connivance of landlords: and not prohibiting as is the intention or withholding all additional profit upon pre-war rental values ...'[114]

The introduction of a revised Courts (Emergency Powers) Bill at this juncture promised to resolve the difficulty without further recourse to the courts. In consequence of the pressure brought to bear by the Workers' National Committee, opposition in the House of Lords was brushed aside and the Government prevailed upon to accept the amendments brought forward by the Labour Party.[115]

[112] 'Memorandum on Amendments to the Courts (Emergency) Powers Bill with the object of amending the Rent & Mortgage Interest (War Restrictions) Act, 1915 (WNC Papers).
[113] J. Kesterton to J. S. Middleton, 8 Mar. 1917 (WNC Papers).
[114] William Ellis to J. S. Middleton, 7 Mar. 1917 (WNC Papers).
[115] Minutes of War Emergency Workers' National Committee, 15 Mar., 29 Mar., 12 Apr., 10 May and 27 June 1917 (WNC Papers).

The Courts (Emergency Powers) Bill, which became law in July 1917, provided for the recovery of all extra rent paid by tenants since the introduction of the Rent Act, 1915, at any time up to January 1918; excess charges made after the passing of the new enactment were recoverable by deductions from subsequent payment at any time within six months. The new Act also provided a penalty—a fine of £10 on summary conviction—to prevent the improper marking of rent books, an important provision since a clear rent book was, for working-class tenants, a universally acknowledged character reference.[116] Thus began that process of piecemeal reform destined to render rent control legislation incomprehensible to all but the finest legal minds; and even they were baffled.[117]

Birmingham tenants were not appeased. The very success of the protracted campaign, which had begun with *Sharp* v. *Chant*, made the apparent simplicity of continued evictions all the more galling. The Trades Council, in a resolution forwarded to the Prime Minister and his colleagues, described this 'winkling' of tenants as 'a disgrace to the country and calls for immediate attention'.[118] The action of a local firm in seeking to eject several servicemen's families in order to find accommodation for their own workpeople, condemned by Kesterton as a form of 'legal barbarity', led to demonstrations.[119] The provocative claim to have alone obtained 3,000 eviction orders, recklessly bandied about by the somewhat irresponsible secretary of the Birmingham & District Property Owners' Association, was one which infuriated tenants were not disposed to question,[120] for it seemed consistent with their own experience. The 36 orders for ejectment, affecting some 398 tenants, made during September, 1917, coinciding with the unrest at Barrow, could hardly fail to stimulate agitation for the application of Regulation 2A(2) to the Birmingham district.[121] The initial expectation that Birmingham and Coventry might be treated separately for this purpose proved illusory.[122] The

[116] Appendix iii, Minutes of War Emergency Workers' National Committee, 5 July 1917 (WNC Papers).

[117] On this, see *Report of Committee on the Increase of Rent & Mortgage Interest (War Restrictions) Acts* (PP 1920, XVIII), para. 29; J. D. Crawford, *Reflection and Recollections* (1936), pp. 103-12.

[118] Minutes of Birmingham Trades Council, 27 June 1917.

[119] *Birmingham Daily Post*, 26, 27, and 28 June 1917.

[120] See Correspondence of A. J. Wilson, *Birmingham Daily Post*, 29 June 1917.

[121] On evictions in Birmingham, *HMM*, V, 5, p. 30.

[122] Cf. 'Munitions Council Daily Report', 26 Oct. 1917 (PRO Mun. 1/2).

officials of the Central Billeting Board arrived in Birmingham early in the new year to a city that was in a state of very considerable ferment. When questioned, the solicitor representing the organized tenants and Trades Council, stated:

> that this matter has caused such an amount of feeling in Birmingham that twelve Tenants' Associations had been formed in the City each with a membership of about 1,000 and that it was proposed to establish an Association in each ward of the City.
> The object of these Associations was to prevent any increase in rent and to assist tenants to resist applications for evictions. They claimed that evictions should be abolished so long as the rent was paid.
> He stated that no effort had been made to canvass the City to induce persons to join this Association, but directly the idea was mooted there was a rush of applicants for membership.

The lawyer was convinced that, notwithstanding the limitations of Regulation 2A(2), responsibility for ejectments should be removed from the hands of an unsympathetic judiciary and vested in the Ministry of Munitions, although on reflection he agreed that 'serious trouble' would result from any subsequent evictions, and that this disorder might be abated if the Minister acted through the local Court.[123]

The visitors were sceptical. Birmingham differed from Coventry and Barrow in that its work-force was not composed exclusively of munitions workers. In these circumstances, it was felt that the uneven impact of the suggested Regulation might actually exacerbate the unrest: 'It may be a source of trouble if one portion of the Birmingham workers, merely because they happen to be engaged on munitions work, receive some measure of protection which is denied to others. Mr. Kesterton was fully alive to this point, and appeared apprehensive of the possible results.' And yet, having found 'no great hardship prevailing over evictions in spite of the alleged attitude of the County Court judge and to a lesser degree, the Magistrates', the investigators concluded that, on balance, a case had been made out for declaring Birmingham a special area. Once again it was the 'very strong agitation on the subject in Birmingham Labour circles' which appears to have been decisive.

The nightmarish possibility of the whole country being scheduled in a like manner could be no longer be dismissed. The Minister was

[123] This and the following paragraph are based on 'Central Billeting Board, Report on Birmingham'. 28-9 Jan. 1918 (PRO Mun. 5/97).

thus advised against the application of the Regulation to the Motherwell area 'as it would almost certainly involve extension to the
whole Clyde district'.[124] Yet something had to be done: the demand
for the suspension of ejectments *tout court* was daily becoming
louder; unrest grew apace.[125] 'The question of the eviction of tenants
of small houses is causing very great trouble', Barnes informed his
colleagues in March, 1918. 'I am getting letters daily and there have
been some ugly incidents in Glasgow connected with evictions.'
Moreover, the agitation was no longer confined to the industrial
districts. In the Home Counties, and especially along the South
Coast, where the well-to-do were buying up homes and evicting
the occupants in order to escape from the London air raids, 'the
matter is exciting a great deal of indignation on the part of poor
tenants'.[126]

The line had to be drawn somewhere; these endless concessions
were unseemly and dangerous. Officials of the Central Billeting
Board, confronted by threatened industrial action at Workington,
informed local militants that 'the Ministry would be prepared to
deal with the matter in a way which seemed most fair to all parties
but that they could not be influenced in the matter one way or the
other by threats of the kind made'. At the same time, their superiors
in Whitehall were informed confidentially that these threats were in
fact the sole consideration. 'From the figures supplied of proceedings
before the Magistrates, there seems to be no case whatsoever for
Workington being declared a "special area" but on the other hand
the agitation has gone so far that we are inclined to think that if the
Regulation is not made, there is a possibility of serious trouble.'[127]
The Government, if it were not to lose all dignity and authority, had

[124] 'Munitions Council Daily Report', 3 May 1918 (PRO Mun. 1/9).
[125] See, for example, A. Seabury to J. S. Middleton, 14 Nov. 1917 and J. Alderson,
Secretary of Stockton and Thornby Trades & Labour Council, to J. S. Middleton, 5
Apr. 1918 (WNC Papers).
[126] 'Increase of Rent & Mortgage Interest (Amendment) Bill', Memorandum by
George Barnes, 14 Mar. 1918 (PRO Cab. 24/25 GT 3913); and see too S. C. Ball,
Secretary of Eastbourne Trades Council, to J. S. Middleton, 26 July 1918 (WNC
Papers).
[127] 'Central Billeting Board, Report on Workington', 14 Mar. 1918 ((PRO Mun.
5/97). The problem at Workington was resolved by the passage of the Amendment
Act of 1918 which obviated the need for the Regulation. It was, however, considered
prudent to bring this to the attention of Arthur Pugh, General Secretary of the Iron
and Steel Trades Confederation, who was prevailed upon to explain the new position
to his constituents: 'Central Billeting Board, Minutes of 14th Meeting', 7 May 1918
(PRO Mun. 5/97).

to make a preemptive intervention. The Minister of Munitions pressed for amending legislation.[128]

A general enactment protecting the sitting tenant in the event of a transfer of ownership would, it was hoped, arrest the growing movement for more extensive controls for working-class success in this sphere had begun to generate similar demands amongst the formerly self-reliant middle classes.[129] These claims were to grow in volume as the difficulties of meeting increased liabilities on reduced incomes exposed the middle strata to some of the unfamiliar insecurities of working-class life. It was to be an important factor in the continuation of rent control after the war. At this juncture, however, Ministers set themselves firmly against further extension of control. Although aware of cases of serious hardship, it was decided that, if the limits of rental fixed in the act of 1915 were revised upwards, 'there is no point at which the increase could well be stopped. There would also probably be strong pressure to continue the Act after the end of the war. It is doubtful whether any stopping place would be found short of giving all existing tenants security for life in the houses they now occupy.'[130] The Increase of Rent & Mortgage Interest (Amendment) Act, which became law in April, 1918, was therefore confined to working-class dwellings. It was a retroactive measure which deprived persons purchasing houses since 30 September 1917, of the right to obtain possession whether for their own occupation or the occupation of persons in their employ. Regulation 2A(2) was thus rendered superfluous, although its withdrawal was long considered impolitic: it was allowed to lapse in 1920.[131]

Reformers had hoped for a more comprehensive enactment penalising those who flouted the law, transferring all proceedings to the County Courts, and closing loopholes in connection with the deliberate manipulation of assessments in order to exact higher rents, a practice which in Warrington threatened to precipitate 'a rent strike that will set the Town ablaze'.[132] The Workers' National

[128] *HC Deb.* 5s. cv (1918), 1021.
[129] Cf. 'Letters and Memoranda on the Sale of Houses and Subsequent Ejectment of Tenants, 1917' (PRO T. 172/481).
[130] 'Increase of Rent & Mortgage Interest (Amendment) Bill' (PRO HO. 45/10808/310841).
[131] Cf. 'Eviction of Tenants', Memorandum submitted to Departmental Committee on Operation of the Rent Acts (PRO HLG. 41/1) and *HMM*, II, 1, p. 235.
[132] 'Report of the Rent Sub-Committee on the Increase of Rent etc. Amending Bill' (WNC Papers). Quotation from A. E. Seabury to J. S. Middleton, 21 Mar. 1918 (WNC Papers).

Committee and the War Rents League prepared to lobby on behalf of such a measure.[133] However, the scope for independent initiative at Westminister had long since been curtailed. 'As you realize,' Middleton informed a correspondent, 'our difficulty about amending Bills is that the whole of Parliament's time is in the hands of the Government, and the old rights of private members to introduce legislation had been swept away. This means of course that we are limited now to pressing our case on Government Departments, and I am afraid that those concerned with this particular question are not particularly pliable.'[134] Ministers, it seemed, responded to nowt but agitation.

IV

The first experiment in state-subsidized housing is generally held to have been initiated by the Housing and Town Planning Act, 1919. The growth of tenant militancy, however, cannot be properly understood apart from the pioneering but now forgotten efforts of the Ministry of Munitions.

The Ministry spent slightly over £4,250,000 on various housing schemes during the war, much of it disbursed in subsidies to local authorities and 'controlled establishments'. Under the post-war ownership scheme, introduced to surmount impediments in the mobilization of labour and materials, the Ministry itself undertook the direct construction of permanent dwellings for subsequent purchase at a market value to be fixed, if necessary, by independent arbitration. The system was less than satisfactory. In the exceptional uncertainties of the period, local authorities were unwilling to commit themselves to a speculative venture; the embittered haggling which followed retarded progress and aggravated labour unrest.[135]

The more sensitive question of rent determination was fraught with even greater difficulties. The economic rent on 70 per cent of expenditure stipulated by the Treasury entailed, in all cases, a very substantial increase over the prevailing standard of rents. This somewhat arbitrary percentage, intended to accustom tenants to inevitably higher post-war rentals, came to be regarded as a vital bridge to the resumption of market forces. It was continuously

[133] Dan Rider to J. S. Middleton, 12 Mar. 1918 (WNC Papers).
[134] J. S. Middleton to A. E. Seabury, 25 Apr. 1918 (WNC Papers).
[135] On the finance of housing schemes, see *HMM*, V, 5, pp. 6-12; and for a revealing insight into the strained relations between central and local government, see 'Central Billeting Board, Report on the Clyde', 12-16 Nov. 1917 (PRO Mun. 5/97).

threatened by soaring building costs and the depressing effect of rent control, centrifugal pressures destined to render the bridge impassable. Officials at the Whitehall end increasingly felt like Horatius confronted by inflationary proletarian hordes to be resisted at all—or nearly all—costs.[136]

The ever-widening discrepancy between pre-war rentals and the rents chargeable on the 70 per cent basis hindered mobility and led to disturbance. The rents of Mid-Lanark houses, approved in January, 1917, provoked the Tenants' Defence Association and Trades Council and could not be enforced until May, the following year. In March 1917 Coventry Corporation succumbed to a rent strike organized by the Stoke Heath Tenants' Defence Association and reduced rents accordingly. In October the Treasury, under protest, accepted a return of between 45 and 52 per cent on the capital cost of rents for semi-permanent houses at Barrow.[137] Tenant power was irresistible. In the words of the Official History: 'It was not until after the Armistice that a firm stand in the matter of rents could be taken.'[138]

The quality of the accommodation built or subsidised by the Ministry was, in view of the difficult circumstances, rather good. Well Hall Garden Suburb, built for the fastidious Woolwich artisan, 'was designed, without being in any sense luxurious, so as to give an air not only of comfort but of architectural grace'.[139] The two-storeyed brick houses, built at Mid-Lanark, were said to be of 'pleasing appearance' and a credit to the designer, the architect to the Scottish Local Government Board. 'The sculleries are large, the staircases and rooms light, bath rooms are usual and used, and there is an excellent hot water supply.'[140] The absence of a parlour, the principal defect, was remedied at Barrow where the houses were also planned and laid out 'with a view to a aesthetic as well as sanitary considerations'.[141] Working people, it was noted, were

---

[136] See S. C. Turner to G. H. Duckworth, 'Memorandum on the Rents of Permanent Houses', 22 Aug. 1919 (PRO Mun. 5/96).

[137] *HMM*, V, 5, pp. 12-16. On Mid-Lanark, see too 'Memorandum of the Scottish Local Government Board', para 12 (Doc. 20) (PRO Reco. 1/644).

[138] *HMM*, V, 5, p. 2. On occasion, however, the Ministry was prepared to make a stand and drew up plans accordingly: see 'Munitions Council Daily Reports', 11, 14, and 18 Mar. 1918 (PRO Mun. 1/7).   [139] Wolfe, *Labour Supply & Regulation*, p. 91.

[140] G. H. Duckworth to Sir Lionel Earle, 'Memorandum on Threatened Rent Strikes—Mid-Lanarkshire', 9 Aug. 1920 (PRO Mun. 5/330).

[141] 'Inadequacy of Housing Accommodation at Barrow', Memorandum by George Barnes, 26 Sept. 1917 (PRO Cab. 24/27 GT 2130); and in general see S. Pepper and M. Swenarton, 'Home front: garden suburbs for munitions workers 1915-1918', *Architectural Review* clxiii (1978), pp. 366-75.

ready to employ increased purchasing power to raise their standards of domestic comfort. The highest standards were demanded and where expectations were disappointed unrest ensued.[142]

The claustrophobic quality of the 305 houses that comprised the Brewery Fields Estate, Dudley, provoked a good deal of criticism. In addition to the unpleasing 'match box' exterior, tenants had to contend with defective craftsmanship, rising damp, cracked plaster, and leaking roofs, while the paper-thin partition walls gave rise to the derisory commonplace—one nail does for two pictures.[143] In Coventry too scamped work and the want of amenity were influential factors in the formation of the Stoke Heath Tenants' Defence Association.[144]

Tenants of Rosyth Garden City were not at all satisfied with the design and construction of the cold dwellings which the Admiralty had provided for its patriotic servants who had answered the call and given up comfortable homes in the southern port towns to come and work at the northern dockyard. The Rosyth Ratepayers' Association, a non-political body representing the newcomers, in a petition to the Lords Commissioners, spoke of the unsuitable nature of the accommodation provided:

The houses should have been built after the style of those in which we were accustomed to live, prior to our transference to Rosyth, and not according to the ideas of those whose position in life will not compel them to live in them ... As the largest employers of labour in the Country and with a business man (Sir Eric Geddes) at your head, you should know that a satisfied workman is a job half completed.

Ill-fitting doors and windows, inadequate roofing insulation, and the awkwardly situated upstairs lavatories—'Making it very inconvenient at times to a person working in his garden',—were as nothing compared to the discomfort caused by the absence of a rear

---

[142] On patterns of consumption, see, for example, G. H. Duckworth, 'Memorandum on the Barrow Housing Scheme', 12 Oct. 1917 (PRO Mun. 5/96); on standards of accommodation, J. Mavor, Secretary of Rosyth Ratepayers' Association, to Admiralty Superintendent, 21 Nov. 1918 (PRO Adm. 116/2163) and 'Rosyth Housing', Memorandum by Civil Engineer-in-Chief, 3 Feb. 1920 (PRO Adm. 116/2161).

[143] *Dudley Chronicle*, 24 May 1919.

[144] On the defective construction of the Stoke Heath Estate, see correspondence of H. E. Derrick and Report of LGB Enquiry, *Midland Daily Telegraph*, 6 Jan. and 28 Feb. 1919; also *Coventry Herald*, 14 Mar. 1919; on the absence of amenity, *Midland Daily Telegraph*, 21 May 1917. Even the Well Hall Estate was not beyond criticism on these grounds: see PRO Reco. 1/622.

entrance. 'We wonder how many of the houses in which you gentleman have to live have coals, bicycles, prams, manure, etc. carried through the only room in which you have to eat and dine?' The architect's almost perverse disregard of the elements of good sanitation seemed to border on treachery, or so the tenants thought: 'Eminent hygienists tell us that corners harbour dirt, and bring disease. This being the case, the houses here must have been designed by a German, with the idea of spreading disease. There are more corners in one of these houses than in any polygon which you gentleman can conceive.'[145]

Rosyth Garden City, planned before the war to service the new secure North Sea base, had been built with quite exceptional celerity. 1600 of the projected 3,000 dwellings were completed by the close of 1918.[146] In the process corners had been cut and according to one visitor the whole development was 'a very cheap gimcrack version' of 'middle-class Letchworth'.[147] But, in view of the preparation of the post-war housing programme, and the almost reverential regard for the power of precedent, this substantial essay in town planning assumed more than logistical significance. The report of the special subcommittee, appointed by the Scottish Trade Union Congress to examine the scheme, corroborated much of the tenants' complaints. Although lay-out and appearance were not without merit, homes were decidedly small. The bathroom was described as 'an apology, and a very poor one.... It will tax the ingenuity of the grown person to wash by instalments; to bathe must be left to their imagination.'[148] The absence of recreational facilities did nothing to relieve the inevitable discomfort attendant upon such rapid development.[149]

Temporary accommodation was a good deal worse. Nearly 3,000 five-roomed bungalows, distributed throughout nine estates around the Woolwich Arsenal, were, in the words of the Controller of Housing, 'literally human packing cases'. Thrown together from

[145] D. Rafer, Chairman, and F. Burnett, Secretary, of Rosyth Ratepayers' Association to Lords Commissioners of the Admirality, n.d. but Feb. 1918 (PRO Adm. 116/2164).

[146] Alexander McKenna, Assistant Secretary to Scottish Local Government Board. to Secretary of the Admiralty, 17 Jan. 1919 (PRO Adm. 116/2163). On construction and development, see 'Report on Rosyth Housing' by H. Ryle, 9 Apr. 1920 (PRO Adm. 116/2161).

[147] *Workers' Dreadnought*, 9 Aug. 1919.

[148] *Dunfermline Press*, 22 Sep. 1917.

[149] 'Rosyth: Proposal to Erect Cinema Building', Report from Admiral Superintendent to Director of Works, 19 Jan. 1918 (PRO Adm. 116/2164).

inferior timber, some were built without concrete foundations, others without regard to drainage or ventilation; in winter they were cold and damp and virtually uninhabitable. Temporary road surfaces, constantly cut up by heavy army lorries, were frequently impassable. 'The external aspect', wrote Duckworth, 'is hideous.' 'These Estates will need careful supervision to prevent them becoming a slum.'[150] At Holbrook Lane, Coventry, things were better—just. At Dudley such accommodation could only be let with great difficulty.[151] 'Tin Town'. Rosyth, scandalized the First Lord of the Admiralty, Walter Long, who probably knew and cared more for good estate management than naval affairs.[152]

The sixteen-week rent strike that began at Coventry twelve days after the Armistice, initiated a cycle of eighteen months duration in which Ministers were fairly deluged with report of rent strikes, demonstrations, riots, and disorders. That the unrest had been foreseen did little to diminish its impact. A questionnaire drawn up by the Reconstruction Committee on the Rents Acts, appointed in the spring of 1918, recognized in tenant radicalism the emergence of a new and vital political force. Information was sought on this novel phenomenon. Notwithstanding provision for the automatic expiration of the Rent Restriction Acts six months after the declaration of peace, decontrol, it was already clear, would have to take account of working-class susceptibilities. One of the largest of Scottish house-owners, a substantial builder, financier, and architect, and curiously a man of left-wing sympathies, predicted the most fearful chaos should the Government proceed to honour its commitment:

House owners will immediately put up rents in a drastic manner. This will coincide with the coming home of the soldier who will have this dramatic fact of the result of his fighting vividly brought home to him. All the elements calling for a Bolshevik Revolution will be brought into existence....

What would probably happen is that a general strike against rent would be proclaimed, and as the Government would almost certainly capitulate, popular clamour would have demonstrated its power, and had its appetite whetted for greater triumphs.[153]

[150] G. H. Duckworth, 'Notes on a visit to the Woolwich Bungalows', 19 Dec. 1918 (PRO Mun. 5/96); *HMM*, V, 5, pp. 84-6.
[151] Correspondence of Robert McQueen, Chairman of Foleshill Tenants' Association, *Midland Daily Telegraph*, 27 Sept. 1919; *HMM*, V, 5, p. 15.
[152] Memorandum of Civil Lord initialled W.H.L., 14 Sept. 1920 (PRO Adm. 116/2161).
[153] John A. Mactaggart to W. G. Wallace, 20 May 1918 (PRO Reco. 1/646).

Those who abhorred violence took the same view. Dan Rider, a member of the Committee, warned his colleagues that, 'any increase of rent whatsoever will be greatly resisted, ... any increase owing to scarcity will be strenuously opposed as an attempt of one section of the community to profit at the expense of the workers, resulting in widespread discontent and serious upheavals of extreme gravity'. Rider was particularly worried by the consequences of irresponsible and vengeful landlords being loosed upon the nation. 'If Bolshevism is ever popular in this country', he wrote, 'these are the people who will have to be thanked for it.'[154] 'If an attempt were made to increase rents generally,' said an official of the South Wales Miners' Federation, 'it would meet with organised opposition and would mean revolution.' William Mellor, the mild-mannered secretary of the Manchester and Salford Tenants' Defence Association, was not only convinced that such attempts would provoke disturbance, but felt justified in taking part in it. The advocates of 'normalcy' misunderstood both the economic and political situation. Sidney Webb, who was not given to apocalyptic visions, had no doubt that the discontinuance of rent control, even if graduated, would be disastrous: 'Apart from its uselessness in producing those houses [an] increase in rent would cause such political and industrial disturbance as to be politically impossible. He confidently predicted that no Cabinet would adopt it.'[155] Even if fears of revolution were, as a matter of policy, deliberately enlarged (and the archives of the Workers' National Committee hint at deft orchestration),[156] there is ample evidence of the new and radical spirit by which working-class tenants were now possessed.

The complaint at Coventry was long-standing. The six-hundred hastily erected houses that comprised the Stoke Heath Estate, had been built to accommodate employees of the local Ordnance Works. On taking possession in September 1916, tenants organized to

[154] Committee on Increase of Rent Act, 'Memorandum of Suggestions' by Dan Rider (Doc. 58) (PRO Reco. 1/646).

[155] Committee on Increase of Rent Act etc.: Minutes of 8th Meeting, 5 Nov. 1918 (PRO Reco. 1/645).

[156] Rider had been discreetly primed by Sidney Webb, who had also arranged for him to confer with the two additional witnesses who were to reinforce Webb's statement before the Reconstruction Committee: see S. Webb to D. Rider, 2 Oct. 1918; J. S. Middleton to William Mellor, 29 Oct. 1918 and Middleton to W. Harris and W. Mellor, 2 Nov. 1918; and see too 'Memorandum on the Points to be Insisted on by Witnesses before the Rent and Mortgages Restrictions Act Committee'; also Circular letter of Manchester Trades Council (WNC Papers).

contest the projected rents which, in view of the unfinished condition, were acknowledged as excessive.[157] The concessions offered by the Corporation were not, however, considered satisfactory, and in the course of the protracted negotiations which followed, opinion on both sides hardened.

Early in the new year tenants were balloted; support for direct action was overwhelming.[158] The Corporation capitulated after an eleven-day rent strike. An interim settlement was then concluded. Tenants agreed to accept the 1*s*. 1*d*. per week rent reduction that was offered in place of the full 3*s*. demanded, on condition that the rents would be again reviewed upon completion of the scheme when the total capital cost had been ascertained.

At the end of the financial year the agitation was renewed. Repairs were not, as promised, executed with sufficient expedition. Contractors moving clumsily from house to house caused great inconvenience and were a constant irritant. Tenants on shift-work were especially vexed by the endless disturbances. In May 1918 Stoke Heath Tenants' Association submitted a claim for compensation coupled with a demand for a further revision of rents.[159] The Corporation's offer of arbitration, made seven months later, came too late to avert a second rent strike.[160]

Tenants were not in the least intimidated when, in its sixth week, the secretary of the association received a letter from the Town Clerk coupling substantial concessions with the threat of proceedings. A thousand people assembled that evening to consider the correspondence: 'As usual, the gathering was called by bells and bugles. The communication was read, and when the last paragraph, relating to distraint, was reached there was much groaning and hissing.'[161] Their determination to resist was encouraged by knowledge of extensive support within and beyond Coventry. At the end of 1918 the association had changed its name to incorporate some of these

[157] The official history erroneously ascribes the formation of the Stoke Heath Tenants' Association to Mar. 1917: *HMM*, V, 5, p. 13. However, as early as the previous October representations were being made to the Corporation: *Midland Daily Telegraph*, 27 Oct. 1916. See too 'Report on Industrial Welfare Conditions in Coventry by Miss Anderson and Miss Markham', Nov. 1916 (mimeographed), pp. 4-5 (PRO Reco. 1/802).

[158] *Midland Daily Telegraph*, 3 and 7 May 1917.

[159] *Midland Daily Telegraph*, 24 May 1918.

[160] See correspondence of A. P. Read and J. Gooding, Chairman and Secretary of Stoke Heath Tenants' Associations' *Midland Daily Telegraph*, 1 Jan. 1919.

[161] *Coventry Herald*, 10 Jan. 1919.

new elements. Henceforth it became the Stoke Heath and Municipal Dwellings Defence Association.[162] In addition to local trade unionists, Stoke Heath tenants received moral and material support from tenants in Tottenham, Tooting, Nottingham, and Wolverhampton, and were especially heartened by news of the launching of a similar rent strike at Woolwich.[163] In the County Court counsel for the eleven selected tenants, including the principal officers of the association, summoned by the Corporation, spoke darkly of the certain disorder that would attend any attempt to enforce the adverse judgement made.[164] This was no idle threat; already opponents had been burned in effigy.[165] The orderly crowds on that occasion, however, formed a marked contrast to the tumultuous incident, which attracted much odium in the previous strike, in which a recalcitrant tenant, who declined to display the usual No Rent poster, was subjected to this and other kinds of 'rough music'.[166] Although the Tenants' Defence Association took exception to intimidation and was loath to encourage violence, the authorities were left in no doubt that distraint would be resisted. The Corporation wisely refrained from further acts of provocation.

The Tenants' Defence Association had not foreseen the prolongation of the dispute, and no preparation had been made to bank the accumulated arrears which, by the fourteenth week, amounted to £3,710.[167] The presence of relatively large sums of money in those houses in which the rents had not been consumed may well have created a sense of unease and a willingness to seek to escape from the entrenched position adopted. The Corporation too was keen to move away fron confrontation, and had in vain appealed to the Government for a subsidy for this purpose. It was finally agreed that the Local Government Board be invited to hold an inquiry to help settle the matter, and then, if necessary, to seek arbitration.[168] Christopher Addison, the Minister, was more than willing to oblige.

Four months after the strike first begun, Stoke Heath tenants voted overwhelmingly to accept the offer of a 5*d.* per week reduction.[169]

[162] *Midland Daily Telegraph*, 16 Dec. 1918.
[163] *Midland Daily Telegraph*, 6 Jan. and 17 Feb. 1919.
[164] *Coventry Herald*, 14 Feb. 1919.
[165] *Coventry Herald*, 17 Jan. 1919.
[166] Correspondence of F. E. Latham, Secretary of Stoke Heath Tenants' Association, *Midland Daily Telegraph*, 19 and 22 May 1917; *HC Deb* 5s. cxiii (1919), 847.
[167] *Midland Daily Telegraph*, 28 Feb. 1919.
[168] *Midland Daily Telegraph*, 20 Feb. 1919.
[169] *Midland Daily Telegraph*, 14 and 15 Mar. 1919.

The settlement, which fell 6*d*. short of the original target, encountered a brief but abortive resistance organized by a number of malcontents.[170] The overall impression was one of success. On the morrow of victory Coventry Tenants' Defence League, an advisory body formed by the Trades Council in 1915, merged with the Stoke Heath Association to strengthen the campaign against rent decontrol which was then getting under weigh.[171]

'See what they've done at Coventry. They haven't paid any rent for months because it was set too high.' The words of a defiant tenant registered the power of example upon the anxious officials who called at her home at the end of the first week of the Woolwich rent strike.[172] The strike, which began in February 1919, was not, however, the first of such outbursts. Shortly after arrival in August, 1915, the first 200 tenants, artisans and trade unionists to a man, united to combat excessively restrictive conditions of tenure; payment of the 5*s*. key money, imposed subsequent to their having obtained tenancy, was also withheld. The action met with a partial success. Withdrawn in so far as it affected the protesters, the demand was retained in the case of new tenants. The campaign for outright abolition, a matter of principle rather than hardship, persisted.[173]

The authorities, in search of a settlement, proposed that the total sum in question be handed over to the control of trustees appointed jointly by the Office of Works and the Tenants' Association for the erection of a much needed social centre. Although later withdrawn, the proposal possessed considerable attraction. Jack Mills, the future Labour MP for Dartmouth, who was then resident on the estate and chairman of the Tenants' Association, warmed to the idea. 'They should remember', he told one meeting, 'that the Association does not exist only to oppose the powers that be! Its chief object was to promote the happiness and well-being of the residents.' Will Crooks, Vice-President of the Association, was no less enthusiastic. The central problem, as he saw it, was the absence of neighbourliness. 'In London the people next door were frequently strangers to us. Many were broken in life because of the want of sympathy and the interest which would only be given by those close at hand.'[174] The

---

[170] *Midland Daily Telegraph*, 17, 18, and 20 Mar. 1919.

[171] *Midland Daily Telegraph*, 23 Mar. 1919.

[172] G. H. Duckworth, 'Notes on a Visit to the Woolwich Bungalows on the Occasion of a Rent Strike', 22 Feb. 1919 (PRO Mun. 5/96).

[173] See *Woolwich Pioneer*, 3 Dec. 1915, 20 Feb., and 10 Mar. 1916.

[174] *Woolwich Pioneer*, 17 Mar. 1916.

Well Hall Garden City provided an unprecedented opportunity for the development of those bonds of friendship and mutuality which then still meant something to the labour movement. Such sentiments were widely shared amongst the newcomers. One of them even saw the Promised Land in the not too distant future:

The Well Hall Garden City Tenants' Association is a unique body: it owes a great deal to the unique circumstances which surround it. The tenants are not only united in being all under the same landlord, but they are also united in being under the same employer. All their interests are in common. The Tenants' Association is the nucleus of many bodies which will spring up on the estate; we shall have athletic, literary, debating and social clubs, all under the wings of the association. The women will be organised; the children will be catered for; the maypole will be set up on Lovelace Green and some of the happiness of the past will be won back to become the hope of the future. What form is the political organisation of the tenants going to take?

What will be its policy at election times? These are questions which the future alone can answer, but of one thing we may be quite positively sure—a new growth will result; an added inspiration will be present which will surprise many who are wedded to the old methods of political organisation.

... It may well be that in Well Hall we have the germ of a city of the future. It is built on a romantic spot. Near by is the old home of Sir Thomas More who wrote 'Utopia'. The Utopia of the future is springing up on the very soil where Sir Thomas More lived. It may not fulfill all that he hoped for but it will approximate very closely to Whitman's ideal of the great city ...[175]

Meanwhile, the Association was preoccupied with the more mundane details of everyday life: excessive rentals and the want of educational and shopping facilities. The first two items were matters for negotiation with the authorities; the last was within their own province. Preparations were made for the formation and communal management of a co-operative store.[176]

The Well Hall Garden City Tenants' Association, which in due course came to recruit at least 700 of the 1,298 tenants who comprised the estate, represented the cream of the working class. The inhabitants of ubiquitous bungalows, 'hutments' in the common parlance of the period, were a class apart.[177] Although reluctant to become

---

[175] *Woolwith Pioneer*, 24 Mar. 1916.   [176] *Woolwich Pioneer*, 12 May 1916.

[177] Tenancies of permanent dwellings built for and by the Ministry of Munitions were, as a matter of policy, confined to the better-off elements beneath the servant-keeping classes: 'The Housing Department of the Ministry of Munitions: Interim Statement with regard to its Constitution, Principles, etc.' by G. H. Duckworth, 7 Apr. 1919 (PRO HLG. 46/106); membership of tenants' association from *Woolwich Pioneer*, 5 Nov. 1920.

identified with these lesser folk, the Garden City Association, having been approached on several occasions, agreed that a hutments section of the Association should be formed. 'It would quite ments section of the Association should be formed. 'It could quite with the main body for the removal of common grievances and in their mutual interest.'[178] At the first concert, organized by the Bostall and Churchfield Tenants' Association early in 1918, the 'gratifying fact' was announced that 436 members had joined out of a possible 495 hutments.[179] The movement grew in numbers; and in their radicalism, too, the hutments people surpassed the parent body.

The first of the post-war rent strikes at Woolwich was organized by the Government Hutments Tenants' Protection League, a body which represented a fusion of the various tenants' associations that had been formed on the numerous estates that stretched from Greenwich to Abbey Wood. The strike was a protest against the dilatory response to previous representation for a 5s. (50 per cent) reduction of weekly rents. An abatement of 2s. 6d. had been granted in recognition of the difficulties of heating the damp flimsy bungalows, 'dirty little chicken houses', in the expressive phrase of the observer, but this concession, due to expire after three months, was dimissed as little more than a sop, and, perhaps, a sign of weakness.[180]

The deputation that waited upon the Minister two months earlier, in December 1918, had not created a good impression. Duckworth, Controller of Housing, thought the deputies of dubious character, indolent or self-interested, and their constituents inferior to the model citizens of the Well Hall Garden Suburb. He also thought concessions inadvisable. Not only were the complainants able to pay the rents, but there was a lengthy waiting list of people who were more than willing to pay; lower rents, moreover, would hasten the process of slum formation:

The reduction of rents is further to be avoided because of the deteriorating effect that it would have upon the existing tenancies. It is important for the morale of the Estate that the fairly comfortable working class should be retained in order to maintain the character of the settlements. As it is, the tenants are of a less thrifty class than the tenants of the permanent houses,

[178] *Woolwich Pioneer*, 2 June 1916.
[179] *Woolwich Pioneer*, 22 Feb. 1918.
[180] *Woolwich Pioneer*, 14 Feb. 1919.

with lower rents the better tenants will tend to leave and be replaced by a poorer and rougher class from Woolwich or from Inner London.[181]

The 'better type', according to the official historians, had already decamped leaving the 'very rough element' in possession. The lumpenproletariat, who dominated the Tenants' Protection League, according to this extravagantly mendacious account, then proceeded to foment riots and demonstrations, 'chiefly with a view to terrorising the rent-paying householders, who formed the majority, into joining the strike'.[182]

Now it is true that the composition of the estate was changing rapidly and that the Tenants' Protection League never enjoyed the active support of 50 per cent of the residents.[183] It is also the case that many were anxious and confused. One woman, for instance, told the collector that, 'the "League of Nations" had instructed her husband not to pay'; another tenant said: 'We must stick by our class. The League had told us not to pay, and you know what it is to be called a blackleg.' Duckworth, who recorded these observations, concluded, on the basis of a visit to twenty-eight houses, that 'There is an evident nervousness at the possible results of refusing to pay. At the same time there is a strong feeling of loyalty to their own class and a fear of intimidation which in some cases has been sufficient to prevent payment.' Duckworth, who considered the leaders of the Tenants' Protection League 'men of no repute', did not indicate whether these fears were with or without foundation. There is nothing in the extant records of the Ministry of Munitions or in the newspapers, unlikely to have missed such superb 'copy', which is in any sense consistent with the official version of the Woolwich Terror; there were no disorderly demonstrations, and the riots are illusory.

The Controller of Housing and his subordinate were in fact convinced that 'there was no real feeling of injustice at the back of the agitation,... that the refusals were half-hearted, and would yield with a very few exceptions to a clear instruction from the Ministry'. The intransigents, it was further agreed, would have to be summoned in court. 'There would also be a row in the local Press of which the Minister should be warned.'[184] The four-week rent strike was not

[181]   G. H. Duckworth, 'Notes on a Visit to the Woolwich Bungalows', 19 Dec. 1918 (PRO Mun. 5/96).   [182] *HMM*, V, 5, p. 87.
[183]   On composition of estates, see 'Government Housing Schemes: Well Hall Estate Management', Memorandum by J.B.C., 2 Mar. 1920 (PRO Works 22/24/9).
[184]   Quotations from G. H. Duckworth, 'Notes on a Visit to the Woolwich Bungalows on the Occasion of a Rent Strike', 22 Feb. 1919 (PRO Mun. 5/96).

finally called off, however, until, following the fifth deputation to the Ministry of Munitions, the temporary half-crown allowance had been consolidated as a permanent remission of rent.[185] Thereafter the Tenants' Protection League concentrated upon the broader movement for housing reform and continued the development of a thriving social life on the estate which had from the outset absorbed a good deal of its energies.[186]

'How did the Woolwich and Coventry strikes come off?' The meeting at which this rhetorical interlocution occurred replied to the platform with one voice: 'They won'.[187] The gathering, organized by the Municipal Tenants' Protection Association, was unanimous; The Dudley rent strike began shortly afterwards. It collapsed four weeks later when the Local Government Board inquiry, for which the tenants had pressed, concluded that the rent increases imposed by the Corporation were reasonable and ought to be paid.[188]

Tenants of Rosyth Garden City were made of sterner stuff. They had to be for they faced a far more formidable adversary, the Admiralty. The development and management of the project had been entrusted to a specially appointed intermediary, ostensibly an independent public utility, the Scottish National Housing Company. But the tenants well understood the distinction between the organ-grinder and the monkey.[189] The rents for three and four-apartment houses ranged from 8*s.* to 13*s.* per week, and were considered to be double the rents charged for five- and six-roomed houses in the English dockyard town whence most of the tenants came. This in itself was a major grievance, for the tenants had come North on the firm understanding that rents at Rosyth would not be higher than those to which they were accustomed.[190] Discontent here, as elsewhere, was aggravated by the widening differential between controlled and uncontrolled rents. In order to attract skilled labour to the adjacent Crombie Ordnance Works, the Lords Commissioners,

[185] *Woolwich Pioneer*, 21 Mar. 1919.

[186] Correspondence of Geo. Haley, Organiser of Government Hutments Tenants' Protection League, *Woolwich Pioneer*, 25 Apr. 1919; on development of social life, see, for example, *Woolwich Gazette and Plumstead News*, 28 Oct. 1919.

[187] *Dudley Chronicle*, 7 June 1919.   [188] *Dudley Chronicle*, 5 and 12 July 1919.

[189] Cf. 'Scottish National Housing Company', Memorandum for the Sub-Committee of the Admiralty Reconstruction Committee, by John W. Stone, 5 Oct. 1918 (PRO Adm. 116/2163); also Minute of B. W., 23 June 1921 (PRO Adm. 116/2161).

[190] *Forward*, 26 July 1919; 'Report of 3rd Development Houses', Memorandum by H. H. Bruce, 22 June 1918 (PRO Adm. 116/2163).

ever since 1900, had offered generous subsidies to their workmen with the result that rents were considerably lower than those which obtained in the Garden City, a point which 'seems somehow to be a bone of great contention with the tenants', and one that was continuously 'thrown back at the Admiralty'.[191] An added twist to this already complex problem of rent relativities was provided by the 'inconvenience allowance' granted to upwards of 4,000 workers who, in consequence of the deficient accommodation in the Garden City, commuted daily from Edinburgh, Dunfermline, Inverkeithing, and other allegedly lower-rented districts.[192] Rising building costs, moreover, meant that newly-completed houses at the Garden City, especially those with the much prized parlour, were more expensive than the existing stock, a fact which gave further cause for concern.[193]

Ever since the first houses had become available in the spring of 1916, the excessively high rentals at the Garden City aroused criticism. In March 1917 a deputation, representing trade unionists and residents, was received by E. G. Pretyman, Civil Lord of the Admiralty, who was couteous and sympathetic but not particularly forthcoming. He did, however, promise that rents would be reviewed at the end of the war when overtime might not be sufficient to allow tenants to meet their liabilities.[194]

The promise was not to be forgotten and nor was the matter allowed to rest there. The Rosyth Ratepayers' Association, in addition to the organizing of concerts, flower shows, gardening competitions and other pastimes, continued to press for the provision of more adequate schooling and shopping facilities, allotments, and for various structural improvements.[195] At the same time, their Lordships were requested to reconsider the proposed erection of superior accommodation for dockyard foremen and other

[191] Minute of H. H. Bruce, 2 June 1919; 'Rosyth Housing', Minute from Civil Engineer-in-Chief, 11 June 1919 (PRO Adm. 116/2162).

[192] 'Notes of a Conference between Representatives of the Local Government Board and the Scottish National Housing Company' 3 May 1919; 'H. M. Dockyard, Rosyth, Memorandum Regarding Workmen's Trains, Inconvenience Allowances, Housing' etc. On conflicting estimates of comparative rentals, see J. Mavor, Secretary of Rosyth Ratepayers' Association, to First Civil Lord of the Admiralty, 2 August 1919 and Alex. Blair, Chief Valuer, Scotland, to Civil Engineer-in-Chief, 29 August 1919 (PRO Adm. 116/2162).

[193] W. Graham Greene to Secretary, Local Government Board, Edinburgh, 25 April 1917 (PRO Adm. 116/2170).

[194] 'Rosyth Housing,' Memorandum initialled H.T.G., 21 March 1917 (PRO Adm. 116/2170).

[195] *Dunfermline Press*, 4 August and 29 September 1917.

'subordinate officers' which seemed destined, and was intended, to perpetuate and extend invidious distinctions from the industrial to the domestic sphere.[196] These efforts were not without some success. But on the crucial proposal for a half-crown rent reduction there was no progress. Relations were, moreover, soured by the Scottish National Housing Company's dilatory response to the tenants' complaints, the net effect of which was to intensify the demand for the Admiralty to abandon its unconvincing performance as Pilate, assume direct managerial responsibility, and dispense with market considerations in the matter of rents.[197]

In March 1918 the Ratepayers' Association took a new tack. New or vacant accommodation in the Garden City, hitherto reserved for the exclusive use of Admiralty employees, was henceforth to be 'blacked'; and by the close of the year there were seventy-five unlet houses.[198] The reduction in overtime thereafter quickly led to an escalation of the campaign as the difficulty of making ends meet became more acute.[199] Rank subordination could not, of course, pass without a salutary rejoinder. The authorities decided to put a number of vacant houses upon the open market, having first raised the rents by £5 per annum. The predictable response was overwhelming; ten Dunfermline policemen thus obtained tenancies.[200] The associated tenants were not intimidated. In April 1919 Rosyth ratepayers called for a 50 per cent reduction and threatened to withhold rent in support of their demand.[201]

The eight-week rent strike that began at the end of the following month involved a minimum of 700 of the 1600 tenants before the end of June, and possibly double that number by the end of July. It placed the Admiralty in something of a quandary; to grant a special allowance might ease the problem of differentials but amounted to a

[196] F. J. Burnett, Secretary of Rosyth Ratepayers' Association to Lords Commissioners of the Admiralty, 16 August 1917 (PRO Adm. 116/2170).

[197] 'Rosyth Housing: Report from Admiral Superintendent to Secretary of the Admiralty' 15 March 1918 (PRO Adm. 116/2164).

[198] Minute of Civil Engineer-in-Chief, 27 March 1918 (PRO Adm. 116/2164); also 'Memorandum on Rosyth Garden City Rents' September 1920 (PRO Adm. 116/2161); and Henry H. Bruce to A. F. Pease, 2nd Civil Lord of the Admiralty, 17 December 1918 (PRO Adm. 116/2163).

[199] 'Rosyth Housing: Question of Rents', Memorandum and Minute (PRO Adm. 116/2163).

[200] Burgh of Dunfermline, *Case on the Appeal of the Scottish National Housing Company Ltd. & Others for the Opinion of the Judges under the Valuation of Land (Scotland) Acts*, pp. 14, 15, 96, 114-16 (PRO Adm. 116/2162).

[201] *Rosyth & Forth Mail*, 10 Apr. 1919.

de facto wage increase, which was not desirable; whereas a reduction
of rentals 'would probably re-act upon other Home Dockyards and
create demands for equal consideration of the emolument of the
mass of Admiralty employees generally'.[202]

First, however, order had to be restored. Any doubts as to the
futility of further negotiations, and there could have been few, were
scotched by the disastrous encounter between Lord Lytton, Civil
Lord, and the tenants' representatives at the end of June. Lytton
was evidently ruffled by the unaccustomed intransigence with which
he was confronted. 'The Civil Lord replied that agreement appealed
to him, but threats did not. No rent meant no home.'[203] Proceedings
were begun against a number of tenants shortly afterwards. The
case was heard three weeks later. On 29 July 1,580 men struck work
to attend Dunfermline Sheriff Court. The procession was headed by
the Dockyard Band; flags and other emblems of solidarity were
displayed, but there was no carnival atmosphere. A vigilant official
espied the apparently furtive presence of Sylvia Pankhurst in court
who, like everyone else, behaved with the utmost decorum.[204]

The Admiralty, in taking a firm line, was not acting in isolation.
No branch of government, and least of all a service department,
could fail to have been aware of the tense political climate after the
Armistice. It was not for nothing that king and country were so
preoccupied with the Housing Question, for upon its resolution had
come to depend all the hopes for the post-war stability that was so
firmly embedded in the concept of Reconstruction.[205] Indeed, it was
a commonplace of the period that nothing provided a more congenial
milieu for the activities of those ubiquitous agitators than the crisis
in housing.

That the mounting unrest amongst government tenants might,
unless speedily checked, come to constitute a most serious challenge
to authority could not, then, be dismissed. The force of example, so

[202] Minute of D.D.R., 26 June 1919 (PRO Adm. 116/2162); *Forward*, 9 Aug.
1919.
[203] 'Notes of a Meeting which the Civil Lord had with the Rosyth Ratepayers'
Association', 30 June 1919 (PRO Adm. 116/2162).
[204] Telegram from Hewitson to Admiralty, 29 July 1919, (PRO Adm. 116/2162).
[205] On His Majesty's concern, see Lord Stamfordham to Addison, 11 June 1919
(Addison Papers, Box 41); on the symbolic importance of the housing programme,
Philip Abrams, 'The failure of Social Reform, 1918-1920', *Past and Present* No. 24
(1963), p. 43. The ideological element in the provision and design of this programme
is re-examined in Mark Swenarton, *Homes Fit for Heroes: The Politics and Architecture of Early State Housing in Britain* (1981).

strikingly demonstrated during the war-time rents agitation, had still to be reckoned with. The dramatic entrée of Glaswegian house-wives in 1915 had not been forgotten and was invariably cited with approbation during subsequent campaigns. On the eve of the Wool-wich rent strike the chairman of the Stoke Heath Tenants' Associa-tion had visited the Arsenal as well as the substantial colony of hutments at Walthamstow where, he was given to understand, the occupants also intended taking action.[206] Although systematic linkage between the various centres was denied, the aggrandizing tendencies of the Stoke Heath Association within Coventry suggested that such connections might not be too difficult to forge. But what-ever the precise degree of collaboration, there is no doubt that, from the authorities' point of view, the events at Stoke Heath had pro-duced an adverse reaction amongst tenants elsewhere. In addi-tion to the Woolwich and Dudley rent strikes, resistance was en-countered at Avonmouth Garden Suburb, Bristol while Lanarkshire tenants proved troublesome as ever.[207] In March 1920, however, the Ministry of Munitions finally secured judgement in the High Court and thereby broke the well-organized rent strike that had begun almost a year earlier amongst the occupants of the 456 hutments at Holbrook Lane, Coventry.[208] But by that time the delay had somewhat blunted the hoped-for salutary effect. Mean-while tenants, buoyed up by previous success, prepared for the bigger struggle that lay ahead. The admirable organization formed at Stoke Heath, said one of them, 'was only an expression of coming events'.[209]

A similar sentiment voiced at Rosyth was, in view of the spokes-man, altogether more ominous. Amongst the numerous veterans, male and female, who addressed the tenants during the course of the rent strike, was a strong contingent from the Glasgow Labour Party Housing Association, amongst whom Mr Patrick Dollan was as ever conspicious. The struggle, Dollan observed in the course of one of several speeches, was a matter of the utmost importance for working-class tenants everywhere in Scotland, a dress rehearsal for

[206] *Midland Daily Telegraph*, 18 Feb. 1919.

[207] James F. Hope to Hon. Waldorf Astor M. P. (draft), 9 May 1919 (PRO HLG. 46/106); G. H. Duckworth to Sir Lionel Earle, 'Memorandum on Threatened Rent Strikes—Mid-Lanarkshire', 9 Aug. 1920 (PRO Mun. 5/330); Directorate of Intel-ligence, A Survey of Revolutionary Movements in Great Britain in the Year 1920 (1921), p. 40 (PRO Cab. 24/118 CP 2455).

[208] *Coventry Herald*, 11 Apr. 1919; *HMM*, V, 5, p. 54; Attorney-General v Lund & Others, *The Times*, 31 Mar. 1920.

[209] *Coventry Herald*, 17 Jan. 1919.

the national rent strike that was then under consideration.[210] The authorities did not doubt it.

But there were varying shades of red. 'Shop Steward', writing in *The Worker*, advised tenants to extend the struggle. 'The point at which to organise their forces is the point of production', he remarked, 'let them link up with the workers' committee movement there, and fight this question as workers.... You can refuse to pay your rent if you like, but the law will empower your landlord to arrest your wages, and it will be your industrial might and solidarity that will count then.' Although apparently unaware of the complexities involved in the legal process—servants of the Crown were exempt from arrestment—the industrial implications of the struggle were most significant.[211] Trade union officialdom, alarmed by the decision to strike work and attend court in support of the fourteen tenants against whom proceedings had been taken, were apprehensive lest spill-over from the rents agitation react unfavourably upon an important wage claim about to be submitted to the rank-and-file for confirmation. The District Secretary of the Engineering and Shipbuilding Federation expressed his concern thus:

There is an element behind the movement who were the leading lights in the Clyde Workers Committee who are determined to make this movement if possible an industrial one, and speakers who have been down urging this are Dollam [*sic*] of Glasgow, Guy Aldred of Communist Fame and McManors [*sic*] S.L.P., and my object in writing you is to get in touch with the Admiralty and try to stop the evictions. I would respectfully suggest an Arbiter be sent here to hear the case and report, because if something is not done to stop the extremists I and my Committee are afraid the Ballot Vote and its issue on the 95/- rate will be a fiasco so far as this base is concerned, because we are of opinion if the powers behind the strike are successful to any extent in making this an industrial question, the power of Trade Unions here will be irrevocably lost.[212]

These fears were heightened by the menacing presence of John Maclean who, it was observed, had addressed the tenants in 'a highly revolutionary tone'.[213]

[210]   *Rosyth & Forth Mail*, 24 July 1919.
[211]   On attendant difficulties of arrestment, see (PRO Adm. 1/8594/147, and for an outline of the process, see my article, 'Wage Arrestment in Victorian Scotland', *Scottish Historical Review*, LV (1981). Quotation from *The Worker*, 24 May 1919.
[212]   J. Arlned Wood to F. Smith Esq (Copy), 25 July 1919 (PRO Adm. 116/2162).
[213]   Telegram from Dockyard, Rosyth, to Admiralty, 12 Aug. 1919 (PRO Adm. 116/2162).

Those in nominal control of proceedings considered any direct intervention from the Admiralty inadvisable. The dispatch of distinguished counsel to represent the Scottish National Housing Company could but magnify the importance of the case and might tend to further incitement. A 'low profile' was both prudent and sufficient.[214] It proved sound advice and a verdict was secured without difficulty. The ejectment order was suspended for one month in the hope that some agreement might then have been reached.[215] An arrangement was subsequently concluded for the repayment of the outstanding arrears.[216]

The rent strike collapsed. Impecunious workers began to drift away, sometimes without first having cleared their debts, an absentminded practice which, it was suggested, the arrestment of wages would do much to deter. Others removed as and when alternative accommodation became available.[217] The Rosyth Ratepayers' Association was not, however, dissolved. The agitation continued.[218]

H. M. Dockyard, Rosyth and its attendant establishment was a permanent installation, the future of which was affected but not jeopardized—at least not immediately—by the economies that accompanied the re-establishment of the armed forces upon a peacetime footing. The Admiralty willy-nilly would have to come to more satisfactory terms with its disaffected tenants. The position of the Ministry of Munitions, then in process of demobilization, was quite different. Here tenant unrest represented a major impediment to the smooth dismantling of a costly and redundant war machine.

Coventry Corporation, following the first Stoke Heath rent strike, had reneged upon a post-war ownership scheme which previously it had been willing to undertake.[219] The unresolved rent problem on these munitions estates had a similar deterrent effect upon other would be municipal purchasers.[220] Neither the Office of Works nor

---

[214] Thomas Carmichael, Admiralty Solicitor, to Treasury Solicitor, 6 Aug. 1919 (PRO Adm. 116/2162).   [215] *Rosyth & Forth Mail*, 7 Aug. 1919.

[216] Telegram from Civil Engineer-in-Chief to Navy Works, London, 4 Oct. 1919 (PRO Adm. 116/2162).

[217] David W. Deas, Secretary Scottish National Housing Company, to Secretary, HM Dockyard, Rosyth, 27 Dec. 1919 (PRO Adm. 1/8594/147); *Rosyth & Forth Mail*, 8 Dec. 1920.

[218] H. Witchener, Secretary of Rosyth Ratepayers' Association, to Walter Long, 25 Feb 1920 (PRO Adm. 116/2162).

[219] 'Memorandum on the Present Position of Various Housing Schemes in which the Ministry is Interested', 2 June 1917 (PRO Mun. 5/96).

[220] 'Housing Department, Memorandum of Meeting held on 9 Aug. at Ministry of Munitions' (PRO HLG. 46/106).

the Ministry of Health wished to assume responsibility for their administration. Attempts to liquidate this substantial liability through sale by auction also proved unavailing. No purchaser could be found, and the Treasury refused to give them away.[221] The difficulty in this respect was aggravated by the post-war extension of rent control in consequence of which it proved impossible to effect a sale without having first obtained vacant possession. The retention of empty dwellings for this purpose provoked severe criticism from the local authorities, fostered unrest amongst the working classes and encouraged resort to the growing practice, especially among ex-service men, of taking forcible possession of unlet premises.[222]

Although demolition was considered desirable on almost every conceivable ground—administration, cost, design, structure—the short-life properties, which comprised the bulk of the accom-modation built by the Ministry of Munitions (none of it in compliance with local bye laws) had to be retained. On political grounds, if no other, it was impossible to raze the dwellings and displace the occupants in the absence of alternative accommodation.[223] Until the housing shortage was overcome not only was the state compelled to remain in business as one of the largest of landlords but to continue the building of such hutments in order to relieve the most pressing districts. The Office of Works, to whom responsibility had, by Cabinet fiat, been transferred in July 1920 was thus burdened with the administration of some thirty-six estates. These consisted of approximately 9,880 houses representing an increase of 34 per cent within two years of the assumption of department responsibility. 'I am quite convinced', wrote a remarkably prescient official in 1923, 'that there is no chance of the Government getting rid of these Housing Estates for twenty years at least.'[224] In 1946 disposal of the remaining estate was still pending.[225]

The predicament had been foreseen. The desire to avert such an

[221]   On attendant difficulties of disposed, see memoranda (PRO Works 6/394/1).
[222]   See Memoranda on 'Ministry of Munitions Housing Schemes: Sales by Auction', 28 and 30 Aug. 1920 (PRO Works 6/394/1).
[223]   'Ministry of Munitions Schemes Administered by HM Office of Works', 28 Jan 1922 (PRO Works 6/394/1).
[224]   'Establishment, Lands and Accommodation Directorate, Estate Management Section', Memorandum initialled A.D., 24 Nov. 1922. Quotation from J.E. to J.C. Carr, 1 Jan. 1923 (PRO Works 22/41).
[225]   Note by A. S. Cunliffe, 29 May 1947 (PRO Works 6/394/1).

outcome was not the least of the factors influencing official response to tenant unrest. Until the onset of depression, the punitive measures taken against tenants at Woolwich, where the organizer of the Hutments Tenants' Protection League was subsequently evicted, and at Holbrook Lane, Coventry, seemed to have some effect. But from the summer of 1920 onwards the position began to deteriorate. 'Arrears have increased, protests and claims for reduction of rentals have been frequent and it has been found necessary to take Court action in many cases.' In 1922 the outlook seemed grim: further cases for possession or arrears were anticipated 'in large numbers'.[226] Ministers, placed in the invidious position of having to sanction these proceedings, found the whole business a source of acute embarrassment.[227] The wooden huts, in particular, were a financial disaster and a political liability. With an estimated life of from only ten to fifteen years, those built in 1915/16 were already showing distinct signs of wear and tear by the end of the war. The Earl of Crawford and Balcarres, First Commissioner of Works, despaired. In a memorandum, submitted to the Cabinet in the summer of 1921, he drew attention to the scandal in the making:

As residential amenity decreases, the political burden will grow. We are already subjected to continuous and concerted pressure to reduce rents. Trifling increases arouse indignation. A group of huts at Woolwich was seized twelve months ago by 100 squatters who live in utter squalor and pay no rent. One may foresee a growth in this kind of difficulty and it is difficult to devise remedies against a well-organised rent strike.[228]

The position at Woolwich remained tense throughout the early twenties. Administration required the skills of the diplomatist and such qualities were rare. However, it was not the only problem estate. The Admiralty, it seemed, had fared somewhat better in its relation with Rosyth tenants. The firm line taken appeared to have been an unqualified success. Yet the rent strike had not been an unmitigated failure and the fear of similar outbursts was sufficient in the next two years to limit the increases which might otherwise have

[226] 'Establishment: Lands & Accommodation Directorate, Estate Management Section', Memorandum initialled A.D., 24 Nov. 1922 (PRO Works 22/41).

[227] Earl of Crawford & Balcarres, First Commissioner of Works, to Sir Howard Frank, Director of Lands, War Office, 10 June 1921 (PRO Works, 6/394/1); Cabinet Minute (25), 5, 7 Apr. 1924 (PRO Cab. 23/47).

[228] 'Ministry of Munitions Cottages now Administered by HM Office of Works', Memorandum by First Commissioner of Works, June 1921 (PRO Works 6/394/1).

been imposed.[229] In addition to the political outcry, the desire to avert organized resistance was uppermost in naval minds and a restraining influence in regaining possession of the homes occupied by those who had been made redundant as part of the post-war economies.[230]

These concessions, however, raised a more fundamental problem. 'The principle at stake in Rosyth is no mere local one', wrote Patrick Dollan, during the course of the rent strike, 'for if the dockyard men win they will strike a blow for cheap housing all over the country. The houses at Rosyth are the kind of houses the Government intends to build all over the land, and the rents established in the Fife village will be the basis of the standard for fixing rents for new houses in Scotland.' The conclusion was obvious: 'It rests with all of us then to give the tenants every support, knowing that what is won for Rosyth is won for the whole country. The last rent strike in Govan won a reform for the entire working class in Britain, and the Rosyth conflict may have a similar result.'[231] Dollan was not the sole commentator to have divined the meaning of the rents agitation. The growth of such radicalism, it was recognized, foreshadowed the permanent subsidizing of working-class housing and thus the demise of private enterprise. The Stoke Heath rent strike was viewed as a harbinger of things to come:

Whenever tenants imagine they have a grievance, full well knowing the pliability of councillors, and the vote-catching tactics which many of them are ever ready to adopt, the Coventry method will be followed. The Utopianism which pervades the imagination of housing idealists for ideal cottages to be let at rentals which are quite inadequate to defray interest on the capital outlay is, we fear, likely to be shattered after the cottages are in occupation. Tenants leagues will be common and no rent strikes will be engineered, so that reduction of rents can be enforced and the burden transferred to other rate-payers...[232]

Birmingham property-owners, who were badly shaken by the 'ugly and disturbing' events at Stoke Heath, subsequently employed such arguments against the post-war housing programme. In a pamphlet, sub-titled 'REMEMBER COVENTRY, MAY 12, 1917', and

[229] Minute of L. R. Saville, Civil Engineer-in-Chief, 5 Apr. 1921 (PRO Adm. 116/2161).

[230] V. W. Baddeley to Admiral Superintendent, Rosyth, 13 Mar. 1922 (PRO Adm. 116/2160).

[231] *The Worker*, 31 May 1919.

[232] *Municipal Engineering & Sanitary Record*, 6 Feb. 1919.

printed in bold red type, they warned: 'No person who takes an intelligent interest in local government will fail to appreciate the deep and sinister significance of this fact, and the municipality which shapes its policy without reference to all that is involved in the Coventry strike is heading for disaster.'[233] A similar apprehension was shared by the authorities who were acutely conscious of the fact that, hitherto in the matter of rents, tenants had got the better of them. As one official observed:

Purely financial considerations are not in question ... The working man now pays without a murmur, £50 for a piano and £50 for a fur coat for his wife, for which in pre-war times, he would have paid £25 and £20. And these payments are not exceptional. The consideration of rentals is not, therefore, connected in any way with inability to pay, and is purely affected by political considerations ... such as the fixation of rents under the Restriction of Rents & Mortgage Act and the fears of labour trouble if the workman chooses to consider the payment of an economic rent as a suitable occasion for a strike.[234]

What was so disheartening was that, so far from pacifying the working-class tenant, concessions seemed merely to generate fresh demands which invertebrate politicians seemed unwilling to resist. Shortly after the Armistice, for example, it was decided that, in the exceptional conditions which then obtained, the 30 per cent subsidy on housing built by the Ministry of Munitions should be continued 'as an insurance payment'. Duckworth was disgusted, particularly by Addison, who, he claimed, 'was afraid of facing the question of rentals'.[235]

The refusal to face up to this question threatened the re-establishment of housing upon an economic footing, hitherto the dominant concern within the Ministry.[236] The urgency of the question was underlined by the launching of the Government's post-war housing programme in view of which, the official historians noted, administration of the munitions estates 'assumed a new importance'.[237] The full significance of the rents agitation will be better understood

[233] Birmingham & District Property Owners' Association, *The Housing Question, Remember Coventry, May 12, 1917* (Birmingham, c. 1920), pp. 10-11.

[234] Memorandum from G. H. Duckworth to A.F.S., 22 Aug. 1919 (PRO Mun. 5/96).

[235] *HMM*, V, 5, p. 14. Quotation from G. H. Duckworth to G. I. H. Lloyd, 14 Jan. 1921 (PRO Mun. 5/330).

[236] 'Draft Memorandum on the Rents of Permanent Houses', Sept. 1918 (?), (PRO Mun. 5/96).

[237] *HMM*, V, 5, p. 2.

in conjuction with a fresh appraisal of the character of state-subsidized housing in Britain.

V

The provision of subsidized working-class housing was not in principle a matter of party political rivalry. The inevitability of some degree of state assistance had been accepted by both Conservative and Labour parties before the war. B. S. Rowntree, who rather favoured a minimum wage, revised his opinion after joining the second Reconstruction Committee. The report of the Royal Commission on Housing in Scotland, published in September 1917, with its unequivocal support of extensive state intervention, reinforced the kind of progressive opinion which he represented. Conservative enthusiasm, it is true, did not survive the war intact, but it was more than offset by the remarkable surge of labourist *étatisme*.[238] Theoretical hostilities to subsidies were jettisoned *tout court*; the labour movement called for 1,000,000 houses to be let at pre-war rents. The figure was immaterial. Henceforth, housing need was to be calculated not merely in accord with the war-related deficit but also in terms consistent with current standards of public health and inclusive of replacement need. Whatever its source and whatever the magnitude, the shortage would have to be made good.[239] No other political party thought in such heroic terms. The scope and purpose of state intervention remained a matter of the deepest contention.

Dr Addison, though he predicted serious disorder, failed during the war to convince his most important Cabinet colleagues of the need for all but the most minimal post-war housing programme.[240] Moreover no adequate preparations were made, even for that. The Local Government Board, dominated by an unimaginative, geriatric establishment, and presided over by the reactionary incompetent Hayes Fisher, was consistently obstructive, the Treasury

[238] On rank-and-file apathy towards housing subsidies within the Conservative Party, see Keith Feiling, *Life of Neville Chamberlain* (1947), p. 108; Iain Macleod, *Neville Chamberlain* (1961), pp. 90-2.

[239] For an excellent summation of Labour Party thought in this connection, see 'Statement Submitted by Mr Sidney Webb on behalf of the War Emergency Workers' National Committee (WNC Papers).

[240] See 'Housing: Notes on Ministerial Conference', 27 Nov. 1917 (Addison Papers, Box 72).

cautious.[241] Addison was humiliated. 'I had the bitterest experience which any man could have', he later wrote of his tenure as Minister of Reconstruction. 'For my part I would rather sweep a crossing than repeat such experience'.[242] This supremely important and well-documented discord, however, involved differences of degree.

From its inception the housing programme was viewed as a finite emergency measure to make good the shortage caused by the cessation of building during the war. There never was any intention to enter into an open-ended commitment to provide according to need, let alone to supersede private enterprise.[243] Until the introduction of Wheatley's Housing (Financial) Provisions Act, 1924, which firmly hitched the local authorities to a continuing fifteen-year programme of subsidized construction, state assistance was still framed in terms of the return to 'normalcy'. Dr Addison was no exception. The Housing Act, 1919, which certainly represented a major advance on the scope of previous proposals, was nevertheless thought of as a once-and-for-all intervention.[244]

Rent control in this context was little more than an awkward appendage. Addison regarded it as a matter of administration, a 'difficult and thankless task' and a distraction with which he did not care to be burdened.[245] The architect of state-subsidized housing, following the advice of the Reconstruction Committee on the Rent Acts, envisaged an orderly withdrawal at the end of a seven-year transitional period during which rents would be gradually decontrolled. In order to smoothe the planned evacuation, rents of state-assisted schemes were to be fixed so as to give an economic return on a capital outlay of two-thirds of the actual cost at which

[241] See attached memorandum, Addison to Lloyd George, 8 July 1919 (Addison Papers, Box 12); Addison's Diary Notes, 8 Feb. 1919 (Addison Papers, Box 99); also 'Priority of Housing Among After War Problems', Draft Memorandum by R. L. Reiss, n.d. (PRO Reco. 1/584).

[242] Addison to Lloyd George, 3 Mar. 1920 (Addison Papers, Box 8).

[243] See, for example, Reconstruction Committee, Memorandum [Printed] on Housing in England & Wales, May 1917; 'Notes on Our Proposals concerning Housing in England and Wales', by B. S. Rowntree, 3 Aug. 1917; 'Housing Policy', Memorandum by Addison, 10 Dec. 1917 (Addison Papers, Box 72); *Housing in England & Wales: Memorandum by the Advisory Panel on the Emergency Problem* (PP 1918, XXVI), p. 3.

[244] Cf. John Bradbury, Permanent Secretary to the Treasury, to Secretary of Local Government Board, 24 Apr. 1919 (PRO HLG. 49/1).

[245] 'Rents and Liabilities of Landlords and Tenants', Memorandum by the President of the Local Government Board, 19 Feb. 1919 (PRO Cab. 24/76 GT 6836). Quotation from Addison to Marquis of Salisbury, 15 Apr. 1920 (Addison Papers, Box 38).

the houses were built, on the assumption that the period of readjustment would be over by 1927 by which time prices would be two-thirds of the present level. This entailed a series of heavy rent increases: 'we cannot contemplate the possibility of dispensing with private enterprise in the future'. It was not a strategy calculated to arouse widespread enthusiasm. Assailed by the left as the worst kind of rack-renting landlord, the housing programme would be condemned by the right as a profligate impediment to the restoration of market forces and sanity. 'It may be hoped,' wrote A. V. Symonds, the philosophical Under Secretary at the Local Government Board, 'that these opposite contentions may be mutually destructive.'[246] Chamberlain's introduction of the infamous 'filtering-up' concept, a restatement of a nineteenth century fiction, endorsed the determination to preserve the limited nature of the state's commitment.

The success of this flawed conception had already been jeopardized by the famous 'penny-rate' formula which placed a premium upon municipal extravagance. It had always been feared that local authorities, in the absence of any incentive towards economy, would come to regard house building as the activity which should be permanently subsidized by the state. At the time, however, Ministers, fearing for the very stability of the state, were inclined to be generous and caution was thrown to the winds.[247] But this was not the sole setback. Even before the introduction of the Housing Bill in March 1919 it was decided to extend rent control.

The Committee, appointed by Addison in April 1918 to examine the Rent Acts in relation to the post-war housing programme, was deeply conscious of the responsibility it had incurred. 'The problem upon which our advice is sought is an exceedingly difficult one', it reported at the end of the year. 'The policy adopted may determine whether housing is to continue on an economic basis, or whether it is to be permanently subsidised; and thus, in effect, to become a State enterprise.'[248] The difficulty was not, of course, one of intent.

---

[246] The principles embodied in this strategy are stated with crystalline clarity in Ministry of Health, *General Housing Memorandum No. 8: Financial Assistance to Local Authorities* 1919, paras. 18-22; also see *Ministry of Reconstruction, Report of the Committee on the Increase of Rent & Mortgage Interest (War Restrictions) Acts* (PP 1919, XII), paras. 30-3. Quotation from 'Rents', Memorandum by A.V.S., 31 Mar. 1919 (Addison Papers, Box 11; also in PRO HLG. 49/1).

[247] Paul Barton Johnson, *Land Fit for Heroes* (Chicago, 1968), pp. 345-7; also see Laurence F. Orbach, *Homes for Heroes, A Study of the Evolution of British Public Housing, 1915-1921* (1977).

[248] *Ministry of Reconstruction, Report on Rent & Mortgage Interest etc. Acts*, para 24.

Nobody, discounting Sidney Webb and the Labour Party, desired such enterprise. The contemporary view can be summarized thus. Controls could not be raised while the shortage persisted; but the housing shortage persisted because controls were not raised. The strategy, outlined above, seemed to offer a resolution of the crisis. The danger was that, in the interval, Ministers might be forced off course and compelled to sacrifice private enterprise in order to placate a rising popular clamour.

The Committee heard some pretty blood-curdling evidence. Glasgow property owners braced themselves for a final show-down. The mistake of 1915 was held to have consisted in the imposition of small but irritatingly frequent rent increases; the error would not be repeated. Even before the end of hostilities Glasgow Landlords' Association pressed for a massive 40 per cent increase. Tenants were no less bellicose. If the Government wanted trouble, said Dollan, all it need do was to sanction an increase of this magnitude.[249] 'It was friction which caused the passing of the Act originally', said M'Bride. 'Greater friction will be caused if it is allowed to expire.' 'People', he declared, 'must be housed whether they can pay or not, and the state must bear the deficit. The loss must be written off by the State as a health investment'.[250] He added, ominously: 'Our Association believes that there should be no consideration or provision made for the resumption of House-Building or House-Owning by private enterprise'.[251] The Clyde Rent War had begun.

The Report of the Reconstruction Committee was submitted to the Minister on 31 December 1918, and reached the Home Affairs Committee two months later. Its principle recommendation, that control be continued for a further two and a half years, was dismissed by the Attoney-General, Sir Gordon Hewart, as 'an alarming pro-position'. The Home Secretary was no less disturbed. 'Mr Short considered that hardships were being felt more by the landlord than the tenant'. Addison, still as ever trying to disclaim departmental responsibility—'The question does not, as a matter of fact, come within the province of the Local Government Board'—thought it a capital suggestion, one which 'in the case of rentals below £35 per

[249] Committee on Increase of Rent Act: MS Minutes of 5th Meeting, 17 Sept. 1918 (Doc. 48) (PRO Reco. 1/645); *Herald*, 12 Jan. 1918.
[250] Committee on Increase of Rent Act: MS Minutes of 6th Meeting, 18 Sept. 1918 (Doc. 49) (PRO Reco. 1/645).
[251] 'Memorandum from Glasgow Labour Party Housing Association', by Andrew M'Bride, July 1918 (Doc. 41) (PRO Reco. 1/645).

annum (i.e. working class) would help to keep things quieter with the particular class of inhabitant.' The chairman, H. A. L. Fisher, favoured a one year continuation. Anything else, he told the House when introducing the new measure, 'would be dangerous and against public policy'.[252] It was a bizarre intervention. No one seriously expected the housing shortage to be made good within twelve months but it fulfilled a psychological need. It kept alive the belief that decontrol was still 'practical' politics and not the mere empty rhetoric and stale slogan it was destined to become. But it did nothing to allay unrest.

The battle lines, though drawn sharpest on Clydeside, stretched southwards well beyond the Tweed. The casualties were considerable. The actual number of evictions sanctioned by the courts, it is true, were negligible; but who can compute the anxiety and suffering caused by the upwards of 30,000 applications for possession made annually in the first few years of the peace.[253] The sheer desperation of working-class tenants is evident from the numerous accounts of the seizure and occupation of vacant premises that took place up and down the country. Moss Side Tenants' Defence Association, under the direction of two Manchester Labour councillors, initiated a policy of obtaining forcible possession of such properties in order to house ex-servicemen and their families. East Ham Trades Council, working in conjunction with the People's Protection League and the local branch of the National Union of Ex-Servicemen did likewise. Unemployed ex-servicemen in Woolwich, Swansea, Peckham, Brighton, and Barrow were reported as having made similar 'captures'.[254] It was, said one county court judge, 'nothing more or less than anarchy'.[255]

The more responsible elements within the judiciary, however, could not be indifferent to the plight of the poor people appearing before them. In conditions of acute housing scarcity, such as obtained in post-war Britain, controls, however tightly drawn, would inevitably be breached sooner or later; and without doubt the temptation so to do was facilitated by the loosely-drawn provisions affecting security of tenure embodied in the Rent Act passed in

[252] Home Affairs Committee 20 (1), 21 Feb. 1919, (PRO Cab. 26/1); *HC Deb*. 5s. cxiii (1919), 801.
[253] See *HC Deb*. 5s. clxxii (1924), 621, 951.
[254] *Manchester Evening News*, 7 June 1920; *The Times* 25 Oct. and 9 Dec. 1920; *Woolwich Herald*, 3 Dec. 1920; *Barrow Guardian*, 18 Nov. 1922.
[255] *The Times* 10 Mar. 1922.

April, 1919.[256] The resultant pressure upon the judiciary was intolerable. Fresh legislation had to be enacted before the year was out.

The severity of the crisis formed the subject of an astonishing correspondence between a Minister of the Crown and one of the several metropolitan county court judges who had been consulted in framing the technical provisions of the additional legislation. In December 1919 His Honour wrote:

My object in writing now is to urge the *extreme expediency* in the public interest of the Bill being passed into law before *Christmas*. For some months past I and other judges to my knowledge, have been dealing with pitiful problems that are presented to us daily, viz: cases where the landlord's right to evict is clear, but the tenant's inability to find other accommodation is equally clear, by various methods (such as adjourning the summons for 1, 2 or 3 months, or making orders for possession suspended for similar periods) which in my opinion are of very doubtful validity in law. So far, in my experience, the power of the Judge to make such orders has not been questioned, but this may happen any day, and if it is seriously questioned I much doubt whether it can be maintained.... In the hope of the situation being relieved by the passing of the Bill aforesaid, I and other Judges have made many orders suspended to a date in January. I shudder to think what will happen if that date comes before the Bill has been passed. I and other Judges are at present straining our powers to breaking point (and beyond it I fear!) to avoid the terrible alternative, viz: evicting families by dozens into the streets or the workhouse. I need not dwell upon the serious addition to the present state of 'unrest' that such happenings would produce.[257]

Dr Addison, the recipient, was more than aware of the gravity of the situation. In the previous month he had drawn the Cabinet's attention to the dangers arising from the inadequacies of the Rent Acts. Reform was urgent. 'The trouble is a deep and widespread one', he warned. 'The matter brooks no delay as evidence is accumulating of social unrest and threatened disturbance on these evictions or threatened evictions.'[258] The Lord Chancellor concurred: 'unless steps were taken disorder might break out at any moment'. Whatever the response of the hard-faced men—and it was thought

---

[256] *Report of the Committee on the Increase of Rent & Mortgage Interest (War Restrictions) Acts* (PP 1920, XVIII), para. 10.

[257] James Scully to Addison, 14 Dec. 1919 (Addison Papers, Box. 38).

[258] 'Trouble arising from eviction or threatened eviction of tenants of small dwellings', Memorandum by the Minister of Health, 24 Nov. 1919 (PRO Cab. 24/93 CP 184).

that the proposed measure would be 'severely criticised' in the House of Commons—there was no option but to legislate. 'The only justification', said Sir Claud Schuster, private secretary in the Lord Chancellor's office, 'was the necessity of maintaining public order'.[259] This was the dominant but not the sole factor underlying the successive extensions of rent control during this period.

The desperate shortage of accommodation with which the nation was confronted at the end of the war was not an exclusively working-class problem; the cessation of building also adversely affected the middle classes. Those with sufficient capital who formerly might have purchased properties within the protected limits, in view of the difficulties attendant upon obtaining vacant possession, began to compete for more expensive accommodation. Scarcity drove prices up; middle-class tenants and leaseholders, even before the end of hostilities, were being told 'to purchase or quit'.[260] 'The profiteering that has taken place in connection with this class of property,' wrote Dan Rider, 'has been beyond belief.'[261] This widespread, though not universal, problem was particularly acute in the London suburbs.[262] In Scotland the difficulty was largely confined to the Glasgow region. A sample analysis of the valuation roll of houses rented at £30 to £40 (ie above the limits of protection) disclosed an average rent increase of 9 per cent from 1915 to 1918; in the following twelve months, however, there was an increase of 10 to 15 per cent over the previous year.[263]

The outcry was considerable. White-collar workers called for a quinquennial extension of the Rent Acts.[264] Shopkeepers and other small businessmen, hit hard by the phenomenal upward spiral in post-war property values, were particularly active.[265] The Glasgow

[259] Home Affairs Committee 46 (2), 25 Nov. 1919 (PRO Cab. 26/2).

[260] Walter T. Jerrad to W. G. Wallace, 6 May 1918 (PRO Reco. 1/644); 'Instances of House-Grabbing of which the War Rents League have full particulars' (WNC Papers).

[261] Committee on the Increase of Rent Act: 'Memorandum on Suggestions' etc. by Dan Rider (Doc. 58) (PRO Reco. 1/646), see too G. D. H. and Margaret Cole, *Rents, Rings and Houses* (1923), pp. 19-23.

[262] 'Alleged victimization of tenants of houses above the rental limits fixed by the Increase of Rent etc. Act, 1915', Memorandum by the President of the Local Government Board, 28 Feb. 1919 (PRO Cab. 24/76 GT 6902); also Cab. 24/75 GT 6817.

[263] Home Affairs Committee 20 (1), 28 Feb. 1919 (PRO Cab. 26/1).

[264] A. Lynes, Secretary of the Postal & Telegraph Clerks Association, to J. S. Middleton, 14 Dec. 1918 (WNC Papers).

[265] On problems affecting business premises, see evidence of Patrick Howling and A. C. Melluish of the Town Tenants' League, Departmental Committee on Operation of the Rent Acts: MS Minutes of Evidence, 18 Mar. 1920 (PRO HLG. 41/9). There is a wealth of relevant material submitted in evidence to the *Select Committee on Business Premises* (PP 1920, VI).

Labour Party was quick to recognize its political importance; the flexibly astute M'Bride sought to enlist the support of his fellow shopkeepers behind the working-class campaign for fixity of tenure.[266] Yet old habits died hard. One embittered Glaswegian bourgeois, though sorely in need of protection, felt that, in consequence of rent control, relative class positions had been so transformed that he no longer felt middle class: 'I don't think that the term should be applied to us now as the working man is now the top dog, and gets off scott free.'[267] Others pocketed their pride, and Ministers felt the pressure. Indeed, pundits were convinced that the general inflation was driving the disaffected middle classes into the arms of the Labour Party.[268] The Prime Minister was told that, as an electoral force, 'the *greatest asset of the Labour Party* ... has been the sympathy which it has received from the middle classes'. The report continued: 'This result is more economic than political.... The middle classes see no salvation except by supporting those who have already gained concessions.'[269] The relative radicalization of the middle classes in this period, a complex phenomenon which has yet to find its historian, without doubt owed something to the housing crisis.[270] Its most dramatic manifestation was provided by the Mitcham by-election of 1923 when A. G. Boscawen, the Minister of Health, whose Rent Bill proposed the withdrawal of higher rented houses from the protection enjoyed since April 1919, lost his seat in a normally safe constituency, as indeed did two other junior Ministers who had the misfortune of contesting equally safe Tory seats at the same time.[271] The Home Counties no less than the Gorbals or the East End had a vested interest in the retention of rent controls.[272]

[266] Departmental Committee on Operation of the Rent Acts: MS Minutes of Evidence, 15 Mar. 1920, pp. 1-6 (PRO HLG. 41/8); and see too *Forward*, 28 Feb. 1920. Glaswegian trade unionists, however, wished to see the shopkeepers stew in their own juice: Minutes of Glasgow Trades Council, 10 Feb. 1920.

[267] Alexander Livingstone to Sir Robert Horne MP, 6 Feb. 1919 (Addison Papers, Box. 8).

[268] 'Report on Revolutionary Organisations in the United Kingdom, No. 17', 18 Dec. 1919 (PRO Cab. 24/95 CP 319). See too Holford Knight, 'The Black-Coated Poor', *Contemporary Review* CXVII (1920), pp. 689-95.

[269] Frederick Guest to Lloyd George, 29 Jan. 1920 (Addison Papers, Box 123).

[270] Cf. remarks of Dan Rider, Onslow Committee on the Rent Restrictions Acts: MS Minutes of Evidence, pp. 160-1 (PRO HLG. 41/23).

[271] C. L. Mowat, *Britain between the Wars* (1955), p. 165.

[272] On disproportionate concentration of controlled middle class housing in the greater London region, see Memorandum by A. V. Symonds, 12 Feb. 1923, Rent & Mortgage Interest Restrictions Bill Papers, 1923 (PRO HLG. 29/128).

The upshot of the conjoint pressure of middle and working classes was that, by 1924, legislation affecting rents had been enacted on at least five occasions, and that so far from having been removed, restrictions were more extensive than ever. The limits of rental were doubled in 1919 and trebled the following year with the result that there was something like half a million more houses under control in 1920 than there had been five years earlier.[273] Nevertheless, it was confidently assumed that these temporary reversals would not long impede the scheduled return to normality.[274]

The continued uncertainty, however, had an adverse effect upon progress in this sphere. In addition to the discouragement of private enterprise rent control, by depressing the general level of rents, aggravated the problem of obtaining an economic return on new building and thus increased the deficits on state-assisted schemes. The experience of the Ministry of Munitions in this respect seemed all-too likely to be repeated. The working classes, it was to be feared, were unlikely to behave reasonably: 'those tenants who were most insistent in the demand for improved amenities would in many cases be the first to protest against any addition to the rents of their houses'.[275] This observation, recorded during the course of the Rosyth rent strike, found ample supporting evidence. Although enforced without violent opposition, the 40 per cent increase sanctioned under the Rent Act, 1920 (in order to permit owners to maintain their properties in a proper state of repair), was said to have 'inflamed the minds of the working classes'.[276] At Woolwich it precipitated a five-week rent strike organized by the Well Hall Garden City Tenants' Association, and supported by 90 per cent of the residents, that ended in an uneasy truce following independent arbitration.[277] In Scotland it encountered a one-day general strike.[278]

[273] *Report of Inter-Departmental Committee on the Rent Restrictions Acts* (PP 1930-1, XVII), pp. 15-20.
[274] 'Calculation of Housing Subsidy by Estimates', Memorandum initialled C.G., 22 Jan. 1923 (PRO HLG. 49/1/3).
[275] Cf. Duncan Graham, Secretary Lanarkshire Country Miners' Union, to Secretary of War Cabinet, 20 Nov. 1918 (PRO Cab. 24/70 GT 6348). Quotation from '(Housing) Finance Committee, Report No. 5', 16 July 1919 (Addison Papers, Box 11).
[276] 'Directorate of Intelligence, A Survey of Revolutionary Movements in Great Britain in the year 1920 (1921)', p. 22 (PRO Cab. 24/118 CP 2455).
[277] *Woolwich Pioneer*, 24 Sept., 1 Oct., 5 and 19 Nov. 1920; *The Times*, 2 Nov. 1920.
[278] On the abortive rent strike it was meant to initiate, see Iain Maclean, 'The Labour Movement in Clydeside Politics 1914-1924' (University of Oxford Unpublished D. Phil thesis, 1971), Ch. xiii.

The president of the National Federation of Property Owners took steps to enlist the support of the press in order to deflate the mounting agitation for a national rent strike, then considered a very real possibility.[279]

The difficulties of bridging the gap between the rents of pre-war and post-war houses was not, then, a mere matter of administration but a political question of the first magnitude. If, as Sidney Webb asserted, cost was to be discounted and pre-existing custom taken as the only basis for a 'fair rent', the state would have to subsidize house-building in perpetuity.[280] Dr Addison and his colleagues were determined to resist such commitment.

The rules for fixing the rents of houses built by subsidy under the Act of 1919 reflected this concern. In order to obtain approval from the Ministry of Health (and hence indemnity against loss beyond the produce of a penny rate), rents charged by the local authorities had to be fixed in accordance with the principle that in 1927 the amount charged represent an economic return on two-thirds of the actual cost of building. The local authorities were enjoined to 'use every endeavour' to obtain such a return 'as early as possible'.[281] However, the local authorities, uncertain of their ability to obtain the stipulated return, and anxious lest a surcharge be incurred, were unwilling to proceed without further assurances. Addison, desperately keen to get building operations started, was in no position to bargain. The rules were promptly modified; henceforth the local authorities were to charge the best rent that was 'reasonably obtainable'.[282]

In practice the Ministry set out with no other principle than to exact the highest rents possible.[283] Until the slump began to bite with unconscionable severity this determined stand was not without success. 'The firm line adopted by the Ministry, which has resulted in agreement being reached with over 450 authorities', a proud official remarked, 'has undoubtedly had great educational effect on

[279] *National Federation of Property Owners & Ratepayers, Report of 43rd Conference* (1921), p. 15.

[280] Committee on Increase of Rent Acts: MS Minutes of 8th Meeting, 5 Nov. 1918 (Doc. 69), PRO Reco. 1/645).

[281] Ministry of Health, *General Housing Memorandum, No. 8*, Oct. 1919.

[282] Ministry of Health, *General Housing Memorandum No. 18*, Dec. 1919; also see *Local Authorities (Assisted Housing Schemes) Regulations, 1919*, pp. 9-10.

[283] S. C. Alford to A. McKenna, 23 Nov. 1923 (PRO HLG. 49/871); and see too E. S. Strohmerger to O. E. Niemeyer (copy), 26 Nov. 1920 (Neville Chamberlain Papers, University of Birmingham Library, NC 7/11/13/9).

the minds of Local Authorities and has done much to remove the loose ideas in many areas that a new and improved house subsidised by the State would be obtainable at the prevailing rent of a hovel.'[284] There were, of course, back-sliders; and not always from the local authorities.

Although keen to complete the Garden City development, the Lords Commissioners of the Admiralty, chastened by the unrest amongst Rosyth residents, were reluctant to court further trouble through an over-zealous adherence to the spirit of the new housing programme.[285] As one senior officer wrote: 'if endless discontent and unlimited friction are to be avoided, the rents in the Garden City must be fair and reasonable compared with those of similar houses else-where'.[286] Treasury officials, to whom the whole business was anathema,[287] were not on the whole disposed to make concessions to errant departments. 'It is the essence of the policy embodied in the Housing Act', the Admiralty was reminded, 'that the level of rents of workmen's dwellings should be gradually raised nearer to the new economic level.'[288] There could be no permanent departure from this vital principle.

But in face of industrial depression and mounting unemployment it proved increasingly difficult to hold the line. Arrears amongst working-class tenants, council and private, grew at an alarming rate. In Glasgow, arrears in many cases mounted to one fifth of the annual rent. But for relief measures, the position in East London might have been as bad. On the former munitions estates accounts were heavily in the red.[289] Complaints against high council house rents were legion.[290] Local authorities, responding to the outcry,

[284] Memorandum on 'Rents', n.d. but 1921 (PRO HLG. 49/871).

[285] J. W. S. Anderson to Secretary, HM Treasury, 25 Oct. 1919 (PRO Adm. 116/2162); V. W. Baddeley to Secretary, HM Treasury, 4 Nov. 1921 (PRO Adm. 116/2160).

[286] 'Report from Admiral Superintendent to Secretary of the Admiralty', 9 Aug. 1921 (PRO Adm. 116/2160).

[287] 'Rent fixing', the Chancellor was advised, 'is going to be so difficult (like other forms of Government interference) that we ought to get out of it at the earliest opportunity': Note by O. E. Niemeyer, 27 Nov. 1920 (PRO T. 172/1160).

[288] G. L. Barstow to Secretary of the Admiralty, 28 Jan. 1920 (PRO Adm. 116/2162).

[289] *Report of Committee on the Rent Restrictions Acts* (PP 1924-5, XV), p. 14; *Unemployment in East London: Report of a Survey made from Toynbee Hall* (1922), pp. 16-18; *Third Report of Committee on National Expenditure* (PP 1922, IX), p. 84; *First and Second Reports from the Select Committee on Public Accounts* (PP 1924-5, VI), q. 1187.

[290] A. Sayle, *The Houses of the Workers* (1924), p. 163; G. W. Rhodes, 'Housing Developments in Leeds, 1919-1939', (University of Leeds Unpublished MA thesis, 1954), pp. 19-32.

pressed the Ministry of Health to relax its stringent regulations. The subsequent reduction of council rents at St. Giles, Lincoln, precipitated a rent strike on the contiguous estate, administered by the Office of Works, which had stubbornly refused to lower its absurdly high rents. In consequence of this impudent defiance, the reduction known to be necessary was delayed for twelve months in which time officials, having first reasserted their authority, satisfied themselves that the unrest was of a non-political character, and concluded that distress must therefore be genuine. Meanwhile disaffection had spread from the 'baser sort' who had engineered the rent strike to schoolmasters, government officials, and bank clerks. Here indeed was conclusive proof of real hardship and deprivation![291] At the 'Well Hall Republic', to quote *The Times*'s nervous caption, where the £5,000 arrears accumulated from the previous rent strike had yet to be repaid, fresh trouble broke out.[292] It was this incident which occasioned the interesting admission that the housing subsidy, anticipating the likelihood of rent strikes, had been fixed with an allowance for such eventualities, and that local authorities need have no fear of being saddled with untoward deficits as a result.[293] This was, perhaps, one of the most important aspects of the post-war rents agitation. The discontent voiced by the various tenants' associations, too numerous to chronicle, was not, then, without effect. Until Chamberlain and Wheatley tightened incentives to local economy, too much weight was thought to have been attached to such pressure, and the Ministry too ready to make concessions. But for that, rents would have been substantially higher.[294] However, at the time the foregoing observation was recorded, the possibility of an imminent disengagement from the housing sphere was fast receding. Following the advent of the first Labour Government state provision came to be accepted, albeit reluctantly amongst the rank and file of the Conservative party, as an inescapable duty.

[291] On this interesting and well-documented episode, see PRO Works. 6/399/2.

[292] On the continuing unrest at Woolwich, see James Bird, Clerk of the LCC, to Secretary, Office of Works, 12 May 1921; 'Memorandum by director of Lands & Accommodation on Woolwich Estates', 24 May 1922 (PRO Works 22/4/9) and Arthur B. Bryanson, Town Clerk, Metropolitan Borough of Woolwich, to Sir John Baird, First Commissioner of Works (copy), 4 Jan. 1923 and draft reply initialled L.E., 26 Jan. 1923 (PRO HLG. 49/1/3). Quotation from *The Times*, 5 Oct. 1922.

[293] Arthur Michael Samuels MP to Minister of Health, 7 Feb. 1923 and A. G. Boscowen to Samuels, 19 Feb. 1923 (PRO HLG. 49/3).

[294] Minute by S. C. Alford to Mr Strohmerger, 20 May 1926 (PRO HLG. 49/874).

12

Conclusions

The wartime rents agitation, unlike the shop stewards movement, gave rise to no important theoretical innovations; its rewards were material and durable. The war transformed the hitherto uneven struggle between landlord and tenant. The state was compelled to intervene to redress the balance. Combat in which various tenants' associations were pitted in isolation against adversaries assured of the ultimate support of the law became a thing of the past. Henceforth the conflict was nationalized. The persistence of the agitation no doubt owed something to the manner in which the key bridgehead had been established. The capitulation of the Government in 1915, it was rightly noted, 'undoubtedly strengthened the belief in the minds of many of the men that concessions could be obtained by striking which it was not possible to secure in any other way'.[1] Nevertheless, the resurgence of tenant unrest after the introduction of rent control does represent a rather puzzling phenomenon.

Until the latter stages of the war, house rents remained frozen. On the face of it, the outcry which culminated in the introduction of Regulation 2A(2) and its supersession by the Rent Act, 1918, was not at all commensurate with the number of evictions in England and Wales. The data collected by the Central Billeting Board disclosed no serious hardship arising from this cause. The widespread and continued agitation seemed to be without foundation. Contemporaries were perplexed. The question arises: was it the case that working people had nothing to fear but fear itself? Such a proposition, though not implausible, amounts to nothing more than a description of popular apprehension. The new element in the situation resides not in the fear but in the response to insecurity; and this will be better understood if viewed as part of a larger process of radicalization that developed out of the campaign of 1915.

The remarkable success of that campaign came as something of a revelation to both landlord and tenant. The extent to which possession

[1] *HMM*, II, 4, p. 105.

of residential property had become bound up with the preservation of a private-enterprise economy is thrown into relief by the often exaggerated expectations which the very idea of the rent strike aroused. Its shock-value was considerable. 'It was an instrument which would arouse consternation in the Government and the well-to-do', wrote Sylvia Pankhurst, who viewed it as a most dramatic medium for the projection of the pre-war suffragette campaign. Similarly, the abortive national rent strike, organized by the left-wing National Union of Ex-Servicemen in 1920, was not part of the rents agitation as such; rather landlords were considered the most convenient target for the proposed campaign against inflation and profiteering. 'Poplarism' too was distinguished by a willingness to resort to rent strikes both to secure the release of the imprisoned councillors and to persuade Ministers to sanction the extraordinary expenditure on relief incurred in that poverty-stricken area of London.[2]

The hopes of the militants were the fears of the reactionaries. The Russian Revolution cast a dark shadow over the prospects for private property in Britain. In the Soviet Union, it was noted, workers lived rent-free.[3] Alderman Sir George Bean, chairman of Dudley Corporation Housing Committee, was convinced that the time was at hand when British workers would enjoy a similar privilege. The proposed rent strike amongst council tenants, he said, constituted 'the first attempt at Bolshevism in Dudley'. The Woolwich rent strike, declared the *Municipal Engineering and Sanitary Record*, presaged the abolition of rent. The spread of tenants' associations seemed a most menacing development. In Manchester, they were said to be 'hot beds for Bolshevism' composed of 'worthless people, utterly wrong and miserably insignificant'. In Barrow too they were a magnet for subversives of all sorts.[4]

The universal significance attached to the private ownership of

[2] Sylvia Pankhurst, *The Suffragette Movement* (1931), p. 528; on National Union of Ex-Servicemen, see *The Times*, 29 July and 20 Aug. 1920, *The Communist*, 19 Aug. 1920, and 'Report of Ministry of Labour', 28 Aug. 1920 (PRO Cab. 24/111 CP 1811); on 'Poplarism', 'Reports on Revolutionary Organisations in the U.K.', 22 and 29 Sept. 1921 (PRO Cab. 24/128 CP 3333 and CP 3550), and 'Statement Made by the Chairman to Sir Alfred Mond on the Occasion of the Deputation on 20 June 1922' (Poplar Municipal Alliance Papers, Tower Hamlets Central Library).

[3] *Manchester Evening News*, 10 June 1920.

[4] *Dudley Chronicle*, 7 June 1919; *Municipal Engineering & Sanitary Record*, 17 Apr. 1919; *Report of 42nd Conference of National Federation of Property Owners* (1920), pp. 29-30; 'Report on Revolutionary Organisations in the U.K.', 18 Dec. 1919 (PRO Cab. 24/95 CP 319).

house property symbolized in the foregoing extravagance, obscures much that is of interest. Owners of house property were politically marginal figures. Starved of capital, suffocating beneath the mountainous weight of local taxation, and subject to damaging attacks from left-wing critics, these proprietors sought—not without success—to conceal their nakedness behind an ideological fig-leaf. The landlord's largely untrammelled right to the enjoyment of his property depended more on the inertia of the working class than on the political power wielded by the various property-owners' associations. Indeed, the growth of such bodies was a recognition that the system could not long withstand a concerted challenge. The attempt to masquerade as ratepayers' associations was indicative of their vulnerability. It postponed the day of reckoning.

Until the outbreak of war, the dominant threat to private property in Britain was posed by Mr Lloyd George's determination to press ahead with extensive social reforms financed out of involuntary contributions levied upon the owners of real estate. After 1914 it was displaced by the previously latent challenge posed by working-class tenants; and in 1915 the spell was broken. The collapse of this once hallowed symbol of authority was not lost on contemporaries. W. C. Anderson noted the transformation:

Time was when the landlords had everything their own way, when they could bully and threaten and domineer without challenge, when tenants appeared to accept their position as creatures of meaner destiny and baser clay. Whether there has been much change in the spirit of landlordism may be doubted, but at all events there has been a big change in the spirit of the tenants. New and liberating movements have been at work and the temper and outlook of the people have undergone something in the nature of a revolution. The landlords are no longer looked upon as the custodians of a heaven sent and eternal system not to be tampered with by the vulgar and profane. The present arrangement is definitely challenged by hundreds of thousands of discriminating and undiscriminating minds ...[5]

Discriminating minds were, perhaps, *au fait* with the detail of the new legislation; undiscriminating minds simply knew that henceforth they had something to protect.

The tenants' defence associations, spawned in the course of the struggle for the Rent Act, together with the trades councils and other organized vigilants, were quickly absorbed with the enforcement of the new measure. The Workers' National Committee was

[5] *Forward*, 3 Nov. 1915.

overwhelmed by the insatiable demand for information. 'There appears to have been something like a conspiracy on the part of the Press to keep from the people the fact that the Bill has passed the Lords', Middleton, its hard-worked secretary, complained, as Slessor laboured to produce a comprehensive leaflet outlining the provisions of the new law.[6] The diffusion of this useful knowledge was of paramount importance. But, though he strained every sinew, the lawyer was unable to accommodate all the urgent claims of anxious affiliates. William Mellor, who pressed for even greater expedition, was almost in despair: 'I am being worried to death by correspondence respecting the position of Tenants now that the Rent Bill has passed', he wrote Middleton in January, 1916.[7] The months that followed brought little respite. W. C. Anderson, Middleton wrote in answer to an inquiry, the following year, 'is so overwhelmed with correspondence arising out of the Rent Restrictions Act that he cannot reply to all the intricate points raised'.[8] Dan Rider had to give up a short-lived column in the *Daily Herald* in order to cope with the resultant 50,000 inquiries.[9]

Tenants were less and less inclined to suffer in silence, and prepared to put to the test that part of the labour litany which underlined the unity of knowledge and power. Birmingham Trades Council's determined prosecution of *Sharp* v. *Chant* was symptomatic of the new assertive mood. Trades unionists and tenants' associations were everywhere keen to expose illegal exactions and bring the protection of the law within reach of their otherwise defenceless constituents. This was a formidable task. Popular antipathy towards any involvement with the courts (notwithstanding Dr Philip's important qualifications in the sphere of criminal law) remained a major constraint.[10] The desire to minimize contact with the judicial process, and thus to reduce insecurity, was not the least of the factors underlying the repudiation of Fair Rents Courts in 1915 and the subsequent insistence upon the application of Regulation 2A(2). Above all, summary eviction retained an awful

[6] J. S. Middleton to A. Jenkins, 31 Jan. 1916; and see too leaflet published by Newcastle Labour Representation Committee, *Increase of Rent & Mortgage Interest (War Restrictions) Act* (1916) (WNC Papers).

[7] William Mellor to J. S. Middleton, 17 Jan. 1916 (WNC Papers).

[8] J. S. Middleton to John McGillivray, 7 May 1917 (WNC Papers).

[9] Departmental Committee on the Operation of the Rent Acts: MS Minutes of Evidence, 8 Mar. 1920, p. 35 (PRO HLG. 41/5).

[10] On working class willingness to prosecute offences against property, see David Philips, *Crime and Authority in Victorian England* (1977), pp. 124-9, 285-6.

association with a court appearance. 'In the background', Rider remarked, 'there always lurked the fear of being summoned to that strange place, the Court, and being ordered to give up their homes.'[11] The arcane nature of the proceedings and the ritual, even in the inferior courts, together constituted a massive form of intimidation which landlords well understood. The unorganized tenant remained at the mercy of unscrupulous landlords. The rewards attendant upon participation could be substantial, however. In consequence of the systematic campaign to recover excess rents undertaken by organized labour in Hull, more than £10,000 was returned to some 5,000 tenants.[12] The sensitizing effect of the innumerable campaigns to redress abuses conducted by local labour movements was at the bottom of brushfire agitation sparked by Mr Churchill's extraordinary intervention at Barrow in the summer of 1917. The resultant success encouraged tenants to probe further the apparent weaknesses of the authorities.

The wartime tenants' struggles were not without a bearing upon that still unexplained phenomenon, the radicalization of working-class women. These were years which witnessed an unprecedented effort on the part of groups such as the Women's Labour League to tap that vast reservoir of expertise which working-class women alone possessed, and to involve them in the design and planning of the homes to be built for themselves and their returning heroes.[13] The daughters of the proletariat, however, were not passive participants; in 1915 they were at the forefront of the no-rents agitation. Thereafter the Glasgow Labour Party Housing Association went out of its way to accommodate these most valuable recruits on terms of equality.[14] The Glasgow Women's Housing Association felt it now possessed sufficient confidence to subordinate the claims of women to those of class; henceforth it became the Glasgow Workers' Housing Association.[15] The effect of their exemplary and widely-publicized conduct in 1915 was evident in subsequent actions. The 'street captains', pioneered by housewives at Govan and Partick, reappeared with bells and klaxons during the post-war rent strikes

[11] Rider, *Ten Years Adventures*, p. 47.

[12] F. Potter, Secretary of Hull Trades Council, to J. S. Middleton, 12 Apr. 1917 (WNC Papers).

[13] See leaflet published by Women's Labour League, *The Working Woman's House* (1917) and 'Report on the Work of the Housing Sub-Committee of the Women's Labour League', by Marion Phillips (WNC Papers).

[14] See correspondence of Andrew M'Bride, *Forward*, 4 Mar. 1916.

[15] *Forward*, 20 May 1916.

at Dudley and Rosyth.[16] The transformation was the subject of much comment. 'Women's minds had changed considerably', said Jack Sheppard, the industrial militant. 'The School Board man doesn't frighten mothers into a fit nowadays, and we have women banding together and refusing to pay rent'. An official of the Workers' Union, addressing a meeting of Rosyth tenants, made much the same point. 'Women', he said, much to the evident amusement of the audience, 'were the best men in this case'. Naïve and self-seeking politicians were convinced that the War Rents League was able to 'deliver' the female vote.[17]

The rents agitation, then, provided a potent source of radicalization amongst working-class women. Whether or not it provided a similar entrée for other previously disadvantaged groups is less clear. Were, for example, poor unskilled workers, those who, before the war, might have been more inclined to wrap a poker round an insistent landlord's head, increasingly disposed to organize in tenants' and other associations to achieve their objectives? The evidence on this point is not as yet sufficient to offer a pronouncement. The activities of the Government Hutments Tenants' Protection League at Woolwich and the rent strike organized by the Foleshill Tenants' Association at Holbrook Lane, Coventry, were the product of exceptional circumstances and a reflection of the geographically uneven impact of state intervention on the economy.

The concentration of production aggravated the pre-existent housing shortage in most of the major arms manufacturing centres. The minimal provision of state-subsidized accommodation coupled with measures designed to foster greater diversification would, it was hoped, suffice to resolve the crisis. From the outset it was recognized as impolitic for the state to act simultaneously as both employer and landlord.[18] The estates built by the Ministry of Munitions were formally managed by the local authorities. But, as was seen, the parallel arrangements made by the Admiralty at Rosyth barely concealed the special relationship which had thus been created. Tenants in these districts, all in one way and another employed on

[16] *Dudley Chronicle*, 21 June 1919; *Rosyth & Forth Mail*, 12 and 26 June and 3 July 1919.
[17] *Woolwich Pioneer*, 14 Feb. 1919; *Rosyth & Forth Mail*, 15 May 1919; Rider, *Ten Years Adventures*, p. 81.
[18] 'Woolwich Housing Schemes: Extract from the Report of the Proceedings of a Conference held on 8 Jan. 1915 of Representatives of the Local Government Board, War Office and Office of Works' (PRO Works 22/24/9).

vital war work, were therefore in a position to exert an unusual amount of leverage. The dominant concern for the resumption of market forces, evident in the preservation of what proved to be an ever-widening differential between controlled and uncontrolled rents, provoked the very unrest it was the object of policy to forestall.

In a period of rapidly rising prices, rent reductions rather than wage increases were considered by many workers a less inflationary means of maintaining living standards.[19] The post-war rent strikes in part reflect this preference. They are also indicative of a new confidence which turned into desperation in face of the unemployment that scarred a generation.

The authorities, though not always favourably disposed, could not but help remark upon the changed outlook among working-class tenants. 'It must be understood that although there is a War Rents Act, it does not mean that tenants are absolutely the masters of the situation' said Judge Granger, KC. 'There are still some rights left to the landlord.' His Honour Judge Crawford took a no less jaundiced view. 'In the eyes of many of these people', he wrote, 'a landlord was fair game. He had had his innings, it was now their turn, and they intended to make the most of it.' Crawford, like many others, found it difficult to reconcile the habits of a lifetime in defence of the sanctity of contract with the creation of statutory tenancies. Coke and Blackburn, he felt, must have turned in their graves. 'There seems to be an impression abroad now that working men can enter into contracts and disregard them at their pleasure', said an irascible County Court Judge, when giving judgement for the Ministry of Munitions against the organizer of the Government Hutments
Tenants' Protection League.[20]

Those charged with the making of policy tried to adopt a more enlightened view. Duckworth recognized in the emergence of organization amongst tenants a novel phenomenon with which authority would have to come to terms. A full account of the wartime experience, he argued, merited inclusion in the official history of the Ministry of Munitions and not merely on historio-

---

[19] See evidence of Harry A. Johns, Chairman, Rosyth Ratepayers' Association, Burgh of Dunfermline, *Case on the Appeal of the Scottish National Housing Co. and Others for the Opinion of the Judges under the Valuation of Land (Scotland) Acts*, p. 105 (PRO Adm. 116/2162).

[20] *Woolwich Pioneer*, 18 May 1917; J. D. Crawford, *Reflections and Recollections* (1936), pp. 86, 107-8; *Woolwich Pioneer*, 20 June 1919.

graphical grounds. Such an account, he felt, would 'afford instructive reading in view of possible rent strikes in the future'.[21] Those halcyon days before the lamps went out, when tenants submitted without protest, were over.

Even on the assumption of immediate post-war decontrol, there was a dawning recognition within Whitehall that the old autocracy could not be restored in its entirety. Legislation prepared within the Ministry of Reconstruction acknowledged the need of new machinery for the settlement of disputes between these fractious parties.[22] In the event, desirable safeguards were to be grafted painfully in piecemeal fashion upon an endless stream of rent acts. This process of *ad hoc* emendation, perhaps a political need and psychological necessity,[23] was not without its pitfalls. Ministers feared that tenants, when properly advised, would no longer hesitate to embark upon litigation in order to exploit the opportunities presented by the drafting errors that invariably crept into these increasingly complex enactments, and indeed much post-war militancy can be ascribed to such initiatives.[24]

High council rents and the uncertain future of rent control provided a continuous impulse towards organization throughout the inter-war years. This phase of the struggle still awaits its historian. The contours, however, are reasonably clear. The attempt of the

---

[21] G. H. Duckworth, to G. I. H. Lloyd, 13 July 1920; also see Duckworth to Lloyd, 10 Jan. 1921 (PRO Mun. 5/330). The official history, it should be noted, was a work of reference rather than scholarship: on manner of compilation, see D. Hay, 'The Official History of the Ministry of Munitions, 1915-1919', *Economic History Review*, 2nd Ser. XIV (1944).

[22] PRO Cab. 24/76 GT 6836.

[23] Symptomatic of this was the fact that the administration of the Rent Acts was never vested in any single department of state: *Report of Inter-Departmental Committee on the Rent Restriction Acts* (PP 1937-8, XV), para. 24. On the subsequent failure to integrate rent control with housing policy, see M. J. Barnett, *The Politics of Legislation* (1969).

[24] For one example, see the remarkable campaign of the Stapleford Tenants' Association, *Long Eaton Advertiser*, 17 June, 15 July, 5, 12, and 26 Aug., 30 Sept., 7 Oct., 4, 11, and 25 Nov. and 2 Dec. 1921; also see Crawford, *Reflections and Recollections*, pp. 81-2; 'Legislation for the Coming Session', Memorandum by the Minister of Health, 31 Jan. 1922 (PRO Cab. 24/132 CP 3668); Home Affairs Committee 105 (2), 23 Feb. 1922 (PRO Cab. 24/6); 'Increase of Rent & Mortgage Interest Restriction (Continuance and Amendment) Bill', Memorandum by the First Commissioner of Works, 6 Mar. 1923 (PRO Cab. 24/159 CP 139 (23)). The most important of these initiatives, that of the Clydebank Housing Association, is outlined in B. Moorhouse, M. Wilson, and C. Chamberlain, 'Rent Strikes—Direct Action and the Working Class' in R. Milliband and J. Saville (eds.), *The Socialist Register* (1972), pp. 136-8.

National Labour Housing Association (former Workmen's National Housing Council) to transform itself into a powerful federation of tenants' associations never amounted to very much, it is true.[25] But the rents agitation did not fade without trace. The Scottish Labour Housing Association lost none of its vitality nor did the War Rents League. Birmingham & District Tenants' Federation continued to expand so that, by the beginning of the 1930s, it comprised 'something like 33,000 tenants', though membership had fallen by a third before the end of the decade.[26] New bodies too sprang up. Some were a mere flash in the pan; others more durable. Glasgow Council of Tenants' Associations, for example, with twenty-nine affiliates, claimed to represent 'nearly 30,000 householders', the bulk of them council tenants.[27] The 7,500-strong Stepney Tenants' Defence League, formed in 1934, had grown prodigiously by the eve of war.[28] In the summer of 1939, 60,000 tenants were said to be on rent strike and their numbers were growing daily.[29]

The varied work of the tenants' associations was made possible only by the extraordinary devotion of their elected officials. These were often drawn from local worthies: councillors, guardians, members of assistance committees etc.—people such as Mrs Christina Moody, 'Glasgow Tenant's K.C.', a noted member of the Co-operative Party and a leader of the Scottish Labour Housing Association, or W. C. Woodward of the Lozzells Tenants' Association, who served for six years on Birmingham City Council, five of them as chairman of the sanitary committee, and was 'acknowledged as the authority in the Midlands on Tenants' questions, being freely termed "The Rent Act Expert" '.[30] Such expertise developed out of the policing of the rent acts. These complex pieces of legislation provided ample scope for abuse. Indeed, their very complexity constituted a form of intimidation. Tenants, fearful of involvement in a suspect legal process, were, in the absence of expert guidance,

[25]   On this, see National Labour Housing Association, *Annual Reports* (1918-24). The Association folded at the end of the decade.

[26]   Inter-Departmental Committee on Rent Restrictions Act, 1930-1: MS Minutes of Evidence, q. 5962 (PRO HLG 41/44); Rent Restrictions Acts Committee: MS Minutes of Evidence, q. 2995 (PRO HLG 41/64).

[27]   *Glasgow Herald*, 23 Mar. and 20 Apr. 1933.

[28]   *Evening News*, 27 June 1939 (Tubby Rosen Press Cuttings Collection).

[29]   *News Chronicle*, 28 June 1939 (Tubby Rosen Press Cuttings Collection).

[30]   *Forward*, 20 Sept. 1930; Constance M. Hood, Secretary of Birmingham & District Tenants' Federation, to E. C. H. Salmon, Secretary to Rent Restrictions Acts Committee, 7 Mar. 1931, p. 832 (PRO HLG 41/44).

prone to sacrifice their rights. The provision of such advice formed the staple of all tenants' associations.

The prevention of eviction, was *the* major concern. The disruptive effects of war upon people and property: the cessation of house-building, the creation of statutory tenancies, a straightened middle class and a more homogeneous working class—all combined to propel landlord and tenant relations to the forefront of post-war politics. It is not without significance that the prevention of eviction was to constitute one of the earliest of the rocks on which the first Labour Government foundered. No longer was eviction for non-payment of rent a process confined to the lowest of the low. The dispossession of respectable folk, unemployed ex-servicemen and out-of-work tradesmen, charged the issue with a new meaning.

The Rent Act of 1923 made a precarious situation desperate. The provision for decontrol on vacant possession, creeping decontrol as it was called, positively encouraged landlords to harass and evict sitting tenants. In theory there was nothing to fear. The new legislation provided express safeguards against precipitate action. No judgement or order for recovery or possession was to be given unless the Court 'considers it reasonable' to make such an order. But was it reasonable to grant possession against a family of nine who had occupied the same house for twelve years simply because the owner's son, whose needs were not pressing, was about to get married? 'Surely, Sir', the secretary of East Birmingham Tenants' Association wrote his MP, 'this kind of hardship could never have been anticipated in the legislation of the 1923 Rent Act; if so, then I can only say that if some measure is not adopted to provide alternative houses in such cases, then we feel something serious must happen ...'[31] Neville Chamberlain, architect of the new legislation, thought 'the outcry about evictions to be grossly exaggerated'.[32] The figures, however, suggest a want of sensitivity and imagination rather than the callous indifference levelled at him by opponents. Still, the 35,000 actions for possession or ejectment entered in the county courts in the eight months following the introduction of the Act of 1923 did give cause for concern.[33]

The position in industrial Scotland was even more serious.

[31] A. H. Platt to Neville Chamberlain, 16 Nov. 1923, (Chamberlain Papers, NC 5/13/127).

[32] Political Diaries, 7 Apr. 1924 (Chamberlain Papers, NC 2/21/10).

[33] *Return of Proceedings in Actions for Possession or Ejectment in the period of 1st August 1923 to 31st March 1924 in County Courts* (PP 1924, XIX).

Table 8: Cases heard in Glasgow Rent Court 1917–1933

Year	Cases	Decrees
1917/18	9,748	4,498
1918/19	6,890	3,080
1919/20	7,321	3,061
1920/1	23,855	9,446
1921/2	24,664	5,367
1922/3	20,298	2,657
1923/4	29,722	4,520
1924/5	24,175	3,343
1925/6	23,135	2,788
1926/7	20,785	2,832
1927/8	20,820	3,175
1928/9	22,473	4,403
1929/30	25,177	4,442
1930/1	26,342	4,359
1931/2	30,252	5,127
1932/3	32,472	5,506

Source: *HC Deb.* 5s. cclxxxiv (1933), 177–8

Landlord and tenant on Clydeside virtually broke down in the early 1920s. The Rent Acts seemed merely to exacerbate tension; neither party was satisfied with their operation. The plight of the unemployed was aggravated by the fact that, unlike the Boards of Guardians, Parish Councils in Scotland did not include a rent allowance in allocating relief. In Glasgow alone the numbers involved in summary eviction proceedings was no less than in pre-war years. But the response of labour was decidedly different. Robert Smillie, who held no brief for the destructive classes, condemned eviction for non-payment of rent as a moral outrage that ought to be abolished forthwith. Glasgow Trades Council organized a series of protest marches.[34] Parish Councils were pressed to relax their rules and grant additional assistance to unemployed tenants who were in arrears.[35] The eviction or threatened eviction of the unemployed excited the same fierce passions as were once aroused by the dispossession of servicemen's dependants in wartime. Thomas Munro, Clerk of Lanarkshire County Council, warned that 'it would be disastrous even dangerous to the public peace' if restraint were not

[34] Onslow Committee on the Rent Acts: MS Minutes of Evidence, pp. 29-32 (PRO HLG 41/26); *Glasgow Herald*, 2 July 1923.
[35] Minutes of Glasgow Trades Council, 14 June 1923; *Glasgow Herald*, 4 July 1923.

shown in such cases. And his was not a lone voice. Charitable funds were mobilized to avoid evictions and prevent disorder. Ministers were urged to set an example and speak out to prevent the jobless from joining the homeless.[36] The Secretary of State, however, refused to intercede.[37] Tenants were encouraged to organize and resist; Wheatley expressed himself willing to go to prison to secure justice.[38] The minority government of which he became a member shortly afterwards was none the less ill-prepared for the crisis in the making. What should have been a relatively straightforward measure for the protection of unemployed tenants, for which a majority might have been found, was badly botched on the floor of the House.[39] The government was humiliated; tenants were left to their own devices.

Between landlord and tenant there stretched an unbridgeable gulf. No basis could be discovered for the kind of voluntary arrangement which in Birmingham or South Wales did something to reduce tension in the early 1920s. In the absence of informal joint committees for the settlement of disputes out of court, the provision of adequate legal assistance became a matter of some urgency.[40] In 1920 permission was secured from the Sheriff-Principal for the appointment of a Lay-Advocate to advise and assist tenant-defendants in the summary eviction court.[41] Officials of the Scottish Labour Housing Association could not, however, cope with the sheer volume of transactions. Militants, especially members of the National Unemployed Workers Movement, who scorned legal defence work, were encouraged to press the formation of local Councils of Action to organize physical resistance to eviction.[42] Even the factors were appalled. A spokesman, taxed with the fact that more than 600 cases were trundling through the Glasgow Rent Court each week, readily agreed that something ought to be done:

[36] *Glasgow Herald*, 7 Dec. 1922. Quotation from PRO Cab. 27/119 CU 240.

[37] *Glasgow Herald*, 19 June 1923.

[38] On resistance, see *The Worker*, 3 and 10 Mar. 1923; on Wheatley, *Glasgow Herald*, 25 Jan. 1923.

[39] David Marquand, *Ramsay Macdonald* (1977), pp. 321-4.

[40] On joint committees, see Onslow Committee on the Rent Acts: MS Minutes of Evidence, pp. 91, 183-4 (PRO HLG 41/25); *HC Deb*. 5s. clxiv (1923), 2463-4; Birmingham & District Property Owners' Association, *Twenty First Annual Report* (Birmingham, 1922), p. 73.

[41] *HC Deb*. 5s. cclxxix (1933), 1012.

[42] On the cleavage of opinion, see 'Report on Policy Re Arrears of Rent due to Unemployment', Minutes of Glasgow Trades Council, 1 Feb. 1922; also Minutes, 21 Feb. 4 July, 1 Aug. and 11 Sept. 1923.

'Better provision for the conduct of rent cases is an obvious necessity. The factors join with the tenants in that matter. We have usually to wait four weeks before we can get a case heard!'[43] It was 1931 and the worst was yet to come. In the following year 35,000 cases were to pass through the rent court.[44] The need for the appointment of a public defender, for the extension of legal assistance, for improvement in court procedure, above all the need for the provision of adequate maintenance to avoid eviction, remained the dominant preoccupation of Scottish tenants down to the outbreak of war.[45]

The position as to distress and sequestration also gave cause for concern. Once again the Scottish tenant came off worse. Although wartime legislation against the levying of distress without leave of the court had been consolidated into the Rent Act of 1920, procedural difficulties in the Small Debt Court limited the Sheriff's power to direct repayment of arrears by instalments with the result that tenants were still sold-up and evicted.[46] In England and Wales, by contrast, bailiffs were rather less active. In order to forestall the accumulation of arrears property owners tended to apply for leave to distrain secure in the knowledge that, rather than contemplate the loss of his or her home, the defaulter would consent to repay the debt by regular instalments.[47]

Property-owners, however, still spoke fondly of the good old days, before the war, when the bailiffs could be put in without fuss. So long as the status of rent control remained uncertain, tenants continued to fear the bum bailiff as one would a vicious dog on a short leash. Creeping decontrol fuelled these fears. Once a property passed out of control it became subject to the ordinary law of distress. The expansion of municipal housing, the great building boom of the thirties and the impact of official slum clearance policies further diminished the stock of controlled housing.[48] In 1920 when rent control was at its peak all but a handful of the

[43] *Forward*, 12 Dec. 1931.

[44] *HC Deb*. 5s. cclxxix (1933), 1012.

[45] *Forward*, 13 Feb. and 7 May 1932; *HC Deb*. 5s. cccxxxviii (1938), 2565.

[46] 'Distress for Rent', Memorandum by Sir Arthur Jennings (copy), n.d., 1932, Rent Restrictions Bill Papers 1933 (PRO HLG 29/198); Minutes of Glasgow Trades Council, 17 Dec. 1923, 9 Jan. 1925; 'Small Debt Decrees—Instalments—and Arrestment of Wages Limitation', Memorandum by Wm. Adamson, 13 Mar. 1924 (PRO Cab. 24/165 CP 181 (24)).

[47] W. H. Whitelock to H. H. George, 11 June 1923, Rent & Mortgage Interest Restrictions Bill Papers 1923 (PRO HLG 29/128).

[48] New properties were not, of course, affected by rent restrictions.

nation's 8 m. dwellings were affected; fifteen years later controlled housing constituted about forty per cent of an enlarged housing stock—about 4½ m. out of 11 m. houses; and as the percentage fell officials began to prepare for the return to market forces. But for Hitler's inconsiderate intervention rent control might have ended in 1945.[49]

No such restoration was, however, possible if, as tenants' spokesmen alleged, bailiffs were little better than bullying terrorists.[50] At the Cabinet's insistence a small departmental committee of the Ministry of Health was set up to investigate. No evidence could be found of widespread harsh or improper conduct in the use of distress proceedings. At the same time the committee recognized that oppressed tenants were the least likely to co-operate with such a tribunal; further protection was therefore recommended.[51]

In conditions of acute housing shortage the temptation to evade rent restrictions frequently proved irresistible. The recovery of illegal increases remained a major preoccupation. 'The reports of local tenants' associations', said the Birmingham *Town Crier*, 'invariably record substantial sums reclaimed for landlords who have been exacting more than they were entitled to.'[52] In one year alone £3,000 was recovered by the Tenants' Federation from landlords who had been overcharging.[53] Such efforts, however impressive, pale into insignificance in comparison with the achievements of Stepney Tenants' Defence League which, within six months, claimed to have refunded £20,000 of excess charges and gained £18,000 in rent reductions.[54]

No less urgent was the vexation and discomfort due to negligence on the part of proprietors. Homes, though occupied and yielding a regular income, were too often unfit for human habitation. Here the tenants' associations acted as intermediaries forwarding complaints to the local authorities and thereby keeping 'a whole army' of sanitary inspectors in gainful employment.[55] This was of particular

[49] Statement 18A, 'The Rent Restrictions Acts' (PRO HLG 41/103).

[50] Rent Restrictions Acts Committee: MS Minutes of Evidence, 1 July 1937, pp. 3, 14, 23, 35, (PRO Cab. 27/638).

[51] See 'Departmental Committee on Distress for Rent, (Draft) Majority Report (1938)' (PRO HLG 41/87).   [52] *Town Crier*, 23 May 1924.

[53] Inter-Departmental Committee on the Rent Restrictions Acts, 1930-1: MS Minutes of Evidence, q. 6051 (PRO HLG 41/44).

[54] *Reynolds' Newspaper*, 19 Mar. 1939 (Tubby Rosen Press Cuttings Collection).

[55] Inter-Departmental Committee on the Rent Restrictions Act, 1930-1: MS Minutes of Evidence, q. 6735 (PRO HLG 41/44).

importance in view of the fact that the 40 per cent increase in rent sanctioned by the Rent Act of 1920 was to enable proprietors to undertake necessary repairs and not simply a windfall. Provision was therefore made for the suspension of the increase where the county court was satisfied—by certificate of the sanitary inspector—that the house was in a state of disrepair. In London it was a dead letter.[56] So long as the expiration of controls seemed imminent, tenants fearing the wrath to come were unwilling to exercise their rights. At the polling booth it was another matter. Embittered tenants, Chamberlain feared, would be driven to support the 'mad legislation' proposed by the Labour Party.[57]

The Rent Act of 1915 was not a tenants' charter but an emergency measure due to expire on the morrow of victory. The failure to raze controls threatened the whole basis of the post-war housing programme. Neither Coalition nor Conservative governments regarded subsidies as a permanent feature of housing policy. State assistance was framed in terms of the return to normality: once the war-related deficit had been made good, the state would withdraw from the housing field. Rent decontrol was vital to the success of this strategy. At the same time the rents agitation precluded the simple restoration of the *status quo ante*. The retention of protection was the key to the removal of restrictions. 'In the absence of this', wrote one observer shortly after the Armistice, 'the movement for the establishment of rent courts would receive a substantial impetus.'[58] The revolt of the middle classes at Mitcham in February 1923, confirmed the truth of this forecast.

Support for some form of rent court was readily forthcoming from local authorities, enlightened judges and other exponents of progressive opinion. Fair rent courts, it was realized, instead of an insidious form of socialism, might be the means of de-politicizing a troublesome issue and thereby smoothing the path towards a gradual lifting of restrictions.[59] 'The absence of such courts', declared the *Municipal Journal*, 'has undeniably caused the people who rent houses to clamour for the continuation of the Rent Restriction Act

[56] E. Martin to J. Maude, 10 Nov. 1932, Rent & Mortgage Interest Restrictions (Amendment) Bill Papers 1933, (PRO HLG 29/197).

[57] Neville Chamberlain to Dr John Robertson, 8 Mar. 1924 (Chamberlain Papers, NC 5/13/548).

[58] S. A. Smith, 'Rent Problems', *Surveyors' Institution, Transactions* LII (1919-20), p. 368.

[59] *Municipal Journal*, 16 Feb. 1923; *Daily News*, 22 Feb. 1923.

... with such courts a reign of peace could be secured between landlords and tenants ...'[60] Proprietors were assured that tenants need not be the sole beneficiaries; for it was by no means axiomatic that a fair rent meant an uneconomic rent. On the contrary: private ownership might revive 'if there was some guarantee that fair rents for homes could be fixed': 'To be candid, we can understand the fear of property owners that they will be swamped by a too ready sympathetic consideration of tenants' complaints. There is undeniably too much favouritism in court where landlords are involved, and tenants invariably score. This unfairness, indeed, might have been taken for a first class argument for the establishment of special courts which should be formed to deal impartially with rents'.[61] Conservative politicians, however, winced at anything which prolonged restrictions. The instinctive feeling that rent courts and rent control represented the thin edge of the socialist wedge persisted in spite of electoral setbacks. 'I feel that if a Conservative government, returned to power at a General Election six months ago with an absolute majority, cannot do anything substantial towards decontrol, no government will ever be able to do it.' So wrote Lord Onslow shortly after the Mitcham defeat.[62] Onslow, chairman of the ill-starred committee of inquiry whose advice had actually provoked the rebellion in the suburbs, felt, on reflection, that to proceed with decontrol by stages or through the appointment of fair rent courts, would serve merely to start additional focuses of agitation. Instead, he proposed a short-lived experiment in decontrol by arbitration. 'I am of the opinion', he wrote, 'that no attempt should be made to establish a court of law or anything on the lines of what are generally known as fair rent courts; the analogy would be more on the lines of the Military Service Tribunals (without the Appeal).' These tribunals, operating briskly, could dispose of the matter within twelve months.[63]

Neville Chamberlain, who had succeeded the luckless Griffith Boscawen as Minister of Health, was no less keen to restore the free movement of rents without delay. The new Minister, however, recognized the need to retain some form of protection until the

[60] *Municipal Journal*, 2 Mar. 1923.

[61] *Municipal Journal*, 6 Apr. 1923.

[62] Minute of Onslow to the Minister, 3 Apr. 1923, Rent & Mortgage Interest Restrictions Bill Papers 1923 (PRO HLG 29/128).

[63] Memorandum by Lord Onslow, n.d., Rent & Mortgage Interest Restrictions Bill Papers 1923 (PRO HLG 29/128).

housing shortage had been considerably reduced. The Rent Bill of 1923 therefore provided for the continuation of protection for five years beyond the termination of controls (due to expire in 1925).[64] The principal form of protection, however, proved contentious.

Proprietors and their supporters on the back-benches took exception to the provision for the formation of reference committees to be set up after the abolition of controls. These committees, comprising representatives of property-owners and tenants and an independent chairman, were to try and settle disputes without the intervention of the courts. Reference committees were nothing more than a temporary expedient to reduce pressure on the courts during the transition to economic rents. The stratospheric level of summary eviction proceedings and the unrest engendered thereby made such provision seem both humane and politic.

Landlords were not convinced. 'The wrong sort of people may easily capture such committees, and use them for all sorts of fads and agitations and even worse', wrote the secretary of the Land Union.[65] The Glasgow Property Owners' Association was no less adamant: 'The Association objects most emphatically ... to the setting up of reference committees to control rents and induce further litigation and ill-feeling between landlord and tenant indefinitely. The institution of reference committees is simply an institution of rent courts which, once set up, will most probably become permanent.'[66] Samuel Talbot, a substantial Birmingham proprietor and a leading figure in Unionist politics, put the case bluntly. If landlords could not obtain justice from a Conservative government, he warned, they would be compelled to look elsewhere.[67] Against such fears rational debate was futile.

Chamberlain's programme, was, in any case, overtaken by the march of events. Restrictions could not be lifted in 1925 nor for many years thereafter. The whole episode, however, left a bitter taste. Reference committees and fair rent courts remained improper subjects for conversation among true defenders of private

---

[64] *HC Deb.* 5s. clxiv (1923), 2221-32.

[65] R. B. Yardley to Neville Chamberlain, 21 June 1923, Rent & Mortgage Interest Restrictions Bill Papers 1923 (PRO HLG 29/128).

[66] Memorandum of Property Owners' & Factors' Association, Glasgow Ltd. as to the Rent & Mortgage Interest Restrictions Bill, 14 June 1923, Rent & Mortgage Interest Restrictions Bill Papers 1923 (PRO HLG 29/128).

[67] S. T. Talbot, *The Rent Bill 1923: Observations* (Birmingham, 1923), p. 14.

property.[68] Support for such courts served merely to differentiate those who wished to hasten decontrol from those who sought to preserve it. And these views were not confined to the Tory back-benches. Within the Ministry of Health such courts came to be viewed with the deepest suspicion: fair rent courts were seen not as a demand for social justice but as a piece of legerdemain, a cunning attempt on the part of Labour to perpetuate rent control after the formal withdrawal of restrictions.[69]

Tenants' associations were represented at the various official inquiries which preceded the periodic renewal of restrictions. Time and again their officers proposed remedies for the numerous abuses which deprived tenants of the protection of the law. Above all they were concerned to arrest the policy of creeping decontrol initiated in 1923: 'We have seen the terrible effects which have invariably followed de-control; increased rent, the power of ejectment, the burden of all repairs, cleansing and decorating, key money and premiums, and restrictions of every kind are included in the terms of tenancy, clearly showing that if the "Rent Acts" are allowed to expire, hundreds of thousands of law-abiding subjects will be involved in like conditions.'[70] In its submission to the Ridley Committee of 1937, Birmingham Tenants' Federation maintained that experience had shown that '... the weapon of decontrol has brought widespread resentment against landlords, a sullen resentment that is smouldering and longing to burst into fire but dare not because of the insecurity of their tenure is a great living reality which they dare not risk its plunging them and their families into the street or back into the irksome everyday quarrels of sub-let rooms [sic].'[71] Besides the insistence upon tighter restrictions, tenants' associations campaigned throughout the period for the maintenance of rent controls until the housing shortage had been overtaken. Bitter experience left no doubt as to the consequence of decontrol in times of scarcity.

[68] Section 10 of the Rent Act of 1933 empowered local authorities to appoint advisory rent committees and to publish information for the assistance of landlords and tenants as to rights, duties and procedure under the principal Rent Acts. It was not much used: Memorandum on Rent Restrictions Committees of Local Authorities, n.d. (PRO HLG 41/104).

[69] 'Tenancy Courts', Memorandum to Mr Elliot, n.d. but 1938, Increase of Rent & Mortgage Interest (Restrictions) Bill Papers 1938 (PRO HLG 29/248).

[70] Birmingham & District Tenants' Federation, *Delegates Conference in Digbeth Institute* (Circular, Mar. 1928) (Birmingham Reference Library Pressmark 520968).

[71] Rent Restrictions Acts Committee: MS Minutes of Evidence, p. 411 (PRO HLG 41/64).

Tenants' associations not only contended that the relaxation of controls was disastrous but supported their claims with systematic evidence.[72] It was the outcry provoked by such revelations which led to the appointment of the Inter-Departmental Committee on the Rent Acts in 1931.[73] The Committee found that, as regards working-class tenants, the Rent Act of 1923 had been an unmitigated failure. No "filtering-up" had taken place: on the contrary, de-control by possession placed a premium upon immobility; private enterprise had no incentive to provide for the lower end of the housing market and the local authorities could not afford to make such provision. Nor had friction diminished. All that had happened was that an eighth of working-class houses, 'rather more than ¾ million' houses, had been decontrolled and exorbitant rents imposed. Official statistics disclosed an ever-widening disparity between controlled and decontrolled rents: on average decontrolled rents were 85-90 per cent above the pre-war rent as compared with the 50 per cent increase in the rents of controlled houses.[74] The relaxation of controls had it seemed, been a ghastly mistake.

The uncertain status of the tenants' associations posed problems of exceptional complexity in the definition of working-class politics. Stalwarts accustomed to organizing the worker at the point of production often found it difficult to accommodate the consumer in the community.[75] In some areas, most notably Clydeside, tenants' associations were a simple extension of the labour movement. In Birmingham, by contrast, where deep roots within the community were not struck, it was found mutually convenient for tenants to eschew politics and co-operate with labour as independent allies.[76] Such distinctions were not always apparent to adversaries who persisted in viewing tenants' associations as hotbeds of subversion. The dramatic interventions of the National Unemployed Workers'

[72] See, for example, Sparkbrook, Sparkhill & Midland District Tenants' Association, *General Secretary's Sixteenth Annual Report* (1932) in Rent & Mortgage Interest Restrictions (Amendment) Bill Papers 1933 (PRO HLG 29/197).

[73] Minute of H.H.G., June 1932, Rent & Mortgage Interest Restrictions (Amendment) Bill Papers 1933 (PRO HLG 29/197).

[74] *Report of Inter-Departmental Committee on the Rent Restrictions Acts* (PP. 1930-1, XVII), pp. 17-18, 28.

[75] Cf. H. Y. Brockhouse, 'Report and Suggestions to the N.A.C.', 10 June 1918, Minutes of National Administrative Council, 1918, fos. 20-1 (Minutes and Papers of the Independent Labour Party, British Library of Political and Economic Science).

[76] On this, see my article, 'Tenants and Politics: The Birmingham Tenants' Federation During and After the First World War', *Midland History*, VI (1981), pp. 131-2.

Movement or the well-publicized happenings in the 'Little Moscows' provided just sufficient evidence to make this kind of prejudice seem plausible.[77] Intelligent Conservatives, however, feared that it was the landlord rather than the Communist who was the real recruiting sergeant for socialism.[78]

The struggle for tenants' rights between the wars was, then, a radicalizing experience. How far, though, did such struggles provide a platform on which broader connections might be established and the level of political consciousness raised? P. J. Dollan was impressed by the defensive character of the post-war conflicts. The demand for pre-war rents, he argued, was simply the voice of economic necessity. 'Tenants only organised to reduce rents when economic conditions compel them to seek relief in that way.'[79] Identification with the tenants had, however, helped to consolidate the political base of the Labour Party in Scotland. The Communist Party too, during the 1930s, came to participate in these struggles with similar success.[80]

Tenant's associations played an important role in the shaping of social policy in inter-war Britain. Achievements, though not spectacular, were by no means negligible: harassment and intimidation were checked, wrongs redressed, law enforced. In the 1930s advisory services of this kind were exceptional. The rents agitation, moreover, created a climate of opinion in favour of increased protection which it was simply impolitic to ignore. Key money, for example, an immoral rather than an illegal exaction, was, as Neville Chamberlain put it, just one of those questions which 'arouse so much adverse comment and make it so difficult to advocate the termination of the Rent Restrictions Act'. Proprietors were urged 'to do everything in [their] power to prevent actions of this kind by landlords who are certainly injuring their own case'.[81] Above all, tenants' associations had upheld the (then novel) belief that, rent control or no rent control, tenants had rights that ought to be protected.

[77] On this, see Stuart Macintyre, *Little Moscows, Communism and Working Class Militancy in Inter-War Britain* (1980).
[78] Laurence J. Libgott to Neville Chamberlain, 25 Jan. and 4 Mar. 1924 (Chamberlain Papers, NC 5/13/454-456).
[79] *Forward*, 11 July 1925
[80] Communist intervention is examined in Steven Schifferes, 'Tenants' Struggles in the 1930s' (University of Warwick, MA Dissertation, 1975).
[81] Chamberlain to A. J. Wilson, 21 Dec. 1926 (Chamberlain Papers, NC 5/13/410).

Bibliography

UNPUBLISHED SOURCES

Public Record Office, London:
Cabinet Papers & Memoranda
Admiralty Papers
Home Office Papers
Metropolitan Police Papers
Ministry of Housing and Local Government Papers
Ministry of Munitions Papers
Ministry of Works Papers
Ministry of Reconstruction Papers
Treasury Papers
War Office Papers

Scottish Record Office:
Records of Scottish Development Department

Bishopsgate Institute, London:
Minutes of the General Council of the Reform League

Bodleian Library, Oxford:
Christopher Addison Papers

Corpus Christi College, Oxford:
R. C. K. Ensor Papers

London School of Economics:
William Beveridge Munitions Collection
Charles Booth Papers
J. S. Mill-Harriet Taylor Papers
Passfield Papers
Minutes and Papers of Labour Representation Committee
Webb Local Government Collection
Independent Labour Party Papers

University of Birmingham Library:
Neville Chamberlain Papers

Leeds City Archives:
Minutes of Leeds Trades Council
Minutes of Leeds Labour Representation Committee

Labour Party Archives, Transport House:
War Emergency Workers' National Committee Minutes & Papers

Mitchell Library, Glasgow:
Minutes of Glasgow Trades Council

Tower Hamlets Central Library:
Poplar Municipal Alliance Minutes & Papers

National Housing & Town Planning Council, London:
Minutes of the National Housing & Town Planning Council

Peabody Trust, London:
Minutes of Board of Governors

In the possession of Harold Knee, Surrey:
Minutes of the Workmen's National Housing Council

Birmingham Reference Library:
Minutes of Birmingham Trades Council

National Museum of Labour History:
Tubby Rosen Press Cuttings Collection

THESES

Abel, E. K., 'Canon Barnett and the First Thirty Years of Toynbee Hall' (University of London Ph.D., 1965)

Berridge, V. S., 'Popular Journalism & Working Class Attitudes, 1854–86; a study of *Reynolds's Newspaper, Lloyds' Weekly Newspaper* & the *Weekly Times*' (University of London Ph.D., 1976)

Englander, D., 'The Workmen's National Housing Council, 1898–1914' (University of Warwick MA, 1973)

Hole, W. V., 'The Housing of the Working Classes in Britain, 1850–1914: A Study in the Development of Standards and Methods of Provision' (University of London Ph.D., 1965)

Jordan, J. R. 'Homes for Heroes: Housing Problems at the end of the First World War' (University of Kent MA, 1971)

Kaijage, F. K., 'Labouring Barnsley 1816–56: A Social and Economic History (University of Warwick Ph.D., 1975)

Lincoln, W. E., 'Popular Radicalism and the Beginnings of the New Socialist Movement in Britain 1870–1885' (University of London Ph.D., 1977)

Maclean, Iain, 'The Labour Movement in Clydeside Politics 1914–1924' (Oxford D.Phil., 1971)

Mallier, A. T., 'Housing in Coventry: The Development of Municipal Action, 1890–1908' (University of Birmingham M. Soc. Sc., 1969)

Offer, Avner, 'Property and Politics, A Study of Landed and Urban Property in England between the 1880s and the Great War' (University of Oxford, D.Phil., 1978)

Rhodes, G. W., 'Housing Development in Leeds, 1919–1939' (University of Leeds MA, 1954)

Schifferes, Steven, 'Tenants Struggles in the 1930s' (University of Warwick MA, 1975)

Steffel, R. V., 'Housing for the Working Classes in the East End of London, 1890–1907' (Ohio State University Ph.D., 1969)

Wilding, P. R. 'Government & Housing: A study in the development of social policy 1906–1939' (University of Manchester Ph.D., 1970)

Zoond, Vera, 'Housing Legislation in England 1851–1867' (University of London MA, 1931)

OFFICIAL PAPERS

Annual Reports of the Local Government Board, 1872–1914

Reports of the Select Committee of the House of Commons on Public Petitions, 1836–1900*

Civil Judicial Statistics for Scotland, 1899–1925

Hansard, *Parliamentary Debates*, 1836–1939

PP 1817, VI: *Report of Select Committee on the Poor Laws*

PP 1818, V: *Report of the House of Lords Committee on the Poor Laws*

PP 1833, XXII: *Fifth Report of the Commissioners appointed to enquire into the Practise and Proceedings of the Superior Courts of Common Law relative to provincial Courts in England for the Recovery of Small Debts*

PP 1834, X: *Select Committee on Handloom Weavers*

PP 1834, XVI: *Select Committee on Metropolitan Police*

PP 1834, XXVII, XXVIII: *Royal Commission on the Poor Laws*

* Not published as a command paper

PP 1834, XXVI; 1835, XXXV: *Report of Law Commission, Scotland*

PP 1836, XXXIV: *Poor Enquiry—(Ireland) Appendix G, Report on the State of the Irish Poor in Great Britain*

PP 1837, XII: *Select Committee on Metropolitan Police Offices*

PP 1837–8, XV: *Select Committee on Metropolitan Police Offices*

PP 1837–8, XXI: *Select Committee on the Rating of Tenements*

PP 1837–8, XXVIII; 1839, XX: *Fourth & Fifth Annual Reports of the Poor Law Commissioners*

PP 1842, XXVI: Edwin Chadwick, *Report on the Sanitary Condition of the Labouring Population of Great Britain in 1842*, ed., M. W. Flinn (Edinburgh 1965)

PP 1843, XX: *Report of the Poor Law Commissioners on Local Taxation*

PP 1850, XIX: *Select Committee on the Savings of the Middle and Working Classes*

PP 1851, XXIII: *Report to the Board of Health in reference to the Sanitary Condition of Agar Town, St. Pancras and other parts of the Metropolis*

PP 1854, XXV: *Report of Commissioners enquiring into the outbreak of Cholera in Newcastle, Gateshead and Tynemouth*

PP 1854, XXXV: *Second Report on the Operation of the Common Lodging Houses Act*

PP 1854, XXXV: *Report of the General Board of Health on the Administration of the Public Health Acts*

PP 1859, VII: *Select Committee of the House of Lords on the Rates and Municipal Franchise Acts*

PP 1864, LII: *Parish of Bethnal Green: Copies of Depositions and Correspondence relating to charges against Dr. Moore*

PP 1866, XXXIII: *Eighth Report of the Medical Officer of the Privy Council*

PP 1868–9, VII: *Select Committee on Registration of Voters*

PP 1868–9, IX: *Select Committee of the House of Lords on the Operation of the Law of Hypothec in Scotland*

PP 1868–9, XI: *Select Committee on Poor Rate Assessments*

PP 1870, VIII: *Select Committee on Local Taxation*

PP 1871, XXV; 1872, XXVI: *Royal Commission on Friendly and Benefit Building Societies*

PP 1873, X: *Select Committee on the Present Scarcity and Dearness of Coal*

PP 1874, LIV: *Hypothec (Scotland): Return on the Number of Sequestrations for Urban Subjects*

PP 1881, VII; 1882, VII: *Select Committee on Artisans' and Labourers' Dwellings Improvement*

PP 1884–5, XXX: *Royal Commission on the Housing of the Working Classes*

PP 1887, XIII: *Select Committee on Town Holdings*

PP 1887, LXXI: *Statements of Men Living in Certain Districts of London*

PP 1887, LXXXI: *Further Reports from Her Majesty's Minister at Washington on the Homestead and Exemption Laws in the U.S.*

PP 1888, LXXXII; 1890–1, LXIV: *Evictions (London & Suburbs)*

PP 1890, XVII: *Fifth Report of the Select Committee of the House of Lords on the Sweating System*

PP 1892, XXIV, XXXV, XXXVI: *Royal Commission on Labour*

PP 1895, IX: *Select Committee on Distress from Want of Employment*

PP 1895, XV: *Royal Commission on the Aged Poor*

PP 1898, XLI, XLV; 1899, XXXVI; 1901, XXIV: *Royal Commission on Local Taxation*

PP 1903, XXX: *Royal Commission on Physical Training (Scotland)*

PP 1905, LXXXIV: *Memoranda, Statistical Tables & Charts prepared in the Board of Trade ..... Changes in the Cost of Living in Large Towns*

PP 1906, CIV: *Transcript of Shorthand Notes taken at the Public Inquiry into the General Conditions of the Poplar Union*

PP 1906, CIV: *Report to the President of the Local Government Board on the Poplar Union by J. S. Davy, Chief Inspector to the Board*

PP 1907, XXXVI; 1908, XLVII: *Report and Minutes of Evidence of Departmental Committee on House Letting in Scotland*

PP 1909, XXXVIII; 1909, XXXIX; 1910, XLIX: *Royal Commission on the Poor Laws and Relief of Distress*

PP 1913, LXVI: *Report of an Enquiry by the Board of Trade into Working Class Rents, Housing, Retail Prices and Standard Rates of Wages in the U.K.*

PP 1914–16, XXXV: *Report of the Departmental Committee on Increase in the Rentals of Small Dwelling Houses in the Industrial Districts in Scotland*

PP 1917–18, III: *Report of Committee on Public Accounts*

PP 1917–18, XIV: *Report of Royal Commission on the Housing of the Industrial Population of Scotland*

Report of Royal Commission on the Housing of the Industrial Population of Scotland; Minutes of Evidence, 4 vols. HMSO (Edinburgh, 1921)

PP 1917–18, XV: *Reports of Commission of Enquiry into Industrial Unrest*

PP 1918, XXVI: *Housing in England & Wales: Memorandum by the Advisory Panel on the Emergency Problem*

PP 1919, XII: *Ministry of Reconstruction: Report of the Committee on the Increase of Rent & Mortgage Interest (War Restrictions) Acts*

PP 1920, VI: *Select Committee on Business Premises*

PP 1920, XVIII: *Report of Committee on the Increase of Rent & Mortgage Interest (War Restrictions) Acts*

PP 1922, IX: *Third Report of Committee on National Expenditure*

PP 1924, XIX: *Returns on Evictions in England, Wales and Scotland*

PP 1924–5, VI: *First and Second Reports from the Select Committee on Public Accounts*

PP 1924–5, XV: *Report of Committee on the Rent Restriction Acts*

PP 1930–1, XVII: *Report of Inter-Departmental Committee on the Rent Restrictions Acts*

PP 1937–8, XV: *Report of Inter-Departmental Committee on the Rent Restrictions Acts*

PP 1964–5, XVII: *Report of the Committee on Housing in Greater London*

MUNICIPAL PAPERS

Annual Reports of Medical Officers of Health of Metropolitan Vestries and Borough Councils, 1855–1918 (copies in Greater London Record Office)

Annual Reports of Medical Officer of Health for the City of Birmingham, 1900–18

Annual Reports of Medical Officer of Health for the City of Liverpool, 1864–1925

London County Council, Proceedings of the Council, 1890–1914

London County Council Housing of the Working Classes Committee, Agenda Papers (copies in Greater London Record Office; also in Ensor MSS (Unsorted))

City of Birmingham, *Special Housing Enquiry: Report and Minutes of Evidence* (1914)

Glasgow Municipal Commission on the Housing of the Poor, *Report and Recommendations with Minutes of Evidence* (1904)

City of Liverpool, *Commission of Inquiry into the Subject of the Unemployed in the City of Liverpool* (1894)

Borough of Liverpool, *Reports of Dr. Parkes and Dr. Sanderson on the Sanitary Condition of Liverpool* (1871)

London County Council, *London Statistics*, 1890–1916

Petitions to Glasgow Magistrates (Strathclyde Regional Archives)

PERIODICALS

The Annual Register
The Builder

Charity Organisation Review
Contemporary Review
Economic Journal
Fortnightly Review
Journal of the Royal Statistical Society
Labour Annual
Macmillans' Magazine
Nineteenth Century
Quarterly Review
Soots Magazine
Socialist Review
Surveyors' Institution, Transactions

NEWSPAPERS & JOURNALS

Anarchist
Ardrossan & Saltcoats Herald
A. S. E. Monthly Journal & Report
Aston News
Barrow Guardian
Bee-Hive
Bethnal Green Times
Birmingham Daily Mail
Birmingham Daily Post
(Birmingham) *Evening Despatch*
Birmingham Gazette
Cambuslang Advertiser
Christian Socialist
Clarion
Club & Institute Journal
Clydebank & Renfrew Press
Coatbridge Leader
Commonweal
Correspondent
Coventry Herald
Daily Chronicle
Daily Citizen
Daily Herald
Daily News
Daily Sketch

Dudley Chronicle
Dunfermline Press
East End News
Eastern Post
East London Advertiser
East London Observer
Estates Gazette
Fabian News
Forward
Freedom
Freeholder
Glasgow Citizen
(Glasgow) *Daily Record & Mail*
Glasgow Eastern Argus
Glasgow News
Glasgow Property Advertiser
(Glasgow) *Weekly Record & Mail*
Govan Press
Greenock Herald
Hackney & Kingsland Gazette
Handsworth Herald
House & Home
Housing Journal
Justice
Labour and Employment Advertiser

Labour Leader
Labour Standard
Leeds & Yorkshire Mercury
Leeds Weekly Citizen
Liverpool Mercury
Local Government Journal
London
Long Eaton Advertiser
Manchester Evening News
Manchester Examiner & Times
Manchester Guardian
Midland Counties Express
Morning Chronicle
Municipal Engineer & Sanitary Record
Municipal Journal
North Western Daily Mail
Paisley Observer
Paisley & Renfrewshire Gazette
Pollokshaws News
*Poplar Alliance Review**
*Poplar's Local Municipal Review**
Porcupine
Property Owners' Gazette
Property Owners' Journal
Radical
Reynolds' Newspaper

* *Copies in Tower Hamlets Central Library*

Rosyth & Forth Mail
Salford Weekly News
Scotsman
Scottish Typographical Journal
South London Chronicle
Southwark Recorder
Standard
Sunday Chronicle
The Call
The Communist
The Times
The Torch
Town Crier
The Worker
Tottenham & Edmonton Weekly Herald
Tower Hamlets Independent
Voice of Labour
West Central News
West Ham Citizen
(Wolverhampton) *Express & Star*
Woman's Dreadnought
Woolwich Gazette & Plumstead News
Woolwich Herald
Woolwich Pioneer
Workers' Dreadnought
Yorkshire Evening Post
Yorkshire Factory Times
Yorkshire Observer

REPORTS

Annual Reports of the following organizations:
Scottish Trade Union Congress
Artisans', Labourers' and General Dwellings Company
Bermondsey Settlement, Annual Reports
Birmingham & District Property Owners' Association
Mansfield House University Settlement in East London
National Federation of Property Owners & Ratepayers
National Labour Housing Association
Social Democratic Federation

CONTEMPORARY BOOKS, REPORTS ETC.

Addison, Christopher, *The Betrayal of the Slums* (1922)

—— *Politics from Within* 2 vols. (1924)

—— *Four and a Half Years* 2 vols (1934)

Alison, Archibald, *Some Account of My Life and Writings* 2 vols. (London & Edinburgh, 1883)

Banfield, F., *Great Landlords of London* (1890)

Bateman, John, *The Great Landowners of Great Britain and Ireland* (4th edn. 1883)

Beames, Thomas, *The Rookeries of London*, (2nd edn. 1852)

Begg, James, *Happy Homes for Working Men and How to Get Them* (1866)

Bell, G. J., *Commentaries of the Laws of Scotland and the Principles of Jurisprudence* (7th edn. 1870)

Birmingham and District Property Owners' Association, *The Housing Question, Remember Coventry, May 12, 1917* (Birmingham c. 1920)

Bennett, Arnold, *The Card* (Penguin Books edn., 1973)

Blackstone, William, *Commentaries on the Laws of England*, 4 vols. (1844)

Blaiklie, W. G., *Heads and Hands in the World of Labour* (1865)

Booth, Charles, *Life and Labour of the People of London* 17 vols. (1902)

Booth, William, *In Darkest England and the Way Out* (1890)

Burt, Thomas, *Autobiography* (1924)

Chambers, Robert, *Traditions of Edinburgh* 2 vols. (Edinburgh, 1825)

Cross, Alexander, *Explanatory Notes on the House-Letting & Rating (Scotland) Act, 1911* (Glasgow, 1912)

Dewsnup, E. R., *The Housing Problem in England* (Manchester, 1907)

Dickens, Charles, *Sketches by Boz* (1890 edn.)

Dollan, Patrick, *The Clyde Rent War* (Glasgow, 1925)

Duncan, David, ed., *Life and Letters of Herbert Spencer* (1908)

Dundee Social Union, *Report on Housing and Industrial Conditions and Medical Inspection of Schoolchildren* (Dundee, 1905)

Eighth Special Report of US Commissioner of Labour, *The Housing of Working People*, 53rd Cong. 3rd. Sess. (Washington 1895)

Fabian Society, 'Facts for Socialists', *Fabian Tract* No. 5 (1899)

Fenwick, Pascoe, *Better Dwellings for the Workmen of London* (1884)

First Report of the Metropolitan Sanitary Commission (1848)

Fraser, William 'Fluctuations in the Building Trade and Glasgow's House Accommodation', *Proceedings of the Royal Philosophical Society of Glasgow* (1907–8)

Fynes, R., *The Miners of Northumberland & Durham* (Blyth, 1873)

Gavin, Hector, Sanitary Ramblings—*Being Sketches and Illustrations of Bethnal Green: A Type of the Condition of the Metropolis* (1848)

Geddes, Patrick, *Cities in Evolution* (1915)

Goschen, G. J., *Reports & Speeches on Local Taxation* (1872)

Haw, George, *No Room to Live* (1899)

—— *Britain's Homes* (1902)

Hill, Octavia, *Homes of the London Poor* (1875)

—— *Letters to My Fellow Workers*, 1872–1907 (Copies in LSE)

History of the Ministry of Munitions 12 vols (1920–24)

Hole, James, *The Homes of the Working Classes* (1866)

Holmes, Thomas, *Known to the Police* (1908)

Hunter, R., *Law of Landlord & Tenant*, 2 vols (4th edn., 1876)

Liberal Land Enquiry, *Report of Liberal Land Enquiry* 2 vols. (1913–14)

Liberal Publications Department, *The Urban Land Problem—Housing—Wages, Speeches of David Lloyd George* (1913)

Llewellyn Smith H. & Vaughan Nash, *The Story of the Dock Strike* (1889)

Low, Sidney, *The Governance of England* (1904)

Mackenzie, Norman, ed., *The Letters of Sidney and Beatrice Webb* 3 vols. (Cambridge, 1978)

Manchester & Salford Trades & Labour Council, *Report on Increase of House Rents in Manchester and Salford since the Commencement of the War* (Manchester, n.d., 1915)

Marx, Karl, *Capital*, vol. 1 (Moscow, 1959)

Masterman, C. F. G., *In Peril of Change* (1905)

—— *The Condition of England* (1909)

Mayhew, Henry, *London Labour & The London Poor*, 4 vols (1861–2)

Mearns, Andrew, *The Bitter Cry of Outcast London* (1883)

Mudie, Smith, R., *The Religious Life of London* (1904)

Nicol, James, *Vital Social and Economic Statistics of Glasgow*, (Glasgow, 1885 & 1891)

Pember Reeves, Mrs, *Round About a Pound a Week* (1913)

Presbytery of Glasgow, *Report of Commission on the Housing of the Poor in Relation to their Social Condition* (Glasgow, 1891)

Ramm, Agatha, ed., *Political Correspondence of Mr. Gladstone and Lord Granville*, 2 vols. (Oxford, 1962)

Renwick, Robert, *Memorial of Glasgow* (Glasgow, 1908)

Report of a Committee of the Manchester Statistical Society on the Condition of the Working Classes in 1834, 1835, 1836 (1838)

Report of a Committee of Working Men, Improved Homes for Working Men in London (1866)

Report on the Conditions of the Poorer Classes of Edinburgh (Edinburgh, 1868)

Reynolds, Stephen, & B. & T. Woolley, *Seems So! A Working Class View of Politics* (1911)

Riddell, Lord, *More Pages from My Diary 1908–1914* (1934)

Rider, Dan, *Ten Years Adventures Amongst Landlords and Tenants* (1927)

Roberts, Henry, *The Physical Condition of the Labouring Classes Resulting from the State of their Dwellings* (1866)

Robson, E. R., *School Architecture* (1874)

Rowntree, B. S., *Poverty, A Study of Town Life* (1901)

—— & Bruno Lasker, *Unemployment, A Social Study* (1911)

Russell, C., & H. S. Lewis, *The Jew in London* (1900)

Scottish Land, *Report of the Scottish Land Enquiry Committee* (1914)

Shadwell, Arthur, *Industrial Efficiency* 2 vols. (1906)

Shimmin, Hugh, *Liverpool Sketches* (Liverpool, 1862)

Sims, G. R., ed., *Living London* 3 vols. (1902)

Soutter, F. W., *Recollections of a Labour Pioneer* (1923)

—— *Fights for Freedom* (1925)

Thompson, R., *The Law Respecting Landlords, Tenants and Lodgers* (1841)

Unemployment in East London, Report of a Survey made for Toynbee Hall (1922)

Urwick, E. J. ed., *Studies of Boy Life in Our Cities* (1904)

Vyvyan, W. L., ed., *Charterhouse in Southwark: Some Account of the Charterhouse Mission, 1885–1892* (n.d.)

Watts, John, *The Facts of the Cotton Famine* (1866)

Wheatley, John, *£8 Cottages for Glasgow Workers* (Glasgow, 1913)

Wells, H. G., *Anticipations* (1902)

Wilson, A. J., *War Time and Other Legislation affecting Property Owners* (Birmingham, 1918)

Woods, Robert, A., *English Social Movements* (1892)

Wright, Thomas, *The Great Unwashed* (1868)

The Riverside Visitor [Revd. Thos. Wright], *The Great Army, Sketches of Life & Character in a Thames-side District* 2 vols. (1865)

SECONDARY SOURCES

Abrams, Philip, 'The Failure of Social Reform, 1918–20', *Past and Present*, No. 24 (1963)

Allen, C. M., 'The Genesis of British Urban Redevelopment with Special Reference to Glasgow', *Economic History Review* 2nd Ser. XVIII (1965)

Arnstein, W. L., *The Bradlaugh Case: A Study in Late Victorian Opinion & Politics* (Oxford, 1965)

Artizans' & General Properties Company Limited, *Artizan's Centenary 1867–1967* (1967)

Ashworth, William, *The Genesis of Modern British Town Planning* (1954)

Barltrop, Robert, *The Monument, The Story of the Socislist Party of Great Britain* (1975)

Barnett, H. O., *Canon Barnett: His Life, Work and Friends* (1921)

Barnett, M. J., *The Politics of Legislation: The Rent Act 1957* (1969)

Barnsby, G. J., *A History of Housing in Wolverhampton 1750–1975* (Wolverhampton n.d.)

Bealey, Frank, & J. Blondel and P. McCann, *Constituency Politics, A Study of Newcastle-under-Lyme* (1965)

Best, Geoffrey, *Mid-Victorian Britain* (1971)

Blewett, Neal, *The Peers, The Parties and The People: The General Elections of 1910* (1972)

Boase, T. S. R., *English Art 1800–1870* (Oxford, 1959)

Bowley, A. L. & A. R. Burnett-Hurst, *Livelihood & Poverty* (1915)

Bowley, Marion, *Housing & The State 1919–1944* (1945)

Briggs, Asa, *History of Birmingham Vol. II* (1952)

—— ed., *Chartist Studies*, (1959)

—— *Victorian Cities* (1963)

—— *Victorian People* (1965)

Briggs, E. & A. Deacon, 'The Creation of the Unemployment Assistance Board', *Policy & Politics*, II, 1 (1973)

Bristow, Edward, 'The Liberty and Property Defence League and Individualism', *Historical Journal*, 18, 4 (1975)

Brockway, Fenner, *Towards Tomorrow* (1977)

Brotherstone, Terence, 'The Suppression of Forward', *Bulletin of the Scottish Society for the Study of Labour History*, No. 1 (1969)

Brown, Kenneth D., *John Burns* (1978)

Building Societies Association, *Facts & Figures*, 1975

Bunce, J. T., *History of the Corporation of Birmingham Vol. II* (Birmingham, 1885)

Burnett, John, *Plenty & Want* (1966)

—— *A History of the Cost of Living* (1969)

—— *A Social History of Housing, 1815–1970* (Newton Abbot, 1978)

Cairncross, A. K., *Home & Foreign Investment, 1870–1913* (Cambridge, 1953)

Campbell, R. H., *Scotland Since 1707* (Oxford, 1965)

—— & J. B. A. Dow, *Source Book of Scottish Economic and Social History* (Oxford, 1968)

Chalkin, C. W., *The Provincial Towns of Georgian Britain: A Study of the Building Process, 1740–1820* (1974)

Chapman, S. D., ed., *The History of Working Class Housing, A Symposium* (Newton Abbot, 1971)

Checkland, S. G., 'The British Industrial City: The Glasgow Case', *Urban Studies*, I (1964)

Cherry, Gordon E., 'Influences on the Development of Town Planning in Britain', *Journal of Contemporary History*, IV (1969)

—— *Urban Change and Planning: A History of Urban Development in Britain* (Henley-on-Thames, 1972)

Clarke, P. F., *Lancashire and the New Liberalism* (Cambridge, 1971)

Cleary, E. J., *The Building Society Movement* (1965)

Clifford, Frederick, *A History of Private Bill Legislation* 2 vols. (1885–7)

Clinton, Alan, *The Trade Union Rank-and-File: Trades Councils in Britain, 1900–1940* (Manchester, 1977)

Clay, Henry, *The Problem of Industrial Relations* (1929)

Cole, G. D. H. & Margaret, *Rents, Rings & Houses* (1923)

Corbett, J., *Birmingham Trades Council, 1866–1966* (1966)

Cornford James, 'The Transformation of Conservatism in the Late Nineteenth Century', *Victorian Studies*, VII (1963–4)

Cowling, Maurice, *1867: Disraeli, Gladstone and Revolution* (Cambridge, 1967)

—— *The Impact of Labour* (Cambridge, 1971)

Crammond, R. D., *Housing Policy in Scotland 1919–64* (Edinburgh, 1966)

Crossick, Geoffrey, ed., *The Lower Middle Class in Britain 1800–1914* (1977)

—— *An Artisan Elite in Victorian Society: Kentish London 1840–1880* (1978)

Crawford, J. D., *Reflections & Recollections* (1936)

Cullingworth, J. B., *Housing in Transition* (1963)

Daunton, M. J., *Coal Metropolis: Cardiff, 1870–1914* (Leicester 1977)

Davies, E. ed., *John Scott Lidget, A Symposium* (1957)

Durant, Ruth, *Watling, a Survey of Social Life on a New Housing Estate* (1939)

Dyos, H. J., ed., *The Study of Urban History* (1968)

—— *Victorian Suburb* (Leicester 1973)

—— & Michael Wolff eds., *The Victorian City: Images and Realities*, 2 vols. (1973)

Englander, David, 'Tenants and Politics: The Birmingham Tenants' Federation during and after the First World War', *Midland History* VI (1981)

—— 'Wage Arrestment in Victorian Scotland', *Scottish Historical Review* LX (1981)

—— & James Osborne, 'Jack, Tommy and Henry Dubb: The Armed Forces and the Working Class', *Historical Journal*, 21, 3 (1978)

—— 'Landlord and Tenant in Urban Scotland: the background to the Clyde Rent Strike, 1915'; *Journal of Scottish Labour History Society* No. 15 (1981)

Ensor, R. C. K., *England, 1870–1914* (Oxford 1936)

Eversley, David, *The Planner in Society: The Changing Role of a Profession* (1973)

Feiling, Keith, *Life of Neville Chamberlain* (1947)

Ferguson, Thomas, *Scottish Social Welfare 1864–1914* (Edinburgh, 1958)

Fishman, William J., *East End Jewish Radicals, 1875–1914* (1975)

Furbey, R., 'National and Local Differentials in Social Class Relation—Some Evidence from Three Scottish Cities', *Social and Economic Administration*, 3 (1974)

Gainer, Bernard, *The Alien Invasion* (1972)

Garrard, John, A., *The English & Immigration 1880–1910* (1971)

Gartner, Lloyd, P., *The Jewish Immigrant in England 1870–1914* (1960)

Gauldie, Enid, *Cruel Habitations: A History of Working Class Housing 1780–1918* (1974)

George, M. D., *London Life in the Eighteenth Century* (1966 edn.)

Gilbert, Bentley, B., *British Social Policy 1919–39* (1970)

Girouard, Mark, *Sweetness and Light: The 'Queen Anne' Movement 1860–1900* (Oxford, 1977)

Glynn, Sean & John Oxenborrow, *Interwar Britain* (1976)

Gray, R. Q., *The Labour Aristocracy in Victorian Edinburgh* (Oxford, 1976)

Hanham, H. J., *Elections and Party Management: Politics in the Time of Disraeli and Gladstone* (1959)

Harris, Jose, *Unemployment & Politics* (Oxford, 1972)

Harrison, Brian, *Drink & the Victorians* (1971)

Harrison J. F. C., *Early Victorian Britain* (1973: Panther edn.)

Harrison, Royden, *Before the Socialists* (1965)

Hay, Denys, 'The Official History of the Ministry of Munitions', *Economic History Review*, XIV (1944)

Hay, J. R., *The Origins of the Liberal Welfare Reforms* (1975)

Haw, George, *From Workhouse to Westminster: The Life Story of Will Crooks* (1917)

Hennock, E. P., 'Finance and Politics in Urban Local Government in England 1835–1900', *Historical Journal*, VI, 2 (1963)

—— *Fit and Proper Persons* (1973)

Hinton, James, *The First Shop Stewards' Movement* (1973)

Hobson, S. G., *Pilgrim to the Left* (1938)

Holmes, R. S., 'Ownership and Migration from a Study of Rate Books', *Area*. V (1973)

Howarth, E. G., and M, Wilson, *West Ham* (1907)

International Labour Office, *European Housing Problems Since the War* (Geneva, 1924)

Johnson, Paul Barton, *Land Fit for Heroes: The Planning of British Reconstruction 1916–1919* (Chicago, 1968)

Jones, D. J. V., *Before Rebecca: Popular Protest in Wales 1793–1835* (1973)

Jones, G. W., *Borough Politics, A Study of the Wolverhampton Borough Council 1888–1964* (1969)

—— 'Herbert Morrison and Poplarism', *Public Law* (1973)

Joyce, Patrick, *Work, Society and Politics: the Culture of the Factory in Later Victorian England* (1980)

Keith Lucas, Brian, *The English Local Government Franchise* (Oxford, 1952)

—— 'Poplarism', *Public Law* (1962)

Kellett, J. R., *Impact of Railways on Victorian Cities* (1969)

Kendall, Walter, *The Revolutionary Movement in Britain 1900–21* (1969)

Kiddier, William, *The Old Trade Unions* (1931)

Kolthammer, F. W., *Some Notes on the Incidence of Taxation on the Working Class Family* (1913)

Kirkwood, David, *My Life of Revolt* (1935)

Lambert, Royston, *Sir John Simon and English Social Administration* (1963)

Lewis, R. A., *Edwin Chadwick and the Public Health Movement* (1952)

Lewis, J. Parry, *Building Cycles and Britain's Growth* (1968)

Lidgett, John Scott, *Reminiscences* (1928)

McCord, Norman, ed., *Essays in Tyneside Labour History* (Newcastle, 1977)

McKeowen, Thomas, and C. R. Lowe, *An Introduction to Social Medicine* (Oxford, 1966)

Macleod, Iain, *Neville Chamberlain* (1961)

McShane, Harry and Joan Smith, *Harry McShane: No Mean Fighter* (1978)

Marquand, David, *Ramsay Macdonald* (1977)

Marwick, Arthur, *The Deluge* (1965)

Marwick, W. A., *Economic Development in Victorian Scotland* (1934)

—— *A Short History of Labour in Scotland* (Edinburgh, 1967)

Mass Observation, An Enquiry into People's Homes (1943)

Melling, Joseph, ed., *Housing Social Policy and the State* (1980)

Michelet, Jules, *The People*, (Trans. John P. McKay: University Illinois Press, 1973)

Middlemas, R. K., *The Clydesiders* (1965)

Milton, Nan, *John Maclean* (1973)

Morley, John, *Life of Richard Cobden* (1910)

Mowat, C. L., *Britain in between the Wars* (1965)

Offer, Avner, *Property and Politics 1870–1914* (Cambridge, 1981)

O'Leary, Cornelius and Iain Budge, *Belfast: Approach to Crisis, A Study of Belfast Politics, 1613-1970* (1977)

Olsen, Donald J., *The Growth of Victorian London* (1976)

Orbach, Laurence F., *Homes for Heroes: A Study of the Evolution of British Public Housing 1915-1921* (1977)

Pankhurst, E. Sylvia, *The Suffragette Movement* (1931)

—— *The Home Front* (1932)

Pelling, Henry, *Social Geography of British Elections* (1967)

—— *Popular Politics & Society in Late Victorian Britain* (1968)

Pilgrim Trust, *Men Without Work* (Cambridge, 1938)

Philips, David, *Crime & Authority in Victorian England* (1978)

Pollard, Sidney & Colin Holmes, eds., *Essays in the Economic and Social History of South Yorkshire* (Barnsley, 1976)

Pollock, Frederick, *The Land Laws* (1883)

Price, Richard, *An Imperial War and the British Working Class* (1972)

Pritchard, R. M., *Housing and Spatial Structure of the City*, (Cambridge, 1976)

Ravitz, Alison, *Model Estate* (1974)

Richardson, H. W. & D. H. Aldcroft, *Building in the British Economy between the Wars* (1968)

Russell, A. K., Liberal Landslide: *The General Election of 1906* (Newton Abbot, 1973)

Saville, J. & A. Briggs, eds., *Essays in Labour History 1886-1923* (1971)

Sayle, A., *The Houses of the Workers* (1924)

Seaborne, M., *The English School*, 2 vols. (1971-7)

Seymour, Charles, *Electoral Reform in England and Wales* (New Haven & London, 1915)

Shipley, Stan, *Club Life & Socialism in Mid-Victorian London* (History Workshop Pamphlet, Oxford, 1971)

Simon, E. D., *How to Abolish the Slums* (1929)

—— *The Anti Slum Campaign* (1933)

Simpson, M. A. and T. H. Lloyd, eds., *Middle Class Housing in Britain* (Newton Abbott, 1978)

Smith, F. B., *The Making of the Second Reform Act* (Melbourne, 1966)

—— *Radical Artisan, William James Linton 1812-37* (Manchester, 1973)

Stedman Jones, Gareth, *Outcast London* (Oxford, 1971)

—— 'Working Class Culture and Working Class Politics in London 1870-1900: Notes on the Re-making of a working class', *Journal of Social History*, VII (1974)

Sutcliffe, Anthony, 'Working Class Housing in Nineteenth Century Britain', *Bulletin of the Society for the Study of Labour History*, No. 24 (1972)

—— ed., *Multi Storey Living: The British Working Class Experience* (1974)

Swenarton M., *Homes Fit For Heroes* (1981)

Tarn, J. N., 'The Peabody Donation Fund: The Role of a Housing Society in the Nineteenth Century', *Victorian Studies*, X (1966)

—— *Working Class Housing in Nineteenth Century Britain* (1971)

—— *Five Per Cent Philanthropy: An account of housing in urban areas between 1840-1914* (Cambridge, 1973)

Taylor, I. C., 'The Court and Cellar Dwelling: The Eighteenth Century Origin of the Liverpool Slum', *Transactions of the Historic Society of Lancashire & Cheshire*, CXII (1970)

Thane, Pat, e.d., *The Origins of British Social Policy* (1978)

Thompson, E. P., *The Making of the English Working Class* (1963)

—— *William Morris* (revised edn. 1977)

Thompson, Paul, *Socialists, Liberals and Labour* (1967)

Townrowe, B. S., *The Slum Problem* (1928)

Tuckett, Angela, *The Scottish Carter* (1967)

Vicinus, Martha, *The Industrial Muse* (1974)

Vince, C. A., *History of the Corporation of Birmingham Vol. III* (Birmingham, 1902)

Webb, Beatrice, *My Apprenticeship* (Penguin edn., 1971)

Wilding, Paul, 'Towards Exchequer Subsidies for Housing', 1906–1914', *Social & Economic Administration*, VI (1972)

—— 'The Housing & Town Planning Act, 1919: A Study in the Making of Social Policy', *Journal of Social Policy*, 4, 11 (1974)

Winter, J. M., *Socialism and the Challenge of War* (1974)

—— 'The Impact of the First World War on Civilian Health in Britain', *Economic History Review*, 2nd Ser. XXX (1977)

Wohl, Anthony, S., *The Eternal Slum* (1977)

Wolfe, Humbert, *Labour Supply & Regulation* (Oxford, 1923)

Young, Ken, *Local Politics & The Rise of Party* (Leicester, 1975)

Young, Terence, *Becontree and Dagenham* (1934)

Index